Shari‘ah Law: An Introduction

Mohammad Hashim Kamali

ONEWORLD
OXFORD

A Oneworld Book

Published by Oneworld Publications 2008
Reprinted 2010

A CIP record for this title is available
from the British Library

ISBN 978–1–85168–565–3

Typeset by Jayvee, Trivandrum, India
Cover design by Design Deluxe
Printed and bound in the United States of America

Oneworld Publications
UK: 185 Banbury Road, Oxford, OX2 7AR, England
USA: 38 Greene Street, 4th Floor, New York, NY 10013, USA
www.oneworld-publications.com

Shari‘ah Law

CONTENTS

FOREWORD

The term *Sharī'ah*, often translated as 'Islamic law', is among the most hotly debated and contested of Islamic ideas – both among Muslims and more recently as part of a political discourse in the West. Yet all too often, we seem to be talking past one another. The great masters of *Sharī'ah* often seem ill-prepared to convey the nuances and origin of this foundational Islamic discourse to a wide audience. At the same time, there is also a xenophobic perspective in the West that seeks to collapse the *Sharī'ah* into a trans-historical, reified notion that stands for all eternity in opposition to gender equality, democracy, and all that (allegedly) stands at the centre of Western consciousness. Rare have been the scholars who can speak with insight and authority about the *Sharī'ah* to a wide audience. That is, until Mohammad Hashim Kamali.

Dr. Kamali is virtually peerless in his lucid and thorough presentation of *Sharī'ah*. He manages to stay clear of the usual problematic presentations, and indeed transcends them. He begins by problematising the usual presentation of Islam as a religious tradition that is legalistic and ritualistic, as well as a timeless and eternal presentation of *Sharī'ah*. Instead, he looks at the origin, historical development, and contemporary debates about the nature of Islamic law in an imaginative, meticulously documented, yet accessible format. After reading this volume, the reader will be informed not only about the important sources of the *Sharī'ah* such as the Qur'ān and the example of the Prophet, but also about the methodology whereby Islamic rulings are extracted from those sources.

In today's world, intimate knowledge about Islam and Muslims is not a luxury, but a matter of mutual survival. We, Muslim and non-Muslim, are in desperate need to come to know one another intimately. The *Sharī'ah* is not the whole of Islam – there is also mysticism and philosophy and Qur'ān and piety and poetry and much more – but it is one of the foundational discourses of Islam. The series that this book inaugurates is committed to introducing the widest audience possible to the Foundations of Islam in a way that is simultaneously authentic, profound, and accessible. And no one is more worthy of beginning the series than the great contemporary scholar, Mohammad Hashim Kamali.

Omid Safi
Series Editor for *Foundations of Islam*

PREFACE

Notwithstanding its title of *Sharī'ah Law: An Introduction* this volume provides a progressive and graduated treatment of the *Sharī'ah*. The first three chapters offer an introductory discussion which expounds the sources of *Sharī'ah,* its characteristic features, as well as its leading schools and *madhhabs*. The succeeding four chapters on *ikhtilāf* (juristic disagreement), the *maqāṣid* (goals and objectives), legal maxims, and *ijtihād* (independent reasoning) take the discussion a step further, and the approach here is not necessarily confined to introductory and descriptive treatment of the subject. From then onwards the discussion is taken to a more advanced level in its treatment of the *Sharī'ah* and the principle of legality, *Sharī'ah* and democracy, and the role and place of *Sharī'ah*-oriented policy (*siyāsah shari'iyyah*) in our understanding of the *Sharī'ah*.

By revisiting the history and methodology of *maqāṣid* in chapter 6, the book penetrates the subject and provides a more advanced-level treatment of the *maqāṣid,* which has already been touched on in chapter 2. Similarly in the other two chapters on legality and *siyāsah,* the discourse and thematic treatment of the subject aspires to a degree of erudition in the *Sharī'ah*. Chapter 12 on 'adaptation and reform' of the *Sharī'ah* provides, in a similar fashion, a fairly comprehensive yet concise update of twentieth-century developments in *Sharī'ah* in the areas of legislation, teaching and research as well as developments of *fatwā* committees, encyclopedias and university degree programmes. The problematics of *ijtihād* and *fatwā* are discussed and proposals are made for methodological reforms in contemporary *fatwā*-making and *ijtihād*. All in all the book pays attention to topics and issues that are not commonly treated in the available manuals and handbooks of Islamic law in English. The reader may also want to know that a bird's-eye view of the topic arrangement and contents has also been attempted in the concluding chapter of this book which may be read before perusing the whole text. The final chapter of the book bears the title 'Reflections on Some Challenging

Issues'. This chapter is divided into five sections, beginning with a discussion of the secularist debate concerning Islam and the *Sharī'ah*, then the decline of madrasah, followed by gender equality issues, suicide bombing, and what we can learn, on a more general note, from the Qur'ānic principle of *wasaṭiyyah* (moderation and balance) on the issues of our concern.

I take this opportunity to record my appreciation for the help I have been generously given by Mrs Salmah Ahmad of the International Institute of Islamic Thought and Civilisation (ISTAC), my research assistant Nirwan Syafrin, and my colleagues and students at ISTAC and the Ahmad Ibrahim Faculty of Law. I would also like to thank the library staff at ISTAC and the main library at the Gombak campus of the International Islamic University Malaysia. Finally, I am grateful to Professor Omid Safi, Oneworld Publications' series editor, for his reading of the manuscript and valuable suggestions. If there are any remaining weaknesses, they are my own work, but I hope, nevertheless, that this volume will meet its desired purpose of providing a balanced and readable handbook on *Sharī'ah* which also relates meaningfully to issues of contemporary concern to the readers in this discipline.

MHK

1

INTRODUCTION

This chapter begins with advancing a perspective on the origins of *Sharī'ah* in the Qur'ān and the formative stages of its development in the early decades of Islam. Attention is also drawn in following paragraphs to the overly legalistic tendency which the latter-day Muslim jurists (*mutakhkhirūn*) have embraced at the expense sometimes of the spirit of Islam, its moral and devotional teachings on matters of personal conduct. This tendency is manifested in the way authors have expounded the relationship of law and religion so that the *Sharī'ah* is often presented as the core and kernel of religion and the essence of Islam itself. The late Joseph Schacht (d. 1969) actually described the *Sharī'ah* in these words. So the tendency to over-legalize Islam is common across the board in the writings of both Muslims and Orientalists. I believe this to be an exaggeration which does not find support in our reading of the Qur'ān and Sunnah, as I shall presently explain. It is questionable whether Islam was meant to be as much of a law-based religion as it has often been made out to be. The same tendency is noted in relationship to the role of state and religion in Islam. Hence an attempt is also made in the following paragraphs to explore the idea of an Islamic state (*dawlah Islamiyyah*), its origin and related developments, and in this context I have drawn attention especially to the doctrine of *siyāsah shar'iyyah* (*Sharī'ah*-oriented policy) and the role it ought to play in the understanding of an Islamic polity and state. This is followed by an overview of more recent writings on caliphate and Islamic state. The last section of this chapter consists of brief summaries and provides an inkling of what the reader should expect under the various chapters that constitute the bulk of this volume. A slightly different summary of the book also appears in my Conclusion at the end of this volume.

THE ORIGINS OF *SHARĪʻAH*

Sharīʻah literally means a way to the watering-place or a path apparently to seek felicity and salvation. The word occurs only once in the Qur'ān and it is used in contradistinction with *ḥawā* (whimsical desire). The verse thus reads in an address to the Prophet Muhammad:

> Thus we put you on the right way [*sharīʻatan*] of religion. So follow it and follow not the whimsical desire (*ḥawā*) of those who have no knowledge. (45:18)
>
> ثُمَّ جَعَلْنَاكَ عَلَى شَرِيعَةٍ مِّنَ الْأَمْرِ فَاتَّبِعْهَا وَلَا تَتَّبِعْ أَهْوَاءَ الَّذِينَ لَا يَعْلَمُونَ.

In an explanatory note on this verse, 'Abdullah Yusuf Ali's translation reads '*sharīʻatan* in this verse is best translated as "the right way of religion" which is wider than the legal provisions which were mostly revealed in the Madinan period, long after this verse had been revealed'. Since *Sharīʻah* as a legal code did not exist at the time this verse was revealed, the Qur'ānic reference is to its literal sense of belief in Islam (God's appointed way) and avoidance of disbelief. The renowned Qur'ān commentator al-Bayḍāwi noted that the reference to *ḥawā* in this verse is to the pagan beliefs of the people of Makkah who believed in idolatry and association of idols with supernatural powers.

Since *Sharīʻah* is a path to religion, it is primarily concerned with a set of values that are essential to Islam and the best manner of their protection. Islam stands on what is known as the five pillars (*al-arkān al-khamsah*), namely belief in God, ritual prayers, fasting, the hajj and giving the poor due (*zakah*). Faith in God, the manner of worshipping Him and observance of the five pillars of Islam thus constitute the essential concerns of *Sharīʻah*. The manner of worshipping God is expounded in that part of *Sharīʻah* which is known as *ʻibādāt* (devotional matters). Then there is the concern with justice, which is a major preoccupation of *Sharīʻah*. Justice is concerned with the manner in which God Most High wants His creatures to be treated, expounded mainly under the general heading of *mu'āmalāt* (civil transactions). One of the areas of primary concern to *Sharī'ah* is protection and advancement of the five essentials (*al-ḍaruriyāt al-khamsah*), namely of life, religion, property, intellect and family.[1] It is often said that *Sharī'ah* in all of its parts is concerned with the manner of best protecting these values. *Fiqh* is an equivalent term to *Sharī'ah* and the two are often used interchangeably; the two words are, however, not identical. Whereas *Sharī'ah* is conveyed mainly through divine revelation (*waḥy*) contained in the Qur'ān and authentic *ḥadīth*, *fiqh* refers mainly to the *corpus juris* that is developed by the legal schools (*madhhabs*), individual jurists and judges by recourse to legal reasoning (*ijtihād*) and issuing of legal verdict (*fatwā*).

The bulk of the legal rules that later became known as *Sharī'ah* was revealed after the Prophet's migration from Makkah to Madinah, where a new Muslim community and government came into being. During his initial twelve and a half years of campaigns in Makkah, the Prophet was preoccupied with the belief and dogma of Islam, the essence of moral virtue, and not so much with the enactment of legal rules. The legal rules of the Qur'ān were mainly revealed during the ten years of the Prophet's residence in Madinah and mainly towards the end of that period. Since Muslims were a minority in Makkah, they had no power to enforce a law. Thus it is noted that most of the Makkan *sūrahs* of the Qur'ān were exhortative and imbued with warnings of the depravity and evil of idol worshipping and oppressive practices of the pre-Islamic Arabs towards the poor, the orphans, the widows and the needy. Most of the Makkan *sūrahs* are short, brisk and forceful in their appeal to the conscience of the reader and recipient. They talk generally of moral responsibility, man and the universe, the day of judgement, good and evil, spiritual awareness and so on. The persistent appeal of the Qur'ān was for people to change their ways and lead a good moral life. Some basic rules on ritual prayers, alms giving and justice to orphans and widows were revealed in Makkah, but the bulk of the legal verses of the Qur'ān (approximately 350 out of a total of over 6200 verses) were revealed in Madinah.[2] But even in Madinah, it will be noted that the penal rulings of the Qur'ān which later became known as the *ḥudūd* were revealed mainly in sūrah al-Mā'idah during the last two years of the Prophet's life. This gradualist and piecemeal approach to legislation in the Qur'ān, known as *tadarruj* (also *tanjīm*) characterizes the whole of the Prophet's campaign in both Makkah and Madinah.

Much attention was paid to preparation before decisive legal rulings were enacted and enforced.

Two other derivatives of the root word *shara'a* (to begin something, to enact) that occur in the Qur'ān also confirm the foregoing analysis that the Qur'ānic conception of *Sharī'ah* was essentially theocentric. In one of these verses, it is provided:

> The same religion has He enacted for you [*shara'a lakum min al-dīn*] as that which He enjoined on Noah and the one we revealed to you and that which We enjoined on Abraham, Moses and Jesus, namely that you should remain steadfast in religion and make no divisions therein. (42:13)
>
> شَرَعَ لكُم مِّنَ الدِّين مَا وَصَّى بِهِ نُوحًا وَالَّذِي
> أَوْحَيْنَا إِلَيْكَ وَمَا وَصَّيْنَا بِهِ إِبْرَاهِيمَ وَمُوسَى وَعِيسَى أَنْ أَقِيمُوا
> الدِّينَ وَلَا تَتَفَرَّقُوا فِيهِ.

Shara'a in this verse refers, according to Qur'ān commentators, to 'belief in the Oneness of God (*tawḥīd*), prayer, fasting, alms giving and hajj'. For these were in common between all of the scriptures revealed to those Prophets.[3] Thus it is noted that *shara'a* in this verse could not be a reference to a legal code as the laws revealed to these various Prophets were not the same. The word thus refers basically to belief and dogma and not to law as such.

The bulk of the Qur'ān, that is, 85 out of the total of 114 *sūrahs*, was revealed in Makkah and all of it focused on Islam as a faith and structure of moral values. Law and government did not feature in the Qur'ān during the Makki period. The legal rulings of the Qur'ān are of a limited scope and are decidedly peripheral to its dogma and moral teachings. The Prophet himself consistently referred to the Qur'ān as a source of authority and only in his latter years in Madinah did he refer to his own teachings and example (Sunnah) as a guide to conduct. The words *Sharī'ah* and *fiqh* do not occur in the Sunnah in their usual meanings. This can be known, for instance, from the renowned *ḥadīth* of the Mu'ādh Ibn Jabal: when the Prophet was sending Mu'ādh to the Yemen as ruler and judge, he was asked three questions as to what he would refer to when making decisions in his capacity as a judge! Mu'ādh mentioned firstly the Qur'ān, then the Sunnah of the Prophet and then his own considered judgement and *ijtihād*. There was no reference to *Sharī'ah* in this *ḥadīth* nor to *fiqh* as such.[4] The word *Sharīʿah* does not seem to have been used even by the Pious Caliphs (*Khulafāʾ Rāshidūn*) following the demise of the Prophet, nor have they used its equivalent *fiqh* in the sense of a legal code. These terminologies emerged much later and consist mainly of juristic designations that found currency when a body of juristic doctrine was developed over a period of time.

The purpose of this analysis is not to doubt or dispute the substance of *Sharīʿah* or of *fiqh* but to emphasize that identifying *Sharīʿah* in the sense of a legal code as the defining element of an Islamic society and state, which became commonplace in subsequent juristic writings, does not find a strong footing in the source evidence. Islam is a faith and a moral code first and foremost; it stands on its own five pillars, and following a legal code is relative and subsidiary to the original call and message of Islam. The persistent line of emphasis on legalism that has dominated the juristic legacy of Islam and *Sharīʿah* should therefore be moderated. The overarching Islamic principle of divine unity (*tawḥīd*) which requires an integrated approach to values should not simply be subsumed under the rubric of legality that focuses on the externalities of conduct often at the expense of the inner development of the human person.

The literalist tendency of scholastic jurisprudence and its emphasis on conformity to rules evoked strong critique from the Sufis and spiritual masters of Islam. The Sufis turned their attention to the spirit and meaning of religion and God-consciousness in personal conduct. They denounced the *fiqh* tendency of undivided attention to the external manifestations of religion at the expense often of its meaning and message.

Shah Wali Allah Dihlawi (d. 1762), who was influenced by the thought and philosophy of Sufism, saw in Islam a process of progressive development of the inner self of the individual that could lead to greater refinement and stages of closeness to God (a process he expounded and termed as *iqtirābāt*). In his renowned *magnum opus*, 'The Conclusive Evidence from God' (*Ḥujjat Allah al-Bālighah*), Shah Wali Allah criticized the literalist legalism which had characterized Islamic juristic thought and looked at the inner meanings of religion (*asrār al-din*) that was informed by the totality of existential phenomena as a manifestation of the principle of divine unity. In doing so, Shah Wali Allah drew much inspiration from the works of Abū Ḥamid al-Ghazali (d. 1111), the author of the renowned 'Rivivification of the Religious Sciences' (*Ihyāʾ ʿulūm al-Din*), who was also motivated by the idea of restoring the meaning and spirit of Islam to its erstwhile disciplines of learning. Shah Wali Allah's purpose was to ensure greater harmony of the law with the ethical and spiritual dimensions of Islamic teachings. Muhammad al-Ghazālī, who translated *Hujjat Allah al-Bālighah* (2001), wrote in his Introduction to this work: 'Shah Wali Allah understood himself as living in an age of crisis in which the integrity of the various Islamic sciences was threatened by the tendency to abandon broader vision and principles in favour of narrow disciplinary specializations and polemical rejection of other perspectives.' That crisis has not receded, but was exacerbated, when scholastic jurisprudence was brought to fresh prominence by the Ottoman state's adoption of the Ḥanafi school of law as the official school of the empire. This marked the beginning of a new phase in juristic imitation (*taqlīd*) whereby Muslim states specified, as they do to this day, the adoption of one or other of the schools of Islamic law in their constitutions. I hasten to add here, perhaps, that this tendency should now be abandoned, as it has become largely redundant due to the promulgation of statutory codes of law that now expound the applied law for purposes of judicial practice. Specification of a particular school of jurisprudence was deemed necessary when the courts of *Sharīʻah* relied mainly on the manuals of *fiqh*, which often left the judges with the uncertainty as to which ruling, school, or opinion they had to apply to cases under adjudication. In our times, the protagonists of Islamic fundamentalism, especially the radical factions among them, have once again taken legalism as the principal theme of their mission, shown by their persistent demand for conformity to the juristic legacy of Islam and restoration of the *Sharīʻah*.

We note a tendency sometimes that places total emphasis on conformity to rules and statements also in some academic writings that designate Islam as a law-based religion, a nomocracy and so forth, and not enough emphasis on the meaning and purpose of Islam and integration of its values in one's conduct. Declaring a state as Islamic, or *Sharīʻah* as the applied law, has often co-existed with despotism and corrupt governance such that the ethical norms of Islam and its unmistakable stress on personal conduct have been conspicuously absent in the track record of the majority of Muslim political leaders of the post-colonial period. To say that alienation of Islamic values from law and governance has been a source of widespread dissatisfaction is to state the obvious, for this has also been the principal motto of the Islamic resurgence movement of recent decades. Yet due to a variety of factors that I shall later elaborate, the necessary corrective has not materialized. This tendency in Islamic juristic thought, and how it has been manifested in the practice of law and governance, namely to target externality at the expense of meaning and substance is due for a corrective. I shall have occasion to elaborate on this a little further in a section below on 'externality and intent' that has also led to some differences of opinion among the schools of jurisprudence.

THE STATE AND THE *SHARĪ'AH*

When Abū'l-Ḥassan al-Māwardi (d. 1058) defined the caliphate as 'protection of religion and management of temporal affairs' (*ḥirāsat al-d n wa siyāsat al-dunyā*), he did not think of implementing the *Sharī'ah* as a defining element of an Islamic government and state. Al-Māwardi's definition was evidently focused on the preservation and protection of religion. To declare *Sharī'ah* as the principal criterion of an Islamic state initially featured, though somewhat less categorically, in the writings of Ibn Taymiyyah (d. 1328). This was later given prominence by Syed Quṭb (d. 1966) and Abu'l-A'la Mawdudi (d. 1979), Muḥammad al-Ghazāli (d. 1992) and Yūsūf al-Qaraḍāwi who saw the Islamic state essentially as a *Sharī'ah* state committed to the enforcement of *Sharī'ah*.

Ibn Taymiyyah was influenced by the tension that had developed between the norms and principles of the original caliphate and the practice of dynastic caliphs, the Umayyads (660–750) and the Abbasids (750–1258), marked by the Mongol invasion of Baghdad (1258) and the destruction of what had remained of the caliphate. Ibn Taymiyyah emphasized that the Qur'ān and Sunnah did not contain any reference to caliphate as an organizational model or a system of government, and since the rightly guided caliphate had only lasted for thirty years, he ignored the hollowed theory and rhetoric of caliphate and called attention to the *Sharī'ah* and a *Sharī'ah*-oriented policy (i.e. *siyāsah shar'iyyah*). The Wahabi movement of nineteenth-century Arabia that was moulded on Ibn Taymiyyah's thought placed additional emphasis on the *Sharī'ah* -based identity of Islamic governance. Twentieth-century writings on Islamic state and government became even more specific on *Sharī'ah* than what Ibn Taymiyyah had meant by a *Sharī'ah*-oriented polity. As I elaborate in a separate chapter below, Ibn Taymiyyah's idea of *siyāsah shar'iyyah* conveys the message that policy (*siyāsah*) was an integral part of Islamic governance, and that governance in Islam was not a matter simply of rule by the text but of politics and administration by judicious rulers whose decisions were to be guided by the *Sharī'ah*, but that they also took into consideration a variety of factors that could not be encapsulated by the legal text alone. This was a pragmatic and yet principled approach to governance. But we note that Islamic scholarship on constitutional law and governance focused on the observance of *Sharī'ah* in a dogmatic fashion at the expense often of concern for accountability, popular participation, justice and fundamental rights. Instead of engaging in Islamic political thought that would ameliorate the failures of the dynastic caliphate in devising mechanisms and procedures for consultation, democratic rights and accountable governance, with some exceptions, many *Sharī'ah* scholars continued expounding the defunct caliphate and expatiated on theoretical themes of Islamic state as a dogmatic principle rather than a mechanism to serve the people and show commitment to the welfare objectives of its citizens.

SUMMARY OF CHAPTERS

The first of the thirteen chapters presented in this volume are devoted to an exposition of the sources, nature and objectives of the *Sharī'ah*. The discussion here begins with the definition of *Sharī'ah*, which is often used in a general sense that includes not only the law that is contained in the Qur'ān and Sunnah but also the detailed rules of *fiqh* that jurists and scholars have developed through interpretation and *ijtihād*. More specifically, however, *Sharī'ah* is grounded in the revealed laws of the Qur'ān and Sunnah in contradistinction with *fiqh* which is a juristic edifice. This line of discussion is advanced in the early part of the first chapter, which is then followed by an exposition of the sources of *Sharī'ah* under the three main headings of Qur'ān, Sunnah, and *ijtihād*. The remaining portion of this chapter addresses the objectives, or *maqāṣid*, of the *Sharī'ah* which are in one way or another elaborated and pursued by the detailed rules of *Sharī'ah* in all of its various branches. An understanding of the *maqāṣid* is thus important for gaining an insight into the rest of the *Sharī'ah*. *Sharī'ah* is often described as a diversity within unity – diversity in the detailed interpretations of individual jurists and schools that has become a characteristic feature of the *Sharī'ah*, and unity in the goals and purposes that are followed by the detailed elaborations of the law. It is through awareness of its goals and purposes that the unity of *Sharī'ah* is protected and upheld.

'Characteristic features of *Sharī'ah*' is the theme of the next chapter. As the title indicates, the emphasis here is on highlighting the salient features of *Sharī'ah* where the discussion sets the background by explaining the lines of distinction between *Sharī'ah* and *fiqh* and proceeds with an outline of the major themes and classifications of *fiqh*. The chapter then focuses on the salient characteristics of *Sharī'ah*. What it precisely means to say, for instance, that *Sharī'ah* is a divine law of permanent validity which also manifests the unitarian outlook of monotheism (*tawḥīd*) in its juristic formulations. *Sharī'ah* also seeks to protect the interests both of continuity and change just as it also provides mechanisms for the interplay of revelation and reason in the formulation of its rules. Our discussion along these lines is followed by a brief section on the scope respectively of externality and intent, the notion on the one hand of compliance to the rules and the emphasis on the other that a dry conformity to rules that is divorced from the intention and purpose of law should not be encouraged. This kind of disjuncture is occasionally found in some of the outlandish sections of *fiqh*, such as the legal stratagems (*al-ḥiyal*), which is problematic to say the least, and its place in Islamic juristic thought must be reduced to the minimum possible.

Chapter 4 addresses the origins and development of the legal schools (*madhāhib*). The chapter begins with a brief history of scholastic divisions which is followed by a section each on the four leading Sunni schools of law and one also on the Shi'ite school of jurisprudence, explaining the basic features and also major differences in their juristic thought. A section is also devoted to methodologies of legal reasoning in each school, as well as their respective approaches to interpretation of the textual rulings of the Qur'ān and *ḥadīth*.

Chapter 5 addresses juristic disagreement (*ikhtilāf*) which is at once a characteristic feature of the *Sharī'ah* as well as an academic discipline and branch thereof. The law faculty of the International

Islamic University Malaysia, for instance, offers a course of study on *ikhtilāf*. The discussion in this chapter basically supplements the preceding chapter on the *madhāhib*, to say that without differences in *ijtihād* and disagreement over matters of interpretation, and some distinctive contribution to juristic thought, separate *madhhabs* could not have come into existence. The opposite of *ikhtilāf* is general consensus (*ijmāʿ*) and I discuss the respective role and value of both of these in the development of Islamic law. This chapter also advances the view that *ijtihād* and also *ikhtilāf* are valuable, indeed inevitable, features of Islamic law, but we now live in a period of history, perhaps, that emphasizes the need for consensus more than disagreement. It would appear that *ijtihād* has in the past been used as an instrument of disagreement more than of unity and consensus. A greater level of consensus would now seem to be advisable, even necessary, for the revival of *Sharīʿah* and *ijtihād* and the role they ought to play in contemporary laws and governance in Muslim societies.

Chapter 6 is devoted to a discussion of the goals and purposes, or the *maqāṣid*, of *Sharīʿah*. This subject is briefly addressed in the first chapter, but due to the importance of the topic and renewed interest that is shown in it in contemporary writings on *Sharīʿah*, a more detailed presentation of the history and methodology of *maqāṣid* has been attempted in this chapter. My earlier treatment did not address historical developments and the contributions of prominent scholars in this area, to which I turn in this chapter. The discussion here refers more specifically to the works of al-Shāṭibi, al-Ghazāli, Ibn Taymiyyah and some contemporary scholars on the subject. The chapter ends with a section on the importance of *maqāṣid* for *ijtihād*.

Legal maxims of *fiqh*, which is the subject of chapter 7, basically supplements the preceding chapter on the *maqāṣid*, or objectives, of *Sharīʿah*, so much so that they often appear as an extension of one another and a unified chapter in the writings of many Muslim jurists. The reason for this thematic unity between the *maqāṣid* and legal maxims is that the latter are naturally focused on the goals and purposes of the law, and provide theoretical, but also condensed and epithetic, entries into the various fields of *Sharīʿah*. Legal maxims provide an efficient exposition of the goals and purposes of the law either generally or in reference to its particular themes and yet they are a branch of Islamic legal studies in their own right, separately from the *maqāṣid*.

Independent reasoning (*ijtihād*) and juristic opinion (*fatwā*) are the focus of the succeeding chapter, which basically explores the potentials of *ijtihād* and *fatwā*, their resources, and their relevance to addressing contemporary issues encountered in the rapid pace of social change. The chapter also highlights the problematics of *ijtihād* and *fatwā* in modern times. They are both instrumental to relating the resources of *Sharī'ah* to contemporary issues but their utility is hampered by a number of shortcomings that need first to be addressed. *Ijtihād* may consist of a novel interpretation of the text in conjunction with a particular issue that has not been encountered before, or it may consist of taking a step beyond interpretation by applying one or the other of the various doctrines, such as analogy (*qiyās*), considerations of public interest (*istiṣlāḥ*), juristic preference (*istiḥsān*) and so forth that are in reality sub-varieties of *ijtihād* and are designed to provide a structured approach and methodology for it. *Fatwā* normally consists of a response that a qualified jurist provides to a question, a counsel that may consist of a brief answer, agreement or disagreement, and it may resemble *ijtihād* or fall below that level. The chapter ends with an exposition of the problematics of *fatwā* in modern times and gives suggestions for reform.

Chapter 9 bears the title '*Sharī'ah* and the Principle of Legality' which explores the basic requirements of the modern-law principle of legality and the extent of their application in *Sharī'ah*. The principal of legality, also known as the principal of the rule of law (sometimes also referred to as due process) is essentially guided by the idea of government under the rule of law and it applies to almost every area of the law that seeks to protect the citizen against the arbitrary use of power. This principle naturally acquires prominence in the sphere of criminal law, arrest, interrogation and trial proceedings, and the chapter before us raises these questions with regard to the *Sharī'ah* and the extent of its compliance with the constitutional principle of legality.

Chapter 10 focuses on 'Democracy, Fundamental Rights and the *Sharī'ah*', offering a perspective on the extent of harmony or otherwise between the basic postulates of democracy and those of the *Sharī'ah*. Attention is drawn in this connection to a growing support for democracy among Islamic parties and movements and their unprecedentedly increased presence in electoral politics especially since 1999 in the Middle East, Turkey, Pakistan, Indonesia and Malaysia. The chapter also advances a perspective on the position in *Sharī'ah* regarding basic rights and liberties, while addressing some relevant aspects of the Orientalist debate on the subject. There is also a discussion of Islam and civil society, exploring the history of this idea in Muslim society and institutions. The chapter ends with a brief introductory discussion of moderation (*i'tidāl*, *wasaṭiyyah*), an important dimension of Islamic teachings, which is then treated in greater detail in chapter 13.

The next chapter, entitled 'Beyond the *Sharī'ah*: An Analysis of *Sharī'ah*-oriented Policy (*Siyāsah Shar'iyyah*)' explores the place of judicial policy and discretion, political acumen and non-textual or extra-*Sharī'ah* procedures in an Islamic system of governance. The history of government in almost every period and every legal system testifies to the basic truism that rulers and governors, administrators and statesmen did not conduct the affairs of state by reference only to the legal text. Some of the renowned figures of Islamic scholarship have articulated this theme under the rubric of *Sharī'ah*-compliant policy (*siyāsah shar'iyyah*) which is often guided by the spirit, goal and purpose of *Sharī'ah* and the values it upholds rather than its textual formulations. This chapter also briefly addresses the question whether it is really the basic idea of *siyāsah shar'iyyah*, rather than the much talked about Islamic state, that relates to the realities of governance that now obtain in the Muslim world. The chapter ends with a reference to Malaysia and the extent to which Malaysia could be said to comply with the requirements of *siyāsah shar'iyyah*.

Chapter 12 reviews recent developments and reforms of Islamic law in various areas through legislation, teaching and research, the establishment of Islamic law academies, *fatwā* collections, judicial decisions and *ijtihād*. The twentieth century has probably marked a turning-point in the history of Islamic law and the developments we discuss here were spurred to some extent by Islamic revivalism and the persistent call for its renewal and reform. Providing adequate responses to the challenges of modern society and its rapid pace of change is bound to require a sustained engagement in fresh enquiry and research into the sources of *Sharī'ah*.

Chapter 13 of this volume addresses some of the most challenging issues facing contemporary Muslim societies. The chapter comprises five sections beginning with an overview of the secularist debate and some of the Islamic responses given to the challenges it has posed. Gender justice issues are discussed in section two, followed by a review of the decline of the madrasah education, and then the somewhat disturbing phenomenon of suicide bombing. The last section of this chapter reviews the Qur'ānic principle of moderation and balance (*wasaṭiyyah, i'tidāl*) which is a most important yet widely neglected aspect of the teachings of Islam and its broader civilizational perspective. Much of what has been said in these survey-style presentations is based on my own views and responses to these issues.

My conclusion at the very end winds up the book by highlighting its salient themes and my own reflections on them. This chapter actually ties up with the introductory chapter of the book and takes to conclusion some of the points that were raised in the Introduction. Readers without a background in *Sharī'ah* studies might even wish to read the Introduction and Conclusion together before reading the rest of the text.

NOTES

1. Cf. al-Shāṭibī, *Muwāfaqāt*, II, 3–5. Further detail on continuity of themes in the Qur'ān appears in chapter 6 below.
2. Muslim jurists have differed over the precise number of legal verses (*ayat al-aḥkām*) in the Qur'ān, due mainly to their differential approaches to the subject. Some were inclined to increase the number as they often extracted a legal ruling from a historical passage, or even a parable in the Qur'ān, whereas others counted a lesser number as they looked for legal verses mainly in a legal context. Differences over the rules of interpretation among jurists also explain some of their different conclusions. Similar differences obtain, even more widely with regard to the *ḥadīth* which resulted in different accounts of the legal *ḥadīths* (*aḥādīth al-aḥkām*) given by the scholars of *ḥadīth*, whereas some put the total number of legal *ḥadīth* at 3000, others have reduced this number to 1200 *ḥadīth*s.
3. Cf. al-Ṣābūnī, *Ṣafwat al-Tafāsīr*, III, 135.
4. Abū Dawūd, *Sunan* (Hasan's trans.), III, 1091, *ḥadīth* 3585.

2

NATURE, SOURCES AND OBJECTIVES OF *SHARĪʻAH*

NATURE OF *SHARĪʻAH*

Literally, *Sharīʻah* means the path to the watering-place, the clear path to be followed and the path which the believer has to tread in order to obtain guidance in this world and deliverance in the next.[1] In its common usage, *Sharīʻah* refers to commands, prohibitions, guidance and principles that God has addressed to mankind pertaining to their conduct in this world and salvation in the next. The basic purpose of this and all other divine guidance is to enable man to forsake the dictates of *hawā,* that is, the untrammelled lust and proclivity to evil; to lead him to righteousness and truth; to make him upright and worthy of assuming the divine trust of *khilāfah,* the vicegerency of God in the earth. Man is thus entrusted with the responsibility to establish justice and good governance in accordance with the guidelines of *Sharīʻah*.[2]

We noted that *Sharīʻah* is a path in religion; it is not a separate path but one which is a part of it. Religion is thus the larger entity and *Sharīʻah* only a part. Its source of reference, its objectives and values are a part of mainstream Islam. Yet we do not subscribe to the view which characterizes *Sharīʻah* as 'the epitome of Islamic thought, the most typical manifestation of the Islamic way of life, the core and kernel of Islam itself'.[3] It may admittedly not be possible to separate or isolate the *Sharīʻah* completely from religion, or from the basic beliefs and values of Islam, yet as we shall later elaborate, the unity of *Sharīʻah* with the religion of Islam is at the higher level of goals and purposes, and there are aspects of *Sharīʻah* where civilian jurisprudence does recognize levels of distinction within the dogma and belief structure of Islam. Justice for example is a central theme of *Sharī'ah* which applies to both Muslims and non-Muslims and the courts of *Sharī'ah* operate civilian and positivist procedures that do not discriminate on the basis of the religious following of the individual.

Sharī'ah is used in the Qur'ān in contradistinction to *hawā,* or caprice, especially of those who have no knowledge. *Hawā* thus stands at the opposite pole *Sharī'ah,* and the latter is designed to discipline the former and tell the believer that his conduct in society cannot be left to the vagaries of *hawā. Hawā* is tantamount to lawlessness and deviation from correct guidance. It is in this sense that the Qur'ān has warned the people, on no less than twenty-five occasions, of the evil consequences of indulgence in *hawā* and the hold that it can have on their hearts and minds.[4] The Qur'ān thus declares:

> Who is more misguided than the one who follows his *hawā* and neglects the guidance of God? (28:50)
>
> وَمَنْ أَضَلُّ مِمَّنِ اتَّبَعَ هَوَاهُ بِغَيْرِ هُدًى مِّنَ اللَّهِ.

Elsewhere it is provided in the Qur'ān, in an address to the Prophet David:

> We appointed you vicegerent in the earth so that you rule among people with justice and that you follow not *hawā,* which distracts you from the path of God. (38:26)
>
> يَا دَاوُودُ إِنَّا جَعَلْنَاكَ خَلِيفَةً فِي الْأَرْضِ فَاحْكُم بَيْنَ
> النَّاسِ بِالْحَقِّ وَلَا تَتَّبِعِ الْهَوَى فَيُضِلَّكَ عَن سَبِيلِ اللَّهِ
> إِنَّ الَّذِينَ يَضِلُّونَ عَن سَبِيلِ اللَّهِ.

It thus appears that even the Prophet David was not immune from the contagious influence of *hawā.* Since the urge to follow one's desire is natural in human beings, there is a need for definitive guidance which the *Sharī'ah* seeks to provide. To harness *hawā* and prevent its evil influence is at once the function and objective of the *Sharī'ah* of Islam.

It was in view of the legal character of *Sharī'ah* that many have described it as 'God's commandments related to the activities of man', of which those that are related to ethics are taken out and classified under morality (*ādāb* and *akhlāq*). *Fiqh* is the legal science and can sometimes be used synonymously with *Sharī'ah.* The two are, however, different in that *Sharī'ah* is closely identified with divine revelation (*waḥy*), the knowledge of which could only be obtained from the Qur'ān and Sunnah. *Fiqh* has, on the other hand, been largely developed by jurists and consists of rules which are mainly founded on human reasoning and *ijtihād.*[5] *Sharī'ah* is thus the wider circle, and it embraces in its orbit all human actions, whereas *fiqh* is narrower in scope and addresses mainly what is referred to as practical legal rules (*al-aḥkām al-'amaliyyah*). The path of *Sharī'ah* is laid down by God and His Messenger; the edifice of *fiqh* is erected by human endeavour.[6]

Muslim scholars have generally regarded *fiqh* as understanding of the *Sharī'ah*, and not the *Sharī'ah* itself; a certain distinction between them had thus existed from the formative stages of *fiqh*. Note, for example, that the leading schools of law that were developed in the first three centuries were all known as the schools of *fiqh*. They were not known by any such terms as the Ḥanafī *Sharī'ah*, or the Shāfi'ī *Sharī'ah* but consistently as Ḥanafī *fiqh*, Shāfi'ī *fiqh* and so forth. The underlying message was one of unity in reference to *Sharī'ah* but of diversity with regard to *fiqh*. This distinction between the *Sharī'ah* and *fiqh* has been articulated by many twentieth century writers on the subject, including, Muḥammad Mūsā, Asaf Ali Fyzee, Muhammad Asad and many others.[7]

In an attempt to define the precise scope of *Sharī'ah,* Maududi observed that it has reached us in two forms, namely the Qur'ān, which embodies word for word the speech and commandments of God, and the ideal conduct of the Prophet, that is his Sunnah, which explains and clarifies the meaning of the Qur'ān. The Sunnah in conjunction with the Qur'ān constitutes what is called the *Sharī'ah.*[8] This description of the *Sharī'ah* excludes from its scope man-made law and *ijtihād* which is embodied in the works of jurists of various schools of thought. This is merely to establish the principle that juristic opinion and *ijtihād* are not to be equated with the authority of divine revelation. Having said this, however, the invaluable contribution of the great '*ulamā*' of the past to the legal and intellectual heritage of Islam is undeniable and never to be taken lightly. Muhammad Asad is even more specific in narrowing down the *Sharī'ah* to the definitive ordinances of the Qur'ān which are expounded in positive legal terms, known as the *nuṣūṣ* or clear injunctions. It is the *nuṣūṣ* or the clear injunctions of the Qur'ān and Sunnah which constitute the real eternal *Sharīʻah.*[9]

Muslim jurists have drawn a distinction between religious and juridical obligations; only the latter are enforceable through formal sanction by the courts of justice. The religious obligations, as well as the moral recommendations of Islam, are primarily addressed to the individual and they fall outside the court's jurisdiction. The rules of *Sharīʻah* are thus classified into the two main categories of *ʻibādāt* (devotional matters) and *muʻāmalāt* (civil transactions). The former comprises rules which regulate the relationship of man with his Creator, whereas the latter is concerned with relations between man and his fellow human beings. A second and somewhat similar classification of the rules of *Sharīʻah* is concerned with the division of rights into Right of God (*ḥaqq Allah*) and Right of Man (*ḥaqq al-ʻabd*). The former refers to public rights or rights that belong to the community as a whole whereas the latter refers mainly to private rights. Broadly the laws of *Sharīʻah* in the sphere of *muʻāmalāt*, which seek to regulate relations among individuals, constitute the primary concern of government authorities and the judiciary. These are, in other words, justiciable and the individual can seek judicial relief if his rights are violated by others or by the government. The rules pertaining to devotional matters, especially those which consist purely or principally of the Right of God, such as ritual prayers and fasting, etc., constitute religious obligations. Failure to fulfil these calls for moral reprimand in this world and punishment in the next, but they are basically not justiciable in the courts.[10]

Another characteristic feature of *Sharīʻah* is related to *tawḥīd,* belief in the oneness of God, which is the first and foremost article of Islamic faith, indeed the *sine qua non* of Islam. Every discussion of law and morality in Islam must, of necessity, proceed from *tawḥīd.* Its influence on *Sharīʻah* and ethics runs deep, so much so that *tawḥīd* manifests itself in ritual devotion and personal piety, in theology and law, in politics and economics, in faith and deeds, all of which are manifestations of the same all-pervasive principle of *tawḥīd.*[11] God created the universe, and every part of it reflects the unity of its source: every part of it is synchronized with its other parts. From this perspective, *tawḥīd* sets forth 'an ontology, cosmology and psychology of its own in its concept of the Oneness of Being'.[12] Consequently Islam and its *Sharīʻah* do not admit of divisions between the various facets of human life. Religion is inseparable, in principle, from politics, morality and economics, just as the human personality cannot be compartmentalized into religious, political and economic segments. Islam addresses all of these and takes a unitarian approach to human existence, in this way creating a way of life and a worldview of its own. The *Sharīʿah* not only regulates legal rights and obligations, but also non-legal matters, and provides moral guidance for human conduct in general. *Tawḥīd* thus dominates the basic outlook of *Sharīʿah*, which is one of unity in diversity. Worship (*ʿibādah*) in Islam is also a practical manifestation of *tawḥīd*, the belief, that is, in the Omniscience of God and homage to His illustrious presence. Without integrating *tawḥīd* into the essence of Islam, devotional acts become empty rituals devoid of all meaning, which should not be even attempted. Yet for purposes of enforcement the *Sharīʿah* does provide levels of distinction between the legal, moral and religious aspects of its rulings. It thus provides a basic scheme and scale of values by which to evaluate human acts into the obligatory (*wājib*), recommended (*mandūb*), permissible (*mubāḥ*), reprehensible (*makrūh*), and forbidden (*ḥarām*). Only the first and the last of these are determined by clear injunctions of the Qur'ān and Sunnah. The other three categories are supplementary and basically non-legal; they are designed to promote moral virtues and the attainment of excellence in conduct. In this way the *Sharīʿah* concerns itself with all areas of human activity, not always in an imposing and overbearing way, but in the form of moral encouragement and persuasion. It thus helps to provide the individual with a code of reference consisting of moral, legal and cultural values that can be reassuring and purposeful. It is due primarily to the influence of *tawḥīd* that the *Sharīʿah* has been characterized as a coherent body of doctrines that 'guarantees its unity in all its diversity'.[13] Human acts and relationships are measured on a scale of values which is reflective of its unity of origin and purpose.

Furthermore, *tawḥīd* plays a unifying role which binds the community together and constitutes its source of equality, solidarity and freedom. A society in which no other attribute except devotion to God and moral rectitude (*taqwā*) can qualify one individual's superiority over the other is founded on the essential equality of its members in the eyes of their Creator. It is in the nature of a unitarian order of society that the individual should enjoy a wide degree of autonomy and freedom. For *tawḥīd* and belief in the omnipotence of God liberates the individual from bondage of all other powers, as he expects no one else (indeed he must not) to be in control of his destiny in this world or the next.[14]

SOURCES OF *SHARĪʻAH*

The revealed sources of *Sharīʻah* are two, namely the Holy Qur'ān and the Sunnah. There are a number of other sources or proofs which are founded in human reasoning and *ijtihād. Ijtihād* occurs in a variety of forms such as analogical reasoning (*qiyās*), juristic preference (*istiḥsān*), presumption of continuity (*istiṣḥāb*), and even general consensus or *ijmāʻ* which basically originates in *ijtihād.* Analogy and consensus have been recognized by the vast majority of '*ulamā*', but there is disagreement among schools and jurists over the validity and scope of many of the rational proofs that originate in *ijtihād.*

The Qur'ān is neither a legal nor a constitutional document in the sense that legal material occupies only a small portion of its text. The Qur'ān calls itself by such alternative names as *hudā* (guidance), *kitāb* (book), and *dhikr* (remembrance), but not a code of law. By far the greater part of its 6235 verses are concerned with moral and religious themes, devotional matters, man and the universe, the hereafter, and even the history of the bygone events and parables. The legal or practical contents of the Qur'ān, often referred to as the *āyāt al-aḥkām* (legal verses), constitute the basis of what is known as jurisprudence of the Qur'ān *(fiqh al-Qur'ān).* There are about 350 legal verses in the Qur'ān, most of which were revealed in response to problems that were actually encountered. This might explain why these verses are also known as practical rulings (*al-aḥkām al-ʻamaliyyah*), pertaining to the conduct of the individual.

There are approximately 140 verses in the Qur'ān on devotional matters, such as ritual prayers (*ṣalāh*), legal alms (*zakah*), fasting, the pilgrimage (*ḥajj*), charities (*ṣadaqāt*) and the taking of oaths and penances (*kaffārāt*). Another seventy verses are devoted to marriage, divorce, paternity, custody of children, maintenance, inheritance and bequests. Rules concerning commercial transactions, such as sale, lease, loan and mortgage constitute the subject of another seventy verses. There are about thirty verses on crimes and penalties such as murder, highway robbery, theft, adultery and slanderous accusation. Another thirty verses occur on justice, equality, evidence, consultation and the rights and duties of citizens. There are about ten verses on economic matters pertaining to relations between the poor and the rich, workers' rights and so on.[15] It will be noted, however, that the '*ulamā*' are not in agreement over these figures, as calculations of this nature tend to differ according to one's understanding of, and approach to, the contents of the Qur'ān. For it is possible, as al-Shawkāni has aptly stated, for a learned scholar and *mujtahid* to derive a rule of law even from the parables and historical passages of the Qur'ān.[16]

The following may be given as examples of the legal verses in the Qur'ān:

> And give women (that you marry) their dower as a free gift. (4:4)
>
> وَآتُوا النِّسَاء صَدُقَاتِهِنَّ نِحْلَةً.
>
> The divorced women must observe upon themselves a waiting period of three menstrual cycles. (2:228)
>
> وَالْمُطَلَّقَاتُ يَتَرَبَّصْنَ بِأَنفُسِهِنَّ ثَلاَثَةَ قُرُوَءٍ.
>
> O you who believe! Fulfill (faithfully) all your contracts. (5:1)
>
> يَا أَيُّهَا الَّذِينَ آمَنُوا أَوْفُوا بِالْعُقُودِ.
>
> The recompense of an injury is an injury equal to it, but if one forgives and makes reconciliation, his reward is with God. (42:40)
>
> وَجَزَاء سَيِّئَةٍ سَيِّئَةٌ مِّثْلُهَا فَمَنْ عَفَا وَأَصْلَحَ فَأَجْرُهُ
> عَلَى اللَّهِ.

Although the Qur'ān contains specific rulings on such matters as marriage, divorce, inheritance and penalties, the larger part of Qur'ānic legislation consists of broad and comprehensive principles. The specific legislation of the Qur'ān is often designed so as to make its general principles better understood. Being the principal source of *Sharīʻah,* the Qur'ān provides general guidelines on almost every major topic of Islamic law. While commenting on this, Abū Zahrah (d. 1974) concurs with Ibn Ḥazm's (d. 1063) assessment that 'every single chapter of *fiqh* finds its origin in the Qur'ān, which is then explained and elaborated by the Sunnah'.[17] On a similar note, al-Shāṭibī (d. 1388) makes the following observation: 'Experience shows that every learned scholar who has resorted to the Qur'ān in search of solution to a problem has found in the Qur'ān some guidance to assist him on the subject.'[18] That the Qur'ān is mainly concerned with general principles is borne out by the fact that its contents require a great deal of elaboration, which is often provided, although not exhaustively, by the Sunnah.

Qur'ānic legislation on civil, economic, constitutional and international relations is, on the whole, confined to the general principles and objectives of the law. Thus, on the subject of contract, the Qur'ān proclaims a general principle that contractual agreements must be fulfilled (5:1), and in the area of civil transactions and property the believers are enjoined to:

> devour not the properties of one another unlawfully, but let there be lawful trade by mutual consent. (4:29)
>
> يَا أَيُّهَا الَّذِينَ آمَنُوا لاَ تَأْكُلُوا أَمْوَالَكُمْ بَيْنَكُمْ بِالْبَاطِلِ
> إِلاَّ أَن تَكُونَ تِجَارَةً عَن تَرَاضٍ مِّنكُمْ.

Elsewhere it is declared that:

> God has permitted sale and prohibited usury. (2:275)
>
> وَأَحَلَّ اللّهُ الْبَيْعَ وَحَرَّمَ الرِّبَا.

The detailed varieties of contracts and lawful trades, the forms of unlawful interference with the property of others, and the varieties of usurious transactions are matters which the Qur'ān has not elaborated. Some of these have been explained by the Sunnah; as for the rest, it is for the scholars of every age to specify them in the light of the general principles of *Sharīʿah* and the needs and interests of the people.[19] To give another example of the Qur'ānic style of legislation, the Qur'ān characterizes government as a trust and its function is stated in the most general and yet penetrating language as follows:

> God commands you to render the trusts [*al-amānāt*] to whom they are due and when you judge among people, you judge with justice. (4:58)
>
> إِنَّ اللّهَ يَأْمُرُكُمْ أَن تُؤدُّوا الأَمَانَاتِ إِلَى أَهْلِهَا وَإِذَا
> حَكَمْتُم بَيْنَ النَّاسِ أَن تَحْكُمُوا بِالْعَدْلِ.

The concept of trust in this text is broad enough to comprise all aspects of government, from adjudication of disputes to appointment of officials, to fulfilment of rights and obligations, and to allocation of public funds, etc. In every case trust must be handed over to those who are entitled to it, and to those who are competent to discharge it. Furthermore, trust is inseparably linked with responsibility. The Qur'ān, in other words, advocates a responsible system of government which is accountable for its conduct. These are some of the conclusions that Ibn Taymiyyah has drawn from this verse. In his widely acclaimed book, *al-Siyāsah al-Shar'iyyah,* Ibn Taymiyyah pointed out at the outset that the entire bulk of this book is a commentary on this single Qur'ānic verse.[20] The same could be said of the Qur'ānic legislation on the principles of government such as consultation (*shūrā*), justice and equality, which is concerned with an exposition of general principles. In the area of crimes and punishments, the Qur'ān is specific but only with regard to a handful of offences and their penalties. The rest of the Qur'ānic legislation in this area lays down general guidelines which enable the learned scholar *(mujtahid)* to specify the general rulings of the Qur'ān in the light of the needs and conditions of the community.[21] The Qur'ānic style of expounding general principles, without encumbering them with specific details, has in it the seeds of lasting validity and the timeless character of its laws.[22]

A ruling of the Qur'ān may be conveyed in a text which is clear and unequivocal (*qaṭ'ī*) or in a language that is open to different interpretations. A definitive text has only one meaning and admits of no other interpretation. An example of this is the text on the entitlement of the husband in the estate of his deceased wife as follows:

> In what your wives leave, your share is one-half, if they have no child. (4:12)
>
> وَلَكُمْ نِصْفُ مَا تَرَكَ أَزْوَاجُكُمْ إِن لَّمْ يَكُن لَّهُنَّ وَلَدٌ.

The quantitative aspect of this ruling, namely one-half, is definitive and therefore not open to interpretation. The Qur'ānic ruling on the essentials of the faith, the specified shares in inheritance, and the prescribed penalties (*ḥudūd*) are all definitive; their validity may not be disputed; everyone is bound to follow them and they are basically not open to interpretation and legal reasoning (*ijtihād*).

The speculative (*ẓannī*) rulings of the Qur'ān are, on the other hand, open to interpretation and *ijtihād.* The best interpretation is that which can be obtained from the Qur'ān itself, that is by looking at the Qur'ān as a whole and finding the necessary elaboration elsewhere in a similar or even different context. The Sunnah is another source which supplements the Qur'ān and elaborates its rulings. When the necessary interpretation can be found in an authentic *ḥadīth,* it becomes an integral part of the Qur'ān, and both together carry a binding force. Next in this order come the Companions who were particularly well-informed on the Qur'ān, and their understanding and interpretation carries authority above that of other commentators.[23]

An example of speculative ruling in the Qur'ān is the text which provides:

> forbidden to you are your mothers [*ummahātukum*] and your daughters [*banātukum*]. (4:23)
>
> حُرِّمَتْ عَلَيْكُمْ أُمَّهَاتُكُمْ وَبَنَاتُكُمْ.

This text is definitive on the basic prohibition of marriage with one's mother and daughter and there is no disagreement on this point. However, the word *banātukum* (your daughters) could include one's real daughter, step-daughter and illegitimate daughter. A subsequent portion of the text eliminates the doubt with regard to step-daughters, as these are declared forbidden. But the jurists have differed as to whether the prohibition should be extended to illegitimate daughters. The Ḥanafis have upheld that both real (i.e. daughters through marriage) and illegitimate daughters are included in the meaning of this text, but the Shāfi'īs maintain that only the daughter through marriage is forbidden. Similar differences of interpretation could have arisen regarding the exact meaning of 'mothers' had the Qur'ān itself and also the Sunnah not clarified the precise import of the text. Consequently, there remains no doubt that besides the real mother, step-mother and foster mother are all included in the meaning of this text.[24]

The '*ulamā*' are unanimous to the effect that the Sunnah is a source of *Sharī'ah* and that its rulings with regard to lawful and unlawful (*ḥalāl* and *ḥarām*) stand on the same footing as the Qur'ān. The Sunnah of the Prophet is a proof which is supported by the Qur'ān, and Muslims are enjoined to comply with it. The words of the Prophet, as the Qur'ān tells us, are divinely inspired (53:3). His acts and teachings that are meant to establish a rule of *Sharīʻah* constitute a binding proof. In more than one place, the Qur'ān commands obedience to the Prophet and makes it a duty of the believers to submit to his judgement and his authority without question. Note for instance,

> Whoever obeys the Messenger verily obeys God. (4:80)
>
> مَّنْ يُطِعِ الرَّسُولَ فَقَدْ أَطَاعَ اللَّهَ.

and

> Whatever the Messenger gives you, take it and whatever he forbids you, avoid it. (59:7)
>
> وَمَا آتَاكُمُ الرَّسُولُ فَخُذُوهُ وَمَا نَهَاكُمْ عَنْهُ فَانتَهُوا.

Al-Ghazālī explains the purport of these verses in that some of the divine revelations which the Prophet received constitute the Qur'ān whereas the remainder are embodied in the Sunnah. The words of the Prophet are proof for anyone who heard the Prophet saying them. As for us and the generality of Muslims who have received them through the verbal and written reports of narrators, we need to ascertain their authenticity.[25] The proof of authenticity may be definitive and proven by continuous testimony (*mutawātir*), or it may amount to a preferable conjecture in the form of a solitary report (*āḥād*). In either case, the Sunnah in principle commands obedience. All the rulings of the Prophet, especially those which correspond with the Qur'ān and corroborate its contents, constitute binding law.[26]

As a source of *Sharīʻah,* the Sunnah enacts its rulings in the following three capacities. Firstly, it may simply reiterate and corroborate a ruling which originates in the Qur'ān. A substantial part of the Sunnah is in fact of this variety. All *ḥadīth* pertaining to the Five Pillars of the faith and such other topics like the right of one's parents, respect for the property of others, and also *ḥadīth* which regulate homicide, theft and false testimony, etc., basically reaffirm the Qur'ānic principles on these subjects.[27] Secondly, the Sunnah may consist of an explanation or clarification of the Qur'ān: it may clarify the ambivalent (*mujmal*), qualify the absolute (*muṭlaq*), or specify the general (*ʻāmm*) of the Qur'ān. Once again, a substantial part of the Sunnah falls into this category, in which case the Sunnah basically explains and interprets the Qur'ān. The foregoing two varieties between them constitute the largest bulk of the Sunnah, and the '*ulamā*' are in agreement that both of these are integral to the Qur'ān; they may not be separated nor taken independently from the Qur'ān.[28] Thirdly, the Sunnah may consist of rulings on which the Qur'ān is silent, in which case the ruling in question originates in the Sunnah itself. This variety of Sunnah, referred to as founding Sunnah (*al-sunnah al-mu'assisah*), constitutes an independent source of *Sharī'ah.* To give some examples, the prohibition regarding simultaneous marriage to the maternal and paternal aunt of one's wife, the right of pre-emption (*shuf'*), and the grandmother's entitlement to a share in inheritance all originate in the Sunnah as the Qur'ān itself is silent on these points.[29]

There is some disagreement among the '*ulamā*' as to whether the Sunnah in all of its varieties should be seen as a supplement to the Qur'ān. The affirmative view on this is based on the premise that even the original rulings of the Sunnah can be related to the general objective and purpose, if not the specific contents, of the Qur'ān. The majority view on this is, however, that there is no necessary conflict in maintaining that the Sunnah is a supplement to the Qur'ān as well as a source of *Sharī'ah* in its own right.

Ijtihād means striving or exertion by the *mujtahid* (one who carries out *ijtihād)* in deriving the rules of *Sharī'ah* on particular issues from the sources. Normally such rules are not self-evident in the sources and their formulation necessitates a certain amount of effort on the part of the *mujtahid. Ijtihād* may consist of an interpretation of the source materials and inference of rules from them, or it may consist of an opinion regarding the *Sharī'ah* ruling on a particular issue. Since the divine revelation has come to an end with the demise of the Prophet, *ijtihād* remains the main instrument of interpreting the divine message and relating it to the changing conditions of the Muslim community.

Ijtihād is validated by the Prophet himself and there are many *ḥadīths* on the authority of *ijtihād.* But the one *ḥadīth* which provides clear authority on this subject, as Al-Ghazālī points out, is the *ḥadīth* of Mu'ādh bin Jabal. Upon sending Mu'ādh as judge to the Yemen, the Prophet asked him about the source on which he would rely in making decisions. In reply, Mu'ādh referred first to the Book of God, and then to the Sunnah of the Messenger of God; in the event where he failed to find the necessary guidance in either, then he would formulate his own *ijtihād.* The Prophet approved of this and was well-pleased with Muʻādh's response.[30]

The *Sharīʻah* in principle admits that legal rules may be changed and modified in accordance with changing circumstances. There is little doubt that abrogation (*naskh*) has occurred in both the Qur'ān and Sunnah due primarily to the change of conditions in the life of the community, especially following the Prophet's migration to Madinah. Abrogation entails the repeal, and often replacement, of one legal text by another. The question arises as to whether a text can be modified on other grounds such as *ijtihād,* man-made legislation and custom.

If the text is on devotional matters (*ʻibādāt*), the general view is that it cannot be changed. But if it concerns worldly transactions, the majority of jurists have held that it is open to interpretation and *ijtihād.* The jurist may consider the meaning of the text, the effective cause (*ʻillah*) on which it was originally founded, and the welfare (*maṣlaḥah*) of the community so as to construct a fresh *ijtihād.* If the text is specific and does not admit of *ijtihād,* the dominant view is that no change should be attempted.[31] But even so, instances can be found in the precedent of the caliph ʻUmar ibn al-Khaṭṭāb (d. 644), where such changes have been made, in a few cases at least, even in the presence of a clear text.[32] Based on these, and the Qur'ānic principle of removal of hardship (*rafʻ al-ḥaraj*), al-Qarāfī (d. 1283) has reached the conclusion that the actual living conditions of the people must be taken into account: 'All the rules of *fiqh* which are founded in custom are liable to change with the change of custom in which they were originally founded.'[33] The substance of this conclusion has been adopted in the *Majallat al-Aḥkām* which provides that 'public usage is conclusive and action must be taken in accordance with it' (Art. 37), and that 'it is undeniable that the rules of law vary with the change of time' (Art. 39).

Ijtihād in our times operates in the following three capacities:

a. With regard to the textual rulings of the Qur'ān and the Sunnah which are open to interpretation and are speculative (*ẓannī*) in respect of either meaning (*dalālah*) or transmission (*riwāyah*) or both, the sphere of *ijtihād* is limited to finding the correct interpretation that is in harmony with the letter and objectives of the law. Should there be an apparent conflict between two textual rulings of this type, the *mujtahid* may select and prefer one to the other in accordance with the accepted rules that govern conflicting evidences.

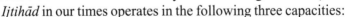

b. With regard to matters on which there is no clear text or *ijmā'*, *ijtihād* is to be guided by the general objectives of the *Sharī'ah* (*maqāṣid al-Sharī'ah*). This type of *ijtihād* is usually referred to as *ijtihād bi al-ra'y* or *ijtihād* which is founded in opinion.
c. In regard to matters which have been regulated by the existing rules of *fiqh* that may originate in analogical reasoning (*qiyās*), juristic preference (*istiḥsān*) and other varieties of *ijtihād*, and the *mujtahid* reaches the conclusion that they no longer serve the objectives of *Sharī'ah* owing to social change, he may attempt fresh *ijtihād*. In doing so, the *mujtahid* is once again to be guided by the general principles and objectives of *Sharī'ah* so as to construct a ruling which is best suited to the prevailing circumstances and responds to the legitimate needs and interests of the people.[34]

OBJECTIVES OF *SHARĪ'AH* (*MAQĀṢID AL-SHARĪ'AH*)

The Qur'ān is descriptive of the objectives of *Sharī'ah* when it declares

> O mankind, a direction has come to you from your Lord; it is a healing for the (spiritual) ailments in your hearts and it is guidance and mercy for the believers. (10:57)
>
> يَا أَيُّهَا النَّاسُ قَدْ جَاءَتْكُم مَّوْعِظَةٌ مِّن رَّبِّكُمْ وَشِفَاءٌ
> لِّمَا فِي الصُّدُورِ وَهُدًى وَرَحْمَةٌ لِّلْمُؤْمِنِينَ.

The message here transcends all barriers that divide humanity; none must stand in the way of the mercy and beneficence that God has intended for all human beings. This is confirmed in another passage where the Qur'ān describes the purpose of the Prophet's mission to be mercy not only to mankind, but to all of God's creatures (21:107). 'Mercy' is perhaps a poor translation of *raḥmah* which conveys compassion, kindness, goodwill and beneficence. Ibn Qayyim al-Jawziyyah (d. 1356) explains that the *Sharī'ah* aims at safeguarding people's interest in this world and the next; 'In its entirety, it is justice, mercy and wisdom.'[35] In order to attain these objectives, the *Sharī'ah* identifies three areas which constitute the component parts of mercy, namely to educate the individual, to establish justice and to realize benefit (*maṣlaḥah*) for the people.[36] The remainder of this chapter looks into each of these separately.

Educating the Individual (Tahdhīb al-Fard)

The primary focus of Islam is on the individual in the sense that it inspires the believer with faith and instils in him the qualities of being trustworthy and righteous. It is through reforming the individual that Islam aims at achieving its social goals. Acts of devotion (*'ibādāt*) are a part of the Islamic educational programme; they are all designed so as to educate the believer, to enable him to be a useful member of society and refrain from causing harm to others. The *'ibādāt* in all of its varieties aims at purifying the mind and heart from corruption, selfishness and over-indulgence in material pursuits. This is indeed the declared purpose of the ritual prayer (*ṣalāh*), as the Qur'ān proclaims:

> Surely prayer keeps one away from indecency and evil, and certainly the remembrance of God is the greatest (form of devotion). (29:45)
>
> إنَّ الصَّلَاةَ تَنْهَى عَنِ الفَحْشَاءِ وَالمُنكَرِ وَلَذِكْرُ اللَّهِ أَكْبَرُ.

Ṣalāh involves both mental and physical training; it leads to inner perfection and it is a means for man to gain proximity to his Creator. While performing the ritual prayer the worshipper concentrates in full attention; he is not free to do what he likes or act in any way that would disrupt the continuity of the prayer. There is no turning to any side, no glancing, laughing, eating or drinking while one prays, all of which involves an exercise in self-control. The whole body must be calm and stable before the phrase '*Allahu akbar*' is uttered. The first chapter of the holy Qur'ān, which is recited from memory, reads in part,

> We worship only Thee, O God, and beg only Thy help.
>
> إيَّاكَ نَعْبُدُ وإيَّاكَ نَسْتَعِينُ.

Here we do not use the word 'I' but 'we' to show that prayer not only concerns the individual but the well-being of the community as a whole.[37]

There is a definite time in which to discharge the obligation of *ṣalāh*, and performing early morning prayer even a minute after the sunrise makes it void, and one cannot offer the excuse of being sleepy. The purpose of observing punctuality is to educate the individual; then we are commanded to face the *ka'bah* in *ṣalāh*. Why should we face the *ka'bah* while the Qur'ān clearly tells us

> whichever direction you turn, there is the face of God. (2:115)
>
> فَأَيْنَمَا تُوَلُّوا فَثَمَّ وَجْهُ اللَّهِ.

It is meant to be a social education for all to face in one direction. For turning to any direction one may wish causes indiscipline and confusion. Imagine the scene if everybody in the congregation faced different directions! Cleanliness in body and attire and decency in clothing are the requirements of every *ṣalāh*. Furthermore, performing *ṣalāh* in congregation nurtures a unified purpose, equality and solidarity among worshippers as well as facilitating social encounter in a peaceful environment. And finally the *ṣalāh* ends by uttering the phrase, 'Peace and the blessing of God to His worthy servants'; a declaration of goodwill towards one's fellow human beings. These objectives are even more vividly present in fasting, the pilgrimage of *ḥajj*, and alms giving, all of which train the individual in self-discipline, sacrifice and sensitivity to the wellbeing of others. The pilgrimage is particularly educational in broadening the individual outlook beyond the confines of a particular locality and encourages a sense of awareness of the wider interests of Muslims worldwide.[38]

There is a great deal in the Qur'ān and *ḥadīth* on promotion of self-discipline and morality through God-consciousness (*taqwā*), honesty (*ṣidq*), fulfilment of promises (*wafā' bi'l-'ahd*), pleasant manners (*ḥusn al-khuluq*), humility (*tawāḍu', ḥayā'*), sincerity (*ikhlāṣ*), beneficence (*iḥsān*), co-operation in good work (*ta'āwun*), courage (*shajā'ah*) and manliness (*murū'ah*). There is even greater emphasis in the sources of Islam on avoidance of oppression (*ẓulm*), lying (*khidhb*), perfidy, turpitude and degrading conduct (*radhā'il*), arrogance (*takabbur*), hypocrisy (*riyā'*) and so forth. Educating the individual in good values and moral excellence may thus be characterized as a cardinal goal and objective of Islam.

Justice (ʻadl)

Whereas the basic objective of Islam and its *Sharīʿah* concerning the individual is purification of character, in the social sphere it is to establish justice. This Islamic concept of justice is not confined to a merely formal or regulatory justice, but makes it a part of the faith, character and personality of believers.

ʻAdl literally means placing things in their right places where they belong. It is to establish an equilibrium by way of fulfilling rights and obligations and by eliminating excess and disparity in all spheres of life.[39] The *Sharīʿah* seeks to establish justice not only in its corrective and retributive sense of adjudicating grievances, but also in the sense of distributive justice, establishing an equilibrium of benefits and advantages in society.[40] This is indeed obvious from the objective and comprehensive approach that the Qur'ān has taken towards justice. It is the one over-riding objective that characterizes the Qur'ānic message as a whole, as the Book declares:

> We sent Our Messengers with evidences and revealed the Book and the balance through them so as to establish justice among people. (57:25)
>
> لقَدْ أَرْسَلْنَا رُسُلَنَا بِالْبَيِّنَاتِ وَأَنزَلْنَا مَعَهُمُ الْكِتَابَ
> وَالْمِيزَانَ لِيَقُومَ النَّاسُ بِالْقِسْطِ.

The phrase 'Our Messengers' is in the plural, and the whole tenor of this declaration suggests that justice is a goal, not only of Islam, but of all revealed religions; it is of central importance to all prophetic missions; and it comprises in its scope all people regardless of their religious denominations. The Book of God and the *Sharīʿah* have thus been revealed to provide valid criteria for justice so that justice is not distorted by ignorance and bias.[41]

The Qur'ānic standards of justice are objective in that they are not tainted by considerations of racial, tribal, national or religious sentiments. The Qur'ān addresses justice as one of its major themes, which is referred to in at least fifty-three instances where the people are urged to be just to others at all levels, whether personal or public, in words and in conduct, in dealing with friends or foes, Muslim or non-Muslim, all must be treated with justice: To quote but a few injunctions of the holy Qur'ān:

> O believers! Stand out firmly for justice as witnesses to God, even if it be against yourself, your parents and relatives and whether it be against rich or poor. (4:135)
>
> يَا أَيُّهَا الَّذِينَ آمَنُوا كُونُوا قَوَّامِينَ بِالْقِسْطِ شُهَدَاء لِلَّهِ
> وَلَوْ عَلَى أَنفُسِكُمْ أَوِ الْوَالِدَيْنِ وَالأَقْرَبِينَ إِن يَكُنْ
> غَنِيًّا أَوْ فَقِيرًا فَاللَّهُ أَوْلَى بِهِمَا.

> And let not hatred of a people divert you from the path of justice. Be just as it is closest to excellence in piety (*taqwā*). (5:8)
>
> وَلاَ يَجْرِمَنَّكُمْ شَنَآنُ قَوْمٍ عَلَى أَلاَّ تَعْدِلُوا اعْدِلُوا
> هُوَ أَقْرَبُ لِلتَّقْوَى.

> And when you speak (make sure that you) speak with justice. (6:152)
>
> وَإِذَا قُلْتُمْ فَاعْدِلُوا.

Elsewhere the Qur'ān demands justice together with benevolence (*iḥsān*):

> Surely God enjoins justice and doing good (to others) (*iḥsān*). (16:90)
>
> إِنَّ اللَّهَ يَأْمُرُ بِالْعَدْلِ وَالإِحْسَانِ.

The juxtaposition of justice and *iḥsān* in this verse opens the scope to considerations of equity and fairness, especially where the linguistic confines and technicality of a legal text might lead to rigidity in the administration of justice. Justice must be attempted in the spirit of *iḥsān,* that is, even when it is not demanded by anyone; the attempt should be in equity and good faith, which will gain the pleasure of God. Ibn Qayyim al-Jawziyyah grasps the essence of justice in the Qur'ān when he observes that justice must be followed and upheld wherever it is found, within or outside the declared provisions of the law: Justice is the supreme goal and objective of Islam. God has sent scriptures and Messengers in order to establish justice among people. When there are signs which indicate the path to justice, it is in accordance with the law of God to aim towards it. Hence 'any path that leads to justice and fairness is an integral part of the religion and can never be contrary to it'.[42] What Ibn Qayyim is saying is that even if nothing could be found in the *Sharīʿah* to show the direction towards justice, it should still be attempted and that the essence of such efforts would always be in harmony with the *Sharī'ah.*

In their relations with non-Muslims, the Muslims are directed to be just:

> God forbids you not to do good and be just to those who have not fought you over your faith nor have evicted you from your homes. God loves those who strive for justice. (60:8)
>
> لَا يَنْهَاكُمُ اللَّهُ عَنِ الَّذِينَ لَمْ يُقَاتِلُوكُمْ فِي الدِّينِ وَلَمْ
> يُخْرِجُوكُم مِّن دِيَارِكُمْ أَن تَبَرُّوهُمْ وَتُقْسِطُوا إِلَيْهِمْ
> إِنَّ اللَّهَ يُحِبُّ الْمُقْسِطِينَ.

According to al-Ṭabarī, the ruling of this verse extends to all nations and followers of all faiths, indeed to the whole of mankind.[43] While quoting this and other Qur'ānic injunctions on the subject, Sayyid Quṭb draws the conclusion that justice is an inherent right of all human beings under the *Sharī'ah.*[44]

It would thus appear that injustice is abhorrent to the letter and spirit of the Qur'ān. There may be some rules of *fiqh* which were once formulated in a different set of historical conditions and may now be deemed to be unjust. Our attitude towards such anomalies should, in my opinion, be guided by Ibn Qayyim al-Jawziyyah's penetrating assessment which I quoted earlier that such rules do not belong to the *Sharī'ah* even if they are claimed to be a part of it. They should therefore be revised through *ijtihād* in the light of the broad objectives of *Sharī'ah* and the prevailing interest of society.

Considerations of Public Interest (Maṣlaḥah)

A principal objective of the *Sharī'ah* is realization of benefit to the people concerning their affairs both in this world and the hereafter. It is generally held that the *Sharī'ah* in all of its parts aims at securing a benefit for the people or protecting them against corruption and evil. In his pioneering work, *Al-Muwāfaqāt fī Uṣūl al-Sharī'ah,* al-Shāṭibī has in fact singled out *maṣlaḥah* as being the only overriding objective of *Sharī'ah* which is broad enough to comprise all measures that are beneficial to the people, including the administration of justice and *'ibādāt.* He placed a fresh emphasis on *maqāṣid al-Sharī'ah*, so much so that his unique contribution to the understanding of the objectives and philosophy of the *Sharīʿah* is widely acknowledged. While highlighting unity in the origin and basic purposes of *Sharīʿah*, al-Shāṭibī points out that God instituted the *Sharīʿah* for the benefit of mankind both in this world and the next. This is a primary objective of the Lawgiver and a unifying factor which can be seen in all of the detailed rulings of *Sharīʿah*.[45]

Despite some disagreement as to the details of al-Shāṭibī's views, the basic outline of his doctrine of the *maqāṣid al- Sharīʿah* has been generally upheld.[46] The '*ulamā*' are thus in agreement that there is no ruling in the entire *Sharīʿah* that does not seek to secure a genuine benefit; that all of the commandments of *Sharīʿah* aim at realizing benefits, and that all of its prohibitions are designed so as to prevent corruption. The obligatory, praiseworthy and permissible *(wājib, mandūb* and *mubāḥ*) in this way aim at realizing benefits and the reprehensible (*makrūh*) and the forbidden (*ḥarām*) aim at preventing corruption and evil. Should there arise a conflict between two injunctions due to the circumstances of their enforcement, priority should be given to that which obtains the higher benefit. Rescuing a drowning man, for example, takes priority over performance of obligatory prayer. Similarly, if the act of rescuing necessitates breaking of obligatory fasting, then this is permissible.[47]

We have already explained as to how the *Sharīʿah* seeks to secure benefits in the sphere of '*ibādāt*. These are not only aimed at gaining the pleasure of God but also to prevent corruption and facilitate benefit to both the individual and society. The *Sharīʿah* encourages the benefits of this world side by side with those of the hereafter. The individual is urged to be a useful member of society, so that hard work and lawful earning, supporting one's family, and even the pursuit and dissemination of knowledge are all equated with acts of devotion. Conversely, even an act of devotion which is attempted as a means of escape from useful work and contribution to society loses much of its spiritual merit.[48]

The benefits are generally divided into three types, namely the essentials (*ḍarūriyyāt*), the complementary (*ḥājiyyāt*) and the so-called embellishments (*taḥsiniyyāt*). The *Sharīʿah* in all of its parts aims at the realization of one or the other of these benefits. The essential benefits are defined as those on which the lives of the people depend, and their neglect leads to total disruption and chaos. They are the overriding values of life, faith, intellect, property and lineage. These must be protected and all measures that aim at safeguarding them must be taken, whether by the individual, or by government authorities. The complementary interests on the whole supplement the essential interests and refer to interests whose neglect leads to hardship but not to total disruption of normal life. To ban profiteering (*iḥtikār*), for example, or the sale of alcohol so as to prevent its consumption, and to grant concessions that the *Sharī'ah* has granted in regard to *'ibādāt* for the traveller and the sick, all fall under the category of *ḥājiyyāt.*[49] The embellishments refer to interests whose realization leads to improvement and the attainment of that which is desirable such as cleanliness, avoiding extravagance, and measures that are designed to prevent proliferation of false claims in the courts, etc.

In order to be valid, *maṣlaḥah* must fulfil certain conditions, one of which is that it must be genuine (*ḥaqīqiyyah*) as opposed to that which is plausible (*wahmiyyah*).[50] The *Sharī'ah* only protects the genuine benefits which, as al-Ghazālī points out, are always related to the protection of the five essential interests as noted above. Any measure which secures these values falls within the scope of genuine *benefits* and anything which violates them is corruption or *mafsadah* and preventing the latter is also a benefit.[51] Protecting the faith, for example, necessitates prevention of sedition (*fitnah*) and propagation of heresy. It also means safeguarding freedom of belief in accordance with the Qur'ānic principle that

> there shall be no compulsion in religion. (2:256)
>
> لَا إِكْرَاهَ فِي الدِّين.

Similarly, safeguarding the right to life includes protecting the means which facilitates an honourable life such as the freedom to work, freedom of speech and freedom of travel. Protecting the intellect necessitates promotion of learning and safeguards against calamities which corrupt the individual and make him a burden to society. Furthermore, safeguarding the purity of lineage entails protection of the family and creation of a favourable environment for the care and custody of children. And lastly protecting property requires defending the right of ownership; it also means facilitating fair trade and lawful exchange of goods and services in the community.[52]

In order to ensure objectivity in the determination of the benefits, reference is to be made to considerations of public interest whose validity is independent of relative convenience and utility to particular individuals. This is so, as al-Shāṭibī explains, because the

Sharī'ah is eternal and timeless in its validity and application. Hence the interest which it seeks to uphold must also be objective and universal, not relative and subjective. Relativity in this connection implies equating *maṣlaḥah* with personal predilections (*ahwā' al-nufūs*), personal benefits (*manāfi'*), prejudice and passionate desires all of which render the *maṣlaḥah* relative and subjective. When a benefit is determined on these grounds, it becomes anomalous and is also likely to conflict with other benefits. The objectivity of *maṣlaḥah* is measured by its relevance and service to the essential benefits, which are clearly upheld by *Sharī'ah.*[53] *Maṣlaḥah* is basically a rational concept and most of the benefits of this world (*maṣāliḥ al-dunyā*) are identifiable by human intellect, experience and custom, even without the guidance of *Sharī'ah.* This is true also of evil and corruption which are generally ascertainable by human intellect. The *Sharī'ah* only provides a set of criteria and guidelines so as to prevent confusion between personal prejudice and *maṣlaḥah.* This is, however, not the case regarding benefits pertaining to the hereafter, and those which combine the benefits of this world and the next, for these can only be identified by the *Sharī'ah.*[54]

And lastly, our discussion of the objectives of *Sharī'ah* would be deficient without referring to the two principles of *Sharī'ah,* namely removal of hardship (*raf' al-ḥaraj*), and prevention of harm (*daf' al-ḍarar*), both of which are integral to the general concept of *maṣlaḥah.* The Qur'ān declares that

> God never intended to make religion a means of inflicting hardship. (22:78)
>
> وَمَا جَعَلَ عَلَيْكُمْ فِي الدِّينِ مِنْ حَرَجٍ.

This is confirmed elsewhere where it is provided in more general terms that 'God never intends to impose hardship on you'; and then it is declared in an affirmative sense that 'God intends to make things easy for you' (5:6 and 4:28). The purport of these declarations is confirmed in a report from the Prophet's widow, 'A'ishah, who stated concerning the Prophet that

> He did not choose but the easier of two alternatives so long as it did not amount to sin.[55]
>
> إنه ما خيّر من الأمرين إلا أيسرهما ما لم يكن إثما.

These are in turn reflected in a legal maxim that 'hardship begets facility' which has been adopted in Article (17) of the *Majallat al-Aḥkām.*[56]

In a similar vein, prevention of harm is a general purpose of the *Sharīʻah* of Islam as the following *ḥadīth* declares:

> Harm shall neither be inflicted nor reciprocated in Islam.[57]
>
> لاضرر وضرار فى الاسلام.

The substance of this *ḥadīth* is upheld in a number of other *ḥadīths* and it is observed that this *ḥadīth* grasps the essence of *maṣlaḥah* in all of its varieties.[58] Najm al-Dīn al-Ṭūfī, a Ḥanbali jurist (d. 1316) has gone so far as to maintain that this *ḥadīth* provides a clear text on *maṣlaḥah.*[59] The *ḥadīth* has in turn been adopted in toto as a legal maxim in *Majallat al-Aḥkām,* and has given rise to the formulation of other legal maxims such as 'the prevention of evil takes priority over the attraction of benefit', that 'harm must be eliminated'; and that 'a particular harm may be tolerated if it were to prevent a general one'.[60]

CONCLUSION

Judging by the precedent and example of the leading Companions, and the renowned '*ulamā*' of jurisprudence, we find that our contemporary scholars feel constrained in attempting legal reconstruction and *ijtihād* in tandem with the rapid pace of social change. This is partly due to the long history of unquestioning imitation (*taqlīd*) which seriously disrupted the natural growth of *fiqh* and arrested the efflorescence of *ijtihād. Ijtihād* must continue at all times so as to keep the law abreast of the needs and changing conditions of society. The renowned closure of the door of *ijtihād* at around the beginning of the eleventh century has led to stagnation. Consequently a gap has developed between the *Sharīʻah* and the living conditions of people in many present-day Muslim societies. The ominous result of this alienation was that with the ongoing changes of history, especially following the industrial revolution in the West and its imported consequences in the Muslim lands, a certain mentality gained roots that the *Sharīʻah* was no longer capable of accommodating the rapid pace of social change.

The experiment in modernity and westernization in recent decades has led to disenchantment as it failed to produce the desired results in the Muslim world and has even added some new problems.[61] There is now an awareness on the part of Muslims of the need to renew their links with their own heritage and find their own solutions to the issues which concern them. The tendency today is not just a return to the *Sharī'ah,* which is a most tangible part of that heritage, but to try to relate the *Sharī'ah* to the living conditions of the people. This would necessitate imaginative reconstruction and *ijtihād* entailing revision and modification of the rules of *fiqh* so as to translate the broad objectives of the *Sharī'ah* into the laws and institutions of contemporary society.

NOTES

1. Cf. '*Sharī'ah, The Encyclopedia of Islam.*
2. Cf. Madkūr, *Madkhal,* 11, al-Ṣābūnī, *al-Madkhal al-Fiqhi*, 20.
3. Joseph Schacht, *An Introduction*, 1.
4. Sa'di Abū Ḥabīb, *Dirāsah fi Manhaj*, 454.
5. Cf. Madkūr, *Madkhal*, 17, N.P. Aghnides, *Muhammadan Theories of Finance*,1.
6. Cf. Muhammad Asad, *The Principles of State, 12*; A. A. A. Fyzee, *Outlines of Muhammadan Law*, 22.
7. Cf. Fyzee, *Outlines of Muhammadan Law*, 16; Kamali, 'The Sharī'ah: Law as the Way of God', in ed. Cornell, *Voices of Islam*, I, 149.
8. S. A. A. Maududi, *The Islamic Law and Constitution, 69.*
9. Muhammad Asad, *The Principle of State,* 13.
10. Cf. al-Ṣābūnī, *al-Madkhal al-Fiqhi, 27;* Maḥmūd Shaltūt, *Al-Islām,* 405.
11. Cf. S. Parvez Manzoor, 'Environment and Values', 155.
12. al-'Attas, *Islam and Secularism,* 167.
13. Schacht, *An Introduction,* 200.
14. Cf. Humayun Kabir, *Science,* 56.
15. Shaltūt, *Al-Islām,* no.10, 494; Khallāf, *'Ilm*, 32.
16. Al-Shawkāni, *Irshād al-Fuḥūl,* 250.
17. Abū Zahrah, *Uṣūl al-Fiqh,* 80.
18. al-Shāṭibī, *Al-Muwāfaqāt fi Uṣūl al-Sharī'ah,* III, 219.
19. For more examples see Badrān Abū al-'Aynayn, *Bayān al-Nuṣūs*, 2–3.
20. Ibn Taymiyyah, *Al-Siyāsah al-Shar'iyyah,* I.
21. For details see M. H. Kamali, *Jurisprudence,* 38 ff.
22. Cf. al-Ṭāhir b. 'Āshūr, *Maqāṣid al-Sharī'ah,* 94.
23. Cf. Khallāf, *'Ilm*, 34: Abū Zahrah, *Uṣūl,* 71
24. For more examples see Kamali, *Jurisprudence,* 27 ff.
25. al-Ghazālī, *Al-Mustaṣfā,* I. 83.

26. Khallāf, *'Ilm,* 34.
27. See for detail Muṣṭafa al-Sibā'i, *Al-Sunnah,* 379; Khallāf, *'Ilm,* 39.
28. Badrān, *Bayān,* 7.
29. Ibn Qayyim, *I'lām al-Muwaqqī'in,* II, 33; al-Sibā'i, *Al-Sunnah,* 380.
30. Abū Dāwūd al-Sijistān, *Sunan Abū Dāwūd,* III, 1019, *ḥadīth* no. 3585; al-Ghazālī, *Mustaṣfā,* II, 63-64.
31. Cf. Madkūr, *Madkhal*, 107, Maḥmaṣṣāni, *Philosophy,* 109.
32. For details see Mahmaṣṣāni, *Philosophy,* 109 ff.
33. Ibid., 67.
34. Ibid.
35. Ibn Qayyim, *I'lām,* III, 1.
36. Madkūr, *Madkhal,* 85–6.
37. Cf. Abū Zahrah, *Uṣūl*, 289.
38. Cf. Abū Zahrah, *Uṣūl*, 289; Madkūr, *Madkhal*, 22.
39. For further detail see Motahhari, *Spiritual Discourses,* 65–6.
40. Cf. 'Abd al-Salām, *Qawā'id* I, 72; Motahhari, *Spiritual Discourses,* 68. Cf. Abū Zahrah, *Uṣūl*, 289.
41. Cf. Sa'di Abū Ḥabīb, *Dirāsah fi Minhāj*, 749.
42. Ibn Qayyim, *Al-Ṭuruq al-Ḥukmiyyah*, 16.
43. al-Ṭabarī, *Tafsīr al-Ṭabari*, XXVIII, 43.
44. Sayyid Quṭb, *Fi Ẓilāl al-Qur'ān*, 11, 689.
45. Khalid Mas'ud, *Islamic Legal Philosophy*, 221.
46. Cf. Abū Zahrah, *Uṣūl*, 297.
47. 'Abd al-Salām, *Qawā'id*, I, 66.
48. For details see Madkūr, *Madkhal*, 13.
49. Abū Zahrah, *Uṣūl*, 295.
50. For details on the condition of *Maṣlaḥah* see M. H. Kamali, 'Have we Neglected the *Sharī'ah* Law Doctrine of *Maṣlaḥah*?', 287–304.
51. Al-Ghazālī, *Mustaṣfā*, I, 139–40.
52. Abū Zahrah, *Uṣūl*, 220.
53. Mas'ud, *Islamic Legal Philosophy*, 233–4.
54. 'Abd al-Salām, *Qawā'id,* 1, 5 & 10.
55. Muslim, *Mukhtaṣar Ṣaḥīḥ Muslim*, 412, *ḥadīth* no. 1546.
56. Cf. Mahmaṣṣāni, *Philosophy*, 154.
57. Ibn Mājah, *Sunan Ibn Mājah*, 11, 784, *ḥadīth* no. 2340.
58. Khallāf, *'Ilm*, 90; Abū Zahrah, *Uṣūl*, 222.
59. See for detail Kamali, *Jurisprudence*, 360 ff.
60. Abū Zahrah, *Uṣūl*, 302; Madkūr, *Madkhal*, 116; al-Ṣābūni, *Madkhal*, 269 ff.
61. See for detail John Robert Voll, *Islam, Continuity and Change,* 277.

3

CHARACTERISTIC FEATURES OF *SHARĪʿAH*

INTRODUCTORY REMARKS

Sharīʿah has often been described as a diversity within unity, diversity in detail and unity over essentials. The finality of the divine revelation of the Qur'ān and its timeless validity has had a unifying effect which ensured continuity in the understanding of fundamentals. The *Sharīʿah* originates in the Qur'ān and it consists of both specific rulings and broad principles of legal and moral import. The clear and specific injunctions of the Qur'ān and Sunnah constitute the core of the *Sharīʿah* and the understanding that they impart is expected to be self-evident. In this area, classical jurists, and jurists of all ages, have differed very little. Our own understanding of this part of the *Sharīʿah* too must be based directly on the Qur'ān and Sunnah, as there is in principle little room for interpretation over the self-evident aspects of the revealed law. Any discussion over the understanding of *Sharīʿah* is therefore bound to be concerned, not so much with the self-evident aspects of the *Sharīʿah,* but with the parts that are open to interpretation and parts which were understood differently by the ʻ*ulamā*' of different ages. In our attempt at characterizing the *Sharīʿah,* we need first to describe the *Sharīʿah* by the terms in which it has described itself before turning to the views of the leading jurists.

In view of the fact that a much larger portion of the Qur'ān is open to interpretation, unanimity and consensus in this area has been difficult to obtain. But even so the jurists of different ages were able to identify a broad line of agreement over interpretations on which they could find supportive evidence in the precedent of Companions or the *ijtihād* of leading ‘*ulamā*’. Unity over some interpretational aspects of the *Sharīʻah* is thus reflected in their general consensus, or *ijmāʻ*, whereas diversity over detail is the subject matter of *ikhtilāf* (disagreement). This chapter is brief on the attributes of *Sharīʻah* which are founded in the clear testimony of Qur'ān and Sunnah; it focuses instead on how the leading ‘*ulamā*’ have differed in interpreting the *Sharīʻah* in areas where it is open to such an exercise.

I note that the attempt to ascertain an understanding of *Sharīʻah* depends on the attitude taken towards it, whether of literalist conformity or of rationalist understanding, and then the levels of rationalist interpretation which are deemed to be acceptable. It should be obvious to the student of *Sharīʻah* that the leading imāms of the major schools have all understood it to be open to rational enquiry and *ijtihād,* but some of them have relied more extensively on rationalist methods than others. The initial sections of the present enquiry are concerned with the definition of terms *Sharīʻah* and *fiqh*, identification of major themes, whether or not the *Sharīʻah* is open to adaptability and change, and then whether it is also open to the exercise of reason side by side with revelation. What does it precisely mean when *Sharīʻah* is characterized as a divine or a religious law? We also discuss the communitarian and individualist dimensions of *Sharīʻah* and the place of legal stratagems (*ḥiyal*) therein.

SHARĪʻAH AND *FIQH*

Islamic law originates in two major sources, namely divine revelation (*waḥy*) and human reason (*ʻaql*). This dual identity of Islamic law is reflected in the two expressions *Sharīʻah* and *fiqh.* The former bears a stronger affinity with revelation whereas the latter is the product mainly of human reason. *Sharīʻah* demarcates the path which the believer has to tread in order to obtain guidance, whereas *fiqh* means human understanding and knowledge. The *Sharīʻah* thus provides general directives whereas detailed solutions to particular and unprecedented issues are explored by *fiqh.* Since *Sharīʻah* is contained in divine revelation, namely, the Qur'ān and the teachings of the Prophet Muhammad, or his Sunnah, it has a closer affinity with the dogma of Islam, whereas *fiqh* is a rational endeavour and a product largely of speculative reasoning which does not command the same authority as that of the *Sharī'ah*. To say that *Sharī'ah* is contained in the Qur'ān and Sunnah would preclude the scholastic legacy of *fiqh* and its vast literature, especially the parts that do not have a clear origin in the Qur'ān, from the purview of *Sharī'ah*. Some parts of the Qur'ān which consist of historical data and parables, for instance, are not included either. *Sharī'ah* is, however, a wider concept than *fiqh* as it comprises the totality of guidance that God has revealed to the Prophet Muhammad pertaining to the dogma of Islam, its moral values and its practical legal rules. *Sharī'ah* thus comprises in its scope not only law, but also theology and moral teaching. *Fiqh* is thus positive law that does not include morality and dogma. Yet the '*ulamā*' are in agreement on the primacy of morality and dogma in the determination of basic values. By comparison with these, *fiqh* is described as a mere superstructure and a practical manifestation of commitment to those values.

Sharī'ah provides clear rulings on the fundamentals of Islam, its moral values, and practical duties such as prayers, fasting, legal alms (*zakah*), the *ḥajj* and other devotional matters. Its injunctions on the subject of what is lawful and unlawful, *ḥalāl* and *ḥarām*, are on the whole definitive, and so are its rulings on some aspects of civil transactions (*mu'āmalāt*). But *Sharī'ah* is generally flexible with regard to the larger part of *mu'āmalāt*, criminal law (with the exception of the prescribed punishments, or *ḥudūd*), government policy and constitution, fiscal policy, taxation, economic and international affairs. On many of these themes *Sharī'ah* provides only general guidelines, which are elaborated in *fiqh*.

Fiqh is defined as knowledge of the practical rules of *Sharī'ah* which are derived from the detailed evidence in the sources. The rules of *fiqh* are thus concerned with the manifest aspects of individual conduct. The practicalities of conduct are evaluated on a scale of five values: obligatory, recommended, permissible, reprehensible and forbidden. The definition of *fiqh* also implies that the deduction of the rules of *fiqh* from the Qur'ān and Sunnah is through direct contact with these sources. The ability to utilize the source materials of the Qur'ān therefore necessitates a knowledge of Arabic and a certain degree of insight and erudition that would preclude the work of an imitator, or one who reproduces the rules without understanding their implications. A jurist (*faqīh*) who fulfils the requirements of this definition and has the ability to deduce the rules of *Sharī'ah* from their sources is also a *mujtahid,* who is qualified to exercise independent reasoning (*ijtihād*).

The rules of *fiqh* occur in two varieties. First, rules which are conveyed in a clear text such as the essentials of worship, the validity of marriage outside the prohibited degrees of relationships, the rules of inheritance and so forth. This part of *fiqh* is simultaneously a part of *Sharī'ah.* Second, rules that are formulated through the exercise of *ijtihād* on parts of the Qur'ān and Sunnah which are not self-evident. Because of the possibility of errror in this exercise, the rules that are so derived do not command finality. These are not necessarily a part of *Sharī'ah* and the *mujtahid* who has reason to depart from them may do so without committing a transgression. Only when juristic opinion and *ijtihād* are supported by general consensus (*ijmā'*) does *ijtihād* acquire the binding force of a ruling, or *ḥukm*, of *Sharī'ah.*

The *corpus juris* of *fiqh* is divided into the two main categories of devotional matters (*'ibādāt*) and civil transaction (*mu'āmalāt*). The former is usually studied under the six main headings of cleanliness, ritual prayer, fasting, the *ḥajj*, legal alms (*zakah*) and *jihād* (holy struggle), and the schools of law do not vary a great deal in their treatment of these subjects. Juristic differences among the schools occur mainly in the area of *mu'āmalāt.* These are generally studied under the seven headings of transactions involving exchange of values (which subsume contracts), matrimonial law, equity and trusts, civil litigation, rules pertaining to dispute settlement in courts, and administration of estates. This body of the law is generally subsumed under what is known, in modern legal parlance, as civil law. Crimes and penalties (i.e. *al-'uqūbāt*) are often studied under a separate heading next to the *'ibādāt* and *mu'āmalāt.* Rules pertaining to state and government are studied under *al-aḥkām al-sulṭāniyyah* (lit. sultanic rulings), also referred to as *siyāsah shar'iyyah* or *Sharī'ah*-compliant policy. This is parallel to what is now known as constitutional and administrative law. And lastly, rules pertaining to international relations, war and peace fall under what is known as *'ilm al-siyar*. The most detailed exposition of the entire range of classical *fiqh* remains that of Shams al-Dīn al-Sarakhsī's (d. 1087) *Kitāb al-Mabsūṭ* (the expanded book) in thirty volumes. A twentieth-century equivalent is Wahbah al-Zuḥayli, *al-Fiqh al-Islāmī wa Adillatuh*, in eight volumes and over six thousand pages.

MAJOR THEME AND CLASSIFICATIONS

The four Sunni schools of Islamic law, namely the Ḥanafi, Shāfiʿī, Māliki, and Ḥanbali, as well as the Shīʿite schools, as explained in the next chapter, tend to vary little on devotional matters (*ibādāt*) and the rituals of worship. The jurists in all of these schools are on the whole in agreement over the binary division of the rules of *fiqh* into matters of worship (*ʿibādāt*), whose principal objective is exaltation and worship of God Most High, closeness to Him, and earning of reward in the hereafter, and civil transactions (*muʿāmalāt*), whose main objective is realization of benefit to mankind. But the detailed arrangement and classification of subjects under these two headings and addition of new categories beyond the scope of these two vary from one school to another. Unlike the *muʿāmalāt* and customary matters (*ʿādāt*) which are open to rational enquiry and the application of such concepts as ratiocination (*taʿlīl*), analogy (*qiyās*) and juristic preference (*istiḥsān*), the norm in *ʿibādāt* is that they are not open to reasoning and that the textual rulings concerning them are followed at face value. The precise causes (*ʿilal*) of *ʿibādāt* are only known to God and the faithful follows His commands and prohibitions in this area as a matter of devotion and unquestioning submission. The *Sharīʿah* provides specific instructions on *ʿibādāt* but with reference to *muʿāmalāt*, it is basically concerned with an exposition of basic objectives and general principles that are on the whole open to rational analysis and *ijtihād*. The individual must know that a particular act of worship (*ʿibādah*) he performs has been ordained by God; to perform it with deliberation and intent (*niyyah*) can only be done from a position of certainty and knowledge. But since service to God and seeking His pleasure is not the main purpose of *muʿāmalāt*, there is no requirement of *niyyah* and no spiritual reward is earned by them unless they are done for that particular purpose. When someone repays his debt, or fulfils a trust (*amānah*), or provides his wife with maintenance, he discharges a duty, regardless as to whether he had the intention to seek God's pleasure or not, but if he did combine such an intention he may earn a spiritual reward.

The Ḥanafis have classified the laws (*aḥkām*) of *fiqh* into the three categories of *ʿibādāt, muʿāmalāt* and *ʿuqūbāt* (punishments). Each of these are in turn subdivided into about five main headings. The *ʿibādāt* are thus discussed under the main headings of *ṭahārah* (cleanliness), *ṣalah* (obligatory prayer), fasting, the pilgrimage of *ḥajj*, legal alms (*zakah*) and *jihād* (holy struggle). It is quite typical of almost all major works on *fiqh* to begin with a detailed exposition of *'ibādāt.* According to the Ḥanafi jurist, Ibn 'Ābidīn (d. 1834), 'the affairs of religion are founded on dogmatics (*i'tiqādāt*), moral values (*ādāb*), devotional matters (*'ibādāt*), transactions (*mu'āmalāt*), and criminal laws (*'uqūbāt*). The first two are, however, not a part of *fiqh.*'[1] The Ḥanafi *fiqh* thus consists of only the last three. *'Ibādāt* is a proper subject of *fiqh* as they consist mainly of practical observances, whereas dogmatic theology falls outside *fiqh* precisely because they do not partake in practical rulings. All the leading schools have excluded dogmatic theology and moral teachings from the scope of *fiqh.* This also indicates that Muslim jurists have recognized a functional distinction between law, morality and religion. One of the practical consequences of this distinction is that only the legal rules of *Sharī'ah* are justiciable. The allegation therefore that Islamic law does not in any way distinguish law from morality and dogma is not justified.

A total separation between law and morality is neither feasible nor recommended. The *'ulamā'* have nevertheless distinguished the rules of *fiqh* from morality and dogma for the practical reason of defining the court jurisdiction over such matters. Indeed we note this distinction in the very definition of *fiqh* which focuses on practical rules governing the conduct of individuals. The schools of law have also recognized the distinction between the moral categories of recommendable (*mandūb*) and reprehensible (*makrūh*), on one hand, and obligatory (*wājib*) and forbidden (*ḥarām*) on the other. The central feature of this division is to identify what is legally enforceable from that which amounts to moral advice that is basically optional.

The Ḥanafis divide the *mu'āmalāt* into the five headings of transactions involving exchange of valuables (*al-mu'āwaḍāt al-māliyyah*), equity and trusts (*al-amānāt*), matrimonial law (*al-munākaḥāt*), civil litigation (*al-mukhāṣamāt*) and administration of estates (*al-tarikāt*). And lastly, the *'uqūbāt* are studied under the main headings of just retaliation (*qiṣāṣ*) and prescribed offences (*ḥudūd*) whereas the latter is subdivided into the five offences of theft, adultery, slanderous accusation, wine drinking and apostasy.[2]

The Shāfi'īs divide the *corpus juris* of *fiqh* into four parts, namely *'ibādāt,* which pertains to one's well-being in the hereafter, *mu'āmalāt,* which relates to one's survival (*baqā' al-shakhṣ*) in this world, the *munākaḥāt* (matrimonial law) which concerns the survival of the species (*baqā' al-naw'*), and *'uqūbāt* (penal law) which concerns the survival of society and civilization (*baqā' al-madīnah*).[3]

The Mālik jurist Aḥmad b. Muḥammad Ibn Juzay (d. 1339) has attempted in his *Qawānīn al-Fiqhiyyah* a classification of the whole body of *fiqh* under the two main headings of *'ibādāt* and *mu'āmalāt.* Each of these are, in turn, subdivided under ten titles, some of which are not included under either heading by the other schools.[4] The Ḥanbali classification of the themes of *fiqh* resemble that of the Shāfi'īs albeit with minor differences of placing certain subheadings in a different place, based on their perception of a logical sequence between the various themes. It is due to such differences of orientation that we find, for instance, the placement in the Ḥanafi arrangement of marriage (*nikāḥ*) as the first heading in the section on *mu'āmalāt,* but which appears immediately next to *'ibādāt,* for the obvious reason that marriage, being essentially a civil contract, also has a devotional aspect (*jānib ta'abbudī*). The Shāfi'īs and Ḥanbalis on the other hand treat matrimonial law as a separate category altogcthcr.[5]

Notwithstanding such attempts at classification, the *fiqh* remains, in some parts at least, wanting in greater consolidation of themes. Al-Sanhūrī (d. 1971) has drawn attention, for example, to the atomistic style in which the classical jurists have expounded the law of contract. The jurists have not articulated the law of contract as such but studied each contract individually. The common themes that are traceable in all contracts have not been given due prominence. The Ḥanafi jurist al-Kāsānī (d. 1191) thus deals with nineteen nominate contracts, and the manner in which they are treated leaves the reader wondering (a) whether these could all be consolidated in order to highlight the features they all have in common; (b) whether the *fiqh* validates contracts other than these; and (c) whether the *fiqh* recognizes the basic freedom of contract on the basis merely of an agreement which does not violate morality and public interest.[6] Is there, in other words, a need for a general theory of contract? A partial answer to some of these questions can be found in the works of Ḥanbali jurists whose contribution to this theme is outstanding. But even so, as I shall later elaborate, the substance of al-Sanhūrī's critique and the issues he raised still point to a certain tendency in *fiqh* which is perhaps not confined to contracts alone. The atomistic style of treatment of individual but interrelated themes is a general feature of *fiqh,* which is indicative perhaps of a certain awareness on the part of the *fuqahā'* not to be too presumptuous in the advancement of general theories. They have addressed issues and incidents on their own particularist grounds, always imparting the awareness that their interpretation of the divine *Sharīʻah* may or may not be in conformity with the intentions of the Lawgiver. The caution they have exercised had a propensity towards fragmentation in the area of *furūʻ al-fiqh* (branches of *fiqh*).

A measure of thematic consolidation in *fiqh* has taken place through the formulation and development of legal maxims, known as *al-qawāʻid al-kulliyyah al-fiqhiyyah* (on which see below). The jurists of various schools have compiled these in the works that generally bear the title *al-Ashbāh wa al-Naẓā'ir* (resemblances and similitudes). There are over 250 (and according to some over a thousand) legal maxims which consist largely of juridical abstracts and statements of principles that consolidate the isolated and yet logically inter-related rules and incidents of *fiqh* into coherent and integrated formulas.[7]

The remainder of this chapter expounds the salient features of *Sharīʻah* and the structure of values that it seeks to uphold.

SALIENT FEATURES OF *SHARĪʻAH*

This section draws attention to some of the distinguishing features of *Sharīʻah,* such as its identity as a religious law, its tendency to balance continuity and change, its support for rationality, and gradualist approach to social reform. *Sharīʻah* also advocates moral autonomy of the individual, and seeks to balance its individualist and communitarian orientations in the formulation of its laws.

RELIGIOUS AND MORAL PROCLIVITIES OF *SHARĪʻAH*

To say that Islamic law originates in divine revelation implies that adherence to its rules is at once a legal and a religious duty of Muslims. Related to this are the concepts of *ḥalāl* and *ḥarām* (permissible and prohibited), which are both religious and legal categories and involve duty towards God and fellow humans. These two aspects of *Sharīʿah* tend to enforce one another on the whole, yet there is an equally significant but often neglected aspect of *Sharīʿah* which is civilian and positivist in character in the area of *aḥkām* (commands and prohibitions) that guide court decisions and government practice. Judges do not, for example, issue judgements on religious considerations alone just as they are under duty to treat all litigants before them equally, regardless of race and religion. A distinction is also drawn between the religious and legal aspects of obligations. This is why Muslim jurists often write in relation to individuals and cases that their legal status is such, but religiously it is the reverse. For example, in the event where a debt is denied by the debtor and the creditor is unable to prove it in the court of law, the creditor is entitled to take the equivalent of what is due to him from the debtor's property without the debtor's permission. But if the matter is brought before the court, the creditor will not be allowed to take anything unless he proves his claim through normal methods. Consider also a case in which the creditor has waived the debt by way of charity to the debtor without declaring it to the debtor. In this case the creditor is entitled to receive payment judicially but not on religious grounds, as charity may not be revoked and the debtor does not owe him anything in the eyes of God.

This distinction between what is enforceable in the courts of justice and what is not can also be seen in the composition of the renowned scale of five values, namely of obligatory (*wājib*), recommended (*mandūb*), reprehensible (*makrūh*), permissible (*mubāḥ*) and forbidden (*ḥarām*). Only the first and the last are legal categories whereas the much larger part that includes the remaining three categories are not justiciable in the courts. The lawful government is authorized, however, to turn reprehensible into forbidden and recommendable into obligatory if public interest (*maṣlaḥah*) dictates it.

The distinction we attempted between religious and juridical obligations also signifies the difference between adjudication (*qaḍā'*) and a juristic opinion (*fatwā*). The judge (*qāḍi*) must adjudicate on the basis of apparent evidence, whereas a jurisconsult (*muft*) investigates both the apparent and the actual positions and both are reflected in his verdict. In the event of a conflict between the two positions, the *muftī* bases his (*fatwā*) on religious considerations, whereas the judge considers objective evidence only. Hence a pious individual in a court case is not to be treated differently from one of questionable piety or of no apparent religion.

This dual approach to rights and duties can also be seen in the different orientations of legal schools with regard to externality and intent. With regard to civil transactions the Shāfi'īs and Ḥanafis tend to stress the externality of conduct without exploring the intent behind it, whereas the Mālikis and Ḥanbalis are inclined towards the latter. This can be illustrated with reference to the contract of marriage. If a man marries a woman with the sole intention, for example, of sexual gratification and a quick divorce to follow, the marriage is invalid according to the Mālikis and Ḥanbalis but lawful according to the Ḥanafi and Shāfi'ī schools. When the legal requirements of a valid contract of marriage are objectively fulfilled, this is all that is necessary according to the Ḥanafi and Shāfi'ī schools, whereas the other two schools base their judgement on the underlying intent, and maintain that distortion should be obstructed whenever this becomes known.

This difference of attitude can also be seen with reference to legal stratagems (*al-ḥiyal al-fiqhiyyah*) in such cases as the double sale of *'īnah:* A sells a piece of cloth to B for $100 payable in one year and then immediately buys the same for $80 from him paid on the spot. The difference here is a disguised usury (*ribā*) as it amounts to charging an interest of $20 for a loan of $100 for one year which circumvents the rules of *Sharī'ah* by violating their intent. The Mālikis and Ḥanbalis reject such stratagems altogether, but the Ḥanbalis and Shāfi'īs have approved them provided they are free of distortion and realize a benefit.[8]

Furthermore the *Sharī'ah* contains provisions on expiations (*kaffārāt*), which are self-inflicted punishments of a religious character that the courts are not authorized to enforce. In the event, for example, that a person breaks a solemn oath, he may expiate it by giving charity sufficient to feed ten poor persons, or alternatively to fast for three days. Other similar expiations have been provided for in the Qur'ān, none of which is, however, legally enforceable.

Morality and religion are, however, closely inter-related and they also affect the *Sharī'ah*. The Prophet thus declared in a *ḥadīth*,

> I have been sent to accomplish the virtues of morality.[9]
>
> بعثت لأتمم مكارم الأخلاق.

The moral overtones of *Sharī'ah* are also clearly seen in its propensity towards duty (*taklīf*), so that some Orientalists have characterized the

Sharī'ah as 'a system of duties' in contradistinction with statutory law, which often speaks of rights. This is not quite accurate but we will not delve into this issue here. The fact that the *Sharī'ah* proscribes usury, wine drinking, and gambling, proclaims legal alms (*zakah*) as a legal duty and encourages 'lowering of the gaze' between members of the opposite sex, as well as declaring divorce 'the worst of all permissible things', are all reflective of the moral underpinnings of *Sharī'ah*. This can also be seen in the rules pertaining to war where *Sharī'ah* forbids maiming, injury to children, women and the elderly as well as damage to animals, and takes to task those who cause them hardship and abuse. Although these are not justiciable in the court of law, the market controller (*muhtasib*) is authorized to intervene and stop immoral practices. The institution of *ḥisbah* (in charge of promotion of good and prevention of evil) that historically functioned to support moral values was also indicative of the distinction between the moral and legal aspects of *Sharī'ah*.

CONTINUITY AND CHANGE

It is often said that Islamic law is immutable as it is divinely ordained and therefore closed to the notion of adaptability and change. It is submitted on the contrary that the immutability view of *Sharī'ah* is only partially accurate, as the divine law itself integrates adaptability and change in its objectives and it is therefore an inalienable part of its philosophy and outlook. The leading jurists and '*ulamā*' have consistently maintained the view that *Sharī'ah* is resourceful and well-equipped with the necessary tools with which to accommodate social change. The *Sharī'ah* thus recognizes independent reasoning (*ijtihād*) and its sub-categories, such as considerations of public interest (*istiṣlāḥ*), juristic preference (*istiḥsān*), analogical reasoning (*qiyās*) and so forth for the very purpose of adapting the law abreast of the changing needs of society. Textual interpretation (*tafsīr, ta'wīl*) may also be used for the same purpose. Since the greater part of the Qur'ān, including its legal verses (*āyāt al-aḥkām*) consist of general (*'āmm*) and unqualified (*muṭlaq*) expressions, they are on the whole open to interpretation and *ijtihād*.

Sharī'ah aims at striking a balance between continuity and change. While the basic objectives of *Sharī'ah* are permanent, the means attaining them are susceptible to the exigencies of time and circumstance. The fundamentals of the faith and the pillars on which it stands, the basic moral values of Islam, and its clear injunctions on *ḥalāl* and *ḥarām* are on the whole permanent and unchangeable. The injunctions of *Sharī'ah* concerning devotional matters (*'ibādāt*) and some of its specific rulings in the area of civil transactions (*mu'āmalāt*) such as the rules of inheritance, are also unchangeable. But the *Sharī'ah* is generally flexible in regard to the larger part of *mu'āmalāt*, criminal law, government policy and constitution, referred to as *siyāsah shar'iyyah*, fiscal policy, taxation, economic and international affairs. On many of these themes the *Sharī'ah* only provides general guidelines whose details could be determined, adjusted and modified, if necessary, through the exercise of human reasoning and *ijtihād*. The *Sharī'ah* requires, for example, objective and impartial justice and it has laid down certain specific guidelines towards achieving it, but the methods, conditions and procedures that are applied towards the same end may be liable to change in light of the changing experience and conditions of society. The laws of *Sharī'ah,* Ibn Qayyim al-Jawziyyah observed, are of two kinds: Firstly, laws which do not change with the vicissitudes of time and place or the propensities of *ijtihād,* such as the obligatoriness of the *wājibāt* (pl. of *wājib*), or illegality of *muḥarramāt* (pl. of *ḥarām*), the fixed quantities of inheritance and the like. They do not change and no *ijtihād* may be advanced so as to violate the substance and character of the *Sharī'ah* in these areas. The second variety of laws are those which are susceptible to change in accordance with the requirements of public interest (*maṣlaḥah*) and prevailing circumstances, such as the quantum, type and attribute of deterrent punishments (*al-ta'zīrāt*). The Lawgiver has permitted variation in these in accordance with the dictates and considerations of *maṣlaḥah*.[10]

The flexibility of *Sharī'ah* and its amenability to change can be seen in both the language of the text and also the style of Qur'ānic legislation. From the linguistic viewpoint the general (*'āmm*), the absolute (*muṭlaq*), the manifest text (*ẓāhir* – as opposed to the clear text or *naṣṣ*) and the ambiguous (*mujmal* as opposed to a clarifed text or *mufassar*) occupy the larger part of its text and they are generally in need of interpretation; the '*ulamā*' of different periods have attempted to draw a different message from them in the light of their own experiences and concerns.[11] One also notes that Qur'ānic legislation, for the most part, consists of an exposition of general principles, although in certain areas the Qur'ān also provides specific details. Being the principal source of *Sharīʻah,* the Qur'ān lays down general guidelines on almost every major topic of Islamic law. Whenever the Qur'ān provides specific details, as Shāṭibī has observed, it is related to the exposition and better understanding of its general principles.[12] With regard to civil transactions, for example, the textual rulings of the Qur'ān on the fulfilment of contracts, the legality of sale, the prohibition of usury, respect for the property of others, documentation of loans and other forms of deferred payments are all conveyed in broad and general terms. Similarly the Qur'ānic injunctions on the subject of justice, respect for truth, and giving testimony in its cause are confined to general guidelines and no details are provided regarding the duties of the judge, trial procedures and the manner in which testimony is given and verified.[13] On principles of government such as consultation (*shūrā*), equality and basic rights, the Qur'ān is generally brief and does not provide any details. The general principles are laid down and it is for the community and its leaders, the *'ūlu al-'amr*, to elaborate them in the light of prevailing conditions.[14]

In the sphere of crime and punishment, the Qur'ān is specific with regard to the punishment of only five offences, namely murder, theft, highway robbery, adultery and slanderous accusation. As for the rest, it only lays down the broad principles of penal law when it provides, for example, that

> the recompense of an injury is an injury equal to it (42: 40)
>
> وَجَزَاء سَيِّئَةٍ سَيِّئَةٌ مِّثْلُهَا.

and,

> when you decide to punish then punish in proportion to the pain inflicted on you. (16: 126)
>
> وَإِنْ عَاقَبْتُمْ فَعَاقِبُوا بِمِثْلِ مَا عُوقِبْتُم بِهِ.

A careful reading of the Qur'ān further reveals that on matters pertaining to belief, the basic principles of morality, man's relationship with his Creator, and transcendental matters (*ghaybiyyāt*), which are characteristically unchangeable, the Qur'ān is clear and detailed, as clarity and certainty are the necessary requirements of belief. In the area of ritual performances such as *ṣalāh,* fasting and the pilgrimage of *ḥajj*, on the other hand, although these too are meant to be unchangeable, the Qur'ān is nevertheless brief on them, and most of the necessary details have been provided by the Sunnah. This is explained by the fact that ritual performances are of a practical nature which are best taught through practical illustration just as the Prophet has done.[15] The Qur'ān contains specific rulings on matrimonial law, the prohibited degrees of relationship in marriage, divorce and inheritance. These are, for the most part, associated with human nature as they also have a devotional (*ta'abbudī*) aspect in common with the *'ibādāt*, which would explain why the Qur'ānic legislation is specific in these areas.

Another feature of the Qur'ān which is accountable for flexibility and change in the *Sharī'ah* is the presence of speculative (*ẓannī*), in contradistinction with definitive (*qaṭ'ī*), rulings throughout the holy Book. A ruling of the Qur'ān may totally or partially fall under one or the other of these two categories. When the language of the text and the ruling that it conveys is clear, self-contained and decisive, there remains little room for interpretation and *ijtihād*. The speculative portions of the Qur'ān, which account for the larger part of its text, are on the other hand open to interpretation, analysis and development. The best interpretation is that which can be obtained from the Qur'ān itself, then from the Sunnah of the Prophet, then from the precedent of Companions, and lastly through juristic *ijtihād*. In interpreting the *ẓann* portions of the Qur'ān (and also Sunnah) the '*ulamā*' have not only differed in matters of orientation and emphasis, but have often drawn totally different conclusions. Muhammad Iqbal's (d. 1937) incisive observation that the Qur'ān 'embodies an essentially dynamic outlook on life' prompted him to advise his contemporary Muslims to rediscover the original verities of freedom, equality and solidarity, and 'to tear off from Islam the hard crust which has immobilized an essentially dynamic outlook on life'.[16]

The extensive scope of *ikhtilāf* (juristic disagreement) which has grown into a separate discipline of Islamic law is by itself suggestive of the openness of *Sharī'ah* and its capacity to accommodate differences of interpretation, or indeed a plurality of equally acceptable interpretations. The interpretation or *fatwā* so arrived at, that is, a *fatwā* which is the subject of disagreement and *ikhtilāf*, is in principle open to further development and change in accordance with the requirements of justice and *maṣlaḥah*.

In a chapter entitled *taghyīr al-fatwā* (change of *fatwā*), Ibn Qayyim al-Jawziyyah has expressed concern over a certain misunderstanding of the *Sharīʻah* 'by those who have held views, out of ignorance, which inflict hardship and rigidity through laying down conditions that are unjustified and unsustainable'. The *Sharīʻah* is 'founded, in roots and branch, on wisdom and realization of *maṣlaḥah* for the people both in this world and the next. It is justice, mercy and benefit in every part.' Ibn Qayyim continues: 'Any ruling that abandons justice in favour of tyranny, mercy for its opposite, *maṣlaḥah* for corruption (*mafsadah*), and wisdom for futility – would have nothing to do with the *Sharīʻah,* even if it is shown, by some remote interpretation, to be a part of it.'[17] We also note in this connection Ibn Taymiyyah's (d. 1328) view, which is representative of the majority of '*ulamā*', that 'the *Sharīʻah* always contemplates realization of benefits (*al-maṣāliḥ*) for the people; it also aims at minimizing corruption and harm (*al-mafāsid*), which is why the *Sharīʻah* is fit to be applied to all times and places'.[18]

With reference to the rational sources of *Sharīʻah,* it may generally be stated that in their broad outline, the proofs and doctrines of *uṣūl al-fiqh* such as general consensus (*ijmāʻ*), analogical reasoning (*qiyās*), juristic preference (*istiḥsān*), consideration of public interest (*istiṣlāḥ*), and custom (*'urf*) are all designed, in their respective capacities, to relate the *Sharīʻah* to social reality, to serve as instruments of adaptation, and provide formulae for finding solutions to problems as they arise. The methods that are so provided also ensure conformity to the basic principles and philosophy of *Sharīʻah*. All of these in turn rely on rational evidence, considered opinion (*ra'y*) of the qualified jurist and the practicalities of social custom.[19]

As a binding source of law, the collective will and consensus (*ijmāʻ*) of the people and their scholars ensure continuity as well as adaptation to change through the introduction of new laws that reflect the legitimate needs of the community and the vision of its scholars. *Ijmāʻ* is a vehicle, in theory at least, for evolution of ideas and for integrating the educational and cultural achievements of the community into the fabric of *Sharīʻah*.

Analogical reasoning (*qiyās*) extends the textual rulings of *Sharīʻah* to similar cases and issues which fall, not within the letter, but the rationale of a given law. It is a rationalist doctrine, founded in the postulate that the rulings of *Sharīʻah* are based on their effective causes (*'ilal*), and it is through finding the rational purpose of a textual ruling that its extension to a similar case is justified. The *raison d'etre* of juristic preference (*istiḥsān*) is to find an alternative solution to a given problem when the jurist is convinced that applying the existing law is likely to lead to rigidity and unfairness. *Istiḥsān* seeks to refine the existing law and integrate considerations of equity and good conscience into its fabric. The basic idea of *istiḥsān* is that a literal application of the *Sharīʻah* must not be allowed to defeat its higher objectives of justice and fair play.[20] Furthermore, *istiṣlāḥ*, or consideration of public interest, encourages initiative on the part of the jurist and government to take all necessary measures to secure benefit for the community. The legal theory of *uṣūl* also recognizes approved custom (*ʻurf*) as a proof of *Sharīʻah* and a valid basis of judicial decision, especially in the area of *muʻāmalāt*. Custom is essentially pragmatic as it is moulded directly by the experience, needs and conditions of society. Custom and *maṣlaḥah* also constitute the motivating factors behind many a ruling of *ijmāʻ* and *ijtihād*.[21]

There are a number of legal maxims, recorded for example, in the Ottoman *Mejelle* (law code), which proclaim custom as a proof of *Sharīʻah* and a valid basis of adjudication. The rulings of custom often command greater authority than the rulings of non-textually based *ijtihād*. It thus appears that the *Sharīʻah* seeks to incorporate the will and consensus of the community and its customary practices into the fabric of its laws. It seems fitting to conclude this discussion with an observation from Muhammad Iqbal that 'I have no doubt that a deeper study of the enormous legal literature of Islam is sure to rid the modern critic of the superficial opinion that the law of Islam is stationary and incapable of development'.[22]

SHARĪʻAH AND REASON

The '*ulamā*' across the centuries have understood the *Sharīʻah* of Islam to be distinctly reasonable. This is based in the first place on affirmative references in the Qur'ān to the exercise of sound reasoning and judgement. The Qur'ān also refers, on numerous occasions, to the cause (*ʻillah*), the objective and purpose (*ḥikmah*) of its laws especially in the sphere of *muʻāmalāt*. This aspect of the Qur'ān, known as *taʻlīl* (ratiocination), is known from the Qur'ānic address in many places to those who think, who exercise their faculty of reason, who enquire into the world around them and investigate, who possess knowledge, and who draw rational conclusions. The '*ulamā*' thus concluded that the Lawgiver has intended that the meaning, implications and objectives of His laws which are often indicated but not always elaborated in the text should be investigated and comprehensively understood.

Taʿlīl is not valid with regard to *ʿibādāt,* but outside this area the *Sharīʿah* encourages investigation and enquiry into its rules. Ratiocination in the Qur'ān means that the laws of *Sharīʿah* are not imposed for their own sake, nor for want of mere conformity, but they aim at realization of certain benefits/objectives. This also tells us that when there is a change of a kind whereby a particular law no longer secures its underlying purpose and rationale, it must be substituted with a suitable alternative. To do otherwise would mean neglecting the objective of the Lawgiver.[23] According to al-Shāṭibī, the rules of *Sharīʿah* concerning civil transactions and customary matters (*muʿāmalāt wa ʿādāt*) follow the benefits (*maṣāliḥ*) which they contemplate. We note, for instance, that the *Sharīʿah* may forbid something because it is devoid of benefit, but it permits the same when it secures a benefit. A deferred sale, for example, of dirham for dinar is forbidden because of the fear of usury (*ribā*) therein, but a period loan is permitted because it secures a benefit (deferment is harmful in one and beneficial in the other). Similarly fresh dates may not, in principle, be sold for dry dates for fear of uncertainty (*gharar*) and usury (*ribā*) but the Prophet permitted this transaction, known as *ʿarāyā,* because of the people's need for it.[24]

Moreover, instances of abrogation in the rulings of Qur'ān and Sunnah which took place during the lifetime of the Prophet can properly be understood in these terms. Instances are also found in the precedent of Companions where some of the laws of *Sharīʿah* were suspended because they no longer secured the benefit which they had initially contemplated. Since the *ʿillah* and rationale on which they were premised were no longer present they were suspended or replaced with suitable alternatives. We note, for example, that the caliph 'Umar b. al-Khaṭṭāb suspended the *ḥadd* punishment of theft during the year of the famine. The caliph also stopped distribution of agricultural land to Muslim warriors in Iraq despite a Qur'ānic ruling that entitled them to war booty; he also suspended the share of the pagan friends of Islam (the *mu'allafat al-qulūb*) in the revenues of *zakah.* These were persons of influence whose co-operation was important for the victory of Islam. The Qur'ān had assigned a share for them (9:60), which the caliph later discontinued on the ground, as he stated, that 'Allah has exalted Islam and it is no longer in need of their support'. The caliph thus departed, on purely rational grounds, from the letter of the Qur'ān in favour of its general purpose and 'his ruling is considered to be in harmony with the spirit of the Qur'ān'.[25]

The schools of law differed somewhat over the understanding of *ta'līl* but the majority maintain that the *Sharī'ah* is inherently rational as it is founded, in principle and in detail, on the benefits of the people. The benefits that are contemplated may be prompt or may materialize over a period of time. They may consist of a benefit in the positive sense or may seek to prevent an evil. Thus we note in the following Qur'ānic passage where God Most High speaks, by way of *ta'līl,* of the prophethood of Muḥammad:

> We have not sent thee but a mercy for the worlds . . . (21:107)
>
> وَمَا أَرْسَلْنَاكَ إِلَّا رَحْمَةً لِّلْعَالَمِينَ.

Mercy (*raḥmah*) thus justifies prophethood just as it also endorses benefit to the servants of God and prevention of harm to them. We also read with reference to the law of just retaliation (*qiṣāṣ*) that

> in *qiṣāṣ* there is (saving of) life for you: O you men of understanding. (2:179)
>
> وَلَكُمْ فِي الْقِصَاصِ حَيَاةٌ يَا أُولِيْ الأَلْبَابِ.

Similarly, the prohibition of wine drinking and gambling is premised on the rationale of preventing 'hostility and rancour' among people and interference with the remembrance of God (5:91). Legal alms and charities are imposed in order to prevent concentration of wealth among the rich (57:7). These and numerous other instances of *ta'līl* in the Qur'ān have led the Shāfi'ī jurist 'Izz al-Dīn 'Abd al-Salām (d. 1261) to conclude that 'the *Sharī'ah* is premised on securing benefit for the servants of God and none of the '*ulamā*' has opposed this. As for the Ẓāhiriyyah, they too have endorsed this principle in its broad outline except that they do not agree with ratiocination in the sense of ascertaining specific causes for the injuctions.'[26]

In exercising *ijtihād,* the '*ulamā*' have differed in regard to the emphasis they have laid on the manifest text or on its broader meaning and rationale. While some '*ulamā*', like those of the Ẓāhir school, have emphasized close adherence to the text and shunned all discussion of the cause, rationale and objective of the Lawgiver, the majority of '*ulamā*' have validated analogy and with it also the search for the effective causes of the laws. It is almost certain that the leading *mujtahids* among the Companions did not speak of ratiocination, causation or *'illah,* as juridical concepts, either in conjunction with analogy or otherwise, beyond the incidental and cursory levels of investigation. Although they resorted to analogical reasoning on numerous occasions they did so without engaging in technicality. They referred to the meanings (*ma'āni*) rather than effective causes or *'ilal* of the laws. Technical elaborations of analogy and its pillars, including the *'illah,* were attempted by the '*ulamā*' of later periods. But even so the basic tendencies that I propose to elaborate here could be ascertained in the works of all leading scholars; they became the focus of attention and were consequently advanced and articulated by the '*ulamā*' of the later periods.

We note in the first place that those who ascertain the meaning and rationale of the law (i.e. *arbāb al-ma'āni*) are distinguished from the proponents of literalism (*arbāb al-ẓāhir*). A second level of distinction is also ascertainable among the *arbāb al-ma'āni,* or semanticists, who are divided into two camps, one of which tended to go beyond the meaning of words towards the spirit and objective of the law and tried to penetrate into its philosophy and rationale. This approach is distinguishable from those of the semanticists who took a more restrictive view of the role of ratiocination in the *Sharī'ah*. Although these too accepted the rationalist theme of ascertaining the purpose and objective of the law, yet in their quest for greater certainty they tended to avoid speculative reasoning in law. Both of these validate analogy and therefore the search for similitudes and their effective causes, but the second group of semanticists differed with the first regarding the wider scope that they acknowledged for rational enquiry in the determination of laws.[27]

The proponents of analogical reasoning and *ta'līl* have also referred to evidence in the Sunnah in support of their positions. It is thus reported that a man from the tribe of Bani Fazārah informed the Prophet that his wife had given birth to a black child, and attempted to accuse her of adultery. The Prophet asked if he had any camels? The man answered that he did. 'What colour are they?' asked the Prophet, and the man answered 'red'. 'Is there a black among them?' asked the Prophet. The man replied that there was. The Prophet then asked: 'why is that so?' To this the man said 'it is perhaps due to genealogical tendency (*naz'at al-'irq*)'. Then the Prophet said that 'this too might have been due to such a tendency'.[28] Similarly when 'Umar b. al-Khaṭṭāb asked if kissing one's wife vitiated the fast, the Prophet asked 'Umar instead: what if a person gargles while fasting? 'Umar answered that this did not vitiate the fast. Then the Prophet said: 'that is also the answer to your first question'. According to another report, the Prophet asked the Muslim forces, which were on the move, not to perform the *salāt al-'aṣr* (afternoon prayer) until they reached Bani Qurayzah. Some followed the obvious meaning and delayed the prayer until they reached Bani Qurayzah while others followed its basic purpose, which they understood to be that they should hurry to reach there early, and with this in mind they performed the *'asr* prayer as usual. The report adds that the Prophet approved of both courses of action, one of which adhered to the letter and the other to the rationale of his order.[29]

The leading figures among Companions who took the source materials of *Sharī'ah* to their rational conclusion and delved deep into the purpose and meaning of the Qur'ān and Sunnah included 'Ā'ishah, 'Umar b. al-Khaṭṭāb, 'Ali b. Abū Ṭālib, 'Abd Allah Ibn Mas'ūd, Zayd Ibn Thābit, 'Abd Allah Ibn 'Abbās and many others. The seven renowned jurists of Madinah, especially Ibn al-Musayyib, Masrūq, 'Alqamah, al-Zuhrī and then also Abū Ḥanīfah, Ibn Abī-Layla, al-Awzā'ī, al-Shāfi'ī, al-Muzanī and numerous other leading figures among the Successors and their followers have also shown propensity to rely on rationality, opinion (*ra'y*) and *ta'līl,* and yet they avoided indulgence in arbitrary opinion. The second group of rationalists who have tended to restrict the scope of their reliance on *ra'y* included the Companion Abū al-Dardā', 'Abd Allah b. 'Umar, and then Ibn Sīrīn, Aḥmad b. Ḥanbal and many others. Having stated this, the list here is only a rough indication of a tendency and does not bear out closer examination, for example, in regard to the contributions of Imām Aḥmad b. Ḥanbal, which is discussed below. Then there soon followed a period where the restrictive approach began to lose ground and found few supporters even after the onset of unquestioning imitation and *taqlīd.*[30]

The literalists (*ahl al-ẓāhir*) who were spearheaded by Dāwūd al-Ẓāhirī (d. 885) and Ibn Ḥazm, adhered to the manifest text and rejected implied and construed meanings as they were also averse to ratiocination and *qiyās.* They saw the *Sharī'ah* as a set of rules, commands and prohibitions, which were to be understood at their face value. They saw the search for *'illah,* purpose and rationale of the laws as indulgence in speculative thought, and repugnant to the spirit of submission to the expressed will of the Lawgiver. Thus they restricted the scope of *ijtihād* to the understanding and elaboration of the clear meanings of the text. Notwithstanding the eminent contribution to scholarship and a rich legacy of original *ijtihād* of some of their scholars, like Ibn Ḥazm al-Ẓāhirī, the Ẓāhirī school eventually lost ground and became extinct.

GRADUALNESS AND PRAGMATISM

The *Sharī'ah* favours a gradual approach to legislation and social reform. This is amply illustrated in the fact that the Qur'ān was revealed over a period of twenty-three years and much of it was revealed in relationship to actual events. As noted earlier, the Makkan portion of the Qur'ān was devoted to moral teaching and dogma and contained little by way of legislation. Legislation is almost entirely a Madinese phenomenon. Even in Madinah many of the laws of the Qur'ān were revealed in stages. The final ban on wine drinking which occurs in sura al-Mā'idah, for instance, was preceded by two separate declarations, one of which merely referred to the adverse effects of intoxication, and the other proscribed drinking during ritual prayer, before it was finally banned. This manner of legislation can also be seen with reference to the five daily prayers, which were initially fixed at two and were later raised to five; the legal alms (*zakah*), which was originally an optional charity, became obligatory after the Prophet's migration to Madinah, and fasting which was also optional at first was later made into a religious duty. Some of the earlier rulings of the Qur'ān were subsequently abrogated and replaced in light of the new circumstances that the nascent community experienced in Madinah.

Islamic law favours realistic reform, and it is averse to abrupt revolutionary changes. This is conveyed in the response, for example, which caliph 'Umar Ibn 'Abd al-Azīz (d. 720), gave to his ambitious son 'Abd al-Malik, who suggested to his father that God had granted him the power to fight corruption in society decisively, once and for all. The caliph advised against such a course saying that Almighty God Himself denounced wine drinking twice before He banned it. 'If I take sweeping action even in the right cause and inflict it on people all at once I fear revolt and the possibility that they may also reject it all at once.' Commenting on this the contemporary jurist, Yūsūf al-Qaraḍāwi, wrote that 'this is a correct understanding that is implied in the very meaning of *fiqh* and would be unquestionably upheld by it'.[31]

The pragmatism of *Sharī'ah* is also manifested in the frequent concesssions it makes concerning those who face hardship, including the sick, the elderly, pregnant women and travellers, for example, regarding daily prayers and fasting. It also makes provisions for extraordinary and emergency situations where the rules of *Sharī'ah* may be temporarily suspended on grounds of necessity. Thus, according to legal maxim, the verdict (*fatwā*) of the jurisconsult must take into consideration the change of time and circumstance. We note, for instance, that people were not allowed in the early days of Islam to charge a fee for teaching the Qur'ān, as this was an act of spiritual merit. But then it was noted that people did not volunteer and Qur'ān teaching suffered a decline. The jurists consequently issued a verdict that reversed the position and allowed remuneration for the teaching of the Qur'ān. Note also the pragmatic verdict of Imām Mālik which permitted the pledging of allegiance (*bay'ah*), for the lesser qualified of two candidates for leadership, if this is deemed to be in the public interest. The nomal rule required, of course, that *bay'ah* should only be given to the best qualified candidate. On a similar note, normal rules require that the judge must be a learned *mujtahid*, but a person of lesser qualification may be appointed should there be a shortage of qualified persons for judicial posts. This also applies to a witness who must be an upright person (i.e. *'adl*). In the event, however, where the only witness in a case is a person of lesser qualifications, the judge may admit him and adjudicate the case if this is deemed to be the only reasonable alternative available. Thus the judge, jurist and ruler are advised not to opt for more difficult decisions in the event where easier options could equally be justified.

INDIVIDUALIST OR COMMUNITARIAN

Islamic law requires that government affairs are conducted through consultation with the community and the government strives to secure the public interest (*maṣlaḥah*). This is the subject of a legal maxim which declares that 'the affairs of Imam are determined by reference to public interest' (*amr al-imām manūṭ bi'l maṣlaḥah*). According to another legal maxim, instances of conflict between public and private interests must be determined in favour of the former. Public interest is thus the criterion by which the success and failure of government is measured from the perspective of *Sharī'ah.*

Notwithstanding the pro-community orientations of *Sharī'ah, Sharī'ah* is also inherently individualist. Religion is a matter primarily of individual conscience and the fact also that the rules of *Sharī'ah* are addressed directly to the *mukallaf,* that is, the legally competent individual. The *Sharī'ah* focus on the individual was evidently strong enough to persuade the Kharijites (lit. outsiders) who boycotted the community in the early decades of Islam, and also a group of Mu'tazilites, the followers of Abū Bakr al-Aṣamm in the eighth century, to embrace the view that forming a government was not a religious obligation. For *Sharī'ah* addressed the individual directly; if every individual complied with its rulings, justice will prevail even without a government. These and other similar views were expressed on the asssumption of a basic harmony between the interests of the individual and those of the community.

Broadly speaking, Islam pursues its social objectives through reforming the individual in the first place. The individual is thus seen as a morally autonomous agent who plays a distinctive role in shaping the community's sense of direction and purpose. The individual is admittedly required to obey the government (4:59) but he obeys the ruler on condition that the latter obeys the *Sharī'ah.* This is reflected in a renowned *ḥadīth* that

> there is no obedience in sin, obedience is only in righteousness.[32]
>
> لاطاعة فى معصية، إنما الطاعة فى المعروف.

We may also quote here two other *ḥadīths* that substantiate the moral autonomy of the individual. In one of these Abu Dhar al-Ghifari reported that the prophet ordered him to

> tell the truth even if it be unpleasant,[33]
>
> قل الحق ولو كان مراً.

and in the other he declared that

> the best form of *jihād* is to tell a word of truth to an oppressive ruler.[34]
>
> أفضل الجهاد كلمة حق عند سلطان جائر.

The dignity and welfare of the individual is of central concern to Islamic law. The five essential values of *Sharīʻah* on which the ʻ*ulamā*ʼ are in agreement, namely faith, life, intellect, property and lineage are all premised on the dignity of the individual, which must be protected as a matter of priority. Although the basic interest of the community and those of the individual may be said to coincide within the structure of these values, the focus is nevertheless on the individual.

The Qur'ānic principle of *ḥisbah* (enjoying good and forbidding evil) is primarily addressed to the individual, man and woman, although it also relates to the community and government. This principle can be seen in a *ḥadīth* which addresses the believers

> if any of you sees an evil, let him change it by his hand, and if he is unable to do that, let him change it by his words, and if he is still unable to do that, let him change it in his heart but this would be the weakest form of belief.[35]
>
> من رأى منكم منكرا فليغيّره بيده، فإن لم يستطع فبلسانه، فإن لم يستطع فبقلبه، وذلك أضعف الإيمان.

Ḥisbah as portrayed in this *ḥadīth* is evidently supportive of the moral autonomy of the individual and validates, in principle, the citizen's power of arrest, but it is only on grounds of caution that the police have subsequently been made the exclusive repository of this power. Muslim jurists have dealt with the details of *ḥisbah*, suffice it to note here that the individual must act with conviction when he believes that the initiative he takes would be beneficial. For if he acts without knowledge, his intervention, however well-intended, might cause a harm equal or greater than the one he is trying to avert.

Another Qur'ānic principle that can be quoted here is that of sincere advice, or *naṣīḥah,* which entitles everyone to advise and alert a fellow citizen, including the head of state and his officials, to something beneficial, or rectify an error on his part. The main difference between *ḥisbah* and *naṣīḥah* is that the former is concerned with events that are actually witnessed at the time they occur, but *naṣīḥah* is not so confined to the actual moment of direct observation and it is, as such, more flexible. The individualist leaning of the *Sharī'ah* is also manifested in the Qur'ānic address to the believers:

> take care of your own selves. If you are righteous, the misguided will not succeed in trying to lead you astray. (5:105)
>
> يَا أَيُّهَا الَّذِينَ آمَنُوا عَلَيْكُمْ أَنفُسَكُمْ لاَ يَضُرُّكُم مَّن ضَلَّ إِذَا اهْتَدَيْتُمْ.

Furthermore, within the context of matrimony *Sharī'ah* upholds the regime of separation of property, and the wife's right to manage her own financial affairs remains unaffected by her marriage. In matters of conscience, although Islam encourages the call to religon (*da'wah*), it proclaims nevertheless that

> there shall be no compulsion in religion. (2:256)
>
> لاَ إِكْرَاهَ فِي الدِّين.

The husband is consequently required to respect the individuality of his non-Muslim wife; he is therefore not allowed to press her into embracing Islam. The individualist propensities of *Sharī'ah* can also be seen in the history of its development as I explain below.

Islamic law is often characterized as a 'jurist's law', mainly developed by private jurists who made their contributions as pious individuals rather than government functionaries and leaders. This aspect of the legal history further manifests the individualist leanings of *Sharī'ah,* which is interestingly also seen as a factor in its stability as it was not particularly dependent on government participation and support. Governments came and went but *Sharī'ah* remained as the common law of Muslims. Another dimension of that picture was that relations between the government and the '*ulamā*' remained generally less than amicable ever since the early years of the Umayyad rule (c. 750). The secularist tendencies of Umayyad rulers marked the end of the Righteous Caliphate and the '*ulamā*' became increasingly critical of this change of direction in the system of government. The '*ulamā*' retained their independence also by turning to prominent individuals among them, which led eventually to the formation of the schools of law that bore the names of their eponyms and made few concessions to the government. The immunities against prosecution, for example, that are enjoyed to this day by monarchs and heads of state, state assemblies and diplomats in other legal systems, are totally absent in Islamic law. No one can claim immunity for his conduct on account merely of social and official status.

Two of the most important principles of Islamic law, namely personal reasoning (*ijtihād*) and general consensus (*ijmā'*) can be conducted, from beginning to end, by the jurists without depending on the participation of the government in power. *Ijtihād* and *ijmā'* manifested the nearest equivalent to parliamentary legislation. *Ijtihād* has been practiced mainly by individual jurists. *Ijmā'* is broadly described as the unanimous consensus of the qualified scholars (*mujtahidūn*) of the Muslim community on the ruling of a particular issue. As such *ijmā'* could be initiated by individual jurists, concluded and made binding on the government without the latter's participation. Neither *ijtihād* nor *ijmā'* were institutionalized and have remained so to this day. The jurist who carries out *ijtihād* also enjoys independence from government and is only expected to act on the merit of each case in line with the guidelines of *Sharī'ah* and his own personal conviction.

EXTERNALITY AND INTENT: THE ISSUE OF *ḤIYAL*

Some differences of orientation in legal thought among the schools can be ascertained with reference to the manifest form as opposed to the essence of acts and conduct. While some are inclined to pay attention to manifest conformity to the letter of the law, others are inclined to credit the intention behind the act, and seek a closer link between the two. But this is indicative only of a general orientation in the sense that they are not mutually exclusive categories, as the proponents of one do not deny validity of the other. The Ḥanafis and Shāfi'īs tend to stress the externality of conduct without delving in the intent behind it, whereas the Mālikis and Ḥanbalis are inclined towards the latter view. A consequence of this difference in attitude can be seen in the approval or otherwise of legal stratagems (*al-ḥiyal al-fiqhiyyah*) in such cases as the catalyst marriage (*zawāj al-muḥallil*), and the double sale of *'īnah*. The former involves marrying a woman who has been finally divorced with the intention merely of legalizing her remarriage to her former husband, which is valid according to the Ḥanafis and Shāfi'īs but not according to the other two schools. We have already explained the sale of *'īnah*. This transaction effectively transforms the permitted act of selling into the forbidden act of *ribā.* In both of these examples, the acts are designed so as to circumvent the rules of *Sharī'ah* by violating their intention. The majority of jurists, including Mālikis and Ḥanbalis, who validate the doctrine of blocking the means (*sadd al-dharā'i'*) have rejected such stratagems but the Ḥanafis and Shāf'īs have upheld them as legally valid and recognize the legal consequences that flow from them.[36] The proponents of such stratagems have expatiated and written extensively on the subject. A new and extensive chapter was thus being written, known as *al-ḥiyal wa al-makhārij*, or legal stratagems and dodges. 'Indeed a mastery of this particular subject', as al-'Alwāni observes, 'became a sign of the *faqīh's* erudition and academic pre-eminence.'[37]

Al-Shāṭib has stated the Māliki position as follows: the Lawgiver enjoins that the intent of the *compos mentis* (*mukallaf*) behind his acts should be harmonious with the purpose of the law. 'Anyone who seeks to obtain from the rules of *Sharī'ah* something which is contrary to its purpose has verily violated the *Sharī'ah* and his actions are null and void.'[38] The Ḥanbali scholar, Ibn Qayyim al-Jawziyyah, has substantially upheld the same position.[39]

Al-Shāṭib elaborates: legal acts are not intended for their own sake but for their meanings (*ma'āni*) which contemplate realization of benefits. The benefits in devotional matters are seeking closeness to God and submission to Him in body and mind. If these benefits are not sought, even the *'ibādāt* are vitiated. A *ṣalah,* for example, which is done merely for ostentation (*ri'ā' al-nās*) is not valid.[40]

The rulings of *Sharī'ah* regarding the *ḥalāl* and *ḥarām* generally involve both the acts and their underlying intentions. A Muslim must therefore not seek to legalize for himself a *ḥarām* even if he obtains a judicial decree to that effect. This conclusion is based on the following *ḥadīth* wherein the Prophet, peace be on him, stated:

> I am but a human being. When you bring a dispute to me, some of you may be more eloquent in stating their cases than others. I may consequently adjudicate on the basis of what I hear. If I adjudicate in favour of someone something that belongs to his brother, let him not take it, for it would be like taking a piece of fire.[41]

إنما انا بشر أنكم تختصمون إليّ، فلعلّ بعضكم أن يكون
ألحن بحجّيّته من بعض فأقضى نحو ماأسمع، فمن قضيت
له بحق أخيه شيئا فلا يأخذه فإنما أقطع له قطعة من النار.

It thus appears that in the event of there existing a discrepancy between the apparent and the concealed (*ẓāhir* and *bāṭin*) while the latter is known to be the truth, it prevails over the former. This aspect of the *Sharī'ah* is well articulated in the *ḥadīth*-cum-legal maxim that 'acts are to be judged by the intentions behind them' (*innamā al-a'māl bil-niyyāt*).[42] With reference specifically to contracts, we read in another maxim of *fiqh:* 'Credit is given in contracts to purposes and meanings not to words and (linguistic) constructs.'[43]

I end this chapter with a comment by al-'Alwāni who made the following assessment: 'Unlike the early Imāms of *fiqh* who worked out legal stratagems solely for the purpose of sidestepping damage or loss, scholars of subsequent ages set themselves to the task of inventing ways to dodge legal responsibilities.'[44]

NOTES

1. Ibn 'Ābid n, *Ḥāshiyah Radd al-Mukhtār 'ala Durr al Mukhtār*, I, 56.
2. Ibid.
3. Al-Tahānawī, *Kashshāf Iṣṭilāḥāt* I, 36.
4. For further detail see Abū Sulaymān, *Tartīb al-Mawdū'āt*, 91 ff.
5. Cf. Abū Sulaymān, n.4 at 17.
6. al-Sanhūrī, *Maṣādir al-Ḥaqq,* I, 78.
7. The earliest collection of legal maxims was attempted by the Ḥanafi jurist, Abū al-Ḥasan al-Karkhī (d. 961) in his work *Uṣūl al-Karkhī.* The best known collections in the Shāfi'ī school include Taj al-Dīn al-Subkī's (d. 1392) *al-Ashbāh wa'l-Naẓā'ir* and of Jalāl al-Dīn al-Suyūti's (d. 1634) work bearing the same title. Ibn Nujaym al-Ḥanafi has also authored a work bearing the same title. The well-known equivalent in the Mālikī school is Shihāb al-Dīn al-Qarāfi's *Kitāb al-Furuq* and in the Ḥanbali school it is Taqī al-Dīn Ibn Taymiyyah's *al-Qawā'id al-Nūraniyyah.* There are many other equally reputable collections of legal maxims in almost every *madhhab.*
8. al-Shāṭibī, *al-Muwāfaqāt fi Uṣūl al-Aḥkām.*
9. Tabrizi, *Mishkāt*, vol. III, *ḥadīth* no. 5097.
10. Ibn Qayyim, *Ighāthah al-Lahfān*, I, 346.
11. See for a discussion of these and other similar terms my *Jurisprudence*, Ch. 4 on rules of interpretation, 117–67.
12. Al-Shāṭibī, n. 8 at III, 217.
13. Cf. Shalṭūt, *al-Islām,* 501.
14. Cf. al-Ṣābūnī et al., *Madkhal*, 73.
15. For further elaboration see my *Jurisprudence,* at 29 ff.
16. Muhammad Iqbal, *Reconstruction*, 149, 156.
17. Ibn Qayyim, *I'lām al-Muwaqqi'īn,* III, 1.
18. Ibn Taymiyyah, *Minhāj al-Sunnah*, I,147.

19. Cf. Zaydān, *Madkhal* at 57; Mūsa, *al-Madkhal* at 82.
20. For further elaboration see Kamali, *Jurisprudence*, where separate chapters are devoted to *ijmā', qiyās* and *istiḥsān* respectively.
21. Cf. Zaydān, *Madkhal*, 69.
22. Iqbal, *Reconstruction*, 164.
23. Cf. Muḥammad Amīn (known as Amir Bādshāh), *al-Taysīr*, I, 360; Shalabi, *al-Fiqh al-Islāmi,* 131.
24. Al-Shāṭibī, n. 8 at II, 305.
25. Cf. Zaydān, n. 18 at 122: 'Abd al-Raḥmān Tāj, *al-Siyāsah al-Shar'iyyah*, 28.
26. 'Abd al-Salām, *Qawā'id al-Aḥkām*, 5, also quoted by 'Aṭiyyah, *al-Naẓariyyah al-'Āmmah*, 102.
27. The two tendencies here come close to the well-known scholastic orientations of '*ulamā*' into the two categories of *Ahl al-ra'y* and *Ahl al-ḥadīth.* But it appears that with the collection and documentation of *ḥadīth* on a massive scale in the post–Shāfi'ī period (i.e. mid-ninth century), a shift of emphasis was noted. The *Ahl al-ḥadīth* had won the day and their basic theme was generally accepted. The *Ahl al-Ra'y* became more assiduous in finding textual authority for their positions and a shift of emphasis in the scope of their reliance on *ra'y* began to develop. See for a discussion *Mawsū'ah* at n. 28 below.
28. See *Mawsū'ah* article, *'al-Ta'rīf bi al-Fiqh al-Islāmi*', I, 130; Abū Zahrah, *al-Shāfi'ī,* 287.
29. *Mawsū'ah,* n. 27 at I, 130.
30. Ibid.
31. al-Qaraḍāwi, *Madkhal*, 131.
32. Tabrizi, *Mishkāt*, Vol. II, *ḥadīth* no. 3665.
33. Ahmad b. Hanbal, *Musnad*, I, *ḥadīth* no. 27.
34. Ibn Majān, *Sunan*, *ḥadīth* no. 4011.
35. Muslim, *Mukhtaṣar Ṣaḥīḥ Muslim,* 16, *ḥadīth* no. 34.
36. Mannā' al-Qaṭṭān, *al-Tashrī' wa al-Fiqh*, 294; 'Aṭiyyah, *Naẓariyyah*, 25 at 30.
37. al-'Alwāni, 'The Crisis of *Fiqh*', 320.
38. Al-Shāṭibī, *al-Muwāfaqāt,* II, 331; see also Zaydan, *Madkhal* at 60–1.
39. Ibn Qayyim, *I'lām,* III, 92.
40. Al-Shāṭibī, *al-Muwāfaqāt,* II, 385.
41. Abū Dāwūd al-Sijistānī, *Sunan Abū Dawūd,* III, 1016, *ḥadīth* no. 3576.
42. Muslim, *Ṣaḥiḥ Muslim,* ed. al-Dīn, p. 287, *ḥadīth* no. 1080.
43. For details see Zaydān, *Madkhal,* at 92.
44. Al-'Alwāni, 'The Crisis', at 327.

4

THE LEADING SCHOOLS OF LAW (*MADHĀHIB*)

A legal school implies a body of doctrine taught by a leader, or imām, and followed by the members of that school. The imām must be a leading *mujtahid*, one who is capable of exercising independent judgement. In his teaching, the imām must apply original methods and principles which are peculiar to his own school, independent of others. A *madhhab* must also have followers who assist their leader in the elaboration and dissemination of his teachings. A *madhhab* does not imply, however, a definite organization, formal teaching, or an official status, nor is there a strict uniformity of doctrine within each *madhhab*. The membership of the present-day *madhhabs* is ascertainable on the basis of both individual confession and a loosely defined association of a country or a group to a particular *madhhab*. 'Legal school' is a fitting description of *madhhab* simply because law is the main area in which the schools have widely disagreed. Their differences on the principles of the faith, at least among the Sunni schools, are negligible. But disagreement on subsidiary matters (*furū'*) extends to a great variety of themes.

The first major division occurred between the Sunni and the Shī'i schools of law barely three decades after the death of the Prophet, about 660. The secession of the Shī'ah from the main body of the Muslims, the Sunnis, took place on political grounds, owing mainly to their differences on the nature and devolution of political authority. The Sunnis accepted as legitimate the leadership of the four 'Rightly Guided' caliphs, the *Khulafā' Rāshidūn*. But the Shī'ah claimed that 'Ali, the fourth caliph and the cousin and son-in-law of the Prophet, had a superior claim to leadership over any of his three predecessors, hence their name, the Shīʻah 'party' of ʻAli. The Sunni schools, namely the Ḥanafi, Māliki, Shāfiʻī and Ḥanbali, basically confine their differences to matters of interpretation.

Theological and juristic controversies which arose in the early period of Islam led to the formation of numerous groupings. The range of contested issues must have been extremely diverse: some five hundred schools and sects are said to have disappeared at or about the beginning of the ninth century. The real formation of Islamic law, at the hands of individual jurists, starts in the latter part of the seventh century. This period is followed in the early eighth century by the emergence of two geographical centres of juristic activity in the Ḥijāz and Iraq. Each of these was further divided into two centres: Makkah and Madinah in the Ḥijāz, and Basra and Kufa in Iraq. Of these four centres, usually referred to as the early schools of law, Madinah and Kufa were the most important. With their further development in the latter half of the eighth century, geographical schools gave way to personal schools, named after an individual master whom the members of the school followed.

The early schools of law adopted two different approaches to jurisprudence. The jurists of Makkah and Madinah, cities where the Prophet had lived and Islam had its origin and early development, laid emphasis on tradition as their standard for legal decisions. They thus acquired the name *Ahl al-ḥadīth,* or 'partisans of tradition'. Being away from the Ḥijāz and with limited access to *ḥadīth*, the Iraqi schools, on the other hand, resorted more readily to personal opinion (*ra'y*), which is why they acquired the name *Ahl al-Ra'y,* or 'partisans of opinion'. This group had a tendency to imagine hypothetical cases in order to determine their legal solutions. They had a flair for scholasticism and technical subtlety. The *ahl al-ḥadīth,* on the other hand, were averse to abstract speculation; they were more pragmatic and concerned themselves with concrete cases. Abū Ḥanīfah was the leading figure of the Iraqi school, whereas Mālik, and after him al-Shāfiʻī, led the Ḥijāzi school of legal thought.

Al-Zarqā has questioned, however, the claim that the *Ahl al-Ra'y* gained strength in Iraq because the *ḥadīth* had not yet become widespread in Iraq. On the contrary, he wrote that many of the prominent Companions and also Muslim soldiers were present in Basra and Kufa especially during the time of the fourth caliph ʻAli. Included among them were ʻAbd Allah b. Masʻūd, Saʻd b. Abi Waqās, ʻAmmār

b. Yāsir, Abū Mūsā al-Ash'ari, Mughīrah b. Shu'bah, Hudhayfah b. al Yamāni, 'Imrān b. Haṣīn and many others.[1] The leading schools are each discussed separately as follows.

THE *ḤANAFĪ* SCHOOL

Abū Ḥanīfah Nu'mān ibn Thābit (d. 767), the founder of the Ḥanafi school, was born in Kufa, where he studied jurisprudence with Ibrāhīm al-Nakha'ī and Ḥammād ibn Abī Sulaymān. He delivered lectures to a small circle of students who later compiled and elaborated his teaching. Abū Ḥanīfah has left no work except a small volume on dogmatics, *Al-Fiqh al-Akbar* (The Greater Understanding). His teachings were documented and compiled mainly by two of his disciples, Abū Yūsuf and al-Shaybāni. The Ḥanafi school was favoured by the ruling Abbasid dynasty. Abū Yūsuf, who became the chief justice of the caliph Hārūn al-Rashīd (r. 786–809), composed, at Hārūn's request, a treatise on fiscal and public law, the *Kitāb al-Kharāj*.

Muḥammad ibn Ḥasan al-Shaybāni, a disciple of both Abū Ḥanīfah and Abū Yūsuf, compiled the *corpus juris* of the Ḥanafi school. Six of his juristic works, collectively called the *ẓāhir al-riwāyah,* or works devoted to principal matters, became the basis of many future works on jurisprudence. All of the six works were later combined in one volume entitled *Al-Kāfī* (The Self-Contained), by al-Marwazī, better known as al-Ḥākim al-Shahīd (d. 965). This was subsequently annotated by Shams al-Dīn al-Sarakhsī (d. 1095) in thirty volumes, entitled *Al-Mabsūṭ* (The Extended). Ḥanafi law is the most humanitarian of all the schools concerning the treatment of non-Muslims and war captives, and its penal law is considered to be more lenient.

Abū Ḥanīfah is known for his extensive reliance on *ra'y* and *qiyās* (personal opinion and analogy), a propensity which is also noted in the somewhat theoretical bent of Ḥanafi jurisprudence. Compared to the Ḥanbalis, for example, the Ḥanafis were inclined not only to address real and actual issues but also theoretical problems which were based on mere supposition. Being a merchant by occupation, Abū Ḥanīfah's contribution to the development of the law on commercial transactions (*mu'āmalāt*) has been particularly noted.[2] Another distinctive feature of Abū Ḥanīfah's contribution is its regard for individual freedom and his reluctance to impose any unwarranted restrictions on it. He thus maintained the view that neither the community nor the government have the authority to interfere in the personal liberty of the individual so long as the latter has not violated the law. Ḥanafi law thus entitles an adult girl to conclude her own marriage contract in the absence of her legal guardian (*walī*), a ruling which is different from that of the majority of other schools. Guardianship over the person of individuals must accordingly be confined to the needs of the ward and there is no such need after the minor has attained the age of majority. Besides, since the Qur'ān grants an adult woman full authority over her property, there is no reason why this should not be the case with regard to her marriage. The Imām has on the other hand stipulated equality (*kafā'ah*) in marriage as well as the provision of a fair dowry (*mahr al-mithl*) for the wife. He has moreover refused to validate interdiction (*al-ḥajr*) of the idiot (*safīh*) and the insolvent debtor on the analysis that restricting the freedom of these individuals is a harm greater than the loss of property that they might otherwise incur. As a precautionary measure Abū Ḥanīfah has stipulated however that the *safīh* must have reached the age of twenty-five before he is entrusted with liberty of action concerning his property.[3] The Imām also held that no one, including the judge, may impose restriction on the owner's absolute right to the use of his property even if it inflicted some harm on another person, provided that this did not amount to exorbitant harm (*ḍarar fāḥish*).

One of the brief but leading statements of Abū Ḥanīfah which represents a principle, not only of his school, but on which there is general agreement, is: 'When the authenticity of a *ḥadīth* is ascertained and established, that is my *madhhab-idhā ṣaḥḥa al-ḥadīth fa-huwa madhhabī.*' A substantially concurrent but more general expression, also attributed to Abū Ḥanīfah, tells us 'when you are faced with evidence, then speak for it and apply it' (*idhā tawajjaha lakum dalīl fa-qūlūībih*).[4] Consequently we find on occasions that the disciples of Abū Ḥanīfah have differed over some of the rulings of the Imām on the evidence they have found, often stating that the Imām himself would have followed it, if he had known of it. A differential ruling of the disciple is thus still regarded as a ruling of the *madhhab,* sometimes in preference to that of the Imām. This eminently objective guideline was upheld during the era of *ijtihād,* but the '*ulamā*' of subsequent periods departed from the spirit of that guidance. The Ḥanafi jurist Ibn 'Ābidīn has thus stated the new position of the school: 'a jurist of the latter ages may not abandon the rulings of the leading Imāms and '*ulamā*' of the school even if he sees himself able to carry out *ijtihād,* and even if he thinks that he has found stronger evidence. For it would appear that the predecessors (*mutaqaddimūn*) have considered the relevant evidence and have declared their preference.'[5] The only exception is made for situations of necessity in which the jurist may give a different verdict (*fatwā*) to that of the established ruling of the school. It was with this in mind, for example, that some of the latecomers (*muta'akhkhirīn*) have declared invalid the variant views of the Ḥanafi scholar, Kamāl al-Dīn Ibn al-Humām (d. 1482) as they did not conform to the rulings of the school.[6]

Another leading statement of Abū Ḥanīfah which represents a principle of his school is: 'No one may issue a *fatwā* on the basis of what we have said unless he ascertains the source of our statement.'[7] The researcher and jurisconsult is thus advised to acquire direct knowledge of the sources of *Sharī'ah* and never to isolate the rulings of the school from the evidence on which they are founded. The message here is one of encouragement for independent enquiry and *ijtihād,* yet the way it was interpreted by the imitators [*muqallidūn*] stands in contrast with the purport of that message: thus it was stated that 'the elders [*al-mashā'ikh*] inquired into the evidence that the Imām and his disciples had relied upon . . . Since we are not competent to inquire into that evidence any further nor have we attained a rank equal to them in conducting the inquiry, it is for us to follow what they have said.'[8]

Although in principle the *mujtahid* (one who carries out *ijtihād*) is entitled to identify as preferable one among the variant rulings of the earlier scholars, even this was later denied on the basis of somewhat questionable analysis: 'Since there is no *mujtahid* in our own time, no such preference should now be exercised between the rulings of the Imām and his disciples. Hence the following order of priority should be applied. Firstly the ruling of the Imām, then that of Abū Yūsuf, then al-Shaybān , then Zufar and then of Ḥasan Ibn Ziyād.'[9]

The limits of propriety and adherence to correct principle would seem to have been stretched to the extreme by such statements as is recorded by al-Karkhī (d. 961), the author of *Uṣūl al-Karkhī,* when he stated the following as one of the normative principles of the Ḥanafi school: 'The principle (*al-aṣl*) [to follow] is that every verse [of the Qur'ān] which opposes the ruling of our scholars is taken to have been the subject of abrogation or of preference. But it is better to resort to an interpretation [*ta'wīl*] that would reconcile such differences.'[10]

Abū Sulaymān has rightly considered this statement to be reflective of 'scholastic fanaticism [*al-ta'aṣṣub al-madhhabi*] taken to extreme'. It is just a little short of subjugating the Qur'ān to the rulings of the school. Another contemporary *Sharī'ah* scholar, al-'Alwāni, considers this kind of indiscriminate imitation (*taqlīd*) as the root cause of the current 'crisis of thought' which consists of 'our loss of direct contact with the Book of Allah and the Sunnah of His Prophet'.[11]

The Ḥanafi school has the largest following of all the schools, owing to its official adoption by the Ottoman Turks in the early sixteenth century. It is now predominant in Turkey, Syria, Jordan, Lebanon, Pakistan, Afghanistan and among the Muslims of India, and its adherents constitute about one third of the Muslims of the world.

THE *MĀLIKI* SCHOOL

The Māliki school was founded by Mālik ibn Anas al-Aṣbaḥi (d. 795), who spent his entire life in Madinah except for a brief pilgrimage to Makkah. Mālik is distinguished by the fact that he added another source of law to those known to other schools, namely the practice of the Madinese (*'amal ahl al-Madīnah*). Since the Madinese followed each generation immediately preceding them, the process would have gone back to the generation that was in contact with the teachings and actions of the Prophet. In Mālik's opinion, the practice of the Madinese thus constitutes basic legal evidence. This pragmatic feature of Mālik's doctrine has been retained to the present in the legal practice (*'amal*) of the Maghreb, which takes more notice than other schools of prevailing conditions and customs. The Māliki school also spread in Andalus due to the continued reign of Māliki rulers there even after the collapse of the Umayyad dynasty in Damascus. The major reference book of the Māliki school is *Al-Mudawwanah* (The Enactment), compiled by Asad al-Furāt, and later edited and arranged by Saḥnūn, who published it under the name *Al-Mudawwanah al-Kubrā* (The Greater Enactment). The Māliki school is currently predominant in Morocco, Algeria, Tunisia, Upper Egypt, the Sudan, Bahrain and Kuwait.

Imām Mālik's reputation as the leading figure of the *ḥadīth* movement is borne out by his life-long experience of residence and teaching in Madinah, and of course, by his renowned work, *al-Muwaṭṭā',* which is often described as a work of *ḥadīth*, but in which the *ḥadīth* are arranged according to the topics of *fiqh.* It is the earliest complete work in the history of Islam after the Holy Qur'ān. Although some of the contemporaries of Imām Mālik like Sufyān al-Thawrī and Ibn Abī Laylā in Kufah, al-Layth Ibn Sa'd in Egypt, and Ibn Jurayj in Makkah have authored works of *ḥadīth*, none has reached us. *Al-Muwaṭṭā'* (lit. The Straightened Path) remains therefore the first complete work that we have.[12] This book is also the earliest work on *fiqh* and has in this respect marked a new chapter in the hitherto almost total preoccupation of Muslim scholars with *ḥadīth* studies (*'Ilm al-ḥadīth*).[13]

Unlike his disciple, Imām al-Shāfi'ī, who articulated in his *Risālah* the legal theory of the *uṣūl al-fiqh,* neither Imām Mālik, nor in fact his elder contemporary, Imām Abū Ḥanīfah, addressed methodological issues. This is not to say that they did not apply methods of deduction such as analogy and juristic preference (*istiḥsān*). Indeed they did, as they also applied a clear order of priority between the sources which al-Shāfi'ī subsequently articulated. Imām Mālik included in the Sunnah, not only *ḥadīth* from the Prophet, but also the precedent of Companions and the common practice of the Madinese. Imām Mālik preferred the latter to solitary, or *āḥād, ḥadīth* on the basis that it was a more reliable indicator of the true Sunnah of the Prophet than a solitary report by odd individuals. For example, Imām Mālik did not accept the *āḥād ḥadīth* which validated the option of cancellation in contracts (*khiyār al-majlis*). This *ḥadīth* provided that

> the parties to a sale are free to change their mind so long as they have not separated – nor left the meeting of the contract.
>
> المتبايعان بالخيار مالم يتفرقا.

The reason was that this *ḥadīth* was contrary to Madinese practice which regarded a contract final upon agreement regardless as to whether the parties remained together or separated. Al-Shāfi'ī's concept of *'amal ahl al-Madīnah* as Shāfi'ī maintained that the only valid Sunnah was the authentic Sunnah of the Prophet which must prevail over popular practice regardless of whether it was in conformity with it or otherwise.[14] Imām Shāfi'ī has taken issue with his teacher Imām Mālik on this, and al-Shāfi'ī's stand is supported by the majority.

Notwithstanding this, from the viewpoint of its diversity and openness, Māliki jurisprudence may be said to be the most dynamic and comprehensive of all the schools.[15] This is borne out by the fact that this school validated literally the entire range of proofs that are upheld by the other three schools. To this the Mālikis have added three other sources, namely the Madinese consensus (*ijmā' ahl al-Madīnah*), *istiṣlāh* (consideration of public interest) and *sadd al-dharā'i'* (blocking the means). Māliki jurisprudence has thus opened the scope and sources materials of *ijtihād* more widely than most and it is in this respect distinguished by its comprehensive approach to the understanding of *Sharī'ah.*[16] Imām Mālik would not rely on personal opinion if he could find authority in *ḥadīth*, but in doing so, he has occasionally relied on weak *ḥadīth.*[17]

Public interest (*istiṣlāḥ*) is identified as a Māliki doctrine, not because it was originated by this school, but because only this school recognized it as an independent proof and gave it due prominence. The other schools do recognize it as a proof but tend to subject it to additional requirements and proofs on which the *Sharī'ah* is more explicit. Imām Mālik on a number of occasions issued *fatwā* on the ground solely of *istiṣlāḥ.* He validated, for example, giving *bay'ah* (pledge of allegiance) to the *mafḍul,* that is, the lesser of the two qualified candidates for the office of the head of state – if this would prevent disorder and chaos afflicting the community. He also validated levying of additional taxes on the wealthy when public treasury runs out of funds, so that the lives and properties of people could be protected.[18]

Another distinctive feature of Māliki jurisprudence is that it has attempted to forge a closer relationship with the practicalities of life in Madinah. This is borne out by its recognition of the Madinese consensus as a source of law, a concept which is only advanced by the Māliki school. The Imām has thus validated, on this basis, the testimony of children in cases of injury between themselves, provided they have not dispersed from the scene of the incident. He also held that the wife of a missing person may seek judicial separation after a waiting period of four years.[19] In a similar vein, Māliki *fiqh* has recognized judicial divorce on ground of injurious treatment of the wife by her husband. The majority ruling on this issue entitles the wife to judicial relief whereby the court may punish the recalcitrant husband.

Mālik law has ruled that if the treatment in question amounted to injury (*ḍarar*), the wife may request the court for dissolution of marriage on that ground. This aspect of Māliki *fiqh* has in recent decades been widely adopted in the reform of divorce law introduced by Muslim countries of the Middle East and Asia.

Another Māliki contribution in this area is in reference to a type of divorce, known as *khul'*, in which the wife proposes dissolution of marriage by mutual agreement against a financial consideration. Being a Qur'ānic concept, *khul'* is basically recognized by all the schools, but it can only be finalized with the husband's approval and consent. Māliki *fiqh* has on the other hand proposed a procedure whereby the wife, in the event of irreconcilable differences, could seek *khul'*, which can be finalized by the court. This aspect of Māliki law has been taken to its logical conclusion by legislation in many contemporary Muslim countries which enable the wife to demand *khul'* as of right and the court is authorized to grant it if all attempts at reconciliation have failed.[20]

Notwithstanding his leading position as the Imām of *Ahl al-ḥadith*, Imām Mālik has relied extensively on personal opinion (*ra'y*). As stated earlier, Imām Mālik has promoted and developed two doctrines of *uṣūl al-fiqh*, namely public interest (*istiṣlāḥ*) and blocking the means (*sadd al-dharā'i'*), which are recognized as Māliki doctrines. They are both eminently rational and rely mainly on personal reasoning and *ra'y*.[21]

In its basic outline the doctrine of *sadd al-dharā'i'* maintains that a means to *wājib* (obligation) partakes in that *wājib*, and whatever that leads to *ḥarām* (forbidden) also becomes *ḥarām*. Similarly the means to *ḥalal* (lawful) is *ḥalal* to the extent of making that *ḥalal* accessible. The Mālikis and Ḥanbalis who are the main advocates of this doctrine have thus declared unlawful the sale of arms at the time of conflict, the sale of grapes to a wine-maker and contracts which lead to usury or *ribā*.[22]

The Māliki jurist al-Qarāfi (d. 1286) has rightly observed that the basic notion of *sadd al-dharā'i'* is generally accepted by all the schools; that it is not, as many seem to think, only advocated by the Māliki school. He elaborated that those means which definitely lead to *ḥarām* and those which are strongly likely to do so, or which lead to an evil (*mafsadah*) in most cases, if not always, are proscribed by all the leading schools. It is due mainly to the additional detail and a degree of prominence that the Māliki scholars have given to this doctrine that it is identified with this school.[23] In Abū Zahrah's (d. 1974) assessment, Imām Mālik was the leading figure not only of *Ahl al-ḥadīth* but also of *Ahl al-ra'y* and his contribution to the juristic heritage of Islam truly transcends the boundaries of scholastic particularities.[24]

None of the leading Imāms have encouraged unquestioning imitation (*taqlīd*) and Imām Mālik has made his standing clear on it by saying 'I am only a human. May be I am wrong and may be I am right. So look into my opinions; if they are in agreement with the Qur'ān and Sunnah, accept them, otherwise reject them.'[25] He has also stated concerning the precedent of Companions: 'abandon what I say in favour of what the Companions have said . . .'[26] Imām Mālik's regard for the precedent of Companions and his perception of the diversity and dynamism of *ijtihād* is also well depicted in the fact that he declined the suggestion by the Abbasid caliph al-Manṣūr to adopt *al-Muwaṭṭā'* as the sole guide of practice in the Abbasid empire. The Imām responded that the Companions had differed among themselves and tolerated disagreement in matters of *ijtihād* and this should be allowed to continue.[27]

THE *SHĀFI'Ī* SCHOOL

This is the third major surviving school, named after its founder, Muḥammad ibn Idrīs al-Shāfi'ī (d. 820). A pupil of Mālik, he formulated the legal theory of *Sharī'ah* in the form in which it has largely been retained ever since. This theory teaches that Islamic law is based on four basic principles, or roots (*uṣūl al-fiqh*): the word of God in the Qur'ān, the divinely inspired conduct or Sunnah of the Prophet, consensus of opinion (*ijmā'*), and reasoning by analogy (*qiyās*). Al-Shāfi'ī studied the works of his predecessors and found that despite the existence of *ḥadīth* from the Prophet, the early jurists occasionally preferred the opinions of the Companions, or ignored a *ḥadīth* when it was contrary to local practice. Insisting on the overriding authority of *ḥadīth*, al-Shāfi'ī said that authentic *ḥadīth* must always be accepted. Whereas Abū Ḥanīfah and Mālik felt free to set aside a tradition when it conflicted with the Qur'ān, for al-Shāfi'ī a tradition could not be invalidated on this ground: he took it for granted that the Qur'ān and *ḥadīth* did not contradict each other.

Al-Shāfiʻī also differed from both Abū Ḥanīfah and Mālik on the meaning of *ijmāʻ*. To al-Shāfiʻī's predecessors *ijmāʻ* meant the consensus of the scholars, but al-Shāfiʻī denied the existence of any such consensus. There could only be one valid consensus – that of the entire Muslim community. He thus restricted the scope of *ijmāʻ* to obligatory duties, such as the daily prayers, on which such a consensus could be said to exist. But the legal theory which prevailed after al-Shāfiʻī returned to the concept of the consensus of the scholars, which it considers infallible in the same way as the general consensus of the Muslims.

Al-Shāfiʻī essentially restricted the sources of law to the Qur'ān and the Sunnah. Should there be no provision in these sources for a particular case, then the solution must be found through the application of analogy, which basically entails extending the logic of the Qur'ān and the Sunnah. Any expression of opinion which is not related to these sources is arbitrary and excessive. Al-Shāfiʻī thus restricted the scope of *ijtihād* (independent reasoning) by subjecting it to the requirements of strict analogical reasoning, hence he considered *ijtihād* and *qiyās* synonymous.

Imām al-Shāfiʻī's impact on the development of *Sharīʻah* is most noticeable in the area of methodology of *uṣūl al-fiqh*. His predecessors and contemporaries had discussed methodological issues but references to such issues remained generally isolated and incidental. Only in Shāfiʻī's *Risālah* do we find an exclusive treatment of the methodology of *uṣūl,* which consequently emerged towards the end of the eighth century as one of the most important disciplines of Islamic learning.[28] Al-Shāfiʻī's role in this regard was hardly exaggerated when Fakhr al-Dīn al-Rāzi compared it to that of Aristotle in logic and to Khalīl Ibn Aḥmad in prosody.[29] Al-Shāfiʻī was the first to write on many new themes of *uṣūl al-fiqh* and it was through his elaboration of such concepts as *bayān* (explanation) and themes such as *ʻāmm* (general), *khāṣṣ* (particular), *al-nāsikh* and *al-mansūkh* (abrogator and abrogated) that the Imām was able to substantiate his views on the basic unity between the Qur'ān and Sunnah. The Sunnah accordingly explains and supplements the Qur'ān in principle and in detail and, for purposes of *ijtihād,* the one must not be read in isolation from the other.

Al-Shāfiʻī generally equated the authority of the authentic Sunnah with that of the Qur'ān, except in regard to matters of belief (*al-ʻaqā'id*) where he stated that the Sunnah did not command an equivalent authority. He rejected the proposition, many had advocated, that the Qur'ān and Sunnah may abrogate one another. Al-Shāfi'ī maintained that since the Sunnah was explanatory to the Qur'ān, abrogation of the Qur'ān was not within the terms of its reference.[30] Al-Shāfi'ī's vision of the basic unity of the revealed sources came close to saying that rejecting the Sunnah also amounted to rejecting the Qur'ān and that accepting the one and rejecting the other was untenable.

In his *Jimā' al-'Ilm* (compendium of knowledge), al-Shāfi'ī explained the onslaught on Sunnah by three groups of people. Firstly, those who denied the authority of Sunnah altogether and held the Qur'ān to be the only source. Secondly those who did not accept the Sunnah unless it was supported and upheld by the Qur'ān. And thirdly those who accepted only the *Mutawātir,* that is *ḥadīth* proven by continuous testimony, as opposed to solitary or *āḥaḍ.*[31] Al-Shāfi'ī firmly refuted all of these and stated that rejecting the Sunnah would leave a vacuum in our knowledge of the essentials of Islam, including, for instance, the five pillars of the faith. To those who only accepted the *Mutawātir* and rejected the *āḥāḍ ḥadīth*, al-Shāfi'ī responded that when the Prophet had a message to deliver he did not necessarily invite all the residents of Madinah to witness it. The Prophet spoke to odd individuals and to multitudes and it would be less than a justice to accept only *ḥadīth* which are reported by a large number. What we do require in all cases is to verify the authenticity of *ḥadīth* through a reliable *isnād* (chain of transmission) and nothing else.[32] The Imām thus refuted the Ḥanafi requirement of plurality of reporters on subjects which are expected to have been widely known (*mā ta'umm bihi al-balwā*) – and also the Māliki requirement that the *ḥadīth* must not be in conflict with the common practice of Madinese. He also rejected the Ḥanafi doctrine of *istiḥān* (juristic preference) and the Māliki doctrine of *istiṣlaḥ* (unrestricted public interest) as they heavily relied on *ra'y.* For his staunch support of Sunnah, the Imām won the appellation in Baghdad of *Nāṣir al-Sunnah* (Champion of Sunnah).[33]

'It is certain', Ibn Taymiyyah (d. 1328) commented, 'that none of the leading Imāms who inspired respect and confidence of the people have deliberately opposed the Sunnah of the Messenger of God in any matter, important or otherwise, and all are unanimous on the obligatoriness of obedience to him. They have all stated that whenever it was known that their ruling came into conflict with Sunnah, it should be abandoned in favour of the Sunnah.'[34] Abū Zahrah observed that only the heretics (al-Zanādiqah) and some Khārijites disputed the authority of Sunnah.[35] It is also suggested that concern over the authority of Sunnah became prominent during the second generation of Successors (*tāb'i tābi'īn*) at a time when forgery in *ḥadīth* had become widely known.[36] Shah Wali Allah Dihlawi (d. 1763) has observed that knowledge of *ḥadīth* in the early period was localized and scholars normally relied on collections that were familiar to their local centres of learning. When a scholar encountered conflict in the *hadīth* of his own town or locality, he tended to exercise a kind of intuitive judgement (*al-firāsah*) to resolve it. Then came al-Shāfi'ī at a time when *ḥadīth* from all localities was brought together and consolidated. Closer examination and comparison of *hadīth* materials revealed instances of conflict and confusion in the vast information that was collected on the subject.[37]

Abū Zahrah draws attention to a somewhat similar situation in modern times whereby questionable factions and groups have emerged, such as the Lahore-based Jamā'at al-Qur'ān, and its equivalents in Egypt, Libya and elsewhere which recognized the Qur'ān as the only valid source of *Sharī'ah* to the exclusion of Sunnah. To this Abū Zahrah has responded: 'would we have another Shāfi'ī and a robust campaigner to set the priorities right again'.[38]

In its general orientation, the *fiqh* of al-Shāfi'ī takes an intermediate stance between the two most dominant movements of his time, the *Ahl al-ra'y* and *Ahl al-ḥadīth*. His objective was to reconcile *fiqh* and *ḥadīth* and strike a balance between the Traditionist stance of the Māliki school and pragmatism of the Ḥanafi. Al-Shāfi'ī took an objective stand over issues at a time when the Traditionists and Rationalists were engaged in bitter controversies defending their respective positions. Al-Shāfi'ī was critical of Imām Mālik's validation of unrestricted *maṣlaḥah* and of Abū Ḥanifah's frequent concessions on details at the expense of general principles.

In Egypt, al-Shāfi'ī wrote his *Kitāb al-Umm* an encyclopedic work which is distinguished by the unique style of combining the *uṣūl* (roots) and the *furū'* (branches) of *fiqh*. He applies systematically the methodology of *uṣūl* which he has articulated in the deduction and exposition of the detailed rules of *fiqh*. He begins his discourse by giving the basic evidence in the sources and advances his theme in progressive stages until it reaches its logical conclusion.

Al-Shāfi'ī's aversion to *taqlīd* is shown in his renowned statement that 'one who seeks knowledge without proof is like a gatherer of wood who goes into the wood at night to collect fallen branches and is bitten by a snake as it was unknowingly taken for another branch'.[39] One of his disciples, Ismā'il al-Muzanī, the author of *Mukhtaṣar al-Muzanī,* has stated that in this book he summarized al-Shāfi'ī's work to impart it to others, together with a reminder that the Imām forbade others from imitating him without investigation and assessment.[40] Al-Rabī' has said that 'I heard al-Shāfi'ī saying: When you find the Sunnah of the Messenger of God opposing what I might have said, follow it and abandon my word.'[41] Statements of this kind, which are also recorded from other leading Imāms, are reminiscent of the fact that the bulk of *ḥadīth* was not yet documented. This was soon to be attempted by al-Bukhāri, Muslim and others around the middle of the ninth century Hijrah.

The Imām developed his Old *madhhab* in Baghdad prior to departing for Egypt, and his New school began upon his arrival in Egypt. The Imām revised many of his earlier *fatwās* with reference to the new environment and customs of Egyptian society.[42] He has explained that the leading Companions, including 'Umar b. al-Khaṭṭāb, 'Ali b. Abū Ṭālib and Ibn 'Abbās, have changed their previous *ijtihād* on issues, and quoted to this effect a portion of caliph 'Umar's renowned letter to his judges as follows: '. . . And let not a judgment that you have rendered yesterday and then upon reflection and reconsideration you find that it was incorrect – deter you from returning to truth. For truth is timeless and returning to truth is better than continuing in falsehood.'[43] Al-Shāfi'ī's new rulings are generally preferred over his older *fatwās* except in two situations: when the older ruling is supported by a reliable *ḥadīth*, and where no new ruling can be found to have been issued on the same subject.[44]

Al-Shāfi'ī emphasized adherence to objective principles, and relied on the apparent and immediate meaning of the text. He also understood the *Sharī'ah* to be concerned with the evident aspects of human conduct. It was therefore not the duty of the judge and jurist to enquire into the hidden meanings of the text nor into the thoughts and motives of individuals. Al-Shāfi'ī has quoted in support evidence from the Sunnah where the Prophet treated the hypocrites on the basis of the words they uttered. When they cited, for example, the testimonials of the faith, the Prophet accepted this on face value and did not question their motives. This attitude of reliance on manifest evidence is also reflected in al-Shāfi'ī's refutation of the Ḥanafi doctrine of *istiḥsān,* which basically upholds the spirit rather than letter of the

Sharī'ah. Instances have thus been recorded of *fatwā* in which the Imām has insisted on adherence to the externalities of the *aḥkām*. This may be illustrated as follows:

> When an upright person brings a claim, say of usurpation [*ghaṣb*] of 100 dirhams against a person who has a reputation for criminality and aggression, but who denies the claim, the claim will be dismissed unless it is proven by normal evidence. Similarly if a person of ill-repute who is known for lying and deception brings a claim of *ghaṣb* against an upright and honest individual, the latter may have to take an oath even if the claim appears false by all indications.
>
> Where a married couple is known to have cohabited for twenty years and then the wife claims that she had not been supported by her husband, the claim must be granted a hearing notwithstanding its apparent incredulity. The husband will be required to provide necessary evidence and the mere fact of cohabitation is not enough to absolve him of the claim.[45]

In a similar vein, al-Shāfi'ī's approach to the interpretation of contracts was almost entirely based on the form rather than intent of the contract. Al-Shāfi'ī thus overruled enquiry into the intention of the parties, even in suspicious circumstances such as the double sale of *'īnah,* and the intervening *nikāh* of *taḥlīl* (an ostentatious marriage designed to legalize a fresh marriage between a divorced couple). The Imām validated both of these and stated with regard to the first 'if we were to invalidate sale on the basis of a fear that it might become a means to something unlawful we would have acted on conjecture'. A man is within his rights to buy a sword even if he intends to kill an innocent person with it. A man may likewise buy a sword from someone he saw using it as a murder weapon. Contracts and transactions are therefore to be judged by their obvious conformity to the law, not by a mere suspicion that they may have violated it. This reliance on the manifest form of contracts and transactions is not peculiar to al-Shāfi'ī, as many others have also shown the same tendency, but al-Shāfi'ī has, in Abū Zahrah's assessment, exhibited it more than most. The rulings of *Sharī'ah* in temporal affairs are generally applied on the basis of obvious facts, and not of hidden phenomena, which are not susceptible to evidence and proof.[46]

Adjudication (*al-qaḍā'*) according to the majority of '*ulamā*', including al-Shāfi'ī, is to be founded on obvious evidence and proof. In stating his position on this point, al-Shāfi'ī has quoted the *ḥadīth* in which the Prophet has stated '. . . I adjudicate on the basis of what I hear' (*fa aqḍi 'alā naḥw ma asma'*). The *ḥadīth* thus indicates that judicial decisions must be based on evident facts and on what people say even if this might enable someone to take what is otherwise unlawful.[47]

Because of his frequent change of opinion and *ijtihād,* al-Shāfi'ī's disciples have recorded different rulings from the Imām on particular issues. It is stated in *al-Umm,* for example, that if a man deceives a woman by presenting a false family pedigree and then it is discovered, he is liable to a *ta'zīr* punishment. Then two other views are recorded on the same issue from the Imām and neither has been given preference. The first view entitles the wife to a choice either to continue the marriage or separate. The second view has it that the marriage will be null and void. *Al-Umm* also contains two rulings on the liability to *zakah* of an insolvent person. According to one view if a person has 1000 dirhams and he is also in debt by a similar amount, he is not liable to pay *zakah.* Al-Rabī' refers to another view of the Imām to the effect that *zakah* will be payable simply because of his being in possession of assets.[48] It is reported that in about sixteen issues, the Imām referred to the prospects of both an affirmative and a negative solution but did not declare his own preference either way.[49]

It has been observed that the plurality of views that al-Shāfi'ī has recorded is indicative of his assiduous pursuit of new solutions and his dynamic intellect. It shows his persistent quest for the truth, which 'could not be said to be indicative of weakness'.[50]

The Shāfi'ī school is now prevalent in Lower Egypt, southern Arabia, East Africa, Indonesia, Malaysia, Brunei, and has many followers in Palestine, Jordan and Syria.

THE *ḤANBALI* SCHOOL

Al-Shāfi'ī's emphasis on the authority of *ḥadīth* was taken further by two new schools which emerged in the ninth century. The first and the only successful one of these was the Ḥanbali school, founded by Aḥmad ibn Ḥanbal (d. 855), the orthodox opponent of the Rationalists, the *Ahl al-ra'y* (the other was the Ẓāhiri school of Dāwūd al-Ẓāhir which is now extinct). Ibn Ḥanbal's reliance on *ḥadīth* was so total that for some time he and his adherents were regarded not as jurists (*fuqahā'*) but as mere traditionists. His main work, *Al-Musnad*

(The Verified), is a collection of some forty thousand ḥadīths. He uses *qiyās* very little and draws mainly on the sacred text. Ibn Ḥanbal's teaching was later refined and developed by his disciples and commanded a widespread following, but in spite of a series of brilliant scholars and representatives over the centuries, the numbers suffered a continuous diminution after the fourteenth century. In the eighteenth century, the Wahhābi, a puritanical movement in the Arabian Peninsula, derived its doctrine and inspiration from the Ḥanbalis and in particular the works of the celebrated jurist and theologian Ibn Taymiyyah. The Ḥanbali school is currently predominant in Saudi Arabia and also has followers in Oman, Qatar, Bahrain and Kuwait.

Ibn Ḥanbal abandoned the *fatwā* of Companions if it came into conflict with a *ḥadīth*, even a weak *ḥadīth*. He thus abandoned the ruling of 'Umar b. al-Khaṭṭāb in respect of granting the right of maintenance to a divorced woman following a final divorce. Instead he followed the *ḥadīth* reported by Fāṭimah bt Qays, in which she said that her husband divorced her and the matter came to the attention of the Prophet, who did not entitle her to any maintenance. Caliph 'Umar had considered this *ḥadīth* to be weak, which is why he did not act upon it.[51] The Imām also abandoned the saying of Ibn 'Abbās regarding the duration of the probation period (*'iddah*) of a pregnant widow to be the longer of the two periods, namely of 130 days, or until delivery. He followed instead the *ḥadīth* of Subay'ah al-Aslamiyyah whose husband died while she was pregnant and the Prophet allowed her to remarry after delivery.[52] Ibn Ḥanbal's extensive reliance on *ḥadīth* was partly facilitated by the fact that by his time, knowledge of *ḥadīth* had become widespread and much progress had been made towards its documentation. Yet it is interesting to note that Ibn Ḥanbal relied extensively on considerations of public interest, or *maṣlaḥah,* and many of his rulings have been validated on this basis. The Imām issued a *fatwā*, for example, which compelled the owner of a large house to give shelter to the homeless. He also validated compelling workers and craftsmen to continue their services in consideration of fair wages (*ujrah bi al-mithl*).[53]

With reference to unquestioning imitation (*taqlīd*), Abū Dāwūd al-Sijistānī has stated that he heard the Imām saying, 'Do not imitate me, nor Mālik, nor Thawrī, nor Awzā'i, but take from where we have taken.'[54] This has prompted Muḥammad Yūsuf Mūsā to pose the question, 'where are we now in relationship to this? And how could we justify the demand, on the part of many a jurist of the later periods, of adherence to their own schools as if it were an obligation under *Sharī'ah*!'[55] But the Ḥanbali '*ulamā*' of all ages have taken a different stand, in principle at least, in regard to *ijtihād,* which they have considered open to anyone who was competent to exercise it. Thus from the viewpoint of principle, *ijtihād* and the presence of independent *mujtahids* is a collective obligation (*farḍ kifa'i*) of the community at any given time. *Ijtihād* must therefore never be allowed to discontinue. As I shall presently explain, permissibility (*ibāḥah*) has meant much more in Ḥanbali jurisprudence than it has in any other school, especially with reference to the freedom of contract.

The schools of law differ as to whether the norm in contract is permissibility or prohibition, or an intermediate position between the two. The majority have tended to restrict the freedom of contract by maintaining that the agreement of parties create the contract but its requirements and consequences are independently determined by *Sharī'ah*. The parties are therefore not at liberty to alter the substance of these nor to circumvent them in a way that would violate their purpose. The parties to contract do not create the law but only a specific contract; their stipulations and terms of agreement should therefore be in conformity with the provisions of *Sharī'ah*. The majority thus maintain that there is no obligation unless the Lawgiver has validated it in the first place. Contracts, in other words, do not create new obligations outside the basic framework that is laid down by *Sharī'ah*. The schools have differed over details. At the one extreme there are the Ẓāhirīs who are more restrictive than most. The Mālikīs and Ḥanafis tend to take a moderate position by making many exceptions to the basic norm of prohibition. The Shāfi'ī position resembles in many ways that of the Ẓāhirīs and both tend to proscribe altering the basic postulates and attributes of contracts through mutual agreement.[56] The Ḥanbalis have differed from the majority by maintaining that the norm regarding contracts and stipulations therein (*al-'uqūd wa al-shurūṭ*) is that they are permissible in the absence of a clear prohibition in the *Sharī'ah*. Ibn Qayyim thus stated:

> The norm regarding the *'ibādāt* is prohibition, which means that they are null and void unless they are specifically validated, and the norm in contracts and transactions is permissibility unless there is evidence to the contrary. God Most High may not be worshipped except in the manner that His Messenger has shown. Because worship is His right over His servants. As for contracts and transactions, they are all permissible unless specifically forbidden.[57]

The Qur'ān has only laid down the general principle that contracts must be fulfilled (5:1); it is also expressive of the central role of consent in commercial transactions and contracts (4:19). The will and agreement of the parties is thus recognized as of primary significance in regard to the requirements of contract; their agreement therefore creates binding rights and obligations.[58]

Ibāḥah under Ḥanbali law can also form the basis of unilateral obligation (*iltizām*), which means that the individual is free to commit himself or herself in all situations where *ibāḥah* can apply. Thus a man may validly stipulate in a contract of marriage that he will not marry a second wife. Since polygamy is only permissible (*mubāḥ*), it may be subjected to stipulations. The other schools disallow this on the analysis that *Sharī'ah* has made polygamy lawful, a position which should not be circumvented nor nullified through contractual stipulations. Any stipulation therefore which seeks to do so is not binding. Ibn Ḥanbal stated that stipulations in a marriage contract must strictly be observed. Consequently when one of the spouses fail to comply with the terms of their agreement, the other would be entitled to seek annulment of the contract.[59] The Imām also validated suspension (*ta'līq*) in contracts, which means that the parties may agree that the contract should take effect on a future date. This is once again at variance with the majority who maintain that contracts which involve transfer of ownership (*'uqūd al-tamlīk*) must be prompt and transfer the ownership in question immediately. Ibn Qayyim stated, on the other hand, that the Imām validated suspended contracts (*al-'uqūd al-mu'allaqah*), including a suspended contract of marriage, indeed all contracts as such.[60]

And lastly, Muslim jurists have differed over the legality of sale in which the price is not specified at the time of contract, but where reference is made to the prevailing market price, when a contractor buys, for example, supplies on a regular basis by reference to the prevailing price and then settles the payment at the end of the month or year. The majority have held this to be invalid, stating that taking possession of such goods does not transfer their ownership. That the exchange amounts to no more than unlawful possession (*qabḍ fāsid*), which is equivalent to usurpation (*ghaṣb*). Ownership therefore remains with the seller. On this issue Ibn Qayyim has stated that 'Imām Aḥmad b. Ḥanbal has validated it and Ibn Taymiyyah has also spoken in its support. They maintain that this transaction has become customary among people and there is nothing in the text, *ijmā'*, or sound analogy to proscribe it.'[61]

SHĪ'ITE SCHOOLS

Shī'ites (lit. followers), refer to the followers of 'Ali, first cousin of the Prophet and the husband of his daughter, Fāṭimah. The Shī'ites maintain that 'Ali was the first legitimate caliph and successor to the Prophet, and therefore reject Abu Bakr, 'Umar and 'Uthmān, the first three caliphs of the Sunni Muslims, as usurpers. The Shī'ites maintain that the Prophet had expressly declared 'Ali as his successor under guidance from God. They are also called the Imamiyyah because they believe that Islam consists in the true knowledge of the Imāms as the rightful leaders of the faithful. In support of this, they also quote the following Qur'ānic verse:

> And when his Lord tried Abraham with words and he fulfilled them, He said: 'I am about to make thee an Imam to mankind,' he said 'of my offspring also?' 'My covenant' said God 'embraceth not evildoers.' (2:118)

> وَإِذِ ابْتَلى إِبْرَاهِيمَ رَبُّهُ بِكَلِمَاتٍ فَأَتَمَّهُنَّ قَالَ إِنِّي جَاعِلُكَ لِلنَّاس
> إِمَامًا قَالَ وَمِن ذُرِّيَّتِي قَالَ لاَ يَنَالُ عَهْدِي الظَّالِمِينَ.

This verse establishes, according to Shī'ite doctrine, the divine character of the Imamate and the conclusion also that the Imām must himself be without blemish or capacity to sin. In this way, the Shī'ites believe in the infallibility (*'iṣma*) of the Imām, whereas the Sunnis, and also one branch of the Shī'ites, the Zaydiyya, do not agree with the idea of infallibility for any Imām. The Prophet has also been quoted as having made the following statement at Ghadir Khum on his way from Makkah to Madinah: 'Whosoever receives me as his master, then let him receive 'Ali. O Lord befriend 'Ali. Be the enemy of all his enemies; help all who help him and forsake all who forsake him.'

In Sunni law the head of state is an elected office, but Shī'i law maintains that leadership, the *imāmate*, descends in the housefold of the Prophet through hereditary succession. Of the numerous Shī'ite schools, only three have survived: Ithnā 'Ashāriyah (Twelver), Zaydi and Ismā'ili. They differ mainly over the line of succession after the fourth imām. The Twelvers, the largest of the three groups, recognize twelve imāms, hence their name, Ithnā 'Asharīyah (Twelvers), as opposed to the Ismā'iliyah, who are also called Sab'iyah (Seveners), as they believe in seven imāms.

For the Sunnis, divine revelation (*waḥy*) manifested in the Qur'ān and the Sunnah ceased with the death of the Prophet. For the Shīʻites, however, divine inspiration (*ilhām*) continued to be transmitted after the death of the Prophet, to the line of their recognized imāms. Accordingly, they maintain that in addition to the Qur'ān and Sunnah, the pronouncements of their imāms, whom they believe infallible (*maʻṣūm*), constitute divine revelation and therefore binding law. The Shīʻites, moreover, accept only those traditions whose chain of authority (*isnād*) goes back to one of their recognized imāms since the imām is divinely inspired. The Shīʻites, basically do not recognize *ijmāʻ*.

The Imamiyyah receive the following twelve as their rightful Imams:

1. ʻAli, the son-in-law of the Prophet;
2. Al-Ḥasan, the son of ʻAli;
3. Al-Ḥusayn, the second son of ʻAli;
4. ʻAli Zayn al-ʻĀbidīn, the son of Ḥusayn;
5. Muḥammad al-Bāqir, son of Zayn al-ʻĀbidīn;
6. Jaʻfar al-Ṣādiq, son of Muḥammad al-Bāqir;
7. Mūsā al-Kāẓim, son of Jaʻfar;
8. Al-Raza, son of Mūsā;
9. Muḥammad at-Taqi, son of Al-Raza;
10. ʻAli al-Naqi, son of Muḥammad Taqi;
11. Al-Ḥasan al-ʻAskari, son of ʻAli al-Naqi; and
12. Muḥammad, son of al-Ḥasan al-ʻAskari, or the Imām al-Mahdi, who is supposed to be still alive; he is the Mahdi, or Guide, which the Prophet prophesied would appear before the day of judgement to establish peace and righteousness in the world.[62] He was born in Baghdad in 872, and believed to have been taken from earth while still eight years of age and lives since then in occultation. Belief in occultation has spread among all branches of Shīʻism which subscribe in the continued life of the Imam they regard as the last and as the one to reappear in the future.[63]

There were two main schisms in the succession of the Imāms, the first upon the death of ʻAli Zayn al-ʻĀbidīn, when part of the sect adhered to his son Zayd, the founder of the Zaydiyya, and the second on the death of Jaʻfar al-Ṣādiq, when he nominated his son, Mūsā al-Kāẓim as his successor, instead of his elder son Ismā'il. Those who upheld Ismā'il's title to the imamate are called Ismā'iliyya. The majority of Shī'ites, however, acknowledge Mūsā al-Kāẓim as the true Imām.

All the Shī'ite groups regard their eminent scholars and *mujtahids* as their leaders and expect them to provide guidance in the absence of the Imam. Whereas the Sunnis have not formalized any procedure for attainment to the rank of *mujtahid*, the Shī'ites have ranked them in a certain order and procedure that is practised in the theological seminaries of Qum and Mashhad to this day.

Until the time of Ja'far al-Ṣādiq, Shī'ism remained political in character, focusing mainly on the issue of succession and lacking a juristic doctrine of its own. It was through the works of two Imāms, Muḥammad al-Bāqir (d. 735) and Ja'far al-Ṣādiq (d. 765) that Shi'ism also became a school of juristic thought.

Much like its Sunni counterpart, Shī'te law consists of legal, moral and religious norms based on the Qur'ān and the Tradition of the Prophet. However, in Shī'ite law, the expounders of the *Sharī'ah* enjoyed charismatic authority in the position of Imām, or the '*ulamā'* and *mujtahids*, in his absence. In one of his renowned statements on the designation of the legitimate Imāms, Ja'far al-Ṣādiq introduced his father as the one who pioneered the Shī'ite school of law as follows:

> Before him [al-Bāqir], the Shī'ites did not know what should be considered as lawful and unlawful except for what they had learned from the common people (reference to Sunnis) until Imam al-Baqir began to explain to them and taught them. Therefore they began to teach others what they had learned from the Imam. That is the way it is. The earth will not be in order without an Imam.[64]

Evidence shows that rejection of legality in the practice of the Companions, especially Abū Bakr and 'Umar al-Khaṭṭāb, was the point of departure for Imām Bāqir to construct his own interpretation of the *Sharī'ah*. Imām Bāqir explicitly rejected the considerable influence of these two figures, and following him, Imām Ṣādiq also ordered his followers to act in accordance with the Qur'ān and the Sunna of the Prophet, but to oppose the practice of commoners (*al-'āmma*, the Sunnis). The community's consensus (*ijmā'*) that played an important role in the precedent of Companions was replaced, in the Shī'ite tradition, by the commonly maintained opinions of the companions of the Imams.[65] With reference to *ḥadīth*, the Shī'ites also rejected the 'six correct books of the Sunnis – *al-ṣiḥaḥ al-sitta*' and replaced them with five collections of their own: *Al-Kāfi; Man la Yastahḍiruhu al-Faqīh; Tahdhib; Istibṣār;* and *Nahj al-Balāgha.* For the Sunnis the transmission of *ḥadīth* can be by any upright person, but the Shī'ites only receive *ḥadīth* through their recognized Imāms. Yet it seems that the Sunni and Shī'ite *ḥadīth* collections differ more in respect of the chain of transmission (*isnād*) and not so much on substantive themes, as one often finds the same *ḥadīth* appearing in both the Sunni and Shī'ite collections.

The Shī'ite law of personal status also differs from its Sunni counterpart on certain points which may be noted as follows.

Under the Sunni law, the words expressed to conclude the contract of marriage may either be explicit (*ṣarīḥ*) or implicit (*kināya*). Under the Shī'ite law they must always be explicit and use the words *nikāḥ* and *tazwij* for a life-long union, and *mut'ah* for a temporary one. The Sunni schools also require the presence of two witnesses for a valid marriage contract, whereas this is not a requirement under the Shī'ite law. Sunni law, on the other hand, does not require the presence of witnesses at the time of pronouncement of a unilateral divorce (*ṭalāq*) by the husband, but witnesses are a requirement of *ṭalāq* under Shī'ite law. Furthermore, Sunni law recognizes regular and irregular (Sunni and Bid'i) forms of *ṭalāq*, and subdivide the former into *ḥasan* (good) and *ahsan* (best), whereas Shī'ite law recognizes only one form of Sunni (i.e. according to Sunnah) or regular divorce. Both schools agree, however, that divorce may either be revocable (*raj'ī*) or final (*bā'in*). And then the Shī'ite law proscribes mixed marriages of a Muslim man to a Christian or a Jewish woman (i.e. a *kitābiya*), which the Sunni law validates. The Qur'ān allows this (5:5) but the Shī'ites determine their position based on an interpretation of a Qur'ānic verse (2:221) which forbids marriage to polytheists (*mushrikā*t). This restriction applies, however, only to a standard marriage but not to *mut'ah*.[66]

With regard to parentage, maternity is established, according to Sunni law, by birth alone, regardless of the presence or absence of a valid marriage between the parents. But under Shī'ite law maternity is only established through a lawful marriage, hence an illegitimate child has no descent, even from its mother, and therefore no right to inheritance. There are also many important differences between the two schools of thought with regard to inheritance, of which the following may be noted.

First, the Shī'ite schools do not give the same degree of prominence to agnatic relatives or *'aṣaba* (i.e. every male in whose line of relation to the deceased no female enters) as do the Sunni schools of law. Hence the Qur'ānic sharers (*dhawu al-furūḍ*) who are mainly female relatives tend to have a greater title, under Shī'ite law, than the male agnates to the residual portion of the estate after an initial but incomplete distribution. Should there be anything left of the estate after the Qur'ānic sharers receive their portions, Sunni law allocates it to the male relatives of the deceased whereas the Shī'ite law distributes the residue proportionately among all the surviving heirs. For example, if the deceased person is survived by his father and daughter, half the estate will go to the daughter and one-sixth to the father. The remaining two-sixths of the estate also goes, under Sunni law, to the father, whereas under Shī'ite law the residue is divided into four parts, of which three are assigned to the daughter and one to the father.

Sunni and Shī'ite laws also differ with regard to partial exclusion or diminution of a share to certain relatives. According to Sunni law, the child, or the child of a son, however lowly, reduces the share of a husband, a wife and a mother from the highest to the lowest appointed for them, while under Shī'ite law, the reduction is affected by any child, whether male or female, in any degree of descent from the deceased. Further when the deceased is survived by a husband or wife, father and mother, the mother's share is reduced, under Sunni law, from a third of the whole estate to a third of the remainder so that the father may have double her share. But under Shī'ite law, the mother's share is not reduced under these circumstances.

With reference to bequests, all the Sunni schools of law validate a bequest of up to one-third of the estate to an outsider who is not a legal heir, and this can be made in favour of anyone, non-Muslims included. A bequest above the limit of one-third does not take effect, under Sunni law, without the consent of the surviving legal heir, and the consent in question must also be given after the death of the testator, whereas under Shī'ite law it may be given either before or after the testator's death. Shī'ite law also permits the testator to bequeath his estate to any person, including a legal heir, within the limit of one-third. Without the consent of the surviving heirs, bequests amounting to more than one-third of the estate must be reduced to the maximum of one-third. Both Sunni and Shī'ite laws thus recognize the validity of bequest and its upper limit of one-third but they differ as to whether the one-third can include a legal heir, and also the time when the legal heir may give consent.[67]

The foregoing provides only a selective treatment of the subject, as differences of detail cannot be addressed here. What has been said, however, should not convey the impression that either the Sunni or the Shī'ite laws are monolithic entities. The Sunni schools of law differ on many issues, as do the Shī'ite schools, but they all tend to be based on their differential understanding of the source data of the Qur'ān and Sunnah and their respective methodological approaches to interpretation. But even the brief outline presented here shows that there are significant differences that can, in many ways, provide the basis of beneficial exchange between the Sunni and Shī'ite schools of law. This has already taken place to some extent in the twentieth-century legislation of some Muslim countries as I have noted elsewhere in this volume and my other works. The twentieth century has also witnessed a tendency on the part of both Sunnis and Shī'ites to highlight their commonalities more than their differences, thus reversing the earlier pattern which was dominated by their differences at the expense almost of the spirit of unity and acceptance of the fundamentals of Islam.

Twelver doctrine was officially adopted in Persia under the Safavids in 1501; it still commands the largest following in Iran, and it has also followers in Iraq, Lebanon and Syria.

According to the Ismā'īli dogma, the esoteric meaning of the Qur'ān and its allegorical interpretation is known only to the imām, whose knowledge and guidance is indispensable to salvation. The Ismā'ilis are divided into two groups, eastern and western. The former are centred in India, Pakistan and Central Asia, and their leader is the present Aga Khan, forty-ninth imām in the line of succession. The western Ismā'īlis follow al-Musta'li, the ninth Fatimid caliph. This line went to the twenty-first imām, al-Ḍayyib, but he became *mastūr* (occult, hidden). This group resides in southern Arabia and Syria.

The Zaydiyah follow Zayd ibn 'Ali (d. 740), the fifth imām in the order of the twelve Shi'i imāms. Imam Zayd was a rival to his nephew, Ja'far al-Ṣādiq, whom the majority of Shī'ites regard as the legitimate heir to imamate. They endorse the legitimacy of the caliphs who preceded 'Ali on the belief that an acceptable leader has a legitimate title notwithstanding the existence of a superior claimant. They regard as legitimate any 'Alid who possessed knowledge and obtained the homage of the community. They also do not subscribe to the notion of infallibity of the imāms, a position which is shared by the Sunnis. Their legal doctrine is the nearest of the Shī'ite schools to the Sunnis, and they mainly reside in the Yemen.

CONSENSUS AND DIVERGENCE AMONG THE SCHOOLS

Disagreement among the Sunni and Shī'ite schools is not confined to differences in *ijtihād* but extends to the sphere of theological doctrines as explained above. Broadly speaking, however, juristic disagreement among the schools is a consequence of the freedom of *ijtihād* which they enjoyed, particularly in the first three centuries of Islam. They have differed mainly in four areas: interpretation of the Qur'ān, acceptance and interpretation of the *ḥadīth*, rationalist doctrines and subsidiary matters. Concerning the Qur'ān, the jurists have disagreed over the abrogation (*naskh*) of some of the Qur'ānic verses by others where two verses provide divergent rulings on the same subject, or when the *ḥadīth* arguably overrules a Qur'ānic verse. While al-Shāfi'ī's doctrine of *naskh* is based on the rule that the Qur'ān can only be abrogated by the Qur'ān and Sunnah only by Sunnah, the other three schools add that the Qur'ān and the Sunnah may also abrogate one another.

The words of the Qur'ān are divided into general (*'āmm*) and specific (*khāṣ*). The jurists have however, disagreed over the meaning and implications of *'āmm* and *khāṣ*. For example, X is unable to pay his debt. His brother Y, pays it while acting on his own initiative and out of goodwill. The question arises as to whether Y who is called *fuḍūli*, or catalyst, is entitled to claim his money back from X. Māliki and Ḥanbali law answer this question in the affirmative on the authority of surah 55:60 of the Qur'ān: 'Is the reward of goodness (*iḥsān*) aught but goodness?' But for the Ḥanafis and Shāfi'īs the words of this verse are too general to be applied to the case in question; hence they deny the *fuḍūli* the right to a repayment.

The scope of disagreement concerning the Sunnah is even wider, for in this area differences extend not only to the interpretation of *ḥadīth* but also to its authenticity. Whereas the Ḥanafis, and to some extent the Shāfi'īs, apply strict rules on the authenticity of *ḥadīth,* the Mālikis and Ḥanbalis are relatively uncritical. Al-Shāfi'ī and Ibn Ḥanbal, for example, accept a solitary (*āḥād*) *ḥadīth*, one which is reported by a single narrator, but Abū Ḥanifah and Mālik accept it only under certain conditions. The jurists have also applied different rules to cases of conflict and abrogation between *ḥadīth*. Whereas the majority would not, for example, allow the abrogation of a *Mutawātir* (a *ḥadīth* reported by numerous narrators) by an *āḥād,* the Ḥanafis permit this in principle.

Disagreement over rationalist doctrines such as *ra'y* (considered opinion), consensus, analogy and *ijtihād* has already been discussed. It may be added here that Ḥanafi law applies *istiḥsān,* or juristic preference, as a doctrine of equity where strict implementation of analogy leads to hardships and undesirable results. The Māliki school, however, adopts *istiṣlāh* (considerations of public interest), which is essentially similar to *istiḥsān,* albeit with some differences of detail. Al-Shāfi'ī rejects both *istiḥsān* and *istiṣlāḥ,* which he considers as no more than frivolous and arbitrary interference with the *Sharī'ah.* Alternately, the Shāfi'īs, the Ḥanbalis, and the Twelver Shī'ah adopt *istiṣḥāb* or deduction by presumption of continuity of the original state, or *status quo ante. Istiṣḥāb,* for example, assumes freedom from liability to be a natural state until the contrary is proved.

Differences of *ijtihād* concerning subsidiary matters need not be elaborated, as the abundance of legal doctrines and schools within the *Sharī'ah* is indicative of such diversity. By the beginning of the tenth century there was a consensus that all essential issues had been thoroughly discussed and finally settled. With this 'closing of the door of *ijtihād*', as it was called, *ijtihād* gave way to *taqlīd,* or 'imitation'. From then on every Muslim was an imitator (*muqallid*) who had to belong to one of the recognized schools. By consensus also the four schools were accepted, and accepted one another, as equally orthodox. Notwithstanding the emergence of prominent scholars in later centuries (including Ibn Taymiyyah and Ibn Qayyim al-Jawziyyah) who objected to *taqlīd*, no one actually provided an independent interpretation of the *Sharī'ah. Taqlīd* remained a dominant practice for about a thousand years until the reform movements of the late nineteenth century (notably the Salafiyyah, whose prominent figure is Muḥammad 'Abduh) and the modernist schools of thought in the present century which challenged *taqlīd* and called for a return to *ijtihād.*

A Muslim may join any orthodox school he or she wishes, or change from one school to another, without formalities. Furthermore, Islamic countries have made frequent use of divergent opinions of other schools, including Shīʿi legal doctrines, in modern legislation. In order to achieve desired results, modern reformers have utilized procedural expedients permitted in the *Sharīʿah* such as *takhayyur* and *talfīq*. *Takhayyur,* or 'selection', enables the jurist to adopt from the various interpretations of the *Sharīʿah* that which is deemed to be most suitable. Reformers in the area of personal status, for example, have frequently adopted a variant doctrine of a recognized school as the basis of reform. Sometimes the view of an early jurist outside the established schools has been selected. Furthermore, legal rules have been occasionally constructed by combining part of the doctrine of one school or jurist with part of the doctrine of another school or jurist. This variation of *takhayyur* is known as *talfīq,* or 'patching', a procedure which has been employed in the modern laws of the Middle East. (For interesting illustrations and details on these procedural devices see Coulson's *A History of Islamic Law.*)

CONCLUSION

Fiqh is essentially dynamic, as it is endowed with the necessary methodology and resources to move abreast of the realities of social change. The long period of stagnation and *taqlīd* has undoubtedly hampered the process of its evolution and created a gap wide enough to put the relevance of *fiqh* to the concerns of modern society seriously in doubt. But *taqlīd* was prompted by a combination of factors including the persistent alienation of the *ʿulamāʾ* and government throughout the many centuries of Umayyad and Abbasid rule. The *ʿulamāʾ* were consequently engaged in their academic pursuits with little involvement in the business of government. The rulers condoned this isolation under the umbrella of *taqlīd* as it left them with initiative and control over public affairs. For essentially similar reasons, one could hardly expect *fiqh* and *ijtihād* to remain viable forces in society during the colonialist domination of Muslims by European powers. It thus appears that the decline of *fiqh* in both these instances had, to a large extent, been due to lack of government participation and involvement in the development of *fiqh*. But the reality of power politics is no proof against the adaptability of *fiqh* and its capacity for growth. As one observer noted, there is no historical precedent to support the suggestion that the *Sharīʿah* cannot be revitalized. The process of its interpretation in the early days of Islam demonstrated that it is not a fixed and permanent entity but capable of change to fit new circumstances.

The course of events in the twentieth century has shown once again that when governments began to introduce legal reforms of family law, they were able to find the resources of Islamic law responsive to the prevailing needs of the community. The Islamic revivalism of recent decades has certainly accentuated the importance of *fiqh* and the role it should play in statutory legislation. Given a favourable pattern of development, the scope of revivalist interest may widen further in the years to come. We are likely to see, however, a mixed pattern of co-existence between Islamic law and existing statutory laws of Western origin, especially in the sphere of public law, which has been dominated by statutory laws of Western origin, but which may see gradual growth of *Sharī'ah*- based legislation.

NOTES

1. Muṣṭafa al-Zarqā, *al-Fiqh al-Islāmī*, 59–60.
2. Cf. Abū Zahrah, *Tārīkh,* 164; al-Nabhān, *al-Madkhal li-Tashrī'*, 239.
3. Abū Zahrah, *Tārīkh,* 381–2; idem, *Abū* Ḥanīfah, 393–400.
4. Ibn 'Ābidīn, *Radd al-Mukhtār*, I, 68.
5. Ibn 'Ābidīn, *Majmū'ah Rasā'il*, I, 24–5.
6. Ibid., I, 24: Ibrāhīm 'Ali, *al-Madhhab 'Ind al-Ḥanafiyyah*, 29.
7. Ibn 'Ābidīn, n. 5, I, 27; Muḥammad Ibrāhīm 'Ali, *al-Madhhab*, 29.
8. Ibn 'Ābidīn, n. 5 at I, 29.
9. Ibid., at I, 26.
10. *Uṣūl al-Karkhī,* 84.
11. Al-'Alwāni, 'The Crisis of Fiqh', 331.
12. Abū Zahrah, *Mālik*, 169.
13. Cf. Al-Nabhān, n. 2 at 261.
14. al-Shāfi'ī, *al-Risālah*, 140.
15. Abū Zahrah, *Mālik,* n. 12 at 376. The sources of law according to the Ḥanafis are the Qur'ān, Sunnah, consensus, analogy, juristic preference and custom. Imām Shāfi'ī basically recognized the first four plus presumption of continuity (*istiṣḥāb*), whereas the Mālikis recognize all of these plus unrestricted public interest (*maṣlaḥah mursalah*), the Madinese *ijmā'*, and *sadd al-dharā'i'*.
16. Ibid.
17. Abū Zahrah, *Abū* Ḥanīfah, 99, quoting also Ibn Qayyim in support of this conclusion.
18. al-Shāṭibī, *al-I'tiṣām,* II, 300, 303.
19. Abū Zahrah, *Mālik,* 188.
20. For details on Māliki law and modern reforms pertaining to *khul'* see my *Law in Afghanistan*, 189 ff.

21. For details on *Maṣlaḥah Mursalah* see M. H. Kamali, 'Have we Neglected the *Sharī'ah* Law Doctrine of *Maṣlaḥah*?' 287–304.
22. Ibn Qayyim, *Ighāthat al-Lahfān*, II, 107. The reader might be interested to know that there is a chapter on *sadd al-dharā'i'* in my *Jurisprudence,* 397–410.
23. al-Qarāfī, *Kitāb al-Furūq,* Section (i.e. *al-farq*), no. 49.
24. Abū Zahrah, *Mālik*, 423.
25. al-Shawkānī, *al-Qawl al-Mufīd,* 44.
26. Ibid.
27. See Ibn Qayyim, *I'lām*, II, 187.
28. Cf. Zafar Ishaq Ansari, 'The Significance of Shāfi'ī's Criticism', 485.
29. Abū Zahrah, *al-Shāfi'ī,* 197.
30. Cf. Abū Zahrah, *Tārīkh,* 461.
31. al-Shāfi'ī, *Jimā' al-'Ilm,* 11 ff.
32. Cf. Abū Zahrah, *Tārīkh*, 464.
33. al-Shahāwi, *Kitāb al-Shahāwi,* 190.
34. Ibn Taymiyyah, *Raf' al-Malām,* 10.
35. Abū Zahrah, *al-Shāfi'ī,* 192.
36. Abū Sulaymān, *al-Fikr al-Uṣūli,* 57.
37. Dihlawi, *al-Inṣāf,* 36.
38. Abū Zahrah, *Tārīkh,* 465.
39. Ibn Qayyim, *I'lām* III, 139.
40. Ibid.
41. Ibid., II, 266.
42. Cf. Abū Zahrah, *al-Shāfi'ī,* 154.
43. Ibid., 155.
44. Ibrāhīm 'Ali, '*al-Madhhab 'Ind al-Shāfi'iyyah*', 5.
45. Abū Zahrah, *al-Shāfi'ī,* 288.
46. Ibid., 292.
47. Al-Shāfi'ī, *Kitāb al-Umm,* VI, 202; Abū Zahrah, *Al-Shāfi'ī,* 290.
48. Ibid., V, 74; Abū Zahrah, *al-Shāfi'ī,* 151–2.
49. Abū Zahrah, *Al-Shāfi'ī,* 156.
50. Ibid., 158.
51. al-Shawkānī, *Nayl al-Awṭār*, VI, 338.
52. Ibid.
53. Ibn Qayyim, *al-Ṭuruq al–Ḥukmiyyah,* ed. Muḥammad Jamīl Ghazi, Jiddah: Maṭba'ah al-Madani, n.d.
54. Ibn Qayyim. *I'lām,* II, 139
55. Yūsūf Mūsā, *al-Madkhal*, 239.
56. Abū Zahrah, *Ibn Ḥanbal,* 233 ff; 'Aṭiyyah, *al-Naẓariyyah*, 39.
57. Ibn Qayy, *I'lām,* I, 344.
58. Ibn Taymiyyah, *Majmū'ah Fatāwā*, III, 239.
59. Abū Zahrah, *Ibn Ḥanbal,* 336.
60. Ibn Qayyim, *I'lām*, III, 338.
61. Ibid., IV, 3, Abū Zahrah, *Ibn Ḥanbal*, 341.
62. Cf. Thomas Hughes, *The Dictionary of Islam*, 574.
63. It is suggested that the idea of 'the return' which is common to Shī'ism bears Judaeo-Christian influence: the belief, that is, about Prophet Elias who was carried off to heaven and will return to save the world from tyranny and injustice.

64. Quoted in Ahmad Kazemi Moussavi, *Religious Authority in Shī'ite Islam*, 10.
65. Idem, 14.
66. Abū'l-Qāsim 'Ali Murtaza 'Alam al-Huda, *al-Intiṣar*, 45.
67. Cf., M.H. Kamali, 'Personal Law', *The Encyclopedia of Religion,* new edn 2005. See also Hughes, *Dictionary of Islam*, 578 f.

5

DISAGREEMENT (*IKHTILĀF*) AND PLURALISM IN *SHARĪ'AH*

It is due mainly to the recognition and tolerance of disagreement among the '*ulamā*' over juristic issues that Islamic law is often described as a diversity within unity; that is, unity in basic principles, and diversity regarding details. A tangible manifestation of *ikhtilāf* in Islamic law is the prevalence of at least seven different schools of jurisprudence which have survived to this day and have followers throughout the Muslim world. Islamic law has in fact nurtured a rich tradition of diversity and disagreement just as it has remained open to the influence of other legal traditions.

Having said this, however, we need to view *ikhtilāf* in conjunction with two other principles of Islam, namely *tawḥīd*, that is, belief in the oneness of God and its far-reaching influence on Islamic legal thought. *Tawḥīd* is the first article of the Muslim faith and a major theme of the Qur'ān. There is only one God. Likewise, there is one Islam, one scripture, one *ummah* (community) and one *Sharī'ah*. A symbolic manifestation of this unity in faith is also evident from the fact that all Muslims pray in the direction of the Ka'bah. Unity in the essence of belief is not open to any level of disgreement. The Qur'ān (21:92) declares Muslims as one nation – *ummatan wāḥidatan* – which is at once the witness and guardian of its own unity. We may have different schools and *madhhab*s, all incorporating equally valid interpretations of the *Sharī'ah*, but this level of plurality does not alter the fact that there is only one *Sharī'ah*, which is manifested in the clear textual injunctions of the Qur'ān and Sunnah. Each of the various schools of law have interpreted the *Sharī'ah* in the light of the needs and realities of their time. None has claimed to be a

Sharīʻah unto itself, but interpretations of the same *Sharīʻah* that is shared by all. *Fiqh* is primarily concerned with the practicalities of conduct and not the essence of belief. *Sharīʻah* is wider than *fiqh* as it comprises in its scope not only practical legal rules but also dogmatic theology and moral teachings. *Fiqh* is thus derived from the *Sharīʻah*; it is neither totally original nor entirely based on personal opinion.[1]

Ikhtilāf basically operates in the realm of *fiqh* which is concerned with practical legal rules. Disagreement over the essentials of the faith, its five pillars, for example, and the essence of moral virtue is not tolerated. This naturally means that the unitarian (*tawḥīdi*) outlook and philosophy of Islam is unmistakably strong, but people tend to notice disagreement more often than consonance and agreement. We also note a gradual strengthening of the voice of unity among Muslims in the course of the twentieth century. There were times, for example, when the schools of law during the era of imitation (*taqlīd*) were emphatic about their own identity to the extent of making a self-righteous assertion of their own interpretations of the *Sharīʻah*. But it is interesting to note that many a prominent Sunni jurist of the twentieth century writes on the juristic legacy of the Shīʻi ʻ*ulamā*ʼ and appreciates their contributions in the spirit of objectivity and acceptance. Note, for example, the late Muḥammad Abū Zahrah (d. 1974) who wrote a book on the life and works of the Shīʻite Imām, Jaʻfar al-Ṣādiq and his contributions to the legacy of Islamic scholarship. The voluminous *fiqh* encyclopedias that appeared in the later part of the twentieth century have also adopted the same catholicity of spirit. The academic style and content of the information that is recorded in several of these valuable works bear no obvious vestige of the narrow scholastic bias of earlier times.[2]

IKHTILĀF AND CONSENSUS (*IJMĀʻ*)

As already noted, *ikhtilāf* is accepted at the level of juristic interpretation, and I shall presently elaborate on its origins and causes, but even at this level the two competing concepts of *ijmāʻ* and *ikhtilāf* need to be seen together, as the one evidently limits the intensity and scope of the other. I would have no difficulty in providing a ready answer to the question as to which of these two carries greater authority and weight.

For we know that *ijmā'* commands normative validity as a proof and source of Islamic law, next to the Qur'ān and the Sunnah.

Notwithstanding the difficulties that we now face over the feasibility of *ijmā'*, in theory at least, it is the only binding proof next to the textual injunctions that is known to Islamic jurisprudence. *Ijmā'* essentially embodies the collective conscience of the Muslim community, their agreement and undivided consensus over the correct interpretation of the text and propriety of *ijtihād*. An individual opinion and *ijtihād*, however authoritative and sound, is not binding on anyone, and everyone enjoys the liberty of having an opinion, and so disagreement is naturally expected before an *ijmā'* materializes over a particular ruling. For *ijtihād* can hardly be visualized without disagreement and it is, in this sense, another name for *ikhtilāf*. But *ikhtilāf,* which is acceptable at this level, must meet two basic requirements, one of which is that each of the opposing views is based on valid evidence, and the other that none of the opposing views leads to what is unfeasible, or entirely unrealistic. Disagreements which fail to meet these requirements have no credibility and should be abandoned.[3] These two conditions also differentiate *ikhtilāf* from what is known as *khilāf*, that is unreasonable disagreement. It thus appears that *ikhtilāf* must have a basis in *ijtihād* in that it is supported by valid evidence.

A great deal of what is known by the name of *ijmā'* begins with *ijtihād*, and disagreement over *ijtihād* is not only tolerated but considered to be beneficial. If the issue over which *ijtihād* is exercised is important to the community as a whole, then it calls for general consideration and scrutiny by the jurists and '*ulamā*'. Two possibilities can then be envisaged: the individual *ijtihād* is not supported by *ijmā'*, in which case it remains an isolated opinion, or else it is elevated to the rank of *ijmā'* when general consensus materializes in its support. In this process *ikhtilāf* is tolerated as a matter of principle and no one is entitled to pressurize a scholar, a jurist or a *mujtahid* so as to prevent him from expressing opinion in accordance with his true convictions. But when there is general consensus over a particular ruling *ikhtilāf* must come to an end, and the scholar or *mujtahid* who might have a different opinion is expected, like everyone else, to abandon his opinion and follow the ruling of *ijmā'*. This is precisely what is meant when we say that *ijmā'* is a binding proof. The *raison d'etre* of *ijmā'* is clearly to put an end to *ikhtilāf* and ultimately to vindicate the outlook and spirit of unity that is of central importance in Islam.

CAUSES OF *IKHTILĀF*

Disagreements among the '*ulamā*' are caused by a variety of factors which may be summarized under three headings: 1) disagreement over linguistic matters that relates to the understanding and interpretation of the relevant text; 2) disagreement over the knowledge and authenticity of *ḥadīth* and 3) disagreement over methodology. The first of these, that is, differences over interpretation, was known during the lifetime of the Prophet, and those questions which were brought to his attention were clarified by the Prophet himself. But the '*ulamā*' have noted numerous instances in the text of the Qur'ān and Sunnah, on which no clear information was recorded from the Prophet or the Companions and the matter therefore remained subject to interpretation and *ikhtilāf.* Disputed issues in the sphere of speculative and general (*ẓanni* and *'āmm*) rulings of the text still remain open to interpretation even if they have received an interpretation in the valid precedent. It may be stated as a matter of principle that disagreement is not valid over the clear and decisive texts of the Qur'ān and Sunnah. But as we have noted, the greater part of the Qur'ān consists of words and sentences that remain open to interpretation.

Disagreements over the meaning of a word may be due to the occurrence of homonyms which carry more than one meaning. The word *qurū'* in the Qur'ān (2:228), for example, has more than one meaning. The text in which it occurs is concerned with the waiting period (*'iddah*) of a divorced woman, which she must observe before she marries again. Her *'iddah* consists of three *qurū'*, which could mean either three menstruations (*ḥayḍ*), or three clean periods (*ṭuhr*) between menstruations. The latter meaning would actually imply four menstruations and, therefore, a longer waiting period. The Companions differed over this and some among them, including 'Uthmān ibn 'Affān, 'Ā'ishah and Zayd ibn Thābit held the latter meaning whereas 'Umar ibn al-Khaṭṭāb and 'Abd Allah ibn Mas'ūd held the former. The '*ulamā*' of Iraq, including the Ḥanafis, have followed 'Umar ibn al-Khaṭṭāb's interpretation whereas the majority of the '*ulamā*' of Ḥijāz, including the Shāfi'ī's, have followed 'Uthmān and 'Ā'ishah, and the *ikhtilāf* has remained unresolved ever since.[4]

To illustrate disagreement over the meaning of words in the *ḥadīth* I refer to a *ḥadīth* on the subject of divorce which proclaims that 'no divorce nor manumission [can take place] in a state of *ighlāq*' (*lā ṭalāq wa lā i'tāq fi ighlāq*). While many have held that the word *ighlāq* means duress, others have held it to mean anger. Ibn Qayyim al-Jawziyyah, concurring with his teacher, Ibn Taymiyyah, is of the opinion that *ighlāq* means obstruction of the faculties of awareness and intent (*insidād bāb al-'ilm wa'l-qaṣd*) and has consequently held that divorce pronounced in a state of insanity, intoxication, extreme anger and even by an imbecile (*ma'tūh*) are all null and void.[5]

The words of the text may sometimes convey both a literal and a metaphorical meaning and there are instances of this in the Qur'ān. For instance, in the context of ritual cleanliness, the ablution (*wuḍū'*) that is taken for obligatory prayers is normally vitiated in various ways, including physical contact with members of the opposite sex. The words that are used in the Qur'ān are ('or when you touch women *aw lāmastum al-nisā'*) then you must take a fresh ablution'. The Ḥanafis understood the word *lāmastum* to mean sexual intercourse, whereas the Shāfi'ī's maintain both the literal and the metaphorical meanings of the word which means that *wuḍū'* is broken not only by sexual intercourse but also by a mere handshake with the members of the opposite sex. Disagreement on this issue has also remained unresolved ever since.[6]

In a similar vein, the Qur'ānic language on the subject of commands and prohibitions is not always value-specific. A word may occur in the imperative mood and it may convey either an obligation (*wājib*), a mere recommendation (*nadb*) or even permissibility (*ibāḥah*), which is far removed from the idea of a command. Thus the Qur'ānic word *faktubūh* (reduce into writing), transactions involving future obligations, or credit-based transactions (see 2:282), is linguistically a command, but documentation here is generally held to be only recommended, not obligatory. Only the Ẓāhiriyyah have held that the text here conveys an obligation and have consequently made documentation a requirement of every loan and deferred transaction.[7] We also read in the Qur'ān command forms such as *kulū wa-'shrabū* (eat and drink, 7:31) and also with reference to the *ḥajj* ceremonies it is provided that when you finish the *ḥajj*, then you [proceed to] hunt – *faṣṭādū* (5:2). The words in both these examples only convey permissibility even though they are in the imperative mood.[8]

A prohibition (*nahy*) in the Qur'ān may likewise convey a total ban, which is the normal meaning of a prohibition, or it may convey a mere reprehension (*karāhiyyah*), or guidance (*irshād*) or indeed a host of other meanings, and the precise import of the words of the text is often determined by reference to supportive evidence in the Qur'ān itself or the *ḥadīth*, and the *'ulamā'* are not always in agreement over the conclusions they have drawn from their readings of the text.[9]

Another cause of *ikhtilāf* among the leading schools of law is due to the variation of localities, customary practices (*'urf*) and cultural environments. The Ḥanafi school was developed in Iraq whereas the Māliki school was mainly developed in the Hijaz, and they have each reflected the cultural leanings and customs of the society in which they had emerged. It is interesting to note, for example, that al-Shāfi'ī's scholastic work was developed initially during the years of his residence in Baghdad and subsequently in Egypt where he resided for several years. It is claimed that he found the customs of the Egyptians so different that he revised and changed a great deal of his earlier rulings, so much so that he is generally known to have developed two schools, the old and the new. Changes of time and place and developments in the customs and culture of society are not confined to these schools but are generally reflected in the works of the *'ulamā'*.[10] *Ikhtilāf* that originates due to cultural and customary differences is not always confined to minor issues as the scope of disagreement among schools and scholars often extends from specific issues to methods of reasoning, attitudes and perceptions over the basic evidence of the *Sharī'ah*.

Another cause of *ikhtilāf* is the ignorance of *ḥadīth*, especially in the early period, that is, prior to the compilation and collection of *ḥadīth* in the mid-ninth century. Some of the disagreements that arose between the Traditionists (*Ahl al-ḥadīth*) and Rationalists (*Ahl al-ra'y*) related to the fact that the scholastic centres of Kufa and Basra in Iraq had not known some of the *ḥadīths* that were known in Makkah and Madinah. This would explain why the *'ulamā'* of Kufa resorted more frequently to *ra'y* and analogy on issues over which they had not known of any *ḥadīth*. Even the *'ulamā'* of Madinah were not at times well-informed of the relevant *ḥadīth* and resorted to Madinese practice (*'amal ahl al-Madīnah*) or to analogy.

This may be illustrated by reference to the *ḥadīth* concerning the option of contractual session (*khiyār al-majlis*) which neither Abū Ḥanīfah nor Mālik, the leaders respectively of the *Ahl al-ra'y* and *Ahl al-ḥadīth*, had implemented in their rulings on the matter. The reason for this is that the *ḥadīth* in question was either not known to them or that they had known it but did not consider it reliable enough since it was a solitary *ḥadīth*. Mālik referred the issue to the Madinese practice which did not correspond with the *ḥadīth*. But when subsequent investigation lent support to the *ḥadīth* and it was recorded by both Bukhārī and Muslim as a *marfūʻ ḥadīth* (i.e. *ḥadīth* that goes back to the Prophet), it was generally followed by the majority of the schools except for the Māliki school, which still disagreed and upheld the Madinese practice.[11] The *ḥadīth* in question provided that 'when two men negotiate a sale, each of them has an option to withdraw until they part company'. The Māliki ruling on this maintains that a contract becomes binding as of the moment the parties reach an agreement, regardless of the moment they part company. Other schools have followed the *ḥadīth* which a jurist who had known a particular *ḥadīth*, or had known it but considered it weak in authenticity, might have relied instead on a manifest – *ẓahir* – text of the Qur'ān or arrived at a ruling by way of analogy to the text. Another jurist might have known a more relevant *ḥadīth* and the result would be differential conclusions over the same issue.[12]

Another level of *ikhtilāf* that originates in *ḥadīth* relates to variation in the reports of different narrators of the *ḥadīth*. A *ḥadīth* is sometimes narrated by more than one narrator, one of which may have conveyed a fuller version than the other, or that one of them might refer to the efficient cause (*ʻillah*) of its ruling and the other does not. The jurist may consequently consider one to be more reliable than the other and various possibilities of *ikhtilāf* can arise in such situations.

The third cause of *ikhtilāf* that is known to the '*ulamā*' is over the methodology and principles of jurisprudence (*uṣūl al-fiqh*). Considerable differences have arisen among schools over the acceptance or otherwise of a certain proof or principle of *uṣūl al-fiqh*. There are differences, for example, with regard to juristic preference (*istiḥsān*) which the majority have accepted as a valid proof and source of the *Sharīʻah* but which the Shāfiʻī's have rejected altogether. *Istiḥsān* is the nearest *Sharīʻah* equivalent of the doctrine of equity in Western jurisprudence and it authorizes a judge and *mujtahid* to find an alternative solution to an issue in the event that strict application of the existing law leads to rigidity and unsatisfactory results. And then with reference to *ijmāʻ* we note that the Mālikis have held the Madinese consensus – *Ijmāʻ ahl al-Madīnah* – to be the most authoritative, or even the only valid form of *ijmāʻ*. The majority, on the other hand, consider *ijmāʻ* as an embodiment of the general consensus of the learned *mujtahids* of the Muslim community without it being necessarily confined to any particular place or region.

The leading schools have also differed over the authority of the *fatwā* of a Companion as a proof and basis of judgement (*ḥukm*). Whereas some have seen the verdict and ruling of a Companion as a true manifestation of the Sunnah of the Prophet and therefore authoritative, others have disagreed and stated that the *fatwā* of a Companion is authoritative over something which the latter has narrated from the Prophet, but not otherwise. Similar differences of orientation have arisen over considerations of public interest – *istiṣlāḥ* – and custom (*'urf*). The Mālikis are the main exponents of *istiṣlāḥ*, and the Ḥanafis of *'urf,* whereas the other leading schools accept them each on a limited basis and the result is usually shown in their different rulings and conclusions on specific issues.

The scope of *ikhtilāf* over methodological principles also extends to rules of interpretation and the implied meaning of word forms such as the general and the specific (*'āmm and khāṣ*). Compare, for instance, the position of the Ḥanafis to that of the majority on the implications of the general and specific rulings of the Qur'ān and Sunnah. The general (*'āmm*) ruling of the text is definitive (*qaṭ'ī*) according to the Ḥanafis but it is speculative (*ẓanni*) according to the majority (*jumhūr*). One of the consequences of this would be that no conflict can arise between the *'āmm* and the *khāṣ*, according to the majority, since the latter will always prevail over the former. But since the Ḥanafis consider the *'āmm* to be also definitive (*qaṭ'ī*), a conflict can arise between one definitive text and another.

The legal schools have also differed over their methodologies of establishing the authenticity of *ḥadīth*, especially the solitary (*āḥād*) *ḥadīth.* It is a report of odd individuals, which remains below a decisive (*mutawātir*) or a well-known (*mashhūr*) *ḥadīth.* The Ḥanafi methodology concerning the solitary *ḥadīth* tends to be more stringent thereby precluding a chain of transmission, or *isnād*, in which there is some weakness that other schools might tolerate. For instance, the Ḥanafis prefer the manifest (*ẓāhir*) of the Qur'ān over the ruling of the *āḥād ḥadīth.* To illustrate this I refer to the subject of guardianship in marriage of an adult woman. The Ḥanafis maintain that the adult female is entitled to conclude her own marriage contract whereas the other three schools require the presence of the legal guardian (*walī*) to validate the marriage. The majority have relied on the solitary *ḥadīth*, which simply declares:

> There shall be no marriage without a guardian.
>
> لانكاح إلا بوليّ.

The Ḥanafis have relied instead on the Qur'ānic verse:

> if he has divorced her, then she is not lawful to him until she marries [*ḥattā tankiḥa*] another man. (2:230)
>
> فإن طَلَّقَهَا فلا تَحِلُّ لَهُ مِن بَعْدُ حَتَّى تَنكِحَ زَوْجًا غَيْرَهُ.

The occurrence of the Arabic word form *tankiḥa* in the feminine singular mode has enabled the Ḥanafis to conclude that an adult woman may contract her own marriage. The text here is characterized as *ẓāhir* (manifest) in respect of guardianship as this is a secondary theme of the text, the main theme being that of divorce, which is why it (i.e. *ẓāhir*) is considered weaker evidence. Yet the Ḥanafis have preferred it to the solitary *ḥadīth* mentioned above, which although definitive in meaning, is less than that in respect of authenticity and proof.[13] The Ḥanafis have also preferred the general (*'āmm*) of the Qur'ān, and at times even a ruling based on analogy (*qiyās*), to a weak *ḥadīth*. With reference to eating out of forgetfulness during the fast of Ramadan, for example, the Ḥanafis, unlike the majority, did not follow the *ḥadīth* which exonerated this and allowed the person to ignore it and complete his fast. The Ḥanafis instead held, by analogy, that a belated fast should be observed. The Mālikis have generally preferred the Madinese practice to solitary *ḥadīth*, which means that fast is not broken by eating due to forgetfulness. Such differences of methodology have naturally had a bearing on the rules which the legal schools have derived from the available evidence.[14]

ETIQUETTE OF DISAGREEMENT (*ADAB AL-IKHTILĀF*)

Islamic jurisprudence (*uṣūl al-fiqh*) is, from beginning to end, concerned with establishing a correct and effective methodology for *ijtihād*, and therefore also for *ikhtilāf*. *Uṣūl al-fiqh* is designed to encourage *ijtihād* in accordance with a set of guidelines. These guidelines go a long way to help distinguish acceptable *ijtihād* from that which is arbitrary and erroneous. For so long as we accept in principle the validity of *ijtihād*, we must also accept *ikhtilāf* within its valid parameters. The Companions were actively engaged in discussing legal questions and frequently differed from one another on matters of interpretation and *ijtihād*, but at the same time they tended to acknowledge and tolerate juristic *ikhtilāf* among themselves. Their method for resolving matters relating to disagreement in *ijtihādi* issues was by having recourse to consultation (*shūrā*), which is a Qur'ānic principle to which Prophet had regularly resorted himself. But they first referred to the Qur'ān and the Sunnah in search of solutions to issues. Only in the absence of a clear ruling in the text did the Companions resort to *shūrā* and *ijtihād*. The following *ḥadīth* is often quoted as a basic authority for *ijtihād*:

> When a judge exercises *ijtihād* and gives a right judgment, he will have two rewards, but if he errs in his judgment he will still have earned one reward.[15]
>
> الحاكم إذا اجتهد فأصاب فله أجران وإن اجتهد فأخطأ فله أجر.

This *ḥadīth* evidently encourages the spirit of tolerance in *ijtihād* by promising a reward even for one who might have inadvertently fallen into error. Since the *ḥadīth* has taken a positive view of such effort, scholars and *mujtahids* are also required to exercise restraint in denouncing a view which they might consider erroneous. This *ḥadīth* also lends support to the conclusion that a judicial decision that is made in the true spirit of *ijtihād* is enforceable and the judge may not be taken to task for it if it later turns out that he had made an error of judgement. Similarly, when a person trusts the integrity and knowledge of a scholar of *Sharī'ah* and acts upon his verdict (*fatwā*) on a legal question but later discovers that the *fatwā* was erroneous, he would have committed no wrong, simply because the *ḥadīth* exonerates an error of that kind in the first place.[16] The reward that is promised is, however, earned only by those whose sincerity and devotion to a good cause are not in question.

The Prophet also directed his Companions to avoid purposeless and destructive disagreement. 'Abd Allah ibn 'Umar has reported that on one occasion the Prophet heard two people arguing over a verse of the Qur'ān apparently on some minor points, such as accentuation and vowelling; the Prophet heard their argument and came out evidently angered with the kind of *ikhtilāf* in which they were engaged and said: 'Verily people were destroyed before you for (their excessive) disagreements over the scripture.'[17]

Yet on another occasion when a similar disagreement had arisen over the recitation of a portion of the Qur'ān, the Prophet noted the sincerity of the disputants and addressed them in these words: 'Both of you are well-meaning.' He warned them, however, to 'avoid excessive disagreement. For people before you were destroyed because of that.'[18]

This *ḥadīth* is quoted by al-Bukhāri in a chapter bearing the title '*Karāhiyyat al-Ikhtilāf*' (the reprehensibility of *ikhtilāf*) which evidently portrays an image of how al-Bukhāri viewed *ikhtilāf.* The expression *halakū* (they were destroyed) occurs in both *ḥadīths* referred to above. *Ikhtilāf* can, in other words, be destructive even if the parties might mean well.

VARIETIES AND STYLE

The '*ulamā*' have classified *ikhtilāf* into the three types of praiseworthy (*maḥmūd*), such as disagreement with the advocates of heresy and misguidance; blameworthy (*madhmūm*), of the kind mentioned in the *ḥādīth* cited above; and one which falls between the two. This last variety of *ikhtilāf* is one that falls in between and it is the most difficult of all to evaluate as it demands greater effort to identify its pitfalls. The hallmark of the distinction between the praiseworthy and blameworthy disagreement is sincerity and devotion, or lack of it, as the case may be. Whether the purpose is a worthy one, such as the advancement of sound *ijtihād*, or one which is tainted with selfish interest and caprice is likely, in the final analysis, to play a crucial role in determining the merit or demerit of disagreement.[19]

In his *Risālah*, al-Shāfi'ī has divided *ikhtilāf* into two types: forbidden disagreement (*al-ikhtilāf al-muḥarram*) and permissible disagreement (*al-ikhtilāf al-jā'iz*). Disagreement is forbidden in matters which are determined by clear textual evidence in the Qur'ān and the Sunnah for anyone who is aware of it. Al-Shāfi'ī then quotes in support the Qur'ānic directive to the believers:

> And be not like those who are divided amongst themselves and fall into disputations (*ikhtalafū*) after receiving clear signs. (3:105)
>
> وَلَا تَكُونُوا كَالَّذِينَ تَفَرَّقُوا وَاخْتَلَفُوا مِن بَعْدِ مَا جَاءَهُمُ الْبَيِّنَاتُ.

God Most High has denounced disagreement in what has been regulated by clear evidence, which consists 'either of a clear text of the Qur'ān or of the Sunnah or analogy thereon'.[20]

As for matters on which the evidence is open to interpretation, which is the sphere of permissible disagreement, al-Shāfiʻī refers to the general rules and guidelines of *ijtihād* which he has discussed in his *Risālah* with the proviso that one should follow evidence that can be found in the Sunnah or by recourse to analogy (*qiyās*).[21]

Ibn Taymiyyah has further distinguished two levels of disagreement, namely substantive disagreement amounting to contradiction (i.e. *ikhtilāf al-taḍād*) and disagreement of variance (*ikhtilāf al-tanawwuʻ*). The former usually consists of two views that are diametrically opposed to one another and they cannot be reconciled. The majority opinion on this type of disagreement is that only one of the opposing views could be right and declared as such but not both. Examples of this type of disagreement among scholars are found on the subject of freewill and determinism in the views of different factions of jurists and mystics. The matter is different in disagreement of variance, which consists basically of variant interpretations, one of which may be recommended while the other is neither denounced nor falsified. This is where preference (*al-tarjīḥ*) finds valid expression, simply because both sides rely on valid evidence. In Ibn Taymiyyah's assessment by far the largest portion of disagreement that has arisen in the Muslim community falls under the latter variety.[22]

The leading authorities of Islamic jurisprudence are on record as praising one another for their sincere contributions and have hardly if ever denounced one another for their different opinions. They have also urged their disciples not to be blind followers of the opinions of the founders of their school of thought but to refer to the sources on which they had relied themselves. The leading authorities have all emphasized adherence to the Qur'ān and the Sunnah as a matter of priority; then they counselled recourse to consensus (*ijmāʻ*) and to analogy (*qiyās*) in the absence of a clear textual ruling on a particular question.[23]

Ikhtilāf is a well-developed area of *fiqh* and works of scholarship on it date as far back as those of the *fiqh* itself. The first extant work on *ikhtilāf* known to us was by Abū Ḥanīfah (d. 767) which bore the title *Ikhtilāf al-Ṣaḥābah* (Disagreement among the Companions). Then his disciple Abū Yūsuf (d. 788) wrote a book entitled *Ikhtilāf Abī Ḥanīfah wa Ibn Abī Laylā*. Al-Shāfiʻī also wrote a book entitled

Ikhtilāf Abū Ḥanīfah wa'l-Awzā'i and has a chapter also on *ikhtilāf* in his *Risālah*. He has similarly recorded in *Kitāb al-Umm* his own disagreements with Mālik on many issues. Ibn Jarīr al-Ṭabari (d. 913) wrote a more general work on *Ikhtilāf* entitled *Ikhtilāf al-Fuqahā'*.

The style and content of these works have also changed over time. Initially the style of writing tended to be somewhat defensive and sought to vindicate the writer's own views or school without discussing the works of other schools and jurists, except perhaps where they took issue with one another. Subsequent works on *ikhtilāf* such as al-Ṭabarī's *Ikhtilāf al-Fuqahā'* and Ibn Rushd al-Qurṭubī's *Bidāyat al-Mujtahid* tended to acquire a comparative style of writing and later still, especially after the eleventh century, that is, following the decline of *ijtihād*, *ikhtilāf* works were influenced by regional developments and the focus was shifted to disagreements within the ranks of the schools, such as those between the leading Imām and his disciples, or the disciples themselves. Ibn 'Ābidīn's *Radd al-Mukhtār* may be cited as an example of this approach. Another development of note in this context is that the writers began to indicate their preferred positions and there emerged a genre of juristic literature on preferences (*al-tarjīḥāt*) which developed as an epiphenomenon of *ikhtilāf*.

Three works that merit special attention are al-Kāsānī's *Badā'i' al-'ṣanā'i'*, 'Abd al-Wahhāb al-Shā'ranī's *Kitāb al-Mīzān* and *al-Mughni* of Ibn Qudāmah for their balanced comparison which highlight not only the disagreements but also the points of unanimity and agreement among the schools of *fiqh*.[24]

Two Examples of Ikhtilāf

I refer here to two examples of *ikhtilāf* which relate to disagreement over the interpretation of the textual directives of the Qur'ān and the Sunnah respectively.

1. Our first illustration refers to the differential rulings of the schools on the revocation of a gift (*al-rujū' fi al-hibbah*) prior to delivery. Imām Mālik and the '*ulamā*' of Madinah have held that it was not permissible and the only exception to this was a gift by one's parents (father and mother) who were entitled to revoke a gift they had given to their offspring during their lifetime. Aḥmad ibn Ḥanbal and the Ẓāhirī school have held, on the other hand, that it is not

permissible for anyone to revoke a gift. Abū Ḥanīfah has held the opposite view which entitles everyone to revoke a gift except when it is granted to a close relative who happens to be within the prohibited degrees of marriage. A general consensus seems on the other hand to have developed to the effect that no one may revoke a gift which was intended as a charity for the sake of gaining the pleasure of God.

The basic ground of disagreement here consists of two *ḥadīths*, one of which declares that

> one who revokes a gift is like a dog that turns back on its vomit,[25]
>
> العائد فى هبته كالكلب يعود فى قيئه.

and the other *ḥadīth*, on the authority of Ṭāwus provides

> it is not permissible for the donor of a gift to revoke it except in the case of the father.[26]
>
> لايحلّ للواهب أن يرجع فى هبته إلا الوالد.

The mother's position is said to be analogous to that of the father. Imām Shāfi'ī is reported to have said: 'had the *hādīth* of Ḍāwus reached me (through reliable) narration, I would have ruled upon it'. As for the view that generally validates revocation of a gift except when the recipient is a close relative is based on a report from the caliph 'Umar ibn al-Khaṭṭāb who has been quoted to the effect that 'a gift granted to a close relative or by way of charity may not be subsequently revoked'.

A reference has also been made in this connection to the moral enormity of revoking a gift and the *ḥadīth* in which the Prophet has said

> I have been sent in order to accomplish what is morally virtuous.[27]
>
> بعثت لأتمم مكارم الأخلاق.

The jurists have compared a gift prior to delivery to a promise (*al-wa'd*) which entails only a moral responsibility but which cannot be legally enforced. The only exception here is a gift that is intended as charity and the exception here has been endorsed by general consensus – *ijmā'*.

The majority of jurists have held that when a father gives a gift to his son and then the son dies after receiving the gift, the father may receive it back through inheritance. It is reported that during the Prophet's time, a man of the Anṣār from Khazraj tribe had given the gift of a garden to his parents and then the parents died leaving the same property in their estate. The matter was brought to the Prophet's attention whereupon he said:

> You have earned the reward for your charity and you may now take it back by way of inheritance.[28]
>
> قد أجرت فى صدقتك وخذها بميراثك.

It thus appears that taking the gift back through inheritance, or indeed after a lapse of time when the return is by mutual agreement, is not reprehensible. The moral enormity attached to the revocation of a gift is, as already stated, prior to delivery. For transfer of ownership of the gifted object is completed upon delivery and possession, and from that point onwards, the matter is no longer a moral issue, but governed by legal rules, which means that any subsequent transfer of ownership must be by mutual consent of the transacting parties.

2. To illustrate juristic disagreemeent that originates from variant interpretations of words in the Qur'ān, I refer to the verse on the type of divorce known as *al-īlā'*. The verse in question provides:

> Those who swear that they will abstain from intercourse with their wives should wait for four months. Then if they go back, God is surely Forgiving, Merciful. And if they resolve on a divorce, God is surely Hearing, Knowing. (2:226)[29]
>
> لِّلَّذِينَ يُؤْلُونَ مِن نِّسَآئِهِمْ تَرَبُّصُ أَرْبَعَةِ أَشْهُرٍ فَإِنْ فَآؤُوا فَإِنَّ اللّهَ غَفُورٌ رَّحِيمٌ.

Īlā' typically occurs when the husband takes an oath of abstention, pledging to abstain from sexual intercourse with his wife. Ibn 'Abbās stated that the pre-Islamic Arabs used to take such oaths frequently, and did so at times when the wife refused to comply with her husband's demand over something; he would then take an oath not to approach her. She was left in a state of suspense for one year, perhaps two or three years, or even longer, during which time she was neither a wife nor a divorcee.[30] Then this Qur'ānic ruling set a limit of four months for the husbands to determine the position of their estranged wive one way or another after the completion of that period. Sa'īd ibn al-Musayyib also explained that 'when a man did not like his wife and yet did not wish to divorce her, he swore that he shall not approach her ever again . . . God Almighty then set a limit to this form of abuse'.[31] The above verse effectively declared that if the husband did not resume conjugal relations with his wife within four months, the wife shall be divorced. The rules of *īlā'* which the jurists have elaborated also apply to instances of deliberate desertion of the wife by the husband without a valid excuse, as I shall presently explain.

The Qur'ān has laid down the basic terms of *īlā'* without providing details as to the specific terms of its application and this is where the jurists have disagreed widely.

Abū Ḥanīfah, Mālik and their followers, as well as al-Awzāʻī and al-Nakhaʻ and many others have held that the Qur'ānic terms of *īlā'* apply equally whether the marriage has been consummated or not, whereas al-Zuhrī, ʻAṭā and Sufyān al-Thawr have held that *īlā'* can only occur after consummation. The jurists have also disagreed as to the implications of the Arabic words *fa-in fā'ū* (if they go back) in the verse as it implies return from a state of anger, hence the interpretation by many Companions, including ʻAli, Ibn ʻAbbās, Saʻīd ibn Jubayr and many jurists of subsequent generations that *īlā'* can only occur when pronounced in a state of anger. The renowned Companion Ibn Masʻūd and numerous prominent ʻ*ulamā*' including Ibn Sīrīn, Mālik, Shāfiʻī and Aḥmad Ibn Ḥanbal have held – and this is the correct view – that like other varieties of divorce, *īlā'* can occur both in a state of anger and in the normal state. Ibn Rushd has confirmed this by saying that the words of the verse are general (*ʻāmm*) and specifying their import to the state of anger would need to be supported by evidence, of which there is none.[32] The jurists have also differed regarding the time period which might have been actually mentioned by the husband when pronouncing *īlā'*. There are four views on this:

1) ʻAbd Allah ibn ʻAbbās held that *īlā'* occurs only when the husband swears that he will never approach her again.
2) Abū Ḥanīfah, his disciples, al-Thawr and the ʻ*ulamā*' of Kufah held that the period of *īlā'* is four months and a divorce occurs on expiry of this time unless the husband resumes marital relations before that time.
3) Mālik, Shāfiʻī and Aḥmad ibn Ḥanbal have held that *īlā'* does not occur unless the period actually exceeds four months. There may, in other words, be a pause, after the four month period, in which a decision has to be made on what to do next.

4) According to another opinion even a single day that is specified in the oath of abstention is enough to bring *īlā'* into effect.[33]

The reason for this disagreement is that the Qur'ān has specified the waiting period for the wife but has not specified any period that the husband might mention himself.

It is also stated that the word *fā'ū* in the verse signifies sexual intercourse when there is no valid excuse on the part of the husband. But if the husband abstains for a valid reason such as illness, travelling or imprisonment, he may resume conjugal relations afterwards. Only when the excuse comes to an end by recovery from illness, or by release from imprisonment, and he still abstains from sexual intercourse, the spouses may be separated on grounds of *īlā'*.

A number of early *'ulamā'*, including 'Ikrimah, al-Nakha'ī and al-Awzā'ī, have held that the husband may revoke the oath of *īlā'*, even when he is ill or in prison, by declaring his intention in words, in the presence of witnesses, and according to Aḥmad ibn Ḥanbal, if the husband is unable to speak, he may revoke *īlā'* by gesture or even in his mind. Abū Ḥanīfah is of the opinion that when unable to attempt sexual intercourse, the husband may just declare in words 'I have returned to my wife. But an opinion attributed to Sa'īd ibn Jubayr says that revocation of *īlā'* (which is called *al-fay'*) does not occur except through sexual intercourse, even when the husband is on a journey or in prison.[34]

Then there is also the question of expiation (*kaffārah*) for breach of oath which the husband needs to make when he returns to his wife. There are two opinions on this, one of which maintains that the position here is analogous to breaking any other oath and the normal *kaffārah* (which is feeding ten poor persons, or fast for ten days) for a breach of oath would apply. Thus when a man says to his wife: 'By God I shall not speak to you' and then he speaks, or says: 'By God I shall not approach you' and then he does, he is in breach of his oath and therefore liable to *kaffārah*. The second opinion on this question is that no *kaffārah* is necessary, and this is because of the wording of the verse that '. . . if they go back, God is surely Forgiving, Merciful' (2:266). Others have held that the reference to mercy and forgiveness here is general and does not absolve the husband from the *kaffārah*.[35] The jurists have also differed over the interpretation of the phrase in the verse which refers to a divorce (*talāq*) that 'if they resolve on a divorce' (*wa in 'azamu 'l-ṭalāq*). Does the divorce that ensues *īlā'* take place automatically or does it occur by means of a judicial decree? Many '*ulamā*' including the leading Companions, 'Umar ibn al-Khaṭṭāb, 'Uthmān, 'Ali, 'Abd Allah ibn Mas'ūd, 'Abd Allah ibn 'Abbās and also several leading jurists including Sufyān al-Thawri and Abū Ḥanīfah, have held that divorce follows automatically, that is, upon the expiry of the four-month period.

There is also disagreement over the nature of the divorce and whether it is a revocable (*raj'i*) or a final (*bā'in*) divorce. Many leading Companions, the majority of the schools and a number of jurists have held that if the husband does not resume marital relations with his wife, he must pronounce a divorce, otherwise the judge may order a revocable divorce. This is because all divorce in the *Sharī'ah* is presumed to be revocable unless there is evidence to prove otherwise. Yet Abū Ḥanīfah has differed from the majority and has held that the divorce that follows is final (*bā'in*).

The Māliki jurist Ibn al-'Arab has stated the Mālik position to the effect that when the husband deliberately abstains from conjugal relations with his wife with malicious intention – even though there is no valid impediment, such as illness, even if he has not taken the oath of abstention by way of *īlā'* his position is analogous to *īlā'*. The wife may accordingly seek judicial relief, after four months of abstention, and the judge may then assign a time, as of the date of the complaint, for the husband to resume marital relations within that period, failing which the rules of *īlā'* will be invoked. For it is said that *īlā'* is not just a verbal pronouncement and may include anything that falls within its meaning, that is, any deliberate act of desertion that is intended to harm and humiliate the wife. Thus when a man swears that he will not speak to his wife, or support her, and so on, and actually acts on his word while intending to harm her, his position is analogous to *īlā'* and the rules of *īlā'* apply to him. This is because the Qur'ān has ordered the husband to

> live with them in fairness (4:19).
>
> وَعَاشِرُوهُنَّ بِالْمَعْرُوفِ.

and therefore any act which is deliberate and harmful is enough to violate the Qur'ānic directive on fair treatment.[36] While referring to this view, the well-known contemporary jurist, Yūsuf al-Qaraḍāwi, has concurred, despite some disagreement that the jurists have recorded about it. There is a view, in particular, that the judge should not order a divorce and should merely advise the husband and admonish him to fear God and cease harming his wife. Al-Qaraḍāwi has stated that if the conclusion is that the husband has violated the spirit of fairness as the Qur'ān has decreed, then the judge must act in order to put an end to abuse.[37]

In both of the above examples, it can clearly be seen that all instances of *ikhtilāf* that the *'ulamā'* have recorded are based on sound evidence and they therefore belong to the category of permissible *ikhtilāf*. I may add here that I have not cited the often-quoted *ḥadīth* which proclaims that

> disagreement of my community is a source of mercy
>
> اختلاف أمتى رحمة.

because of its doubtful authenticity. In his section on *ikhtilāf* in the *Risālah*, al-Shāfi'ī has not referred to this *ḥadīth* nor is it recorded by al-Bukhārī and Muslim, which is why some scholars have expressed reservations about it. But supposing it were authentic then mercy (*raḥmah*) can only be associated with *ikhtilāf* that is within its valid parameters and partakes in sound *ijtihād*.

CONCLUSION AND CONTEMPORARY PERSPECTIVE

The existence of *ikhtilāf* as a well-developed and recognized branch of *fiqh* is naturally indicative of a healthy climate of tolerance among the leading *'ulamā'* and scholars of Islam. The fact that several schools of law have attempted to provide equally valid interpretations of the *Sharī'ah* shows that they have accepted one another and they, in turn, were accepted by the Muslim community at large. All this provides further evidence of the reality of pluralism in Islamic law.

It is also interesting to note that in the formative stages of Islamic jurisprudence during the first three centuries the scholars tend to excel in the degree of latitude and acceptance of *ijtihād*-oriented disagreement. The Companions have disagreed on matters of interpretation and it is even said that they had reached a consensus on this: the agreement to disagree. Their example also finds support among the leading authorities and *'ulamā'* of the era of *ijtihād*. One might expect that subsequent generations of scholars would have preserved and even enriched this valuable heritage. Contrary to such expectations, however, the climate of understanding and openness was subsequently subjected to restrictions during the era of imitation (*taqlīd*) where one finds instances of rigidity and stricture among the lower ranks of the *'ulamā'*. To accept the plurality of the schools of law is indicative of healthy *ikhtilāf*. Hence, for a scholar/imitator to claim total superiority of his school and take an over-critical and dismissive view of other schools is decidedly unsound and contrary to the original spirit of *ikhtilāf*.

Ikhtilāf has played an evidently important role in the development of the rich legacy of *fiqh* and *Sharīʿah* that will continue to provide a lasting source of influence. One can hardly overestimate the inspiring spirit of sound and principled disagreement in our own generation. Yet disagreement has a place in the legal and intellectual heritage of Muslims which should not be exaggerated. A legal order in society can simply not proceed on the basis of never-ending *ikhtilāf*. The value of *ikhtilāf* is therefore relative and not independent of conformity and consensus that must clearly be accepted as the stronger influences which demarcate the limits of acceptable *ikhtilāf*. I say this partly because I believe that the scholastic divisions in the present-day Muslim *ummah*, especially between the Sunni and the Shīʿah, and even among the students of different Sunni legal schools, often tend to violate the spirit of sound *ikhtilāf*. I have seen Muslim youth in university campuses, some of whom have associated themselves with partisan movements, to be restrictive and intolerant of even a mild degree of liberality and openness, or of conservative orientations, as the case may be, that they observe on the part of their peers and associates.

This I believe to be a far cry from the healthy precedent and example that has enriched the intellectual legacy of Islam, and merits constant attention and dignified appreciation and respect. We can simply not afford to be intolerant of our differences and disagreements on various issues.

Yet we also need to be cautious about over-indulgence in *ikhtilāf*. Muslim individuals and scholars could perhaps afford to encourage *ikhtilāf* more widely in certain periods of their history when they enjoyed the confidence that was generated by the superiority of their political power and then a rigorously productive scholarship. But I believe that there is a great need today for Muslims to appreciate the value of unity and consensus while recognizing in the meantime that unity and consensus which emerge out of open deliberation and principled *ikhtilāf* are what deserve our best attention. *Ikhtilāf* and consensus are often inseparable even if they appear to be the opposite.

To say that the Muslim community can totally eliminate disagreement and *ikhtilāf* over all questions is plainly unrealistic and has no historical precedent. The reality of living in a world where disagreements must inevitably exist is one which has dominated the greater part of Muslim history and it is no longer a matter of choice for the contemporary *ummah*. But then the question may still arise as to how Muslims should cope with *ikhtilāf* on issues that they encounter from time to time. I propose to end this section with a tentative response to this question.

The substance of the response that I attempt here is basically the same as has been known to Islamic jurisprudence throughout the ages. The main thrust of the responsibility to resolve *ikhtilāf* accordingly falls on the shoulders of the *'ūlu al-amr*, government leaders and those in charge of the community affairs. They must address and determine *ikhtilāf* by reference to the nature of the questions involved and the urgency or otherwise of providing a solution for them. Thus we read in a legal maxim of *fiqh* the declaration that the 'command of the Imām puts an end to disagreement' (*amr al-imām yarfa' al-khilāf*). The substance of this maxim is upheld in yet another maxim which simply provides that 'the command of the Imām is enforceable' (*amr al-imām nāfidh*). It is a prerogative, therefore, of the lawful government and the head of state to select for purposes of enforcement an interpretation or a ruling of *ijtihād* that is in the best interests of the community. There may be several interpretations of a particular text of the Qur'ān or the Sunnah, or indeed a variety of non-textually based *ijtihād* and opinion relating to the same issue, in which case the leader is within his rights to select one in preference to others. In doing so, the leader, or those in charge of such a selection, must act on the best interests of the people. This is, in fact, the subject of another legal maxim which provides that the 'affair of the Imām is determined by reference to *maṣlaḥah'* (*amr 'l imām manūṭ bi 'l-maṣlaḥah*). Once a *maṣlaḥah*-oriented selection has been made by the ruling authorities, everyone must comply with it: neither the *mujtahid* nor a layman is entitled to deviate from the command of the leader and *'ūlu al-amr*, as this is where disagreement must be laid to rest.

It is, accordingly, the responsibility of the leadership to address issues of *ikhtilāf* that cause tension and disunity in the community generally as well as those that require urgent solutions. We know, of course, from the explicit terms of the Qur'ān that the leaders must resort to consultation, solicit expert opinion and counsel from the community itself, or even outside the community, if this proves to be necessary in order to resolve *ikhtilāf*. Here we may refer once again to the Qur'ānic directive which enjoins the believers to

> ask those who have knowledge, if you yourselves do not know. (16:43)
>
> فاسْألوا أهْلَ الذّكرِ إن كُنتُمْ لا تَعْلَمُونَ.

The search for consultative and well-informed solutions and participatory decisions by the leaders thus summarizes the Qur'ānic directives concerning the determination of *ikhtilāf*.

Consultation in present-day Muslim communities is conducted according to pre-determined procedures at the level usually of representative assemblies which normally uphold the majority opinion. When the authorities in charge have determined a disputed matter in the manner indicated above, it becomes a *Sharī'ah* ruling (*ḥukm shar'i*) and a duty therefore of the citizens to rally behind it and abandon disagreement.

Experience may have shown that due to a high level of sensitivity, certain issues have become a continuous hotbed of tension in the community, and it is possible for leaders to impose a total ban on all manners of disagreement over them. This is once again a legitimate exercise of the same authority that is vested in the lawful government. We note, for example, the provisions in the constitution of Malaysia which totally proscribe disputation and public statements on racial issues as this is proven to be a highly sensitive question in this country. One can find, of course, similar provisions on the limitations that the applied law or the *Sharī'ah* might have imposed on the freedom of speech which may effectively put those issues beyond the realm of disagreement.

To determine a correct procedure for the resolution of disagreement in present-day Muslim societies, one should naturally refer to the constitution and laws of the country or countries concerned. This also means that we do not have a single formula, or a monolithic guideline, to provide us with a unified strategy for the resolution of differences. Often we find that the *Sharī'ah*, or the applied law of a given country, only provide us with general guidelines and leave specific decisions to be made by the experts or those who are in charge of community affairs. This also reminds one of the renowned *ḥadīth* that simply declares 'religion is good advice' (*ad-dīnu al-naṣīḥah*). We cannot expect to have a text to refer to on all our differences, but if we seek good advice, within our own lights or from those who can guide us better, we will act in comformity with this *ḥadīth*.

What I have explored above may still leave us uncertain with regard to certain levels or types of disagreement that the Muslims are experiencing today. Then we need to bear in mind that we have to live with some of the instances of unresolved *ikhtilāf* in juridical and even theological issues that history has left for almost every generation, and of which the present generation is no exception. This is also a function, to some extent, of the circumstantial character of *ikhtilāf* which tends to rise in relationship to new developments and unprecedented experiences. It must remain, by the same token, the responsibility of every generation of Muslims to seize the opportunities they may be endowed with, or which they have at their disposal, to pursue the quest for resolving disagreement within the ranks of the *ummah*, or else to find better ways of coming to terms with it.

NOTES

1. Cf. Al-'Alwāni, *Adab 'l-Ikhtilāf*, 104.
2. Cf. al-Ṣābūnī, et al., *al-Makdkhal al-Fiqhi wa Tārīkh*, 360.
3. Cf. Al-'Alwāni, *Adab 'l-Ikhtilāf*, 104.
4. Cf. Al-Ṣābūnī, *Madkhal*, 316.
5. Tabrīzī, *Mishkāt. ḥadīth* no. 3285; al-Bahnasāwi, *al-Sunnah*, 186.
6. The *Qur'ān*, 5:6.
7. Cf. Abū Zahrah, *Uṣūl al-Fiqh*, 75.
8. Cf. al-Shāṭibī, *al-Muwāfaqāt fi Uṣūl al-Sharī'ah*, III, 88.
9. For illustrations and details see the chapter entitled Commands and Prohibitions in Kamali, *Jurisprudence,* 187–202.
10. Cf. Al-Ṣābūnī, *Madhkal*, 314; 'Aṭiyah, *al-Tanẓīr,* 135.
11. Cf. Bahnasawi, *al-Sunnah*, 183.
12. Cf. Al-'Alwāni, *Adab al-Ikhtilāf*, 110.
13. Kamali, *Jurisprudence*, 123.
14. See for details, *ibid*., 96–108; Bahnasawi, *al-Sunnah*, 187.
15. Abū Dāwūd al-Sijistānī, *Sunan Abū Dawūd*, III, 103, *ḥadīth* no. 3567.
16. Cf. Bahnasawi, *al Sunnah*, 189.
17. Ibn Ḥazm, *al-Iḥkām* V, 66; al-'Alwāni, *Adab al-Ikhtilāf*, 46.

18. Ibn Ḥajar al-'Asqalāni, *Fatḥ al-Bāri,* XIII, 289; Tabrīzī, *Mishkāt, ḥadīth* no. 2212; 'Alwani, *Adab al-Ikhtilāf*, 47.
19. Cf. Al-'Alwāni, *Adab al-Ikhtilāf*, 28.
20. al-Shāfi'ī, *al-Risālah*, 245.
21. Ibid.
22. Ibn Taymiyyah, *Iqtiḍā'*, 124–34; see also for a discussion of *ikhtilāf*, Kamali, *Freedom of Expression*, 144–7.
23. Ibn Taymiyyah, *Iqtiḍā'*, 91.
24. See for details 'Atiyyah, *al-Tanẓīr*, 136–44; al-'Alwani, *Adab al-Ikhtilāf*, 91–3.
25. Ibn Rushd, *Bidāyat al-Mujtahid*, II, 249.
26. Ibid., see also for a discussion Jamāl al-Dīn 'Aṭiyyah, *al-Tanẓīr*, 144–5.
27. Ibn Rushd, *Bidāyat al Mujtahid*, II, 250.
28. Ibid., II, 250; 'Aṭiyyah, *al-Tanẓīr*, 145.
29. See for an early and detailed discussion of this verse, al-Shāfi'ī, *al-Risālah*, 249–54 (sections 1705–52). See also generally on *īlā'* Ibn Rushd, *Bidāyat al-Mujtahid*, II, 74–8.
30. Cf. al-Zuḥayli, *al-Fiqh al-Islāmī*, VII, 536 ff.
31. al-Qaraḍāwi, *Madkhal*, 181.
32. Al-Zuḥayli, *al-Fiqh al-Islāmī*, VII, 545.
33. Al-Shāfi'ī, *al-Risālah*, 250 (section 1718): Ibn Rushd, *Bidāyat al-Mujtahid*, II, 75.
34. Cf. al-Qurṭubī, *al-Jāmi'*, III, 109 al-Qaraḍāwi, *Madkhal*, 184.
35. al-Rāzī, *al-Tafsīr al-Kabīr*, VI, 88; al-Qurṭubī, *Tafsīr al-Qurṭubī*, III, 111, Ibn Rushd, *Bidāyat al-Mujtahid*.
36. Ibn al-'Arabi, *Jāmi'li-Aḥkām al-Qur'ān*, I, 178; Ibn Rushd, Bidāyat al-Mujtahid, II, 76.
37. al-Qaraḍāwi, *Madkhal*, 186–7.

6

GOALS AND PURPOSES (*MAQĀṢID*) OF *SHARĪ'AH*: HISTORY AND METHODOLOGY

In an earlier chapter I discussed some aspects of the objectives of Islamic law (*maqāṣid al-Sharī'ah*, henceforth referred to as *maqāṣid*) in reference to such themes as moral virtue, justice and public interest. In this chapter I present the history of ideas on the *maqāṣid*, including its methodology and its relevance to *ijtihād*. It is important to comprehend the substantive contents of the *maqāṣid* in an effort to address one of its main weaknesses in the eyes of its critics who say that unlike the *uṣūl al-fiqh*, the *maqāṣid* lack a convincing methodology. *Maqāṣid* had on the other hand been the focus of renewed interest and attention in recent decades, borne out by the growth of voluminous literature in Arabic on its various themes. This is due partly to a certain shortfall of the legal theory of *uṣūl al-fiqh* which has shown signs of rigidity and has failed in some ways to provide a workable methodology for contemporary law-making and *ijtihād*. It is felt that the *maqāṣid* can fill that gap – hence my attempt to add a separate chapter on this subject, which seeks to explore the jurisprudence of *maqāṣid* a little further. The discussion that follows also develops the argument as to how and why the *maqāṣid* provides a more versatile tool and a matrix for legislation and *ijtihād*.[1]

I present this chapter in four sections, beginning with a review of the contributions of some of the leading *'ulamā'* to the theory of the *maqāṣid*. The next section looks into the different approaches the *'ulamā'* have taken towards the identification of *maqāṣid*, followed by a section on classification and ranking of the *maqāṣid*. The last section highlights the relevance of the *maqāṣid* to *ijtihād* and the ways in which the *maqāṣid* can enhance the scope and calibre of law-making in modern times.

HISTORY OF *MAQĀṢID*

As a theme of *Sharī'ah* in its own right, the *maqāṣid* did not receive much attention in the early stages of the development of Islamic legal thought and, as such, represent rather a late addition to the juristic legacy of the leading schools. Even to this day many reputable textbooks on Islamic jurisprudence (*uṣūl al-fiqh* – henceforth referred to as *uṣūl*) do not include *maqāṣid* in their usual coverage of topics. This is due partly to the nature of the subject, which is concerned with the philosophy and purpose of the law rather than the specific formulations of its text. Although the *maqāṣid* are obviously relevant to *ijtihād*, they have not been treated as such in the conventional expositions of the theory of *ijtihād*.

Islamic legal thought is, broadly speaking, preoccupied with the concern over conformity to the letter of the divine text, and the legal theory of *uṣūl* has advanced that purpose to a large extent. This literalist orientation of the juristic thought was generally more pronounced among the Traditionists – the *Ahl al-ḥadīth* – compared to the Rationalists – the *Ahl al-ra'y*. The former thus tended to view the *Sharī'ah* as a set of rules, commands and prohibitions addressed to the competent individual (*mukallaf*), and the latter was expected to conform to its directives. The precedent of the leading Companions indicated, on the other hand, that they saw the *Sharī'ah* both as a set of rules and a value system in which the specific rules reflected overriding values. The textualist tradition of the three centuries that followed the early decades of Islam did not take much interest in *maqāṣid* and it was not until the time of al-Ghazālī (d. 1111) and then al-Shāṭibī (d. 1388) that significant developments were made in the formulation of the theory of *maqāṣid*.

The basic outlook that was advocated by the theory of *maqāṣid* was not denied by the leading schools, yet the *maqāṣid* remained on the fringes of mainstream juristic thought. Except for the Ẓāhiris who maintained that the *maqāṣid* are only known when they are identified and declared by the clear text, the majority did not confine the *maqāṣid* to the clear text alone. For they understood the *Sharī'ah* to be rational, goal-oriented and its rules generally founded in identifiable causes. Mere conformity to rules that went against the purpose and outlook of *Sharī'ah* was, therefore, considered unacceptable.[2] There were differences of orientation among the leading schools towards the *maqāṣid*: some were more open to it than others, but elaboration of the goals and objectives of the *Sharī'ah* was generally not encouraged. This unspoken attitude contrasted with the fact that the Qur'ān itself exhibits considerable awareness of the underlying purposes and objectives of its laws and often expounds the causes and rationale on which they are founded. The reticence of the '*ulamā*' in respect of the identification of the *maqāṣid* was partly due to the elements of projection and prognostication that such an exercise was likely to involve. Who can tell, for sure, for example, that this or that is the purpose and overriding objective of the Lawgiver, without engaging in a measure of speculation, unless, of course, the text itself declared it so. But then to confine the scope of *maqāṣid* only to the clear declaration of the text basically made the whole idea unnecessary and redundant, and was in any case not enough, as I shall presently elaborate.

It was not until the early tenth century that the term *maqāṣid* was used in the juristic writings of Abū 'Abd Allah al-Tirmidh al-Ḥakīm (d. 932) and recurrent references to it appeared in the works of Imām al-Ḥaramayn al-Juwaynī (d. 1085) who was probably the first to classify the *maqāṣid* into the three categories of essential, complementary and desirable (*ḍarūriyyāt, ḥājiyyāt, taḥsīniyyāt*) which has gained general acceptance ever since. Juwayni noted that the Prophet's Companions exhibited a high level of awareness of the objectives of *Sharī'ah,* and added that 'one who did not reflect on the *maqāṣid* did so at one's peril and was likely to lack insight into *Sharī'ah*'. Juwayni's ideas were then developed further by his pupil, Abū Ḥāmid al-Ghazālī who wrote at length on public interest (*maṣlaḥah*) and ratiocination (*ta'līl*) in his works, *Shifā' al-Ghalīl* and *al-Mustaṣfā*. Ghazālī was generally critical of *maṣlaḥah* as a proof but validated it if it promoted the *maqāṣid* of *Sharī'ah.* As for the *maqāṣid* themselves, Ghazālī wrote categorically that the *Sharī'ah* pursued five objectives, namely those of faith, life, intellect, lineage and property which were to be protected as a matter of absolute priority.[3]

A number of prominent writers continued to contribute to the *maqāṣid*, not all of them consistently perhaps, yet important to the development of ideas. Fakhr al-Din al-Rāzī (d. 1208) and Sayf al-Dīn al-Āmid (d. 1233) identified the *maqāṣid* as criteria of preference (*al-tarjīḥ*) among conflicting analogies, and elaborated on an internal order of priorities among the various classes of *maqāṣid*. Āmid also confined the essential *maqāṣid* to only five. The Mālik jurist, Shihāb al-Dīn al-Qarāfī (d. 1285) added a sixth to the existing list, namely the protection of honour (*al-'irḍ*) and this was endorsed by Tāj al-Dīn 'Abd al-Wahhāb ibn al-Subkī (d. 1370) and later by Muḥammad ibn 'Ali al-Shawkānī (d. 1834). The list of five essential values was evidently based on a reading of the relevant parts of the Qur'ān on prescribed penalties (*ḥudūd*). The value that each of these penalties sought to vindicate and defend was consequently identified as an essential value. The latest addition (i.e. *al-'irḍ*) was initially thought to have been covered under family lineage (*al-nasl*, also *al-nasab*), but the proponents of this addition relied on the fact that the *Sharī'ah* had enacted a separate punishment for slanderous accusation (*al-qadhf*), which justified the addition.[4] 'Izz al-Dīn 'Abd al-Salām al-Sulami's (d. 1262) renowned work, *Qawā'id al-Aḥkām*, was in his own characterization a work on '*maqāṣid al-aḥkām*' (purposes of injunctions) and addressed in greater detail the various aspects of *maqāṣid* especially in relationship to *'Illah* (effective cause) and *maṣlaḥah* (public interest). Thus he wrote at the outset of his work that 'the greatest of all the objectives of the Qur'ān is to facilitate benefits (*maṣāliḥ*) and the means that secure them and that the realization of benefit also included the prevention of evil'.[5]

Taqī al-Dīn ibn Taymiyyah (d. 1328) was probably the first to depart from the notion of confining the *maqāṣid* to a specific number and added, to the existing list of *maqāṣid*, such things as fulfilment of contracts, preservation of the ties of kinship, honouring the rights of one's neighbour, in so far as the affairs of this world are concerned, and the love of God, sincerity, trustworthiness and moral purity, in relationship to the hereafter.[6] Ibn Taymiyyah thus revised the scope of *maqāṣid* from a designated and specified list into an open-ended list of values, and his approach is now generally accepted by contemporary commentators, including, Muḥammad 'Ābid al-Jābiri, Aḥmad al-Raysūnī, Yūsuf al-Qaraḍāwi and others.[7] Qaraḍāwi has further extended the list of *maqāṣid* to include social welfare support (*al-takāful*), freedom, human dignity and human fraternity, among the higher objectives of *Sharī'ah*.[8] These are undoubtedly upheld and supported by the existing evidence in the Qur'ān and Sunnah. Jamāl al-Dīn 'Aṭiyyah further expanded the range and identified twenty-four *maqāṣid* which he then classified under four headings: *maqāṣid* concerning the individual, those concerning the family, the *ummah* and humanity respectively.[9]

I propose to add protection of the fundamental rights and liberties, economic development, and R & D in technology and science as well as peaceful coexistence among nations to the structure of *maqāṣid*, as they are crucially important and can find support for the most part in the Qur'ān and Sunnah. It would appear from this analysis that the *maqāṣid* remain open to further enhancement which will depend, to some extent, on the priorities of every age.

METHODOLOGY OF *MAQĀṢID*

The methodology of *maqāṣid* is presented in three sections, namely identification of *maqāṣid*, their classification and then the relevance of *maqāṣid* to *ijtihād*.

Identification of Maqāṣid

As already indicated Muslim jurists have differed in their approach to the identification of *maqāṣid*. The first approach to be noted is the textualist approach, which confines the identification of *maqāṣid* to the clear text, commands and prohibitions, which are the carriers of *maqāṣid*. The *maqāṣid*, according to this view, have no separate existence outside the framework of clear injunctions, provided that a command is explicit and normative and it conveys the objective of the Lawgiver in the affirmative sense. Prohibitions are indicative of the *maqāṣid* in the negative sense that the purpose of a prohibitive injunction is to suppress and avert the evil that the text in question has contemplated. This is generally accepted, but there are certain tendencies within this general framework. While the Ẓāhiris tend to confine the *maqāṣid* to the obvious text, the majority of jurists take into consideration both the text and the underlying *'illah* and rationale of the text.[10] Al-Shāṭibī has spoken affirmatively of the need to observe the explicit injunctions, but then he added that adherence to the obvious text should not be so rigid as to alienate the rationale and purpose of the text from its words and sentences. Rigidity of this kind, Shāṭibī added, was itself contrary to the objectives (*maqāṣid*) of the Lawgiver, just as would be the case with regard to neglecting the clear text itself. When the text, whether a command or a prohibition, is read in conjunction with its objective and rationale, this is a firm approach, one which bears greater harmony with the intention of the Lawgiver.[11]

Ever since al-Shāfi'ī's time, *ijtihād* had remained rooted in the utilization of words and sentences of the text, and beyond the text it was basically confined to analogical reasoning. The first of this was a text-bound and literalist approach and the second was tied to the correct identification of the effective cause. The methodology of *qiyās* was also increasingly subjected to technical conditions and requirements. This was the *uṣūli* approach to *ijtihād*. The *maqāṣid* approach which was projected by al-Shāṭibī sought to open the avenues of *ijtihād* from the strictures of literalism and *qiyās*. To construct *qiyās*, one needs to identify an original case, and a new case, and then a precise effective cause, and each of these steps must fulfil a long list of requirements, which are incidentally all a juristic construct that partake in speculative thought. This approach is, moreover, not necessarily focused directly on the purpose of the Lawgiver and the people's interest, or *maṣlaḥah*. The two approaches, namely, of the text, and of the one based on *'illah*, also essentially combined into one, as the *'illah* is extracted from the text, but since the text does not explicitly declare its *'illah* most of the time, the jurist is extracting it through a close analysis of the meaning of words, whether literal or figurative, general or specific (*ḥaqiqi*, *majāzi*, *'āmm*, *khāṣ*) and so forth. To look, for example, at the Qur'ān text on the prohibition of wine drinking, the jurist had to determine the precise meaning of *khamr* (wine) in the linguistic usage of the Arabs that prevailed at the time. For *khamr* referred to the type of wine that was extracted from grapes. Whether the meaning of that expression could be extended to other substances and varieties of wine was a question to be decided! The jurist had to also look into the precise import of the wording of the text that declared the prohibition (i.e. *ijtanibū hu* – avoid it) whether it conveyed a strict ban or a mere reprehension and educational advice. For the Qur'ān is replete with commands and prohibitions that convey different meanings in terms of their precise juridical value. Other questions also arose as to whether the prohibition of *khamr* was an absolute ruling of permanent validity or meant only to address a circumstantial mischief of Arab society of the time. Providing credible answers to such questions could hardly be devoid of speculation and doubt. Similar doubts also arose in the determination of the effective cause (*'illah*) of prohibition, which in this case is intoxication of the kind that overwhelms the intellect and rational judgement. This may be a definitive *'illah* in the case of *khamr* but not so when it is applied to the more mild varieties of intoxicants, such as *nabīdh* – an extract of dates, known at the time, and whether drinking a small amount of wine that did not intoxicate was equally prohibited! Then for each new variety of intoxicant, one had to start a fresh series of investigations and the process was bound to become altogether issue-laden and speculative.

Then there is the *maqāṣid*-oriented approach to the development of *Sharīʻah,* which is premised on realization of benefit (*maṣlaḥah*) and prevention of mischief (*mafsadah*). This takes for granted the rationality of the laws of *Sharīʻah* assuming that *maṣlaḥah* is the one grand *'illah* of all of the laws of *Sharīʻah* that applies universally to all relevant cases. From this basic premise all that the jurist needs to ascertain is the presence of *maṣlaḥah* and what is known as *ḥikmah* (rationale, wisdom) in every new case and new ruling. *Ḥikmah* is the *maṣlaḥah*-oriented name for *'illah*. *'Illah* in the terminology of *uṣūl* is an attribute that obtains in the subject matter of a ruling (*ḥukm*) and it is an indicator of the presence and continued validity of that ruling. Intoxication is thus an attribute and *'illah* of wine (*khamr*) and its presence is indicative of prohibition. In a similar vein, interest or unwarranted increase is the attribute of a usurious sale and the cause of its prohibition. Similarly travel and sickness constitute the *'illah* for breaking the fast in the fasting month of Ramaḍān. As for the *ḥikmah*, it is the reason, motive and rationale of the ruling, which is either to realize a benefit or to prevent a mischief and harm. Hence the *ḥikmah* of prohibition of liquor is prevention of harm that materializes from loss of the faculty of reason, and the *ḥikmah* of prohibition of *ribā* is to prevent exploitation, and the *ḥikmah* of breaking fast in Ramaḍān for the sick and the traveller is prevention of hardship and harm.

Prevention of harm is a benefit, which means that the *ḥikmah* here reflects the larger idea of *maṣlaḥah* and the original *raison d'etre* of the law. To ascertain the *maṣlaḥah* of a law is an easier task for the jurist as unlike the technical issues that are faced in the determination of *'illah*, it is no longer concerned with hidden factors and speculative conclusions. For the purpose is to ascertain benefit and harm to human life which opens the vistas of *ijtihād* and legislation on a self-contained and positivist premise. The jurist is now engaged in evaluative thinking instead of determining the meaning of words, the scope of their application, etc. This rationalist engagement, it may be added here, can draw much support from the causes and occasions of revelation (*asbāb al-nuzūl*) which elucidate the original intent and context of the law. *Asbāb al-nuzūl* is yet another important theme to which the *uṣūl* jurists have paid little attention as it was relegated into a subsidiary factor in relationship to interpretation, analogy and *ijtihād*. In his writings on the hermeneutics of Qur'ān and *ḥadīth*, the late Fazlur Rahman has elaborated the crucial importance of *asbāb al-nuzūl* in devising fresh approaches to the understanding of the text. Muḥammad 'Ābid al-Jābiri has similarly underlined the importance of *asbāb al-nuzūl* to the *maqāṣid*.[12]

To elucidate further the difference between *uṣūl*-based and *maqāṣid*-based *ijtihād*, we may take the Qur'ānic ruling on mutilation of the hand for theft. How can one ascertain the rationality of this law and the limitations also of the *uṣūl*-based approach with regard to the identification of its effective cause and *'illah*? The *uṣūl*-based approach that relies on semantics and analogy would be unable to do this nor to provide a satisfactory response to such questions as to why theft was made punishable with mutilation, not imprisonment or whipping. The analogy-based approach can at best speculate and say that the thief actually stole by using his hand, hence its mutilation. This analogy-based response may well give rise to a question as to why was then adultery not made punishable with mutilation of the relevant organ! And there would be no end to speculation to determine the rationality of these laws. But the *maqāṣid*-based approach does not yield itself to speculative indulgence of the kind in the first place as it detaches itself from analogy and literalism and focuses on the occasions of revelation (*asbāb al-nuzūl*). To formulate a rational response that could explain the punishment of mutilation for theft, the jurist would reflect on the time, place and circumstances in which the law in question originated. The following factors would need to be brought into the picture: firstly, the punishment of mutilation for theft was practised by the Arabs before the advent of Islam. Second, bedouin Arab society consisted largely of nomads who travelled with their camels and tents in search of pastures, and it was not feasible under the circumstances to penalize the thief with imprisonment. Imprisonment necessitates durable structures and guards, feeding and care of inmates and so forth, hence the physical punishment was the only reasonable option. Since there were no protective barriers to safeguard the property of people, society could not afford to tolerate proliferation of theft. Mutilation of the hand of the thief also provided the kind of punishment that disabled the thief from persisting in his wrongdoing, just as it also left a visible mark on the offender to warn people against his menace. Mutilation was thus an eminently rational punishment for theft.

Even after the advent of Islam, the same punishment was retained, as there was no drastic change in the customs and lifestyles of the Arab society. Islam legislated on it and made it subject to many requirements, hence it was no longer a customary practice alone but one that was incorporated in the law. A similar line of analysis can be advanced regarding the punishment of adultery and the conditions that were stipulated concerning the proof of that offence. These conditions, especially the requirement of four eye-witnesses for the proof of adultery were probably feasible in a nomadic society due to the open space and desert setting of the Arabian lifestyle. The question may now arise: would it be feasible to apply the same conditions to a settled society of city dwellers in our own time – which might make proof of adultery next to impossible! Whipping was the suitable punishment for adultery since the Qur'ān legislated on it, and we see no problem in its continued application. The only hesitation we have is over the conditions that were laid down for its implementation that may now be due for a revision, in view for example of the new methods of proof that are now available to be applied instead of, or in addition to, witnesses. This would be in keeping with the rational and *maṣlaḥah*-based approach to *Sharīʻah* that helps to keep the law abreast of the attendant realities of our time.

To premise the rationality of the laws of *Sharīʻah* on the *asbāb al-nuzūl* under the rubric of *maṣlaḥah* would thus open the prospects of rational *ijtihād* in a variety of new cases and circumstances. The *maqāṣid*-based approach is thus likely to open new possibilities for the growth of *ijtihād* and the versatility of the laws of *Sharīʻah* and their continued application to new situations, times and places. None of the approaches we have discussed can supervene nor override the clear text – only that they view the text from different angles and advance differential perspectives towards its understanding and enforcement. They follow the purpose of the text, if not always its letter.

Most of the injunctions of *Sharīʻah* are easily understood, as Shāṭibī reminded us, and their objectives can be known and ascertained from the reading of the clear text. Shāṭibī has similarly concluded that whatever is complementary to the *maqāṣid* and in the service thereof is also a part of the *maqāṣid*. The question then arises: We know that the *maqāṣid* are known from clear injunctions, but can they also be known from a general reading of the text by way of induction? Shāṭibī has given an original response to this question, which is as follows.

Induction (*istiqrā'*) to Shāṭibī is one of the most important methods of identifying the *maqāṣid*. There may be various textual references to a subject, none of which may be in the nature of a decisive injunction. Yet their collective weight is such that it leaves little doubt as to the meaning that is obtained from them. A decisive conclusion may, in other words, be arrived at from a plurality of speculative expressions. Shāṭibī illustrates this by saying that nowhere in the Qur'ān is there a specific declaration to the effect that the *Sharī'ah* has been enacted for the benefit of the people. Yet this is a definitive conclusion which is drawn from the collective reading of a variety of textual proclamations.[13] Shāṭibī then adds that the benefits (*maṣālih*) are to be understood in their broadest sense which should be inclusive of all benefits pertaining to this world and the hereafter, those of the individual and the community, material, moral and spiritual, and those which pertain to the present as well as future generations. This broad meaning of benefits also includes prevention and elimination of harm. These benefits cannot be always verified and ascertained by human reason alone without the aid and guidance of divine revelation.[14]

The inductive method, according to al-Shāṭibī, raised the credibility of one's conclusions from odd incidents to the level of broad and definitive (*qaṭ'ī*) principles. Yet al-Ghazālī, who earlier spoke on the meanings and purposes of the *aḥkām* wrote that 'the companions on the whole pursue the meaning and purposes (*al-ma'āni*), but in doing so they were content with a strong probability and did not make certainty (*al-yaqīn*) a pre-requisite of their conclusions'.[15]

The typical classification of *maqāṣid* into the three categories of essential, complementary and desirable (*ḍarūri*, *hājji*, *taḥsini*), and the conclusion that the Lawgiver has intended to protect these are based, once again, on induction, as there is no specific declaration on them in the textual sources. On a similar note, the ruling of the *Sharī'ah* that the validity of an act of devotion (*'ibādah*) cannot be established by means of *ijtihād* is an inductive conclusion which is drawn from the detailed evidence on the subject, there being no specific injunction on it.[16] It is also the same inductive method which has led the '*ulamā*' to the conclusion that protection of the five values of faith, life, intellect, property and lineage is of primary importance to *Sharī'ah* – there is no textual ruling to specify any category or number of values in that order.

Shāṭibī's inductive method is not confined to the identification of objectives and values but also extends to commands and prohibitions, which may either be obtained from the clear text, or from a collective reading of a number of textual proclamations that may occur in a variety of contexts.[17] Shāṭibī then goes a step further to say that the inductive conclusions and positions that are so established are the general premises and objectives of *Sharī'ah* and thus have a higher order of importance than the specific rules. It thus becomes evident that induction is the principal method of reasoning and proof to which Shāṭibī resorted in his theory of the *maqāṣid* and made an original contribution to this theme.

Shāṭibī's approach to induction is reminiscent of the knowledge that is acquired of the personality and character of an individual that is based on sustained association with that individual and observation of his conduct over a period of time. This kind of knowledge is broad and holistic, as it is enriched with insight, and likely to be more reliable when compared to the knowledge that might be based only on the observation of specific, isolated incidents in the daily activities of the individual concerned.

A comprehensive reading of the textual injuctions of *Sharī'ah* gives rise to such questions as to whether the means to a *wājib* (obligatory) or *ḥarām* (unlawful) should also be seen as a part of the objective that is pursued by that injunction; whether the means to a command, in other words, is also an integral part of that command. Another question raised is whether avoiding the opposite of a command is integral to the goal and objective that is sought by that command. It is said in response that the supplementary aspects of commands and prohibitions are an integral part of their objectives, although disagreements have emerged over details. There is general agreement that the opposite of a command amounts to a prohibition in the event where that opposite can be clearly identified. For instance, in view of the clear Qur'ānic injunction on fasting, and on supporting one's wife, the opposite of fasting, which is not to fast without an excuse, or refusal to support one's dependant would be prohibited in each case. The opposite of some commands may be a little more doubtful to identify. Suppose the master orders his servant to run. Has he then violated this if he only walks fast, or rides a horse, or sends someone else to run for him?

CLASSIFICATION OF *MAQĀṢID*

We have already explained in chapter 2, the classification of *maqāṣid* into the three categories of essential, complementary and desirable (*ḍarūriyyāt, ḥājiyyāt, taḥsiniyyāt*), a broad classification that contemplates the relative merit and importance of the various types of *maqāṣid*.

Maqāṣid have been further classified into the general purposes (*al-maqāṣid al-'āmmah*) and particular goals (*al-maqāṣid al-khāṣṣah*). The general goals are those that characterize Islam and its *Sharī'ah* and they are on the whole broad and comprehensive. Prevention of harm (*ḍarar*) is a general goal of *Sharī'ah* and applies to all areas and subjects. Particular goals are theme-specific and relate to specific subjects. Examples of the particular goals are those that pertain to say family matters, financial transactions, labour relations, witnessing and adjudication and the like.

Another binary classification of the *maqāṣid* is their division into definitive goals (*al-maqāṣid al-qaṭ'iyyah*) and speculative purposes (*al-maqāṣid al-ẓanniyyah*). The former goals are ones that are supported by clear evidence in the Qur'ān and Sunnah, such as protection of property and the honour of individuals, administration of justice, right to financial support among close relatives, and the like. The speculative goals fall below that rank and may be the subject of disagreement. To say, for example, that knowledge of *uṣūl al-fiqh* as one of the *maqāṣid* may well fall under the category of *'aql,* yet it is not a matter of certainty, and may have to be put under the speculative variety of *maqāṣid*. Similarly, to say that even the smallest amount of wine is just as forbidden and so intended by the Lawgiver as a larger amount is a doubtful position simply because it may not intoxicate, which is the effective cause of the prohibition at issue.

Al-Shāṭibī has also classified the *maqāṣid* into the aims and purposes of the Lawgiver (*maqāṣid al-shāri'*) and the human goals and purposes (*maqāṣid al-mukallaf*). To say that securing human welfare and benefit is God's illustrious purpose behind the laws of *Sharī'ah* illustrates the former, whereas seeking employment, for example, in order earn a living illustrates the latter class of *maqāṣid*.[18]

Maqāṣid have also been classified into the primary objectives (*al-maqāṣid al-aṣliyyah*) and subsidiary goals (*al-maqāṣid al-tabʻiyyah*). The former refer to the primary and normative goals that the Lawgiver, or a human agent, has originally intended and they constitute the basic purposes of the laws of *Sharīʻah* in the evaluation of human acts and conduct. For example the primary purpose of knowledge (*ʻilm*) and education is to know God and the proper manner of worshipping Him and also to explore and understand His creation. Similarly the primary goal of marriage is procreation, and the primary purpose of attending lectures is to increase one's knowledge.

The secondary goals are those which complement and support the primary ones. The secondary purpose of marriage, for example, is friendship and sexual satisfaction. The secondary purposes of seeking knowledge can be obtaining academic qualification, personal accomplishment and refinement of one's speech and conduct.[19] It is important therefore to observe the consistency of the secondary goals, with the normative and primary goals as severing the link between them could amount to a distortion that would be unacceptable. When marriage is used, for example, as a means only of sexual gratification without any loyalty and commitment, the purpose of marriage is distorted. Similarly, a ritual prayer that is performed merely for ostentation is not valid. This may be said generally of the laws of *Sharīʻah* and their valid objectives in that the laws of *Sharīʻah* must not be isolated from their proper purposes. Anyone who attempts to distort their consistency by recourse, for example, to legal stratagems (*ḥiyal*) would have distorted the *Sharīʻah* and such stratagems must therefore be avoided. Thus when someone makes a gift of his assets to another at the end of the year and receives back the same later, and the whole exercise is merely intended to avoid the obligation of *zakah* tax, his stratagem will not absolve him from the *zakah*. We do not wish to engage in the subject of stratagems on which the schools and jurists are not in agreement, but to say merely that when an ingenious device or method is used for a beneficial purpose without corrupt intentions, it is no longer a trick or *ḥīlah* but may be said to be a form of *ijtihād*.

Maqāṣid that relate evidently to *ḍarūriyat* may be regarded as definitive (*qaṭʻi*). Those which are identified by induction (*istiqrā'*) from the clear injunctions (*nuṣūṣ*) may also be added to this category.

As for *maqāṣid* that cannot be included in either of these two categories, they may still be seen as definitive if there is general consensus or clear legislation in their support. Additional *maqāṣid* that are identified outside this range may be classified as speculative (*ẓannī*) which may remain in that category unless they are elevated to the rank of definitive through consensus or legislation. In the event of a clash between these, the definitive *maqāṣid* will take priority over the speculative. An order of priority is also suggested among the definitive *maqāṣid* in favour of those which preserve faith and life, and protection of the family comes next, followed by intellect and property. A similar order of priority also applies between the essential *maqāṣid* which take priority over those which are deemed complementary and then those which are considered desirable.

Having said this, there still remains the residual question of how arbitrariness can be avoided in the identification of *maqāṣid*. For the *maqāṣid*, like the benefits (*masāliḥ*), are open-ended and still in need of a more accurate methodology to ensure unwarranted indulgence through personal or partisan bias in their identification. This is a matter to a large extent of correct understanding and it would seem that collective *ijtihād* and consultation would be the best recourse for ensuring accuracy in the identification of *maqāṣid*. It would certainly be reassuring to secure the advice and approval of a learned council as to the veracity of a *maqṣad* that is identified for the purpose of policymaking and legislation. This could be a standing parliamentary committee that comprises expertise in *Sharī'ah* and other disciplines and its task would be to verify, suggest and identify the more specific range of goals and purposes of *Sharī'ah* and law in conjunction with legislation and government policy.

Maqāṣid *and* Ijtihād

Having expounded his theory of the *maqāṣid*, Shāṭibī accentuated the knowledge of the *maqāṣid* as a prerequisite for attainment of the rank of a *mujtahid*. Those who neglect to acquire mastery of the *maqāṣid* do so to their own peril as it would make them liable to error in *ijtihād*. Included among these were the proponents of pernicious innovation (*ahl al-bid'ah*) who only looked at the apparent text of the Qur'ān without pondering over its objective and meaning. These innovators (an allusion to the Kharijites) held on to the intricate segments of the Qur'ān (*al-mutashābihāt*) and premised their conclusions on them.

They took a fragmented and atomized approach to the reading of the Qur'ān which failed to tie up the relevant parts of the text together. The leading '*ulamā*' have, on the other hand, viewed the *Sharī'ah* as a unity in which the detailed rules should be read in the light of their broader premises and objectives. Ṭāhir ibn 'Āshūr, the twentieth century author of another landmark work on the *maqāṣid*, bearing the title *Maqāṣid al-Sharī'ah al-Islāmiyyah*, has also confirmed that knowledge of the *maqāṣid* is indispensable to *ijtihād* in all of its manifestations.[20] Some '*ulamā*' who confined the scope of their *ijtihād* only to literal interpretations have found it possible, Ibn 'Āshūr added, to project a personal opinion into the words of the text and fell into error as they were out of line with the general spirit and purpose of the surrounding evidence.[21] This may be illustrated by reference to the different views of the '*ulamā*' on whether the *zakah* on commodities such as wheat and dates must be given in kind or could it also be given in their monetary equivalents. The Ḥanafis have validated giving of *zakah* in monetary equivalent but al-Shāfi'ī has held otherwise. The Ḥanafi view is founded on the analysis that the purpose of *zakah* is to satisfy the need of the poor and this can also be achieved by paying the monetary equivalent of a commodity. Ibn Qayyim al-Jawziyyah has likewise observed regarding *ṣadaqat al-fiṭr* (charity given at the end of the fasting month of Ramadan) that there are *ḥādīths* on the subject which refer sometimes to dates and at other times to raisins or food-grains as these were the staple food of Madinah and its environs at the time. The common purpose in all of these was to satisfy the need of the poor rather than to confine its payment in a particular commodity.[22]

To give another example, Imām Mālik (d. 795) was asked about a person who paid his *zakah* ahead of time, that is, prior to the expiry of one year, whether he was liable to pay it again at the end of the year. Mālik replied that he was and he drew an analogy with the ritual prayer (*ṣalah*). If someone performs his prayer before its due time, he must perform it again in its proper time. Subsequent Mālikī jurists, including Ibn al-'Arabī (d. 1148) and Ibn Rushd (d. 1126), have reversed this position and stated that early payment of *zakah* was permissible. There was, they added, a difference between *ṣalah* and *zakah* in that the former was bound to specific times, but no such time had been stipulated for the payment of *zakah*. Hence *zakah* may be paid earlier, especially if it is prepaid by only a few weeks or even longer.[23]

It will also be noted that on occasions *mujtahids* and judges have issued decisions in disputed matters, which were found upon further scrutiny to be in disharmony with the goals and objectives of *Sharī'ah.* Instances of this are encountered with reference to contracts. A contract may have been duly signed and made binding on the parties and only then is it found to be unfair to one of the parties due to some unexpected change of circumstance. In that eventuality the judge and *mujtahid* can hardly ignore the subsequent changes and insist merely on the obligatoriness of the said contract on purely formal grounds. For a contract is no longer the governing law of contracting parties if it proves to be an instrument of injustice. Such a contract must be set aside, and justice, which is the goal and *maqṣad* of the Lawgiver, must be given priority over an untenable contract.[24] Instances of conflict between the overriding objectives of *Sharī'ah* and a particular ruling thereof can also arise with reference to the rulings of analogy (*qiyās*). A rigid adherence to *qiyās* in certain cases may lead to unsatisfactory results, hence recourse may be had to considerations of equity (*istiḥsān*) in order to obtain an alternative ruling that is in harmony with the objectives of *Sharī'ah.*[25]

Another feature of the *maqāṣid* which is important to *ijtihād* is the attention a *mujtahid* must pay to the end result and consequence of his ruling. For a *fatwā* or *ijtihād* would be deficient if it fails to contemplate its own consequences (*ma'ālāt*). We note in the Sunnah of the Prophet instances where the Prophet paid attention to the consequence of his ruling often in preference to other considerations. For example, the Prophet avoided changing the location of the Ka'bah to its original foundations which the patriarch Prophet Abraham had laid. The pre-Islamic Arabs of Makkah had evidently changed that location, and when 'Ā'ishah suggested to the Prophet that he could perhaps restore the Ka'bah to its original position, he responded: 'I would have done so if I didn't fear that this may induce our people into disbelief.'[26] In both of these cases, the Prophet did not take what would be thought to be the normal course, that is, to restore the Ka'bah to its original foundations because of the adverse consequences that were feared as a result of so doing.

The normal course in the context of crimes and penalties is, of course, to apply the punishment whenever the cause and occasion for it is present. There may be cases, however, where pardoning the offender appears a preferable course to take, and it is for the judge to pay attention to them and then reflect them in his judgement. Shāṭibī has in this connection drawn a subtle distinction between the normal *'illah* (effective cause) that invokes a particular ruling in a given case and what he terms as verification of the particular *'illah* (*taḥqīq al-manāṭ al-khāṣ*) in the issuing of judgement and *ijtihād*. The scholar and *mujtahid* may be investigating the normal *'illah* and identify it in reference, for example, to the uprightness of a witness, but such an enquiry may take a different course when it is related what might seem appropriate or inappropriate to a particular individual. The judge needs, therefore, to be learned not only in the law and specific evidence but must also have acumen and insight to render judgement that is enlightened by both the overall consequences and special circumstances of each case.[27]

CONCLUSION

The *maqāṣid* are undoubtedly rooted in the textual injuctions of the Qur'ān and the Sunnah, but they look mainly at the general philosophy and objectives of these injunctions, often beyond the particularities of the text. The focus is not so much on the words and sentences of the text as on its goal and purpose. By comparison with the legal theory of the sources, the *uṣūl al-fiqh*, the *maqāṣid* are not burdened with methodological technicality and literalist reading of the text. As such the *maqāṣid* integrate a degree of versatility and comprehension into the reading of *Sharīʿah*. At a time when some of the important doctrines of *uṣūl al-fiqh* such as general consensus (*ijmāʿ*), analogical reasoning (*qiyās*) and even *ijtihād* seem to be burdened with difficult conditions and requirements, the *maqāṣid* can provide a more convenient access to *Sharīʿah*. It is naturally meaningful to understand the broad outlines of the objectives of *Sharīʿah* in the first place before one tries to move on to the specifics. An adequate knowledge of *maqāṣid* thus equips the student of the *Sharīʿah* with insight and provides him with a theoretical framework in which the attempt to acquire detailed knowledge of its various doctrines can become more interesting and meaningful.

NOTES

1. For fuller details on some of these themes see Kamali, 'Issues in the Legal Theory of *Uṣūl*', 1–21; idem, 'Methodological Issues', 1–34; and '*Maqāṣid al-Sharīʿah*', 193–209.

2. Cf. al-Raysūnī, *Naẓariyyah,* 149.
3. al-Ghazāli, *al-Mustaṣfā*, I, 287.
4. Qaraḍāwī, *Madkhal*, 73.
5. 'Abd al-Salām, *Qawā'id* I, 8.
6. Ibn Taymiyyah, *Majmūah Fatawā*, 32:134.
7. Raysūni, *Naẓariyyah*, 44; al-Jābiri, *al-Dīn Wa'l-Dawlah,* 190.
8. Al-Jābiri, *al-Dīn Wa'l-Dawlah*, 173.
9. 'Atiyyah, *Naḥw Taf'īl Maqāṣid*, 10 ff.
10. al-Shāṭibī, *al-Muwāfaqāt fi Uṣūl al-Sharī'ah,* II, 393.
11. Ibid., III, 394
12. Ibid., II, 6; see also Ibn Qayyim, *I'lām al-Muwaqqī'in* vol. I; Qaraḍāwi, *Madkhal*, 8; al-Jābiri, *al-dīn Wa 'l-Dawlah*, 173.
13. Shāṭibī, *Muwāfaqāt*, I, 243; Qaraḍāwī, *Madkhal*, 64–5.
14. Shāṭibī, *Muwāfaqāt* II, 49–51; idem, *al-I'tiṣām*, II, 131–5.
15. Abū Hamid al-Ghazālī, *Shifa al-Ghalil*, 195.
16. Shāṭibī, *Muwāfaqāt*, III, 148.
17. Shāṭibī, *Muwāfaqāt*, II, 5 and II, 223; al-Khādimi, *'Ilm al-Maqāṣid*, 71 f.
18. Shāṭibī, *Muwāfaqāt* II, 400; see also al-Khādimi, *'Ilm al-Maqāṣid* 155 f.
19. Ibid., IV, 179.
20. al-Ṭāhir ibn Āshūr, *Maqāṣid al-Sharī'ah,* 15–16.
21. Ibid., 27.
22. Ibn Qayyim, *I'lām*, III, 12; Raysūnī, *Naẓariyyah*, 336.
23. Cf. Raysūnī, *Naẓariyyah*, 338–9.
24. Cf. al-Zuḥayli, *al-Fiqh al-Islāmī* IV, 32. See for detailed illustrations of this type of *Istiḥsān*, Kamali, *Jurisprudence*, 323.
25. See for details the chapter on *Istiḥsān* in Kamali, *Jurisprudence.*
26. Mālik ibn Anas, *al-Muwaṭṭā'*, *Kitāb al-ḥajj, Bāb Mā Jā' fi Binā' al Ka'bah*; Raysūnī, *Naẓariyyah*, 354.
27. Shāṭibī, *Muwāfaqāt*, IV, 97; *Madhkal*, 186–7.

7

LEGAL MAXIMS OF *FIQH* (*QAWĀ'ID AL-KULLIYYAH AL-FIQHIYYAH*)

This chapter introduces the Islamic legal maxims (*qawā'id kulliyyah fiqhiyyah*) side-by-side with three other related areas of interest, namely *al-ḍawābiṭ* (rules controlling specific themes), *al-furūq* (comparisons and contrasts), and *al-naẓariyyāt al-fiqhiyyah* (general theories of *fiqh*). Developed at a later stage, these genres of *fiqh* literature seek, on the whole, to consolidate the vast and sometimes unmanageable *corpus juris* of *fiqh* into brief theoretical statements. They provide concise entries into their respective themes that help to facilitate the task of both students and practitioners of Islamic law. Legal maxims are on the whole inter-scholastic, and disagreement over them among the legal schools is negligible. Legal maxims also closely relate to the *maqāṣid* and provide useful insights into the goals and purposes of *Sharī'ah* (*maqāṣid al-Sharī'ah*), so much so that some authors have subsumed them under the *maqāṣid.* Yet for reasons that will presently be explained, the legal maxims represent a latent development in the history of Islamic legal thought.

The discussion that follows begins with introductory information on the basic concept and scope of legal maxims. This is followed by a more detailed account of the leading five maxims which the jurists have seen as representative of the entire field saying that all the other maxims can be seen as a commentary on these five. Next we look into the history of legal maxims, and then provide an account of their subsidiary themes, the *ḍawābiṭ* (controllers), the *furūq* (comparisons and contrasts), the resemblances and similitudes (*al-ashbāh wa'l naẓā'ir*), and finally the legal theories, or *naẓariyyāt.*

CONCEPT AND SCOPE

Legal maxims are theoretical abstractions in the form usually of short epithetic statements that are expressive, often in a few words, of the goals and objectives of *Sharī'ah*. They consist mainly of a statement of principles derived from the detailed reading of the rules of *fiqh* on various themes. The *fiqh* has generally been developed by individual jurists in relationship to particular themes and issues in the course of history and differs, in this sense, from modern statutory law rules which are concise and devoid of detail. The detailed expositions of *fiqh* in turn enabled the jurists, at a later stage, to reduce them into abstract statements of principles. Legal maxims represent the culmination, in many ways, of cumulative progress which could not have been expected to take place at the formative stages of the development of *fiqh*. The actual wording of the maxims is occasionally taken from the Qur'ān or *ḥadīth* but is more often the work of leading jurists that have subsequently been refined by other writers throughout the ages. Currency and usage often provided the jurists with insight and enabled them in turn to take the wording of certain maxims to greater refinement and perfection.

Unless they affirm and reiterate a ruling of the Qur'ān or Sunnah, the legal maxims as such do not bind the judge and jurist, but they do provide a persuasive source of influence in the formulation of judicial decisions and *ijtihād*. Legal maxims, like legal theories, are designed primarily for better understanding of their subject matter rather than enforcement. A legal maxim differs, however, from a legal theory in that the former is limited in scope and does not seek to establish a theoretically self-contained framework over an entire discipline of learning. A theory of contract, or a constitutional theory, for example, is expected to offer a broad, coherent and comprehensive entry into its theme. We may have, on the other hand, numerous legal maxims in each of these areas.

Legal maxims are of two types. Firstly those which rehash or reiterate a particular text of the Qur'ān or Sunnah, in which case they carry greater authority. 'Hardship is to be alleviated' (*al-mashaqqatu tajlib al-taysīr*), for example, is a legal maxim which merely paraphrases parallel Qur'ānic dicta on the theme of removal of hardship (*raf' al-ḥaraj*). Another legal maxim: 'actions are judged by the intentions behind them' (*innamā al-a'māl bi al-niyyāt*) in fact reiterates the exact wording of a *ḥadīth*. In his *Kitāb al-Ashbāh wa'l-Naẓā'ir*, which is a collection of legal maxims, Jalāl al-Dīn al-Ṣuyūṭi (d. 1505) has in numerous instances identified the origin, whether the Qur'ān, Sunnah or the precedent of Companions, of the legal maxims he has recorded.

The second variety of legal maxims are those which are formulated by the jurists themselves. Despite the general tendency in legal maxims to be inter-scholastic, jurists and schools are not unanimous and there are some on which the schools of law have disagreed. Legal maxims such as 'certainty may not be overruled by doubt' or '*ijtihād* does not apply in the presence of a clear text (*naṣṣ*)', or 'preventing an evil takes priority over securing a benefit', or 'absence of liability [i.e. innocence] is the normative state' are among the well-known maxims on which there is general agreement.

Legal maxims are different from *uṣūl al-fiqh* (roots and sources of *fiqh*) in that the maxims are based on the *fiqh* itself and represent rules and principles that are derived from the reading of the detailed rules of *fiqh* on various themes. The *uṣūl al-fiqh* is concerned with the sources of law, the rules of interpretation, methodology of legal reasoning, the meaning and implication of commands and prohibition and so forth. A maxim is defined, on the other hand, as 'a general rule which applies to all or most of its related particulars'.[1] This definition, attributed to Tāj al-Dīn al-Subkī (d. 1370) was generally adopted by later scholars. Legal maxims are usually articulated in incisive literary style. It is due partly to the abstract and generalized terms of their language that legal maxims are hardly without some exceptions or situations to which they do not apply even if their wording might suggest otherwise. Some would even say that legal maxims are in the nature of probabilities (*aghlabiyyah*) that may or may not apply to cases to which they apparently apply. Some writers have held that in the legal field, a maxim is only predominantly valid, whereas in certain other fields such as grammar, it is valid as a matter of certainty. It is due to their versatility and comprehensive language that legal maxims tend to encapsulate the broader concepts and characteristics of *Sharī'ah*. They tend to provide a bird's-eye view of their subject matter in imaginative ways without engaging in burdensome details.

A legal maxim is reflective of a consolidated reading of *fiqh* and it is in this sense different from what is known as *al-ḍābiṭah* (a controller) which is somewhat limited in scope and controls the particulars of a single theme or chapter of *fiqh*. *Ḍābiṭah* is thus confined to individual topics such as cleanliness (*ṭahārah*), maintenance (*nafaqah*), paternity and fosterage (*al-riḍā'*) and as such does not apply to other subjects. An example of a *ḍābiṭah* is 'marriage does not carry suspension'; and with reference to cleanliness, 'when the water reaches two feet, it does not carry dirt'.[2] An example of a legal maxim, on the other hand, is 'the affairs of the imam concerning his subjects are judged by reference to *maṣlaḥah*' (*amr al-imām fi shu'ūn al-ra'iyyah manūṭ bi'l-maṣlaḥah*). The theme here is more general without any specification of the affairs of the people or the activities of the imām. Similarly, when it is said, in another maxim, that 'acts are judged by their underlying intentions', the subject is not specified and it is as such a maxim (*qā'idah*) and not a *ḍābiṭah* of specific import. Having drawn a distinction between *ḍābiṭah* and *qā'idah*, we note, however, that legal maxims also vary in respect of the level of abstraction and the scope which they cover. Some legal maxims are of general import whereas others might apply to a particular area of *fiqh* such as the *'ibādāt*, the *mu'āmalāt*, contracts, litigation, court proceedings and so forth. Some of the more specific maxims may qualify as a *ḍābiṭah* rather than a maxim proper, as the distinction between them is not always clear or regularly observed.

THE FIVE LEADING MAXIMS

The most comprehensive and broadly based of all maxims are placed under the heading of '*al-qawā'id al-fiqhiyyah al-aṣliyyah*' or the normative legal maxims that apply to the entire range of *fiqh* without any specification, and the legal schools are generally in agreement over them. Maxims such as 'harm must be eliminated' (*al-ḍararu yuzāl*) (*Mejelle*, Art. 20) and 'acts are judged by their goals and purposes' (*al-umūr bi-maqāṣidihā*) (*Mejelle*, Art. 2) belong to this category of maxims. Being the first codified collection of the Islamic law of transactions, the *Mejelle* was compiled by the Ottoman Turks in (1850) articles drawn mainly from the Hanafi sources of Islamic law. It was completed in 1876 and although Turkey itself abandoned the *Mejelle* within a decade of its compilation, the work has remained in use as a standard reference on Hanafi jurisprudence in many Muslim countries ever since.

The five legal maxims are deemed as the most comprehensive of all on the analysis apparently that they grasp between them the essence of the *Sharīʻah* as a whole and the rest are said to be simply an elaboration of these. Two of these have just been quoted. The other three are as follows:

> 'Certainty is not overruled by doubt' (*al-yaq n lā yazālu bil-shakk*) (*Mejelle*, Art. 4)
> 'hardship begets facility' (*al-mashaqqatu tajlib al-taysīr*) (*Mejelle*, Art. 17)
> 'custom is the basis of judgment' (*al-ʻādatu muuḥakkamtun*) (*Mejelle,* Art. 36).

Each of these will be discussed separately in the following pages.

The first of these may be illustrated with reference to the state of ritual purity (*ṭahārah*). If a person has taken ablution (*wuḍū'*) and knows that with certainty but doubt occurs to him later as to the continuity of his *wuḍū'*, the certainty prevails over doubt and his *wuḍū'* is deemed to be intact. According to another but similar maxim, 'knowledge that is based in certainty is to be differentiated from manifest knowledge that is based on probability only' (*yufarraqu bayn al-cilmi idhā thabata ẓāhiran we baynahu idhā thabata yaq nan*). For example, when the judge adjudicates on the basis of certainty, but later it appears that he might have erred in his judgement, if his initial decision is based on clear text and consensus, it would not be subjected to review on the basis of a mere probability.[3] Similarly a missing person (*mafqūd*) of unknown wherebouts is presumed to be alive, as this is the certainty that is known about him before his disappearance. The certainty here shall prevail and no claim of his death would validate distribution of his assets among his heirs until his death is proven by clear evidence. A doubtful claim of his death is thus not allowed to overrule what is deemed to be certain.[4]

Other supplementary maxims of a more specified scope that are subsumed by the maxim of certainty include the following: 'The norm [of *Sharīʻah*] is that of non-liability' (*al-aṣlu barā'at al-dhimmah*). This is equivalent, although perhaps a more general one, to what is known as the presumption of innocence. This latter expression relates primarily to criminal procedure, whereas the non-liability maxim of *fiqh* also extends to civil litigation and to religious matters generally. The normative state, or the state of certainty for that matter, is that people are not liable, unless it is proven that they are and until this proof is forthcoming, to attribute guilt to anyone is treated as doubtful. Certainty can, in other words, only be overruled by certainty, not by doubt.

Another supplementary maxim here is the norm that presumes the continued validity of the *status quo ante* until we know there is a change: 'The norm is that the *status quo* remains as it was before' (*al-aṣl baqā' mā kāna 'alā mā kāna*), and it would be presumed to continue until it is proven to have changed. An example of this is the wife's right to maintenance which the *Sharī'ah* has determined; when she claims that her husband failed to maintain her, her claim will command credibility. For the norm here is her continued entitlement to maintenance for as long as she remains married to him. Similarly when one of the contracting parties claims that the contract was concluded under duress and the other denies this, this latter claim will be upheld because absence of duress is the normal state, or *status quo*, which can only be rebutted by evidence.[5] According to yet another supplementary maxim: 'The norm in regard to things is that of permissibility' (*al-aṣlu fi'l-ashyā' al-ibāḥah*). Permissibility in other words is the natural state and will therefore prevail until there is evidence to warrant a departure from that position. This maxim is also based on a general reading of the relevant evidence of the Qur'ān and Sunnah. Thus when we read in the Qur'ān that God Most High 'has created all that is in the earth for your benefit' (2:29), and also the *ḥadīth*: 'whatever God has made *ḥalāl* is *ḥalāl* and whatever that He rendered *ḥarām* is *ḥarām*, and whatever concerning which He has remained silent is forgiven' – the conclusion is drawn that we are allowed to utilize the resources of the earth for our benefit and unless something is specifically declared forbidden, it is presumed to be permissible.

'*Al-ḍararu yuzāl* – harm must be eliminated' is one of the leading five maxims and it is a derivative, in turn, of the renowned *ḥadīth* '*lā ḍarara wa lā ḍirār* – let there be no infliction of harm nor its reciprocation'. This *ḥadīth* has also been adopted as a legal maxim in precisely the same words as the *ḥadīth* itself.[6] A practical illustration of this *ḥadīth*-cum-legal maxim is as follows: Suppose that someone opens a window in his house which violates the privacy of his neighbour's house, especially that of its female inhabitants. This is a harmful act which should not have been attempted in the first place and may call for legal action and remedy. But it would be contrary to the maxim under review for the neighbour to reciprocate the harmful act by opening a window in his own property that similarly violates the privacy of the first neighbour.

A similar manifestation of the maxim that harm must be eliminated is the validation of the option of defect (*khiyār al-'ayb*) in Islamic law, which is designed to protect the buyer against harm. Thus when person A buys a car and then discovers that it is substantially defective, he has the option to revoke the contract. For there is a legal presumption under the *Sharī'ah* that the buyer concluded the contract on condition that the object he bought was not defective.

The *ḥadīth* of '*lā ḍarar*' has given rise to a number of additional maxims on the subject of *ḍarar*. To quote but a few, it is provided in a maxim: 'A greater harm is eliminated by [tolerating] a lesser one' (*al-ḍarar al-ashadd yuzālu bi'l-ḍarar al-akhaff*). For example, the law permits compelling the debtor or one who is responsible to support a close relative, to fulfil their obligations and to give what they must, even if it means inflicting some hardship on them. According to another maxim, 'harm may not be eliminated by its equivalent' (*al-ḍarar lā yuzālu bi-mithlih*). (*Mejelle*, Art. 25). This may also be illustrated by the example above of '*lā ḍarara wa lā-ḍirār*'.

Another maxim on *ḍarar* has it that 'harm cannot establish a precedent' (*al-ḍararu lā yakūnu qad man*). Lapse of time, in other words, cannot justify tolerance of a *ḍarar*. For example, waste disposal that pollutes a public passage should be stopped regardless as to how long it has been tolerated. And then also that 'harm is to be eliminated within reasonable bounds' (*al-ḍarar yudfa'u bi-qadr al-imkān*). For example, if a thief can be stopped by the blow of a stick, striking him with a sword should not be attempted to obstruct him. According to yet another maxim 'harm to an individual is tolerated in order to prevent a harm to the public' (*yutaḥammalu al-ḍarar al-khāṣ li-daf' al-ḍarar al-'āmm*) (*Mejelle*, Art. 26).[7] For example, the law permits interdiction on an adult and competent person, including an ignorant physician, or a fraudulent lawyer, in order to protect the public, notwithstanding the harm this might inflict on such individuals.

It is stated in the *Mejelle* that legal maxims are designed to facilitate a better understanding of the *Sharī'ah* and the judge may not base his judgement on them unless the maxim in question is derived from the Qur'ān or *ḥadīth* or supported by other evidence.[8] This is in contrast, however, with the view of Shihāb al-Dīn al-Qarāfi who held that a judicial decision is reversible if it violates a generally accepted maxim.[9] The '*ulamā*' have generally considered the maxims of *fiqh* to be significantly conducive to *ijtihād*, and they may naturally be utilized by the judge and *mujtahid* as persuasive evidence; it is just that they are broad guidelines whereas judicial orders need to be founded in specific evidence that is directly relevant to the subject of adjudication. Since most of the legal maxims are expounded in the form of generalized statements, they hardly apply in an exclusive sense and often admit exceptions and particularization. Instances of this were often noted by the jurists, especially in cases when a particular legal maxim failed to apply to a situation that evidently fell within its ambit, then they attempted to formulate a subsidiary maxim to cover those particular cases.

Legal maxims were developed gradually and the history of their development in a general sense is parallel with that of the *fiqh* itself. More specifically, however, these were developed mainly during the era of imitation (*taqlīd*) as they are in the nature of extraction (*takhrīj*) of guidelines from the detailed literature of *fiqh* that were contributed during the first three centuries of Islamic scholarship, known as the era of *ijtihād*.[10]

The *ḥadīth* of *lā ḍarar* has also been used as basic authority for legal maxims on the subject of necessity (*ḍarūrah*). I refer here to only two, the first of which proclaims that 'necessity makes the unlawful lawful' (*al-ḍarūrāt tubīḥ al-mahẓūrāt*).[11] It is on this basis that the jurists validate demolition of an intervening house in order to prevent spread of fire to adjacent buildings, just as they validate dumping of the cargo of an overloaded ship in order to prevent danger (or *ḍarar*) to the life of its passengers. Another maxim on necessity declares that 'necessity is measured in accordance with its true proportions' (*al-ḍarūrat tuqaddaru bi-qadrihā*). Thus if the court orders the sale of assets of a negligent debtor in order to pay his creditors, it must begin with the sale of his movable goods, if this would suffice to clear the debts, before ordering the sale of his real property.[12]

The maxim 'hardship begets facility' (*al-mashaqqatu tajlib al-taysīr*) is, in turn, a rehash of the Qur'ānic verses: 'God intends for you ease and He does not intend to put you in hardship' (2:185), and 'God does not intend to inflict hardship on you' (5:6) – a theme which also occurs in a number of *ḥadīths*. The jurists have utilized this evidence in support of the many concessions that are granted to the disabled and the sick in the sphere of religious duties as well as civil transactions. With reference to the option of stipulation (*khiyār al-sharṭ*), for example, there is a *ḥadīth* which validates such an option for three days, that is, if the buyer wishes to reserve for himself three days before ratifying a sale. The jurists have then reasoned that this period may be extended to weeks or even months depending on the type of goods that are bought and the position of the buyer who may need a longer period for investigation. According to another, but still related, legal maxim an opening must be found when a matter becomes very difficult (*idhā ḍāq al-amru ittasa'a*). For example, a debtor who accedes to his obligation but is unable to pay must be given time, if this would enable him to clear his debt. The same logic would validate, on the other hand, killing a violent thief if a lesser threat or action is not likely to put a stop to his evil. The judge may likewise admit the best available witnesses even if some doubt as to their uprightness (*'adālah*) persists, if this is deemed to facilitate justice in stressful situations. The maxim under review is also related to the subject of necessity and its related maxim, as quoted above, that 'necessity makes the unlawful lawful'.[13]

The maxim 'acts are judged by their goals and purposes' (*al-umūr bi-maqāṣidihā*) is also a rehash of the renowned *ḥadīth* 'acts are valued in accordance with their underlying intentions' (*innamā al-a'māl bil-niyyāt*). This is a comprehensive maxim with wide implications that the '*ulamā*' have discussed in various areas, including devotional matters, commercial transactions and crime. The element of intent often plays a crucial role in differentiating, for example, a murder from erroneous killing, theft from inculpable appropriation of property, and the figurative words that a husband may utter in order to conclude the occurrence or otherwise of a divorce. To give another example, when someone takes possession of the lost property of another, he could qualify either as a trustee if he intended to return it to its owner, or as a usurper if he intended to keep it unlawfully. Similarly when a person lays a net, or digs a pit, in his own property, and a bird or animal is consequently caught, the game would belong to him if he intended to hunt, but if the net was laid in order to prevent entry, or the pit was intended for some drainage purposes, then the game caught is not presumed to have fallen into his ownership, and it would consequently be lawful for others to take.[14]

The last of the leading five maxims that 'custom is the basis of judgement' is again based on the statement of the Companion, 'Abd Allah Ibn Mas'ūd: 'what the Muslims deem to be good is good in the eyes of God'. This is sometimes identified as an elevated (*marfū'*) *ḥadīth* as the Prophet had himself on numerous occasions upheld customary practices of Arabian society. The court is accordingly authorized to base its judgement on custom in matters which are not regulated by the text, provided that the custom at issue is current, predominant among people and is not in conflict with the principles of *Sharī'ah*. A custom which runs contrary to *Sharī'ah* and reason is therefore precluded. Several other subsidiary maxims have been derived from this, including the one which proclaims 'what is determined by custom is tantamount to a contractual stipulation' (*al-ma'rūf 'urfan ka'l-mashrūṭ sharṭan*) (*Mejelle*, Art. 42). Thus when the contract does not regulate a matter which is otherwise regulated by custom, the customary rule would be presumed to apply. Similarly when someone rents a house or a car, he should use it according to what is customary and familiar, even if the detailed manner of its use is not regulated in the contract. To give yet another example, when the father of a bride gives her a wedding gift of say a set of furniture and later claims that it was a temporary loan (*'āriyah*) and not a gift (*hibbah*) and there is no evidence to prove the claim, credibility would be given to the prevailing custom. If it is found that the father customarily gave such items as gift on such occasions, it would be counted as a gift, even if the father claimed otherwise.[15]

General custom qualifies as a basis of judgement and many jurists have accorded the same value to customs that are confined to a particular area and locality. Technically, however, only the general custom has the strength to take priority over the rulings of analogy (*qiyās*).[16] Custom has thus validated the plucking of ripened fruit that is likely to go to waste, should there be no impediment and no one is there to collect it. This is contrary to normal rules which do not permit taking the property of others. Similarly, people tend to weigh and measure goods and commodities differently in different places, and customary practices concerning them will be recognized by the courts in the locality concerned even if such practices happen to be contrary to normal rules.[17]

According to a parallel, although differently worded, legal maxim, 'the usage of people is a proof that must be followed' (*isti'māl al-nāsi hujjatun yajib al-'amalu bihā*).[18] The word *isti'māl* in this maxim is synonymous with *'ādah* and this maxim is said to contemplate linguistic usages that concern the meaning of words, whether literal, metaphorical, juridical etc. Which of these meanings, if any, should prevail in the event of a conflict arising between them is of concern to this maxim. The first of the two maxims under review (i.e. *al-'ādatu muḥakkamatun*) is thus concerned with actual practices, whereas the second mainly relates to the linguistic usages of words and their meanings. According to yet another supplementary maxim, 'the literal is abandoned in favour of the customary' (*al-ḥaqīqatu tutraku bi-dalālat al-'ādah*) (*Mejelle*, Art. 40). For example, when someone takes an oath that he will never 'set foot' in so-and-so's house, but then he only technically sets his foot in that house without entering it, he will not be liable to an expiation (*kaffārah*) for breaking oath. This is because customarily the expression means entering the house and not the literal meaning that it conveys.[19]

The maxim which declares 'profit follows responsibility' (*al-kharāj bil-ḍamān*)[20] is a direct rendering of a *ḥadīth* in identical words. Thus the yield of trees and animals, etc., belong to those who are responsible for their upkeep and maintenance. Suppose that person A who has bought a machine decides to return it to the seller when he finds it to be defective. Suppose also that the machine has yielded profit during the interval when it was with A, does A have to return the profit he made through the use of the machine to the seller? By applying the legal maxim before us, the answer is that A may keep the profit as the machine was his responsibility during the interval and he would have been responsible for its destruction and loss before he returned it to the seller.[21]

The maxim that a ruling of '*ijtihād* is not reversed by its equivalent' (*al-ijtihād la yunqaḍ bi-mithlih*)[22] has, in turn, been attributed to a statement of the caliph 'Umar Ibn al-Khaṭṭāb which is also upheld by the consensus of the Companions. Supposing a judge has adjudicated a dispute on the basis of his own *ijtihād,* that is, in the absence of a clear text to determine the issue. Then he retires and another judge whether of the same rank or at the appellate level, looks into the case and the latter's *ijtihād* leads him to a different conclusion on the same issue. Provided that the initial decision does not violate any of the rules that govern the propriety of *ijtihād*, a mere difference of opinion on the part of the new judge, or a different *ijtihād* he might have attempted, does not affect the authority of the initial *ijtihād*, simply because one ruling of *ijtihād* is not reversible by another ruling of *ijtihād*. It is further noted that the caliph 'Umar had ruled, in one or two similar cases, contrary to what his predecessor Abū Bakr had done but he did not attempt to declare Abū Bakr's ruling invalid on the analysis that his own *ijtihād* was not necessarily better than that of Abū Bakr.[23]

HISTORY OF LEGAL MAXIMS

Historically, the Ḥanafi jurists were the first to formulate legal maxims. An early Iraqi jurist, Sufyān Ibn Ṭāhir al-Dabbās, collated the first seventeen maxims, and his younger contemporary, Abū al-Ḥassan ʻUbayd Allah Ibn al-Ḥusayn al-Karkhī (d. 951) increased this to thirty-nine. Al-Karkhī's work, entitled *Uṣūl al-Karkhī*, is regarded as an authoritative precursor on the subject among the Ḥanafis, although some scholars regard it as a work in the genre of *uṣul al-fiqh* – as might have been suggested by its title. A more relevant explanation for that title was probably that every one of the thirty-nine legal maxims in it was identified as an *aṣl* (pl. *uṣūl*). Al-Karkhī's collection thus began by recording the first *aṣl* (norm): 'What is proven with certainty may not be overruled by doubt', and it ended with the *aṣl* that 'explanation to a speech is credible for as long as it is given at a time when it can be considered valid, but not otherwise' (*al-aṣlu anna'l-bayān yuʻtabaru bil-ibtidā', in ṣaḥḥa al-ibtidā', wa illā fa-lā*). This may be illustrated as follows: suppose a man divorces two of his wives in a single pronouncement such as: 'you are both divorced'. Later he elaborates that he only meant that one of them be divorced by triple *ṭalāq*. This explanation will be credible only during the probation period of *ʻiddah*, but it will not carry any weight if it is given after that period.[24] Some of the early maxims that were compiled also included the following: 'The norm is that the affairs of Muslims are presumed to be upright and good unless the opposite emerges to be the case.' What it means is that acts, transactions and relations among people should not be given a negative interpretation that verges on suspicion and mistrust, unless there is evidence to suggest the opposite. Another maxim has it that 'question and answer proceed on that which is widespread and common and not on what is unfamiliar and rare'. Once again, if we were to interpret a speech and enquire into its implications, we should proceed on that which is widespread and commonly understood as opposed to what might be said to be a rare understanding and interpretation. And we read in another maxim that 'prevention of evil takes priority over the attraction of benefit' (*dar' al-mafāsid awlā min jalb al-manāfiʻ*). The earliest collection of maxims also included the five leading maxims discussed above.[25]

Al-Karkhī's collection, which is one of the earliest on record, is not all articulated in the incisive and eloquent style that is typically associated with maxims.[26] Some of al-Karkhī's renderings tend to be verbose. His equivalant of the concise maxim 'custom is a basis of judgement', for example, uses twenty-five words to deliver the same message. Many scholars from various schools added to legal maxims over time and the total number of *qawā'id* and *ḍawābit* eventually exceeded twelve hundred.

Next to the Ḥanafis, the Shāfi'īs, and then following them, the Ḥanbalis, then the Mālikis, in this order, as al-Zarqā has noted, added their contributions to the literature on legal maxims. The leading Shāfi'ī scholar, 'Izz al-Dīn 'Abd al-Salām's (d. 1262) *Qawā'id al-Aḥkām fi Maṣāliḥ al-Anām* is noted as one of the salient contributions to this field, and so is 'Abd al-Raḥmān ibn Rajab al-Hanbali's (d. 1392) work *Al-Qawā'id*, both of which have been highly acclaimed. Yet in terms of conciseness and style, the *Mejelle-i Ahkam Adliyye,* an Islamic law code written by a group of Turkish scholars under the supervision of Ahmad Cevdet Pasha (d. 1895), the then Minister of Justice in the 1870s, is said to represent the most advanced stage in the compilation of legal maxims. The introductory section of the *Mejelle* only records ninety-nine legal maxims, which have in turn been elaborated in many other works. One such work is Muḥammad al-Zarqā with the title *Sharḥ al-Qawā'id al-Fiqhiyyah* (1983). The son of this author, and also his commentator, Muṣṭafā al-Zarqā, has noted, however, that the *Mejelle* selection does not necessarily represent a self-contained collection of all the leading maxims. Whereas many fall in that category, there are some which are decidedly subsidiary. The *Mejelle* selection is also not systematic in that maxims which relate to one another do not appear in clusters, but tend to appear on a stand-alone kind of arrangement.[27] The next major attempt on the subject during the Ottoman caliphate was made by Muḥammad Nas b of Damascus. He arranged the maxims according to the headings found in the *fiqh* books and titled his work, *al-Farā'id al-Bahiyyah fi'l-Qawā'id wa'l-Fawā'id al-Fiqhiyyah.*

The development of this branch of *fiqh* is in many ways related to the general awareness of the '*ulamā*' over the somewhat piecemeal and fragmented style of the *fiqh* literature which, like the Roman juristic writings, is issue-oriented and short of theoretical abstraction of governing principles. This is related, in turn, to the fact that *fiqh* was mainly developed by private jurists who were not acting on behalf of governments and institutions that might have exerted a unifying influence. The maxims filled that gap to some extent and provided a set of general guidelines into an otherwise diverse discipline that combined an impressive variety of schools and influences in its fold.

Islamic jurisprudence is also textualist as it is guided by the textual injunctions of the Qur'ān and Sunnah. In developing the law, the jurists have shown the tendency to confine the range of their expositions to the given terms of the text. Theoretical generalization of ideas was generally viewed with caution *vis-à-vis* the overriding authority of the text, and attention was focused on the correct interpretation of the text rather than on developing general theories. Questions are being asked to this day whether Islamic law has a constitutional theory, a theory of contract, or a theory of ownership.

It is only in recent times that Muslim scholars began to write concise yet self-contained expositions of the law in these areas, as I shall presently explain, but first I turn to *al-ashbāh wa'l-naẓā'ir*.

RESEMBLANCES AND SIMILITUDES (*AL-ASHBĀH WA'L NAẒĀ'IR*)

This genre of literature emerged in the writings of the '*ulamā*' sometime during the fourteenth century, well after the formation of the *madhāhib*. Many scholars began to refer to the study of maxims as *al-ashbāh wa'l naẓā'ir*. The term evidently originated in the renowned letter of the caliph 'Umar al-Khaṭṭāb addressed to judge Abū Mūsa al-Ash'ari of Baṣra in which the latter was instructed to 'ascertain the examples and resemblances (*al-ashbāh*) and adduce matters to their likes in giving judgement'. The word *naẓā'ir* (similitudes) does not occur in the letter but was apparently added. *Al-ashbāh wal-naẓā'ir* was later chosen by Tāj al-Dīn al-Subkī, who wrote an important work on legal maxims, as the title of his book. Jalāl al-Dīn al-Suyūṭ (d. 1505) and Zayn al-'Ābidīn Ibn Nujaym al-Ḥanafi (d. 1562) also wrote works that closely resembled one another, both bearing the title *al-Ashbāh wal-Naẓā'ir*. They relied mainly on al-Subkī's writings, with certain modifications that were reflective perhaps, of their respective scholastic orientations. At the beginning of every maxim that he discussed, Al-Suyūṭī identified the source evidence from which the maxim was derived and then added illustration and analysis. Al-Suyūṭī devoted the first chapter of his *al-Ashbāh wa'l-Naẓā'ir* to the five leading maxims and the *fiqhi* issues to which they applied. Then he discussed, in the second chapter, forty other maxims of a more specific type that are derived from the first five. Another chapter in that work is devoted to a selection of most useful and recurrent maxims in the works of *fiqh*, and yet another which discusses maxims on which the jurists are in disagreement. The next two chapters in al-Suyūṭī's work put together clusters of maxims that relate to one another, and those that resemble one another in some ways. The last chapter adds miscellaneous maxims that are not classified in any manner.[28]

Some of the leading maxims that al-Suyūṭī recorded were as follows: 'private authority is stronger than public authority' (*al-wilāyah al-khāṣṣah aqwā min al-wilāyah al-'āmmah*)[29] which evidently means that the authority, for example, of the parent and guardian over the child is stronger to that of the ruler and the judge. Another maxim in al-Suyūṭī declared 'no speech is attributed to one who has remained silent' (*lā-yunsab li'l-sākit qawl*).[30] In a similar vein the maxim 'the attachment follows the principal' (*al-tābi' tābi'*), obviously means that in reference, for example, to contracts and transactions, things which belong to one another may not be separated: one does not sell a yet-to-be born animal separately from its mother, or a living room separately from the house.[31]

Ibn Nujaym divided the legal maxims into two categories of normative or leading maxims, and subsidiary maxims. He only placed six under the former and nineteen under the latter, but discussed a number of other subsidiary rules and maxims in his detailed elaboration and analysis. The sixth leading maxim of Ibn Nujaym that he added to the leading five, was that 'no spiritual reward accrues without intention' (*la thawāb illā bi'l-niyyah*), which is why the ritual prayer, and most other acts of devotion, are preceded by a statement of intention, or *niyyah*.[32] The introductory part of the Ottoman *Mejelle*, which contains ninety-nine legal maxims, was mainly derived from *Al-Ashbāh Wa'l-Naẓā'ir* of Ibn Nujaym.

Despite the general tendency in maxims to be inter-scholastic, the Ja'fari school of Shī'ah has its own collection of legal maxims. Yet notwithstanding some differences of style, the thematic arrangement in that collection closely resembles those of their Sunni counterparts. The first Shī'ite work on maxims was that of 'Allāmah al-Ḥilli (d. 1325) entitled *Al-Qawā'id*, followed by al-Shahīd al-Awwal Jamāl al-Dīn al-'Āmili's (d. 1381) *Al-Qawā'id wa'l-Fawā'id*, which compiled over three hundred maxims, and many more works that elaborated and enhanced the earlier ones. The more recent work of Muḥammad al-Ḥusayn Kāshif al-Ghiṭā', bearing the title *Taḥrīr al-Mujallah,* is an abridgment and commentary on the Ottoman *Mejelle*. In this work, the author has commented on the first ninety-nine articles of the *Mejelle* out of which he selected forty-five as being the most important, and the rest he found to be overlapping and convergent or obscure; but he added eighty-two others to make up a total 127 maxims of current application and relevance especially to transactions and contracts. Al-Ghiṭā' went on to say however, that 'if we were to recount all the maxims that are referred to in the various chapters of *fiqh*, we can add up to five hundred or more'.[33]

COMPARISONS AND CONTRASTS (*AL-FURŪQ*)

Among other related developments of interest to law maxims is the *furūq* literature which occur in almost the opposite direction to that of resemblances and similitudes. The *furūq* literature which, as the word indicates, highlights differences between seemingly similar concepts, or those which have an aspect in common. The *furūq* literature specified the differences between some of the maxims that resembled one another but could be subtly distinguished in some respect. The Māliki jurist Shihāb al-Dīn al-Qarāfī's *Kitāb al-Furūq* discussed 548 maxims, and 274 differences (*furūq*) in this light, and it focuses on distinctions and differences between similar themes and ideas. Occasionally the word *qāʻidah* is used in reference to what is a *ḍābiṭah* or even a specific ruling of *fiqh*. Al-Qarāfī often compares two maxims that address similar themes but which involve subtle differences. He also explains the subjects of his enquiry by referring to its opposites as he believes that this is often a very effective way of highlighting the merits or demerits of particular ideas and maxims. His work is generally regarded as one of the best in the field.[34] Al-Zarqā has noted, however, that *al-Furūq* is not, strictly speaking, confined to legal maxims. This is because the book is dominated by comparisons and contrasts and engages in the explanation of basic *fiqh* themes and issues in a way that almost puts the work in the area of subtantive *fiqh* rather than the maxims of *fiqh*, which is a separate branch of *fiqh* in its own right.[35]

Examples of the *furūq* includes the distinctions between leasing (*ijārah*) and sale, between custody (*ḥaḍānah*) and guardianship (*wilāyah*), between testimony (*shahādah*) and narration (*riwāyah*), between verbal custom and actual custom (*al-'urf al-qawli*, *al-'urf al-fi'li*) and so forth. These are often expressed in rule-like statements that resemble *ḍabiṭah*s as they apply to specific themes, but named *al-furūq* as they usually compare similar themes and highlight the differences between them. Al-Qarāfī's approach represented a new development in the *qawā'id* literature. He has also discussed legal maxims in his other works, namely *Al-Dhakhīrah*, but more specifically in *Al-Iḥkām fi Tamyīz al-Fatāwā 'an al-Aḥkām*. The title itself is, it may be noted, a *furūq*-oriented title referring to differences between *fatāwū* (responsa) and judicial decisions. Ibn al-Shāṭ Qāsim bin 'Abd Allah al-Anṣāri's (d. 1322) work, *Idrār al-Shurūq 'alā Anwār al-Furūq*, is also a work on *furūq*, and smaller works of similar kind were written by some Sḥāfi'ī scholars.[36]

GENERAL THEORIES OF *FIQH* (*AL-NAẒARIYYĀT AL-FIQHIYYAH*)

The next development that may briefly be explained is relatively recent and appears in the modern writings of *fiqh* under the designation of general theories of *fiqh*. A theory in this context implies a self-contained and comprehensive treatment of an important area of the law, such as the theory of necessity, theory of ownership, theory of contract, and so forth. This level of theoretical development marks a departure from the earlier somewhat atomistic style of *fiqh* literature where topics were poorly classified and themes pertaining to a particular area were scattered in different places. The *naẓariyyāt* literature seeks to overcome that and offers a systematic treatment of its subject matter that aims to be self-contained and convenient to use.

The legal theories draw upon the combined resources of *fiqh* in all areas, including the law maxims, the controlling rules and the distinguishers. Yet the legal theories are not expected to reproduce the detailed formulation of these related branches, as theory-oriented works generally seek to be concise and clear of repetition and unnecessary detail; it also incorporates new methods of writing and research which are more effective and less time-consuming.

The *naẓariyyāt* literature is informed by modern methods of writing and research as it also seeks to advance and develop some of the substantive aspects of the *fiqh* doctrines. With regard to the law of contract, for example, 'Abd al-Razzāq al-Sanhūrī (d. 1971) has observed that the *fiqh* literature in this area is focused on the detailed exposition of a number of nominate contracts and treats each contract separately. A perusal of the relevant *fiqh* literature on contracts, al-Sanhūrī noted, leaves the reader askance as to (1) whether these could all be consolidated in order to highlight the features they all have in common; and (2) whether the *fiqh* validates contracts other than these; and (3) whether the *fiqh* recognizes the basic freedom of contract on the basis merely of an agreement which does not violate morality and public interest.[37] Questions of this nature are likely to receive attention in the *naẓariyyāt* literature, which is better consolidated and provide a comprehensive treatment of the theory of contracts.

The *naẓariyyāt* literature is not entirely without precedent in the *fiqh* works. With reference to the theory of contract, for example, we may note that significant progress had been made by the Ḥanbalī '*ulamā*', Ibn Taymiyyah (d. 1328) and his disciple, Ibn Qayyim al-Jawziyyah, whose contributions are widely acknowledged. Ibn Taymiyyah effectively departed from the earlier strictures over the nominate contracts and advanced a convincing discourse, through his own reading of the source evidence, that contracts need not be confined to a particular prototype or number.[38] The essence of all contracts is manifested in the agreement of the contracting parties, who may create new contracts, within or outside the ones that are already known, provided that they serve a lawful benefit and do not violate public policy and morals. Ibn Taymiyyah also wrote a book on legal maxims entitled *al-Qawā'id al-Nurāniyyah*, which treats the subject in an interesting way by looking at the law maxims under the main chapters of *fiqh*. The book thus devotes sections to cleanliness (*al-ṭahārah*), prayers, *zakah*, fasting, the *ḥajj*, and then to contracts and financial transactions, followed by sections on matrimony, etc., and discusses the relevant legal maxims under each heading. These are followed in each part by subsidiary rules (*dawābiṭ*) and disagreements, if any, that may exist concerning them, as well as the author's own views and suggested solutions to such disagreements.[39]

To pursue our discussion of the general theories, it may be added that considerable progress has been made in this area, not only in al-Sanhūrī's writings, but also by numerous scholars, both Arab and non-Arab, who have written widely on contracts and other major themes of *fiqh*. One should also note in this context the emergence of the encylopedias of *fiqh* in the latter part of the twentieth century which marked a milestone in development and succeeded in producing consolidated and reliable works of reference on *fiqh*, and these efforts are still continuing. Yet as a distinctive genre of *fiqh* literature the legal maxims are likely to remain an influential area of the legacy of *fiqh* notwithstanding the encyclopedias.

CONCLUSION

It is probably the abstract and synoptic character of legal maxims that gives them a degree of versatility and timelessness, borne out by the fact that one sees little changes or addition to the early compilations of legal maxims. Contemporary scholars seem to repeat the existing maxims and hardly any new ones have been added to the existing collections. Two factors come to mind to explain this. One is the continued domination of imitation (*taqlīd*) that has had a paralysing effect on the growth of *fiqh* and would probably have had a similar effect on legal maxims. Another and even greater disincentive in this connection has probably been the prevalence of statutory legislation, which seems to have taken on the role that was earlier played by legal maxims. The language and style of statutory legislation show a striking similarity to that of legal maxims as both tend to be concise, and devoid of details, illustration and ratiocination. What could earlier be said in a legal maxim can now be said in the text of a constitution, a civil code or other statutes. Yet these are partial explanations and it still remains to be said that legal maxims and statutes are neither identical nor a substitute for one another. Hence it may be advisable even to put the two side by side and find a supportive role for legal maxims that may supplement and substantiate statutory legislation in the *Sharī'ah*-dominated fields such as personal law and civil transactions.

The *Sharī'ah* law of personal status has remained to be the applied law of most Muslim countries, and development in Islamic banking, finance and insurance has also witnessed a revival of the *Sharī'ah* laws of *mu'āmalāt*. For purposes of better understanding, and consolidation of important *fiqh* concepts with statutory laws, legal maxims that relate to a particular *Sharī'ah*-related statute should, perhaps, be clustered together, somewhat similar to the Ottoman *Majelle*, and added as an appendix, introduction or explanatory memoranda to such statutes to play a role in their interpretation. This will provide *Sharī'ah* judges and lawyers with convenient access to relevant legal maxims and also give the readers and students of such laws a certain insight into the relevant *fiqh* concepts. What is proposed here is also likely in the long run to contribute towards the harmonization and uniformity of the *Sharī'ah* and civil laws.

NOTES

1. Cf. Maḥmaṣṣāni, *Falsafat,* 151; Muḥammad al-Zarqā, *Sharḥ al-Qawā'id*, 33.
2. Cf. al-Ṣābūnī, et al., *Madkhal*, 389.
3. al-Barikati, *Qawā'id al-Fiqh*, 142–3.
4. Cf. Zarqā, *Sharḥ al-Qawā'id*, 382.
5. Ṣābūnī, *al-Madkhal*, 389.
6. *Mejelle*, Art. 19.
7. See also al-Barikati, *Qawā'id al-Fiqh*, 88 and 139.
8. Cf. Maḥmaṣṣāni, *Falsafat*, 152; Zarqā, *Sharḥ al-Qawā'id*, 34.
9. al-Qarāfī, *Kitāb al-Furūq,* IV, 40; see also 'Aṭiyyah, *al-Tanẓīr*, 208.
10. Cf. Ṣābūnī, *Madkhal*, 398.
11. *Mejelle* Art. 17; see also Zarqā, *Sharḥ al-Qawā'id*, 157.
12. Cf. al-Ṣābūnī, *Madkhal*, 100.
13. Cf. Zarqā, *Sharḥ al-Qawā'id*, 163–4.
14. Idem 49.
15. Cf. Zarqā, *Sharḥ al-Qawā'id*, 238; al-Barikati, *Qawā'id,* 125.
16. See for detail Kamali, *Jurisprudence*, 370 f.
17. Cf. Zarqā, *Sharḥ al-Qawā'id*, 221.
18. *Mejelle*, Art, 37.
19. Cf. Kamali, *Jurisprudence*, 369 ff.
20. *Mejelle*, Art. 85. Another substantially similar maxim, albeit in different words, is 'liability for loss proceeds from one's entitlement to profit' (*al-ghanam bi'l-gharamu*). Cf. al-Barikati, *Qawā'id al-fiqh*, 94.
21. Cf. Zarqā, *Sharḥ al-Qawā'id*, 429.
22. *Mejelle*, Art. 16.
23. Cf. al-Barikati, *Qawā'id al-Fiqh*, 56.
24. Al-Barikati, *Qawā'id al-Fiqh*, 65; see also Abū Sulaymān, *Kitābat al-Baḥth*, II, 652.
25. Cf. al-Barikati, *Qawā'id al-Fiqh*, 56.
26. Cf. 'Aṭiyyah, *al-Tanẓīr*, 18; al-Ṣābūnī, *Madkhal*, 387.
27. Cf. Zarqā, *Sharḥ al-Qawā'id*, 43–4.
28. Cf. Abū Sulaymān, *Kitābat al-Baḥth,* II, 677.

29. *Mejelle*, Art. 58.
30. Idem, Art. 66.
31. Idem, Art. 47. See also Zarqā, *Sharḥ al-Qawā'īqāmat al-dīn*, 253.
32. Ibn Nujaym, *al-Ashbāh wa'l-Naẓā'ir*, 67 f.
33. Kāshif al-Ghiṭā', *Taḥrīr al-Mujallah*, 63; 'Aṭiyyah, *al-Tanẓīr*, 75; al-'abūnī, *Madkhal*, 39.
34. Cf. Abū Sulaymān, *Kitābat al-Baḥth*, II, 660.
35. Zarqā, *Sharḥ al-Qawā'id*, 42.
36. See for details 'Aṭiyyah, *al-Tanẓīr*, 131–2.
37. al-Ṣanhūrī, *Maṣādir al-ṭaq* 167, I, 78. see also al-Ṣabūnī, *Madkhal*, 380, n. 2.
38. Much to his credit, the manual that Ibn Taymiyyah wrote on the subject actually bore the title *Naẓariyyāt al-'Aqd* (Theory of Contract).
39. Cf. Abū Sulaymān, *Kitābat al-Baḥth*, II, 678.

8

INDEPENDENT REASONING (*IJTIHĀD*) AND JURISTIC OPINION (*FATWĀ*)

This chapter provides a review of the definition of *ijtihād* and the basic functions of *fatwā* and proposes certain adjustments in respect of their modern applications. It also reviews the methodology of *ijtihād* and the various formulas proposed for this purpose by the leading schools of Islamic law. The chapter then turns to a discussion of the problematics of both *ijtihād* and *fatwā* in modern times and makes suggestions for reform.

Ijtihād and *fatwā* are often used interchangeably, the main difference between them being that *ijtihād* has a greater juridical substance which explains its own evidential basis, whereas *fatwā* often consists of a verdict or opinion that is given in response to a particular question. It is not a requirement of *fatwā* to explain its evidential basis and it may be either very brief or in greater depth and detail. *Fatāwā* (responsa, pl. of *fatwā*) are often sought by individuals who seek a response or legal advice in the context of litigation or a public issue, and the response may be cursory and brief, consisting of a short reply to a question, agreement or disagreement. Where a *fatwā* addresses more complex issues, the jurist often feels the need to probe into the source evidence, in which case it may be equivalent to *ijtihād*. Neither *ijtihād* nor indeed *fatwā* binds the person or persons to whom they may be addressed, unless it is issued by a court in a case under its consideration, in which case the decision would carry a binding force. *Ijtihād* is to be carried out by a qualified person, namely the *mujtahid*, whereas *fatwā* may be issued by a *mujtahid* or by a scholar of lower standing.[1]

Ijtihād literally means striving or exertion; it is defined as the total expenditure of effort by a *mujtahid*, in order to infer, with a degree of probability, the rules of *Sharī'ah* from the detailed evidence in the sources. Two points may be noted in this definition: 1) *ijtihād* is conducted by a qualified jurist in *Sharī'ah*, namely the *mujtahid*; and 2) *ijtihād* is basically envisaged as an individual effort wherein the scholar or *mujtahid* exerts himself to the best of his ability in search of solution to an issue. This definition is evidently focused on the jurist/*mujtahid* who formulates *ijtihād* in his private capacity. This is a feature of the conventional theory of *ijtihād* that is not without some difficulties, as I shall presently elaborate.

Historically, *ijtihād* remained a concern of the private jurist and *mujtahid*. No procedure or machinery was attempted to institutionalize *ijtihād* and identify its *locus* and authority within the state organization. To define and identify the *mujtahid* and the role that *ijtihād* might play in the legislative processes of modern government still remain among the unresolved issues of *ijtihād*. The theory of *ijtihād* specified the qualifications of a *mujtahid* such as knowledge of the sources of *Sharī'ah*, knowledge of Arabic, familiarity with the prevailing customs of society, upright character, as well as the ability to formulate independent opinion and judgement. But the reality remained somewhat elusive and hardly any *mujtahid* volunteered openly to declare himself on attaining this rank. Identification of *mujtahids* by others has often occurred long after the demise of the scholars concerned. There was no procedure specifically designed for the purpose other than a general recognition of the ability and competence of individual scholars by the '*ulamā*' and the community at large. It is revealing to note, in al-Shawkānī's (d. 1839) discussion of *ijtihād*, a reference to Abū Ḥāmid al-Ghazālī (d. 1111), who is on record as having stated that the independent *mujtahid* had become extinct. Al-Shawkānī was obviously not convinced and tersely posed the question 'did al-Ghazālī not forget himself?'[2] Modesty being a moral virtue of Islam, and especially appealing in scholars of high standing, had apparently prompted al-Ghazāli to be almost self-effacing. But he was by no means an exception. As if *ijtihād* could offer solutions to all sorts of problems except defining/identifying its own carrier and agent!

Another problem we face at present is that despite the door of *ijtihād* having been declared wide open, we do not see any effective movement towards making *ijtihād* an engaging process of law and government. A great deal has been said about *ijtihād* for about a century, that is, ever since the days of al-Afghāni and 'Abduh, but the repeated calls for revivification of *ijtihād* have brought about only modest results. With regard to the qualifications that the theory of *ijtihād* has demanded of the *mujtahid*, it is often said that these are heavy and exacting. But this is, in my opinion, just another *taqlīd*-oriented assertion by those who wished to bring *ijtihād* to a close. The qualifications so stated were not excessive and were frequently fulfilled, as al-Shawkānī has stated, by a long series of prominent scholars across the centuries even during the era of *taqlīd*.[3] Furthermore, the uncertainties surrounding *ijtihād* have in modern times been exacerbated by the spread of secularism and the fact that the state has become the sole law-making authority in its own territorial domain. The *mujtahid* has no recognized status. But assuming that there is a certain adjustment of attitude as a result perhaps of the recent decades of Islamic resurgence, then it should be possible to devise a procedure which would integrate *ijtihād* in the legislative processes of government. Universities and legal professions in many Muslim countries are currently engaged in training lawyers and barristers in modern law streams.

To institute an effective programme of training for prospective *mujtahids*, which would integrate studies in both traditional and modern disciplines, should not be beyond the combined capabilities of these institutions. Unless the government takes an active interest in integrating *ijtihād* into its law-making process, *ijtihād* will remain isolated. 'Abd al-Wahhāb Khallāf is right in suggesting that the government in every Muslim country should specify certain conditions for attainment to the rank of *mujtahid* and make this contingent on obtaining a recognized certificate. This would enable every government to identify the *mujtahids* and to verify their views when the occasion so requires.[4]

Two other reform measures need to be taken in order to make *ijtihād* a viable proposition; first, *ijtihād* in modern times needs to be a collective endeavour so as to combine the skill and contribution, not only of the scholars of *Sharī'ah*, but of experts in various other disciplines. This is because acquiring a total mastery of all relevant skills that are important to contemporary society is difficult for any one individual to attain. We need to combine *ijtihād* with the Qur'ānic principle of consultation (*shūrā*) and make *ijtihād* a consultative process. Many observers have spoken in support of collective *ijtihād* although none has suggested discontinuation of *ijtihād* by individual scholars.[5] The private jurist and *mujtahid* should of course be able to exercise *ijtihād* and nothing should interfere with their basic right to do so. But if collective *ijtihād* were to be institutionalized it would naturally carry greater authority and weight. A basic framework for collective *ijtihād* was indeed proposed by Muhammad Iqbal (d. 1937) who suggested in his *Reconstruction of Religious Thought in Islam* that the power to carry out *ijtihād* and *ijmā'* should be vested in the Muslim legislative assembly. The substance of this proposal has since been echoed by numerous other commentators who have spoken in support of the institutionalization of both *ijmā'* and *ijtihād* within the fabric of modern government.

The second point to note is that *ijtihād* was seen as a juristic concept and the preserve therefore, of the jurist-*mujtahid*. This might have been due to the fact that *Sharī'ah* dominated nearly all other fields of Islamic scholarship, but *ijtihād* in the sense of self-exertion is a method of finding solutions to new issues in light of the goals and principles of Islam. It is in this sense a wider proposition which may be exercised by scholars of *Sharī'ah* as well as experts in other disciplines, provided that the person who attempts it acquires mastery of the relevant data, especially in the Qur'ān and Sunnah, pertaining to his subject.

We now propose to offer a new definition for *ijtihād* with a view mainly to overcome the difficulties we noted in the conventional theory of *ijtihād*, and hopefully to make *ijtihād* an integral part of the contemporary legislative processes. This is as follows: *ijtihād* is a creative and comprehensive intellectual effort by qualified individuals and groups to derive the juridical ruling on a given issue from the sources of *Sharī'ah* in the context of the prevailing circumstances of society.

The definition thus proposed incorporates the conventional definition of *ijtihād* but adds emphasis on two points: creative thinking, and the prevailing conditions of society. *Ijtihād* is designed to address new and unprecedented issues in the light of available guidelines in the sources. Creative intellectual exertion also means that existing ideas and teachings of others are not taken at face value nor imitated but scrutinized, and their relevance to new issues independently ascertained. Our proposed definition also departs from the postulate which made *ijtihād* the prerogative only of a *Sharī'ah* scholar-*mujtahid*. There is no reason why this should always be the case. For *ijtihād* may well be attempted collectively by scholars in *Sharī'ah* and other disciplines of vital importance to the community, hence the proviso that it must be comprehensive and inclusive of other viewpoints. Our proposed definition has also envisaged *ijtihād* as a collective endeavour and thus departs from the individualist and subjective bias of the conventional definition.

Ijtihād is the most important source of *Sharī'ah* next to the Qur'ān and Sunnah. The main difference between *ijtihād* and the revealed sources is that *ijtihād* proposes a continuous process of development whereas revelation of the Qur'ān and the Sunnah discontinued with the demise of the Prophet. *Ijtihād* thus remains as the principal instrument by which to relate the Qur'ān and Sunnah to the changing conditions of society.

As a vehicle of renewal and reform, *ijtihād* was always dominated by its dual concern of continuity and change: continuity with the given fundamentals of Islam while keeping pace also with the realities of social change. The two concerns of continuity and change thus characterize the history of *ijtihād* and the role it has played in the development of Islamic law.

METHODOLOGY OF *IJTIHĀD*

In their conduct of *ijtihād*, the Companions of the Prophet did not follow an elaborate methodology and procedure. They took their lead directly from the Qur'ān and Sunnah, and the public interest (*maṣlaḥah*). Their precedent and verdict, often arrived at through consultation and consensus, set a precedent for the next generation of '*ulamā*' and their followers in the succeeding generation, which paved the way, in turn, for the development of *ijmā'* (general consensus) as an important source of law next to the Qur'ān and Sunnah. The second generation of scholars, known as the *tābi'ūn,* further developed the existing legacy of the Companions but they were faced with more complex developments. This was manifested in the territorial expansion of the Umayyad state, the influence of foreign traditions, proliferation and plurality of schools and sects, and also the emergence of self-styled scholars of questionable competence. The '*ulamā*' saw these developments as a threat to the unity of the Muslim community and the integrity of *Sharī'ah* – hence the need for a methodology to regulate *ijtihād*. It was in no small measure due to proposing new methodologies for *ijtihād* that the schools of law justified their individuality and existence.

The schools of law differed widely on the methods they proposed for *ijtihād* and the scope which they acknowledged for the use of personal opinion (*ra'y*) therein. The partisans of *ḥadīth* (*Ahl al-Ḥadīth*) normally referred to explicit text in their search for solutions to new issues, but when they failed to find a text, they tended to exercise restraint and abandon further enquiry. The partisans of opinion (*Ahl al-Ra'y*) especially the Ḥanafis, on the other hand, were inclined to extend the scope of enquiry into the rationale and purpose of the text through the modality of analogical reasoning (*qiyās*). As a method of reasoning, *qiyās* operated on the basis of an effective cause (*'illah*) which was found to be in common between an old case and a new case. The *Ahl al-Ḥadīth* did not agree at first and were critical of reliance on analogy as a basis of legislation. The debate over *qiyās* was concerned mainly with the identification of the effective cause (*'illah*) and the uncertainty that was inherent in this exercise.[6] *Qiyās* represented such a salient feature of the methodology of *ijtihād* that Imām Shāfi'ī equated *ijtihād* and *qiyās* with one another and attempted in this way to narrow down the wider scope of *ijtihād* by identifying *qiyās* as its only valid manifestation.

As a principal mode of *ijtihād*, analogy ensured the conformity of juristic opinion with the textual rulings of the Qur'ān and Sunnah which it sought to extend to similar cases. Personal opinion played a role in the construction of analogy through the identification of an effective cause (*'illah*) between an original case and a new case. For example, the Qur'ān (24:4) penalized slanderous accusation of chaste women of adultery by eighty lashes of the whip. This punishment was then analogically extended also to those who accused innocent men of the same offence because of the commonality of the effective cause, namely of defending the honour of an innocent person, between the original case (women) and the new case (men).

Analogy was thus seen to be the surest way of developing the law in line with the guidelines of the text. But analogy was not altogether devoid of difficulty, especially in cases where the analogical extension of a given ruling to a similar, but not identical, case could lead to undesirable results. Some jurists therefore felt the need for a new formula to overcome the rigidities of analogy. The Ḥanafis consequently developed the doctrine of juristic preference (*istiḥsān*) which enabled the jurist to search for an equitable solution in the event where strict analogy frustrated the ideals of fairness and justice. Al-Shāfi'ī, on the other hand, while strongly in support of *qiyās*, totally rejected *istiḥsān* and considered it to be no more than an arbitrary exercise in questionable opinions.

Although the leading schools have also recognized considerations of public interest (*istiṣlāh*, *maṣlaḥah*) as a source of law, because of its strong utilitarian leanings, they have generally tended to impose a variety of conditions on it. Only Imām Mālik advocated it as a source of law in its own right, which is why it is seen as a Māliki contribution to the legal theory of the sources, the *uṣūl al-fiqh*. Whereas analogy operated within the given terms of the existing law, and juristic preference basically corrected the rigidities of analogy, *iṣtilāh* was not bound by such limitations and it vested the ruler and *mujtahid* with the initiative to take all necessary measures, including new legislation, in order to secure what they considered to be of benefit to the people.

Almost every major school proposed a principle or method to regulate *ijtihād* and ensure its conformity with the overriding authority of divine revelation. Whereas some '*ulamā*', such as the Zāhiris, confined the sources of law to the Qur'ān, Sunnah and consensus (*ijmā'*), the Ḥanafis added analogy, juristic preference, and custom, and the Mālikis added public interest (*istiṣlāh*), and also blocking the means (*sadd al-dharā'i'*). In bare outline, *sadd al-dharā'i'* ensured the consistency of the means and ends of the rulings of *Sharī'ah* by blocking the attempt to use a lawful means towards an unlawful end – such as banning the sale of arms at the time of conflict, or forbidding a sale which may merely disguise a usurious transaction. It also validates preventive measures that are taken even before the actual occurrence of a feared event – such as banning an assembly that is likely to lead to violence. Although some of the obvious applications of this doctrine were generally accepted, the Māliki school applied it more widely than most. The Shāfi'ī school contributed the doctrine of *istiṣḥāb*, or presumption of continuity, which contemplates continuity and predictability in law and in court decisions by proposing that facts and rules of law and reason are presumed to remain valid until there is evidence to establish a change. Certainty may not, for example, be overruled by doubt, and an unproven claim should not affect the basic presumption of innocence and continuity of the existing rights of the people under the *Sharī'ah*.

On a different note, some modern observers have suggested a fresh approach towards *istiṣḥāb*, as this doctrine has the potential to incorporate within its scope the concept of natural justice through the approved mores and customs of society. *Istiṣḥāb* derives its basic validity from the premise that Islam did not aim at a total break with the mores and traditions of the past, nor did it aim at nullifying and replacing all the laws and customs of Arabian society. The Prophet allowed and accepted the bulk of the then existing social values and sought only to nullify or replace those which were repressive and unacceptable. Similarly, when the Qur'ān called for the implementation of justice and beneficence (*'adl wa iḥsān*), it referred, *inter alia*, to the basic principles of justice and good conscience. The *Sharī'ah* has also left many things unregulated, and when this is the case, human action may be guided by good conscience and the general teachings of *Sharī'ah* on equity and fairness. This is the substance of the doctrine of *istiṣḥāb* which declares permissibility to be the basic norm of *Sharī'ah*, and validates conformity with the norms of natural justice, good conscience and approved social custom.[7]

These doctrines are all designed, each in their respective capacity, to regulate *ijtihād* and provide formulae for finding solutions to new issues. The methodology that they propose also ensures the conformity of *fiqh* to the basic principles and objectives of *Sharī'ah.* The idea that the law must evolve and develop within the framework of a certain methodology lies at the root of all of these doctrines.

DECLINE OF *IJTIHĀD*

Until about 1500, Muslim scholars were able to adapt continually in the face of changing conditions and new advances in knowledge. Unfortunately, as Muslim civilization began to weaken about four centuries ago in the face of Western advances, Muslims began to adopt a more conservative stance so as to preserve traditional values and institutions. As a result, many scholars began to view innovation and renewal negatively. The '*ulamā*' of the era of imitation (*taqlīd*) occupied themselves mainly with commentaries, compendia and marginal notes on the books already written by eminent jurists. They added little new to the knowledge of their ancestors and even served the negative purpose of giving an aura of sanctity to the earlier works.

This was a different scenario from that which prevailed during the first three centuries of Islam, known as the era of *ijtihād*, when open enquiry and direct recourse to the sources of *Sharī'ah* was not restricted. The four schools of law that eventually crystallized were initially designed to curb excessive diversity and conflict that had become causes for concern, but they too eventually became instruments of unquestioning imitation and conformity that the schools of law demanded of their followers.

Colonial domination of the Muslim lands also lowered the self-image of Muslims and further encouraged imitation and conservative thinking. *Ijtihād* suffered yet another setback when statutory legislation became dominant and the '*ulamā*' were left with little visible role to play. The era of constitutionalism in the newly independent Muslim countries marked, in effect, a renewed phase of imitation characterized by a wholesale importation of Western laws and doctrines, a trend that was encouraged both by the local elites and their foreign mentors. This was the scenario that eventually gave rise to the Islamic revivalist movement after the 1960s. Westernization and modernity had clearly not borne the same fruits in their new habitat as they had produced in their original home grounds in the West.

The decline of *ijtihād* is also due to methodological problems which call for attention. I summarize and suggest that the theory of *ijtihād* needs to be revised and reformed in respect of the following:

1) To recognize the validity of collective *ijtihād* (*ijtihād jamā'i*) side by side with that of *ijtihād* by individual scholars.
2) To allow experts in other fields such as science, economics and medicine to carry out *ijtihād* in their respective fields if they are equipped with adequate knowledge of the source evidence of *Sharī'ah*. They may alternatively sit together with, or seek advice from, the *Sharī'ah* scholars.
3) In earlier times, *ijtihād* was often used as an instrument of diversity and disagreement. This aspect of diversity appears to be more noticeable in the scholastic works of the era of *taqlīd* after the eleventh century. Although disagreement and diversity must remain valid in principle, there is a greater need now for unity and consensus among Muslims. Scholars and learned bodies should not encourage excessive diversity but try to find ways to encourage unity and bring closer, as far as possible, their juristic positions when attempting *ijtihād* over new issues.
4) *Ijtihād* has in the past been conceived basically as a legal concept and methodology. Our understanding of the source evidence does not specify such a framework for *ijtihād*. Rather we see the

original conception of *ijtihād* as a problem-solving formula of wider concern to Muslims. This would confirm our desire as noted above to broaden the scope of *ijtihād* to other disciplines beyond the framework of *fiqh* and jurisprudence.

5) According to a legal maxim of Islamic jurisprudence, there should be no *ijtihād* in the presence of a clear text of the Qur'ān and *ḥadīth* (*lā ijtihād ma'al-naṣṣ*). This maxim also needs to be revised due to the possibility that the text in question may be given a fresh interpretation in a different context, and that by itself may involve *ijtihād*. Hence *ijtihād* should not be precluded if it could advance a fresh understanding of the text in the first place.

IJTIHĀD AND CONTEMPORARY ISSUES

At the dawn of the twentieth century, Jamāl al-Dīn al-Afghāni (d. 1898) and his disciples Muḥammad Abduh (d. 1905) and Muḥammad Rashīd Riḍā (d. 1935) called for a return to original *ijtihād*, which was well received and won wide support in the succeeding decades. They called upon Muslims to turn away from unquestioning imitation and exercise originality and initiative in their quest for suitable solutions to new issues. The underlying note of this appeal also conveyed the message that *ijtihād* in modern times tends to differ to what it was in medieval times. *Mujtahids* in earlier times lived in a predictable social environment that was preoccupied with issues of marriage and divorce, property, inheritance, *zakāh* and usury and the like. Society was not prone to rapid change and *ijtihād* could be attempted with a degree of predictability that is no longer the case. The much accelerated pace of change and its attendant complexities suggest a multi-disciplinary approach to *ijtihād*. It would seem difficult for a jurist now to address, for example, issues pertaining to new banking products and transactions without some knowledge of modern economics and finance. Technical issues in medicine and science, in labour relations and so on generate different demands on the skills of a modern scholar and *mujtahid*.[8]

Ijtihād in modern times has occurred in the following three forms: through statutory legislation, in the form of *fatwā* by scholars and judges, and through scholarly writings. Instances of legislative *ijtihād* can be found in the modern reforms of family law in many

Muslim countries, particularly with reference to polygamy and divorce which have both been made contingent upon a court order and are no longer the unilateral privilege of the husband. The reformist legislation on these subjects is also based mainly on novel interpretations of the relevant portions of the Qur'ān. One also notes numerous instances of *ijtihād* in the views and legal verdicts of prominent '*ulamā*' including Muḥammad Rashīd Riḍā, Muḥammad Abū Zahrah, Maḥmūd Shalṭūt, Muṣṭafā Aḥmad al-Zarqā, Yūsūf al-Qaraḍāwi as well as important court decisions, as I elaborate below.

Whereas the conventional theory of *ijtihād* looks in the direction of doctrines such as *qiyās* (analogy), *istiḥsān* (juristic preference), *istiṣḥāb* (presumption of continuity) and so forth as noted above, I now need to pay more attention to the goals and objectives of *Sharī'ah* (*maqāṣid Sharī'ah*) as also discussed in an earlier chapter.

Muḥammad 'Abduh emphasized the importance of custom (*'urf*) and the actual societal conditions in the conduct of *ijtihād*. The general welfare of the people also demanded a greater role for considerations of public interest (*maṣlaḥah*) in contemporary *ijtihād*. One of the weaknesses of the *uṣūlī* approach to *ijtihād* was the scant attention it paid to the purposes of *Sharī'ah*. 'Abduh's disciple, Rash d Riḍā, emphasized the need to inform legislation and *ijtihād* with the spirit and wisdom (*ḥikmah*) of the *Sharī'ah* and its goals and purposes (*maqāṣid*). Many people know what is lawful and what is unlawful but they do not always know why a particular act was declared lawful and another unlawful. If the code of law and the goal it enshrines go hand in hand, it will enhance the prospects of better understanding and enforcement.[9] Ubayd Allah Sindhi (d. 1944) observed on a similar note: while the law is not eternal, the goal and wisdom embodied therein create in man the ability to think and to change himself in accordance with his inner motivation and insight. It is due to *ḥikmah* (wisdom) that man seeks new ways for self-improvement, keeping in view the actual conditions of his time as well as maintaining his links with the past.[10] According to Muhammad Iqbal, the teaching of the Qur'ān that life is a process of progressive creation necessitates that each generation, guided but unhampered by the work of its predecessors, should be permitted to solve its own problems.[11] It is also recognized that *fiqh* embodies an important aspect of the Muslim legacy and provides valuable materials for *ijtihād* but it often needs to be re-evaluated and its relevance to modern conditions to be carefully ascertained.[12]

Instances where the *fiqh* provisions need to be reviewed include in the present writer's view, the following:

- Leadership and methods of succession, whether by election by selection, or by coercive power have remained unresolved. Scholars have also spoken in support of the elective method, of consultation (*shūrā*) and participatory government, but these issues have largely remained in the realm of discussion and debate.
- Resolute positions need to be taken against dictatorship and categorical support for constitutional government and democracy. There is wide support now for democracy among Muslims almost everywhere which could also be developed into the general consensus of *Sharī'ah* scholars.
- Islamic law has remained less than categorical on fundamental rights and liberties of the individual, a subject on which medieval *fiqh* scholarship has very little to say. Constitutional rights and liberties should now be reflected and vindicated in the works of *Sharī'ah* scholars and '*ulamā*'.
- The use of violence and issues of relevance to *jihād* and its prevalent distortions call for decisive position-taking by the '*ulamā*' and *Sharī'ah* scholars.
- The disability of non-Muslims in the matter of evidence in the courts of justice. There is no categorical evidence in the sources to disqualify non-Muslims from becoming witnesses in the courts of *Sharī'ah*. However, the majority of *fiqh* scholars have relied on inferential evidence to make the testimony of a non-Muslim inadmissible.
- The generally accepted *fiqh* rulings on the subjects of polygamy and divorce have been influenced by the prevailing conditions of earlier times. Many of these rulings have consequently been modified in the reformist legislation of the *Sharī'ah* in the later part of the twentieth century. Yet firm and decisive positions still need to be taken and developed.
- It is now recognized the death penalty for apostasy in the *ḥadīth* which sanctioned such punishment was meant to be put into effect specifically in the context of hostile and subversive attacks on Islam, on the Muslim community and its leadership in earlier times. This seems to be indicated in the *ḥadīth* itself, confirmed also by the fact that the Qur'ān does not explicitly provide any punishment for apostasy.

Muhammad Iqbal spoke critically of this when he noted that there were cases in India where Muslim women wishing to get rid of undesirable husbands were driven to apostasy. Iqbal then commented that nothing could be more distant from the aims and purposes of Islam 'and the rules of apostasy as recorded in the *Hedaya* do not protect the interest of the faith'. Iqbal added that 'in view of the intense conservatism of the Muslims of India, Indian judges cannot but stick to what are called standard works. The result is that while the people are moving, the law remains stationary.'[13] Iqbal also added that he was in no doubt that a deeper study of the enormous legal literature of Islam was sure to rid 'the modern critic of the superficial opinion that the law of Islam is stationary and incapable of development'.[14]

- Some of the *fiqhi* positions relating to women's rights and their participation in the affairs of government also call for fresh *ijtihād* that should adequately reflect the higher objectives of Islam on equality and justice as well as greater sensitivity to the altered socio-economic conditions of women in the present-day world.

The remainder of this chapter addresses some issues in *fatwā*.

FATWĀ IN MODERN TIMES

An attempt is made in this section to show that *fatwā* under contemporary law is different from the original conception of *fatwā* in the *Sharīʿah*. Literally meaning a 'response', *fatwā* is defined as a response given by a qualified person (i.e. a *muftī*) who expounds the ruling of *Sharīʿah* on a particular issue that is put to him by a person or a group of persons.[15]

Historically *fatwā* began as a private activity that was independent of state intervention and control. The '*ulamā*' who acted as *muftīs* responded to people's questions over issues and gave *fatwā* as a service to the community, and they themselves set their own professional standards usually without government intervention. The *muftīs* acted as legal advisors and counsels in much the same way as the professional lawyers of today. They provided valuable guidance and advice over detailed issues of Islamic law in legal disputes and in court cases for those who were not in a position to consult the law books themselves.

The ruling that is arrived at through *fatwā* is often based on an interpretation of the Qur'ān or Sunnah and the general principles of *Sharī'ah*. In the absence of any evidence in these sources the Islamic scholar (*muftī*) formulates his own best judgement, enlightened by his general knowledge of the *Sharī'ah* and the mores and customs of society. The resulting judgement or verdict consists usually of an opinion that does not bind the person or persons to whom it is addressed, nor does it bind anyone else. The recipient of a *fatwā* is consequently free to go to another *muftī* and obtain a second or even a third *fatwā* over the issue of concern to him, and it is his choice whether or not to comply with any of them. Only in cases where the *fatwā* consists of a clear injunction of *Sharī'ah* and the two or three views given on the issue are found to be concurrent would the *fatwā* bind its audience and recipient, but not otherwise. *Fatwā* that is based on the interpretation and personal opinion of the *muftī* is normally not binding on anyone. This is the main difference between *fatwā* and a judicial ruling (*qaḍā*). *Fatwā* also differs from *ijtihād* in that *fatwā* may be attempted in matters which may have been regulated by decisive evidence or by a mere indication in the Qur'ān and *ḥadīth*. *Ijtihād* on the other hand does not proceed on matters which are covered by decisive evidence in these sources.[16]

Fatwā in many Muslim countries has become a state matter and can no longer be practised by anyone other than an officially employed *muftī* in accordance with a stipulated procedure. Whereas *fatwā* in *Sharī'ah* is not a binding instrument, under statutory law it has generally been given this role. A basically voluntary and investigative concept has been turned into an instrument of mandatory and binding rule-making. *Fatwā* under the *Sharī'ah* is also a vehicle that facilitates the free flow of thought and expression in religious issues, whereas now it has in many countries become an instrument of restriction on freedom of expression in religious matters.

In Malaysia, for example,[17] after approval by the Islamic Religious Council and the Sultan, a *fatwā* only needs to be gazetted to become law, without any requirement for it to be tabled for approval in Parliament or the State Legislature. This is not a new development as the state authorities had *fatwā*-making powers under most of the State Administration of Islamic Law Enactments that have been in force in Malaysia for several decades. The issue took a new turn, however, during the 1990s when legislation on *fatwā* went a step further to declare it an offence for 'any person who gives, propagates, or disseminates any opinion contrary to any *fatwā*'; anyone who does so commits an offence that carries a punishment of up to RM 3000, or imprisonment for up to two years, or both.[18]

Restrictive legislation on *fatwā* is partly related to the changes in the legal and educational systems of Muslim countries. A certain dislocation in the roles of *fatwā* and *muftī* occurred after the spread of Western-style laws and legal education in the Muslim lands. The takeover of legislative and advisory functions by the elected assembly and the legal profession had the overall effect of making the traditional *muftī* more or less redundant. Although *muftīs* continued to function in many Muslim countries, they were being increasingly integrated into the government rank and file. The more elaborate bureaucracy associated with the office of the Ottoman Shaykh al-Islām was discontinued when that office was abolished in 1924. Yet various organizational patterns have emerged and *fatwā* activity has been generally regulated by statutory legislation. In Egypt, the office of the Grand *Muftī* was established in the late nineteenth century, but state *muftīs* were not appointed until the mid-twentieth century in countries such as Saudi Arabia (1953), Lebanon (1955), Malaysia (1955), Yemen (1962) and Indonesia (1975), but since then, they have largely become state functionaries and direct recipients of government orders. In some institutional contexts, *fatwā* is now more closely associated with religious propagation and guidance (*da'wah* and *irshād*) activities.[19]

The state has consequently acquired control of *fatwā*-making activity with the obvious result that certain restrictions have been imposed on the freedom of individual religious scholars and '*ulamā*' in the issuance of *fatwā*. A positive aspect of this development has been a certain procedural regulation for *fatwā*-making which has restrained arbitrary *fatwās* emanating from questionable sources and often playing on people's religious sentiment. A vivid example of this was the late Ayatollah Khomeini's *fatwā* consisting of a death sentence on Salman Rushdie (14 February 1989). This was a controversial procedure that pre-empted normal judicial process on this issue, and it was met with mixed and generally critical response from Muslim scholars in different countries.[20] I do not advocate this kind of unrestrained posture on the issuing of *fatwā*. Yet the kind of control that is exerted over *fatwā*-making through strict and punitive statutory procedures has also given rise to concern over the near-total bureaucratization of *fatwā* in Malaysia and elsewhere in the Muslim world.

Fatwā is meant to keep the *Sharī'ah* in tandem with social reality, but the Malaysian legislation on *fatwā* precludes that, with the likely result of narrowing down the space for public participation in *fatwā*-making. We have often heard about the so-called closure of the gate of *ijtihād* (*insidād bāb al-ijtihād*) which has had debilitating consequences for the viability and growth of the *Sharī'ah*. What we are seeing is the beginning of a similar process that is likely to exacerbate the situation at a time when flexibility and openness are needed. For *fatwā* in Malaysia and elsewhere is being turned into a state matter which is open to discussion and debate only within official circles. This kind of *fatwā*-making procedure basically makes no room for public debate and consultation. This trend should hopefully be arrested and a more flexible procedure adopted to provide opportunity for all concerned, the government agencies, the private scholar and the media, to voice their concerns and constructive criticism of a *fatwā* before it becomes binding in law.

It must be admitted that stipulating a certain procedure for *fatwā* is useful in restraining arbitrary *fatwā*-making. Yet it hardly seems advisable to make that procedure so strict as to render a mere disputation over a state-sponsored *fatwā* a punishable offence. To bring criminal procedure into all of this is also unrealistic.

I therefore propose that the *fatwā* procedure in Malaysia and elsewhere should be revised and moderated. One way to do this would be to integrate the *fatwā* procedure into the mainstream procedure for legislation and subject the *fatwā* to ratification by the legislative assembly and parliament, which may choose to set up a standing committee of *Sharī'ah* experts to report on the proposed *fatwās*. The exceptional status that is now granted to *fatwā* as another source of law-making in the country should thus be terminated.

NOTES

1. For a more detailed review of the classical theory of *ijtihād* see M. H. Kamali, *Principles of Islamic Jurisprudence*, 468–500; for details on the problematics of *ijtihād* in modern times see idem., 'Issues in the Understanding of *jihād* and *ijtihād*', 623 f. Ḍahā Jābir al-'Alwani, *Ijtihād*, 4.
2. al-Shawkānī, *Irshād al-Fuḥūl*, 254.
3. Ibid. For a summary of al-Shawkānī's acount see my *Jurisprudence*, at 491.
4. Khallāf, *'Ilm*, 49–50.
5. Cf. Khallāf, *'Ilm*, 50; Iqbal, *Reconstruction*, 174; al-Ṭamāwi, *Al-Sulṭāt al-Thalāth*, 307.

6. For details on the methodology of *qiyās* see chapter on *qiyās* in Kamali, *Jurisprudence*, 264–306.
7. Ḥasan al-Turābi, *Tajdīd Uṣūl al-Fiqh al-Islāmi*, 27–8.
8. Cf. Jamāl al-Bannā, *Naḥw al-Fiqh al-Jadīd*, 73.
9. Rashīd Riḍā, *Tafsīr al-Qur'ān al-ṭakīm* (also known as *Tafsīr al-Manār*), III, 30.
10. Quoted in Mazheruddin Siddiqi, *Modern Reformist Thought*, 78–7.
11. Ibid., 168.
12. Cf. Ibid., 73.
13. Iqbal, *Reconstruction*, 169.
14. Ibid., 164.
15. '*Fatwā*', in *al-Mawsū'ah al-Fiqhiyyah* published by the Ministry of Awqāf of Kuwait, Vol. 32, at 20; Yūsuf al-Qaraḍāwi, *al-Fatwā Bayn al-Inḍibāṭ wa'l-Tasayyib*, at 11.
16. Cf. Yūsuf al-Qaraḍāwi, *al-Fatwā Bayn al-Inḍibāṭ wa'l-Tasayyib*, 12.
17. Cf. Syariah Criminal Offences (Federal Territory) Act 1997, Art. 9.
18. Ibid., Art. 12; Syariah Criminal Offences Enactment of Johor (sec. 12) and its equivalent provisions in most other states of Malaysia.
19. Cf. Khalid Mas'ud, *Islamic Legal Interpretation*, 27–9.
20. See for a fuller discussion Kamali, *Freedom of Expression*, 294–301; see also a case study of a controversial *fatwā* in Malaysia in idem, 'The Johor *Fatwa*', 99–116.

9

SHARĪʿAH AND THE PRINCIPLE OF LEGALITY

INTRODUCTORY REMARKS

Although the constitutional principle of legality, or government under the rule of law, is not confined to crimes and penalties, these are nevertheless of central importance to the whole notion of legality, which is why criminal prosecution is a focus of our discussion in the following paragraphs.

Criminal procedure is generally predicated on the twin but contrasting objectives of following due judicial process and effective control of crime. Due judicial process tends to focus on providing the accused with various protections to minimize the possibility of unjust or arbitrary criminal convictions. It also seeks to facilitate an efficient administration of justice which promotes objectivity and coherence in trial proceedings. Crime control, by contrast, emphasizes a broader social interest in crime detection and prevention, and tends to limit procedural protections for the accused so as to ensure an efficient prosecution and conviction of the guilty.[1]

Islamic criminal procedure also faces this dilemma and seeks to strike a fair balance between the interests of the accused and those of the society. Specific procedural safeguards are occasionally prescribed by the Qur'ān or the Sunnah, but have generally been left to the discretion of the ruler. Under the doctrine of *siyāsah sharʿiyyah*, or *Sharīʿah*-oriented policy, the ruler is authorized to take measures and devise procedures that are in harmony with the goals and objectives of *Sharīʿah* and secure public interest as best as possible. Simple and direct detection and trial procedures that were deemed adequate for earlier times may not be sufficient for more complex societies where progress in various fields has also opened new avenues for more sophisticated levels of criminality and abuse. The integrity of a procedural system under these circumstances is tested by its openness to refinement and growth. Since procedural matters in the Islamic system of justice are open to considerations of public policy and justice under *siyāsah shar'iyyah*, the process remains, in principle, open to be further developed and refined.

The principle of legality means that no one may be incriminated or punished unless it be on grounds of a legal text which specifically defines the crime and the punishment in question. It also means that the judge may not punish anyone merely on the basis of his whims unless the required legal evidence and proof exist. Moreover, the legal text that is applied must have been in existence at the time when the offence was committed. The law may not, in other words, be enforced retroactively. It also means that only the offender and no one else may be held responsible for his offence. The requirement of due process in interrogation and trial is also designed to ensure that the accused is protected against abuse of power. The principle of legality is thus essentially concerned with the limitation of the power of the state and its operation acquires special significance in the area of criminal law.[2]

LEGALITY AS A PRINCIPLE OF CONSTITUTION

Islamic constitutional theory is explicit on the principle of limitation of the power of the state under the rule of law. The Islamic government is, accordingly, bound to administer and uphold the *Sharī'ah*.[3] There is no place in *Sharī'ah* for arbitrary rule by a single individual or a group. The basis of all decisions and actions in an Islamic polity should not be the whims and caprices of individuals, but the *Sharī'ah*.[4] The '*ulamā*' have unanimously held the view that the head of state and government officials are accountable for their conduct like everyone else, as they are also bound by the decisions of the courts of justice. In response to the question as to how can the decision of a *qāḍī*, who is an employee of the head of the state (Imām), be binding on the Imām, it is pointed out that the judge discharges his duty not as an employee of the Imām, but as a representative of the community whose task it is to implement the *Sharī'ah.* There is, therefore, no recognition of special privileges for anyone, and equality before the law and before the courts of justice is clearly recognized for all citizens alike.[5] It is once again indicative of the high priority that Islam accords to the rule of law that it frees the citizen from the duty of obeying the political authority in matters where the latter violates the law. This is the clear message of the *ḥadīth* which declares:

> There is no obedience in transgression; obedience is in lawful conduct only.[6]
>
> لا طاعة فى معصية، إنما الطاعة فى المعروف.

According to another *ḥadīth:*

> There is no obedience to a creature when it involves disobedience of the Creator.[7]
>
> لا طاعة لمخلوق فى معصية الخالق.

Based on the unequivocal authority provided in a number of similar *aḥadīth*, Mawdūd (d. 1979) has drawn the conclusion that 'Islam confers on every citizen the right to refuse to commit a crime, should any government or administrator order him to do so'.[8] With reference to sovereignty, Maḥmaṣṣānī has concurred with Ibn Khaldūn that the sovereignty of an Islamic state is limited in so far as the state in Islamic law is under obligation to comply with the *Sharī'ah.* Hence when the state issues a command that violates the *Sharī'ah*, the citizen is no longer under a duty to obey that command.[9]

LEGALITY IN CRIMES AND PENALTIES

The *Sharī'ah* safeguards the life, honour and liberty of the individual by laying down a set of principles which are designed to ensure due process in the administration of justice. Included in these is the presumption of original non-liability (*barā'at al-dhimmah al-aṣliyyah*) which simply means that no one is guilty of a crime unless his guilt is proved through lawful evidence.[10] The presumption of innocence is not overruled by a mere accusation, which is not devoid of doubt, simply because doubt does not negate certainty, and what is certain here is the prior innocence of the accused. The principle of legality also entitles the accused to defend himself and attend his own trial. This is established by a *ḥadīth* in which the Prophet (peace be on him) is reported to have given to 'Ali ibn Abū Ṭālib when the latter was sent as judge to Yemen:

> When the litigant presents himself before you, do not pass a judgement unless you hear the other party in the same way as you hear the first.[11]
>
> إذا جلس الخصمان فلا تقض بينهما حتى تسمع من الآخر كما سمعت من الأوّل، فإنك إذا فعلت ذلك تبيّن لك القضاء.

In a similar vein, Islamic law does not permit the judge to sentence a person in the latter's absence. The defendant must, in other words, be present in the court or be represented by an authorized person.[12] There is some disagreement among the Ḥanafīs and Shāfi'īs as to whether an accusation by itself can weaken the force of the original principle of non-liability. The Ḥanafīs maintain that it does, but the Shāfi'īs hold that a mere claim or accusation does not affect the original absence of liability or innocence of the accused. It is important, as al-Ṣāleḥ has rightly noted, that the presumption of innocence is strictly upheld, as the accused will otherwise be faced with the onerous, if not impossible, task of proving that he did not commit the crime.[13]

Anyone, be it the individual or the state, accusing a person of an offence must prove it beyond reasonable doubt.[14] The burden of proof lies on the plaintiff, a principle which is based on the following *ḥadīth*:

> The burden of proof is on him who makes the claim, whereas the oath [denying the charge] is on him who denies.[15]
>
> البيّنة على المدّعى واليمين على من أنكر.

The plaintiff, in other words, may ask the court to put the defendant on oath if the latter denies the claim. If the claimant is required to prove his allegation, then it would follow that until such proof is forthcoming, the defendant is presumed to be innocent. This is also upheld in another *ḥadīth* which provides:

> If men were to be granted what they claim, some will claim the lives and properties of others. The burden of proof is on the claimant, and an oath is incumbent on him who denies.[16]
>
> لو يعطى الناس بدعواهم لادّعى ناس دماء رجال وأموالهم ولكنّ اليمين على المدّعى عليه.

According to Ibn Qayyim al-Jawziyyah (d. 1350), if a claimant supports his claim by evidence, the court will adjudicate in his favour, otherwise the last word is that of the defendant and the court will accept what he says provided he takes a solemn oath to affirm that he is telling the truth.[17]

Punishment is not executed unless there is proof to establish the guilt, and hearsay evidence is not admissible in the execution of penalties. Ibn Taymiyyah (d. 1328) wrote that at the time of the Prophet a woman in Madinah had a bad reputation as regards her sexual conduct, so much so that the Prophet said concerning her: 'If I were to stone anyone without evidence, I would have stoned this woman.'[18] Ibn Taymiyyah also quotes a statement of the caliph 'Umar ibn al-Khaṭṭāb to the effect that no one may be punished on the basis of suspicion and mistrust. Al-Qarāfi (d. 1283) and Ibn Farḥūn have specified that proof means evidence that is sound and free of doubt and loopholes, that has met all its proper conditions and leads to a definite result. Ibn al-Qayyim has observed that offenders are not punished without proof and proof comes either from the offender when he or she makes a confession, or what might amount to a confession, or else it is provided independently. In both cases, the proof must be sound, free of doubt and without recourse to spying.[19]

Confession in crimes, but not in civil disputes, can be withdrawn even after the sentence has been passed or during its execution. Once a confession is so withdrawn, particularly in the prescribed *ḥadd* offences, the punishment may not be carried out. For withdrawal in this manner gives rise to doubt (*shubhah*) which would in turn obstruct the enforcement of punishment.[20] For a confession to be valid, the confessor must also be in full possession of his faculties. Confession must, in addition, be true in that it does not seek to conceal the truth in order merely to protect another person, or a group of persons. When the cause and underlying intention of a mendacious confession is known to the judge, he is under duty to reject it.[21] A valid confession needs to be specific and categorical. If it is ambiguous to the extent that it requires interpretation, it is not admissible. Hence it is not enough if someone says merely that 'I committed adultery' or that 'one of us committed theft'. Both statements are vague as they fail to provide relevant details and do not, therefore, amount to valid proof.[22]

Judicial decisions must be based on apparent truth which is substantiated by valid evidence. The hidden truth, should there be any, is considered to be a matter between the individual and his Creator and it lies beyond the immediate concern of the court. In 'Abd al-Wahhāb al-Sha'rānī's (d. 1565) words: 'God Most High has ordered us to settle disputes among people on the basis of visible proof, and leave the rest to the Day of judgment.'[23] This conclusion is supported by the following *ḥadīth* in which the Prophet is reported to have said:

> I am but a human being. When you bring a dispute to me, some of you may be more eloquent in stating their case than others. I may consequently adjudicate on the basis of what I hear. If I adjudicate in favour of someone a thing that belongs to his brother, let him not take it. For it would be like taking a piece of fire.[24]

> إنما انا بشر أنكم تختصمون إليّ، فلعلّ بعضكم أن يكون ألحن بحجّيّته من بعض فأقضى نحو ماأسمع، فمن قضيت له بحق أخيه شيئا فلا يأخذه إنما أقطع له قطعة من النار.

The Prophet has, in other words, confirmed that he adjudicated disputes only on the basis of the evidence that was presented to him.

Evidence must be allowed to be given in an atmosphere of impartiality. It is a generally agreed rule of the Islamic law of evidence that the judge must avoid indicating to witnesses what should be the content of their testimony; instead, he should hear what they have to say.[25] The Qur'ān demands impartiality in the administration of justice. The witnesses, the judges and the law enforcement authorities are accordingly required to:

> Stand firmly for justice as witnesses to God, even if it be against yourselves, your parents or your relatives, and whether it be (against) the rich or poor, for God can best protect both. Follow not the lust (of your hearts) lest it distract you from the course of justice. (4:135)

> يَا أَيُّهَا الَّذِينَ آمَنُواْ كُونُواْ قَوَّامِينَ بِالْقِسْطِ شُهَدَاء لِلّهِ وَلَوْ عَلَى أَنفُسِكُمْ أَوِ الْوَالِدَيْنِ وَالأَقْرَبِينَ إِن يَكُنْ غَنِيًّا أَوْ فَقَيرًا فَاللّهُ أَوْلَى بِهِمَا فَلاَ تَتَّبِعُواْ الْهَوَى أَن تَعْدِلُواْ.

This Qur'ānic emphasis on impartiality in the administration of justice obviously means that investigation and trial procedures must, from the beginning to the end, be impartial and objective.

The Qur'ānic rule with reference to sentencing is to avoid excess in retaliation and punishment that is out of line with the offence itself. We note, once again, the following Qur'ānic directive, which is addressed to all parties in judicial disputes, including the law enforcement authorities and the state:

> Whoever is aggressive toward you, then your response must be proportionate to the aggression that was inflicted on you. (2:194)
>
> فَمَنِ اعْتَدَى عَلَيْكُمْ فَاعْتَدُوا عَلَيْهِ بِمِثْلِ مَا اعْتَدَى عَلَيْكُمْ.

The Qur'ān further lays down the principle that no one may be accused or punished for an offence committed by another person:

> Everyone is accountable for his own deeds, and no soul shall bear the burden of another. (6:164)[26]
>
> وَلاَ تَكْسِبُ كُلُّ نَفْسٍ إِلاَّ عَلَيْهَا وَلاَ تَزِرُ وَازِرَةٌ وِزْرَ أُخْرَى.

The Qur'ān, addressing the Prophet, lays down:

> We revealed to you the scripture with the truth that you may judge between people by that which God has shown to you, and do not be a pleader for the treacherous. (4:105)
>
> إِنَّا أَنزَلْنَا إِلَيْكَ الْكِتَابَ بِالْحَقِّ لِتَحْكُمَ بَيْنَ النَّاسِ بِمَا أَرَاكَ اللَّهُ وَلاَ تَكُن لِّلْخَآئِنِينَ خَصِيمًا.

This verse was revealed concerning a dispute between a Muslim and a Jew. In this case the Muslim, Ḍu'mah ibn Ubayraq, had stolen a coat of mail. He hid it in the house of a Jew and later accused the latter of theft. He was supported in his false accusation by his tribe. The Prophet cleared the Jew of the charge but Ibn Ubayraq fled and renounced Islam. The following two verses were also revealed concerning the same case:

> Whoever commits a sin only makes himself liable for it . . . and whoever commits a delinquency and then throws the blame thereof upon the innocent, he has burdened himself with falsehood and a flagrant crime. (4:111–12)[27]
>
> وَمَن يَكْسِبْ إِثْمًا فَإِنَّمَا يَكْسِبُهُ عَلَى نَفْسِهِ...وَمَن يَكْسِبْ خَطِيئَةً أَوْ إِثْمًا ثُمَّ يَرْمِ بِهِ بَرِيئًا فَقَدِ احْتَمَلَ بُهْتَانًا وَإِثْمًا مُّبِينًا.

This Qur'ānic principle marked a departure from the ancient Arab tendency to go to excesses in retaliation and revenge. The Arabs sometimes doubled the penalty or claimed more than one life in retaliation. They were also wont to demand exaggerated sums as *diyah* (blood money) and often held the whole tribe responsible for the crime of one of its members.[28] A well-known exception to this principle is the case of *'āqilah* (kinsmen) which is a pre-Islamic Arabian custom that was subsequently taken over on the grounds of Sunnah and consensus (*ijmā'*), and it required the kinsmen of the offender to pay the blood money in unintentional homicide. According to al-Awzā'i (d. 774) and Dāwūd al-Ẓāhirī (d. 884) the offender himself does not participate with his *'āqilah* in the payment of *diyah.* According to Abū Ḥanīfah and Mālik, however, he does participate in the payment of *diyah* whereas, according to al-Shāfi'ī, he participates only if the *'āqilah* are unable to pay the *diyah.* We learn that during the time of 'Umar ibn al-Khaṭṭāb, the *'āqilah* also included colleagues at work (*ahl al-dīwān*).[29] This has led Maḥmūd Shaltūt to the observation that the proper purpose of *'āqilah* is to foster co-operation and mutual help in bearing the consequences of an unintended crime. It is, however, not meant to transfer the responsibility of the offender to another person, which is why the *'āqilah* are not required to participate in the *diyah* of a deliberate crime.[30]

Muslim jurists have formulated a number of legal maxims which complement the principle of legality in the *Sharī'ah.* One of these provides that 'the conduct of reasonable men (or the dictate of reason) alone is of no consequence without the support of a legal text'. This obviously means that no conduct can be declared forbidden (*ḥarām*) on grounds of reason alone or on grounds of the act of reasonable men alone, and that a legal text is necessary to render the conduct in question an offence. No one, therefore, should be deemed a violator because of committing or omitting an act which is not forbidden by the clear provisions of the law.[31] The substance of this principle is also upheld in another legal maxim which declares that 'permissibility is the original norm' (*al-aṣl fi'l-ashyā' al-ibāḥah*).[32] The majority of '*ulamā*' have thus reached the conclusion that all things are permissible unless the law has declared them otherwise. Consequently, no one may be accused of an offence in the absence of a legal text. The third legal maxim under discussion provides that 'no one bears any obligation unless he is capable of understanding the law which imposes it; nor may any one be required to act in a certain manner unless he is capable of knowing the nature of the act he is required to do or avoid doing'.[33] This principle indicates that the law which creates an obligation, or an offence, can only be addressed to a competent person who is capable of understanding it, and that it is physically possible for him to comply with the law when he knows of it. In order to make the knowledge of the law possible for the citizens, the legal text must be published and made accessible to all. Consequently no crime is committed until the text which creates it has been publicly announced and brought to the knowledge of the people.[34] These conclusions are supported by several passages in the Qur'ān. To quote just a few:

> We do not punish until we have sent a messenger (to give warning). (17:15)
>
> وَمَا كُنَّا مُعَذِّبِينَ حَتَّى نَبْعَثَ رَسُولاً.
>
> Nor was thy Lord the one to destroy a population until He had sent in its midst a messenger rehearsing to them Our signs. (28:59)
>
> وَمَا كَانَ رَبُّكَ مُهْلِكَ الْقُرَى حَتَّى يَبْعَثَ فِي أُمِّهَا رَسُولًا يَتْلُو عَلَيْهِمْ آيَاتِنَا.
>
> (All of God's) Messengers gave good news as well as warning so that people should have no plea against God after the (sending of Messengers). God is All-Powerful, All-Wise. (4:165)
>
> رُسُلاً مُبَشِّرِينَ وَمُنذِرِينَ لِئَلاَّ يَكُونَ لِلنَّاسِ عَلَى اللهِ حُجَّةٌ بَعْدَ الرُّسُلِ وَكَانَ اللهُ عَزِيزًا حَكِيمًا.

People are thus accountable for their deeds in consideration of the message and the scripture conveyed to them. The principle contained in these Qur'ānic passages is that without prior warning, scripture and guidance, there shall be no punishment. Thus, according to 'Awdah: 'In the absence of a clear text which may require affirmative action or abandonment of a particular conduct, the perpetrator or abandoner incurs no responsibility and no punishment can be imposed.'[35] Anyone who looks into the *Sharīʿah*, 'Awdah added, will find that there is a clear text for every punishable offence, although the approach may differ with regard to the types of offences, as we shall presently explain.[36] Commenting on the same Qur'ānic passages, Khallāf wrote: 'This is the majority position: that a person who has lived in complete isolation so that no message, law or guidance has been communicated to him is *non-compos mentis* [*ghayr mukallaf*]. Such a person could not, therefore, be rewarded for his good deeds nor could he be punished for his evil conduct and crime. For it is a prerequisite of responsibility (*taklīf*) that the law is communicated to its proper audience.'[37]

There is evidence in the Qur'ān that punishment must not be applied retroactively:

> Say to the unbelievers that if they desist (from unbelief), what they have done in the past would be forgiven. (8:32)
>
> قُلْ لِلَّذِينَ كَفَرُوا إِن يَنتَهُوا يُغْفَرْ لَهُم مَّا قَدْ سَلَفَ.

It is provided elsewhere in the Qur'ān with reference to pre-Islamic marital practices:

> And marry not those women whom your fathers married except for what had already happened in the past. (4:22)
>
> وَلاَ تَنكِحُوا مَا نَكَحَ آبَاؤُكُم مِّنَ النِّسَاءِ إِلاَّ مَا قَدْ سَلَفَ.

Abū Zahrah draws the conclusion from these verses that the Qur'ān forbids applying the penal law of Islam for offences that were committed prior to the advent of Islam. This would, in principle, establish the non-retroactivity of penalties under the *Sharī'ah*.[38] The substance of these verses is once again confirmed in the following *ḥadīth*: When 'Amr b. al-'Aṣṣ embraced Islam, he pledged allegiance to the Prophet and asked if he would be held accountable for his previous transgressions. To this the Prophet replied: 'Did you not know, O 'Amr, that Islam obliterates that which took place before it?'[39]

The Prophet also did not question Abū Sufyān and his wife on their previous conduct, nor did he question the man who had killed his uncle Ḥamzah even though his death had caused him deep sorrow. The only exception to this principle to be noted is that the new law has a retroactive effect when it is in favour of the accused.[40]

The *Sharī'ah* does not advocate a rigid approach in its implementation of the principle of the rule of law. Broadly speaking, *Sharī'ah* employs three different methods for implementing the principle of legality in criminal law. In the case of serious crimes which pose a major threat to society, the *Sharī'ah* specifies both the offence and the punishment. The punishment so specified may fall under the *ḥudūd*, just retaliation (*qiṣāṣ*) and blood-money (*diyah*). For offences which pose a relatively lesser threat to public safety, *Sharī'ah* does not specify the penalty but defines the offence and provides only general guidelines about the punishment. These are the *ta'zīr* offences where the *Sharī'ah* specifies the conduct but empowers the judge to select the type and amount of its punishment, which he deems most suitable, out of a range of approved penalties. *Ta'zīr* offences relate primarily to acts which the *Sharī'ah* has defined as transgression (*ma'ṣiyah*). It is not for the judge to define the offence; he can only specify punishment for a certain conduct the criminality of which has already been determined by a legal text (*naṣṣ*).

While discussing the common misconception that the judge has a free hand in dealing with *ta'zīr* offences, 'Abd al-Qādir 'Awdah points out that the *Sharī'ah* imposes certain restrictions on the powers of the judge. It is, consequently, a mistake to say that *ta'zīr* offences are not regulated by the *naṣṣ* or to suggest that the judge is at liberty to determine both the crime and its punishment. The judge must, first of all, determine whether the conduct is a *ma'ṣiyah* according to the clear texts of the *Sharī'ah.* The offence must then be proved through the legally required evidence. The judge selects only that type of punishment which the *Sharī'ah* has validated. 'Awdah goes on to illustrate this by reference to a number of *ta'zīr* offences and the textual bases on which they rest. The list includes consumption of forbidden substances, breach of trust, cheating in weights and measures, perjury, usury, obscenity and insult, bribery, unlawful entry into private dwellings and espionage. In all of these the Qur'ān and the Sunnah provide the textual authority which renders the conduct a *ma'ṣiyah*. While meting out punishment for any of these offences, the judge must select an approved penalty, ranging from a mere warning to fines and imprisonment, and decide whether the sentence may be suspended or be carried out promptly. The judge, in other words, enjoys discretionary powers in regard to *ta'zīr* offences which 'Awdah characterizes as *sulṭat al-ikhtiyār* (power to select) as opposed to *sulṭat al-taḥakkum* (power to legislate at will). According to the Islamic constitutional theory, neither the judge nor any other organ of government enjoys unlimited powers of this latter type.[41]

In regard to *ta'zīr* offences which violate the public interest (*al-maṣlaḥah al-'āmmah*), the *Sharī'ah* does not specify the nature of the offence but provides only general guidelines on the type of conduct that is deemed to be harmful to society, the reason being that offences of this type are, on the whole, unpredictable and cannot be specified in advance. An act may be permissible and yet the circumstances in which it is committed, or some of its attributes are such that they would violate public interest. While in principle the *Sharī'ah* penalizes only those acts which amount to transgression, it makes an exception by authorizing the judge to penalize the conduct which, though not forbidden by textual authority, and therefore not a *maʻṣiyah*, is prejudicial to public interest and causes harm (*ḍarar*) to society.[42] Examples of this kind of *taʻzīr* are restrictions on the liberty of the insane for the sake of public safety and preventing him from harming the community, or detention without proof of an accused on grounds of public interest, that is, to facilitate investigation and prevent a possible escape of the accused.[43]

In all of this, whether *taʻzīr* contemplates a *maʻṣiyah* (transgression) or *ḍarar* (harm), the punishment must be proportionate to the offence and should remain within the limits of moderation. Based on the authority of the Sunnah, Muslim jurists have further added the proviso that *taʻzīr*, in general, must operate at a level below the severity of the prescribed penalties (*ḥudūd*).[44] *Taʻzir* punishment may also be invoked in the case of prescribed *ḥadd* offences where the specified punishment cannot be enforced due to insufficiency of evidence, or owing to doubt about the fulfilment of their necessary conditions. In both cases, the judge has powers to impose, by way of *taʻzīr*, a lesser punishment as may be considered appropriate.

There is some disagreement among the leading *madhāhib* as to the quantitative limits of *taʻzīr* penalties. While some jurists, especially those of the Māliki school, have specified no limits and have referred the matter to considerations of *maṣlaḥah* and *ijtihād* of the judge, others have held that *taʻzir* penalties in each category must be below the level of the relevant *ḥadd* punishment. This is the view of some Shāfiʻi and Ḥanbali jurists. According to another view, which is upheld by many Ḥanafī, Shāfiʻī and Ḥanbai scholars, *taʻzīr* must not exceed the lowest of all the *ḥadd* penalties across the board, which means that it may not exceed forty lashes of the whip. The fourth opinion on this, which is held by some Ḥanbali ʻ*ulamā*ʼ, is that *taʻzīr* punishment may not exceed ten lashes of the whip absolutely, and there is some authority in the *ḥadīth* in support of this. Having said this, however, *taʻzīr* punishments may also consist of a mere verbal reprimand, imprisonment, and according to some, also of banishment, depending on the nature of the offence, the conditions of the offender and considerations of public interest (*maṣlaḥah*).[45]

THE *ḤUDŪD* DEBATE

The following paragraphs draw attention to the concern over the observance or otherwise of the rule of law in the implementation of the prescribed penalties of *ḥudūd.* Attention is drawn in particular to a certain neglect in the established *fiqh* of the textual dispensations of the Qur'ān concerning repentance and the prospects for rehabilitation and reform. Punishment in Islamic law falls under the general heading of *mu'āmalāt*, that sphere of the law which is concerned with social affairs and transactions. Unlike devotional matters which are mainly regulated by the text, the *mu'āmalāt* are open to considerations of public interest. In almost every area of *mu'āmalāt*, be it commercial law, constitutional law, taxation or international relations, the *Sharī'ah* lays down some basic rules and leaves the rest to be regulated by human legislation based on *ijmā'*, *shūrā*, *maṣlaḥah* and *ijtihād*. In this way the *Sharī'ah* itself leaves room for development of laws based on the ordinances of legitimate goverments and leaders.

The head of state and judge enjoy only limited powers to grant a pardon to a convicted offender, or to order discretionary punishment for unstipulated violations. The deterrent (*ta'zīr*) punishments are open to court discretionary powers to determine the quantitative aspect of the punishment only for conduct which is prescribed by the *Sharī'ah*. The judges have no powers to create an offence, without valid evidence in the sources, on discretionary grounds.

It seems that both the *fiqh* jurists and Islamic fundamentalists substantially concur in their perceptions of *ḥudūd* as fixed and mandatory penalties, yet the latter tend to elevate the ranking of *ḥudūd* to one of the first and foremost agenda of an Islamic government. We have reservations over these positions which we have elsewhere explained but propose only to address here the basic Qur'ānic positions on *ḥudūd*, as considerations of brevity do not permit a fuller treatment of issues.

1) The Qur'ān specifies punishment for four offences, namely theft, adultery, slanderous accusation (*qadhf*) and highway robbery (*ḥirābah*). This by itself is evidence to preclude the two other offences, namely wine-drinking (*shurb*) and apostasy (*riddah*) from the purview of *ḥudūd*. For *ḥadd* by definition is an offence for which the text prescribes a punishment and the Qur'ān specifies no punishment for these two offences. The *fiqh* manuals have, on the other hand, included *shurb* and *riddah* in the category of *ḥudūd*.
2) In all the four instances where the Qur'ān specifies a punishment, it also makes provisions for repentance and reform. This aspect of

the *ḥudūd* has been totally ignored in the juristic discourse of *fiqh*. Our argument is that the Qur'ān has prescribed punishments for these offences which are, however, not fixed and mandatory simply because references to these punishments are immediately followed by provisions on reformation and repentance, a combination which cannot accommodate the idea of fixed and mandatory enforcement. Yet conventional *fiqh* has overlooked this combination and has simply opted for mandatory enforcement. Let us review the four verses under discussion.

(a) Theft (*sariqah*)
As for the thief, male or female, cut off their hands as retribution for their deed and exemplary punishment from God. And God is exalted in power, Most Wise. But one who repents after his crime and amends his conduct, God redeems him. God is Forgiving, Most Merciful. (5:38–9)

وَالسَّارِقُ وَالسَّارِقَةُ فَاقْطَعُوا أَيْدِيَهُمَا جَزَاءً بِمَا كَسَبَا نَكَالاً مِّنَ اللّهِ وَاللّهُ عَزِيزٌ حَكِيمٌ. فَمَن تَابَ مِن بَعْدِ ظُلْمِهِ وَأَصْلَحَ فَإِنَّ اللّهَ يَتُوبُ عَلَيْهِ إِنَّ اللّهَ غَفُورٌ رَّحِيمٌ.

(b) Adultery and Fornication (*zinā*)
As for the woman and the man guilty of *zinā* (adultery, fornication), flog each of them one hundred lashes. Let not compassion move you away in their case from carrying out God's law… unless they repent thereafter and amend themselves, then, God is Forgiving, Most Merciful. (24:2, 5)

الزَّانِيَةُ وَالزَّانِي فَاجْلِدُوا كُلَّ وَاحِدٍ مِّنْهُمَا مِئَةَ جَلْدَةٍ وَلَا تَأْخُذْكُم بِهِمَا رَأْفَةٌ فِي دِينِ اللَّهِ... إِلَّا الَّذِينَ تَابُوا مِن بَعْدِ ذَلِكَ وَأَصْلَحُوا فَإِنَّ اللَّهَ غَفُورٌ رَّحِيمٌ.

(c) Slanderous Accusation
And those who accuse chaste women and fail to produce four witnesses, flog them eighty lashes and accept not their testimony ever after, for they are transgressors – except for those who repent thereafter and reform themselves, then, God is Forgiving, Most Merciful. (24:4, 5)

وَالَّذِينَ يَرْمُونَ الْمُحْصَنَاتِ ثُمَّ لَمْ يَأْتُوا بِأَرْبَعَةِ شُهَدَاءَ فَاجْلِدُوهُمْ ثَمَانِينَ جَلْدَةً وَلَا تَقْبَلُوا لَهُمْ شَهَادَةً أَبَدًا وَأُوْلَئِكَ هُمُ الْفَاسِقُونَ. إِلَّا الَّذِينَ تَابُوا مِن بَعْدِ ذَلِكَ وَأَصْلَحُوا فَإِنَّ اللَّهَ غَفُورٌ رَّحِيمٌ.

d) Highway Robbery
For this offence the text (5:33) prescribes a three-fold punishment which consists of crucifixion, mutilation of limbs and banishment, depending on whether the robber has both killed and robbed his victim or committed the one and not the other crime, or that he only terrorized the people without inflicting any loss of life and property. The text then immediately continues to provide: Except for those who repent before they fell into your power, in which case, know that God is Forgiving, Most Merciful. (5:34)

إِلاَّ الَّذِينَ تَابُوا مِن قَبْلِ أَن تَقْدِرُوا عَلَيْهِمْ فَاعْلَمُوا أَنَّ اللَّهَ غَفُورٌ رَّحِيمٌ.

The *ḥudūd* issues are lengthy and involved. I have discussed them elsewhere in fuller detail.[46] It will be noted, however, that repentance and reform are an integral part of the Qur'ānic text on these offences, but the Muslim jurists have simply turned a blind eye to this aspect of the text, and relegated it into insignificance by subsuming repentance under the ambiguous juristic formulations of Right of God (*ḥaq Allah*) and Right of Man (*ḥaq al-adami*). Thus the argument was advanced that repentance prior to arrest in the case of highway robbers and other *ḥadd* offences absolved the offender from punishment in so far as it related to the Right of God (or community's right) aspect of the offence but not in respect of the Right of Man. It is proposed here that the text does not draw this line of distinction. There is no recognition at all of the division between the Right of God and Right of Man. It is a juristic addition that has introduced unnecessary complication into the reading of the Qur'ān. If we were to take a holistic approach to the Qur'ānic outlook on *ḥudūd* we would simply need to make reformation and repentance an integral part of our reading of the Qur'ān on this subject.

The present writer has elsewhere advanced the argument that the words *ḥadd* and *ḥudūd* are not used in the Qur'ān in the sense of mandatory and fixed penalties, which the jurists later proposed and eventually established. By defining *ḥadd* as a fixed punishment (*uqūbah muqaddarah*) the jurists proposed that the punishment is invariably mandatory and fixed, and by doing so, they left no room for repentance and reform in the adjudication of *ḥudūd* crimes. Our investigation of the Qur'ānic usage of *ḥadd* and *ḥudūd* reveals that the terms are used in a more flexible sense which are not even confined to the context of crime but occur in reference, for example, to divorce in the event when the spouses 'fear they cannot keep to *ḥudūd Allah*', implying the limits of correct conduct in marriage (cf. Qur'ān, 2:229) and in reference also to devotional acts and *'ibadāt* when the text speaks in praise of those who observe the *ḥudūd Allah* (cf. 9:12), and in reference also to atonement (*kaffārāt*) (cf. 58:3–5). Indeed the Qur'ān shows little concern to enforce the *ḥudūd Allah* through the modality of fixed and mandatory punishment. The whole idea of *ḥudūd* in the sense of fixed penalties is, in other words, a juristic construct of a later origin that stands at odds with a holistic reading of the text.[47]

One of the most significant features of the principle of legality is to curb the exercise of arbitrary power in goverment especially of despotic monarchs and autocrats, whose words were law and the principle of legality sought to change it. In the light of this, I now turn to a brief illustration of an aspect of Islamic legal tradition in the work of al-Sarakhsī.

AL-SARAKHSĪ AND THE RULE OF LAW

Shamsuddīn al-Sarakhsī (d. 1090), one of the most distinguished jurists and author of the encyclopedic thirty-volume *al-Mabsūṭ*, reflects a basic attitude in the legal tradition. The following remarks by Sarakhsī appear in the course of his discussing the legal regime of waters and the role of state and ruler in the protection of the rule of law. The question put to Sarakhsī is 'about the validity of the granting by the Emir of Khurāsān to an individual of a right of irrigation from the waters of a great river, when that right was not [so established] before, or if the individual had irrigation for two *kuwwas* [a measure of flow] and the Emir increased this measure and granted him that right over a land which may or may not be on the land of a third party'.

Sarakhsī's answer involves principles of larger impact than the strict watersharing issue at hand:

> If the decision of the Emir harms the public, it is prohibited, and it is permissible if it doesn't, that is, if [the operation] did not take place on the land of a third party, for the ruler [*ṣulṭan*] has a right of

> supervision [*wilāyat naẓar*] without harming the public. So in case there is no such harm, the grant is valid for the grantee, but if harm occurs, the grant would be harmful to the public and the sultan is not allowed to carry it out.

Sarakhsī further explained that

> in the case of harm to the public, each individual can ask for the order's rescission, for the ruler [*imām*] would be nullifying the individual's right [*mubṭilan ḥaqqah*]. The ruler has only authority to collect his right of the public [*wilāyat ist fā ḥaqq al- 'āmma*] and not the authority to impair them, and that only in a way which does not harm the public.

In the particular case at hand, 'the grant should not have taken place . . . and it is not permissible for the Emir of Khurāsān to empty [*aṣfā*] a man's right of irrigation over his land to the benefit of another, and the right must be given back to the original beneficiary and to his heirs'.

It is due to caution exercised in reference to the ruler that Sarakhsī uses this word *iṣfā'* (literally the 'drying' or 'emptying' of a right) instead of usurpation (*ghaṣb*). What is meant by the word *iṣfā'* is usurpation (*ghaṣb*, wrongful seizure) but he kept his tongue and did not use the word. Sarakhsī added that the ruler is equal to others before the law (*al-ṣulṭān ka-ghayrihi shar'an*). Didn't the Prophet say: the hand is responsible for what it took until it gives it back? The granting of ownership to someone other than the right owner is void, and the good which is wrongfully appropriated must be returned to its owner if alive and to his heirs after his death, and so for the sultan's appropriation of what belongs to the people.

This passage epitomizes the complex attitude to the rule of law which the Islamic tradition conveys, yet it confirms clearly that there is a rule of law which is independent of the authority of the ruler, and 'the people' are entitled to protection againt the ruler's impingement on their rights. Evidence of an effective line drawn between several spheres inside and outside goverment is manifold in the history and law books, but Sarakhsī shows how constraints operate on a writer, who must 'keep his tongue' (*hafiẓa lisānah*) while articulating in the meantime the ruler's breach of law.

In the history of Muslim societies, the list of those who spoke their mind is long, and paid a heavy price for it. Sarakhsī is reported to have written the *Mabsūṭ* while in prison for 'a word of advice' to the local ruler.[48] But there is no doubt that an infringement of the rule of law, here connected with administrative expropriation of an individual right, was clear to the jurist.

CONCLUSION

I conclude this chapter by reiterating that criminal judicial procedure in the *Sharī'ah* remains largely open to the prospects of refinement and growth within the general framework of *siyāsah shar'iyyah*. The textual guidelines of the Qur'ān and Sunnah on criminal procedure that I have examined in this chapter generally point in the same direction in so far as Islamic law supports any procedure that advances the cause of justice and fair treatment and does not, in the meantime, violate considerations of public interest. *Siyāsah shar'iyyah* is itself predicated on *maṣlaḥah* and it is, as such, changeable as it must respond to the exigencies of time and circumstance and cannot, as it were, be all predicted and legislated in advance. Even if the broad outlines of *siyāsah shar'iyyah* on criminal procedure were to be codified, the head of the state and judges would still be left with a measure of discretionary powers under *siyāsah shar'iyyah* which they can utilize in response to exceptional and emergency situations that cannot be adequately dealt with under the normal rules of the *Sharī'ah*.

NOTES

1. Cf. Herbert Packer, *The Limits of the Criminal Sanction*, 140 ff.
2. Cf. Maḥmaṣṣānī, *Arkān*, 107–8.
3. al-Nabhān, *Niẓām al-Ḥukm*, 167.
4. Hamid Enayat, *Modern Islamic Political Thought*, 128.
5. Cf. Abū Zahrah, *Tanẓīm*, 34–5; Mutawallī, *Mabādī'*, 387; Ghazāwī, *al-Ḥurriyyah*, 26.
6. Muslim, *Ṣaḥīḥ Muslim*, Kitāb al-Amānah, Bāb Wujūb Ṭā'at al-Umarā' fi Ghayr al-Ma'ṣiyah wa Taḥrīmuhā fi'l-Ma'ṣiyah, *ḥadīth* no. 39. This *ḥadīth* is reported in both Bukhārī and Muslim.
7. Abū Dāwūd al-Sijistānī, *Sunan Abū Dāwūd*, tr. Ahmad Hasan, *ḥadīth* no. 2285.
8. Mawdūdī, *Human Rights in Islam*, 33.
9. Maḥmaṣṣānī, *Arkān*, 94.
10. Abū Yūsuf, *Kitāb al-Kharāj*, 152.

11. Abū Dāwūd, *Sunan*, tr. Ahmad Hasan, *ḥadīth* no. 3582; Maḥmaṣṣānī, *Arkān*, 107.
12. al-Sha'rānī, *al-Mīzān*, 2: 165; see also al-Awad M. Awad, 'The Rights of the Accused', 94.
13. Cf. Al-Ṣāleḥ, 'The Right of the Individual', 66.
14. Maḥmaṣṣānī, *Arkān*, 106.
15. al-Bayhaqī, *al-Sunan al-Kubrā*, Kitāb al-Da'wā wa al-Bayyināt, Bāb al-Bayyinah 'alā al-Mudda'ā wa al-Yam n 'alā al-Mudda'ā 'alayh.
16. Muslim, *Mukhtaṣar Saḥīḥ Muslim*, *ḥadīth* 1053; Ibn al-Qayyim, *al-Ṭuruq al-ḥukmiyyah fi 'l Siyāsah al-Shar'iyyah*, ed. Muḥammad Ḥāmid al-Faqī, 94.
17. Ibn al-Qayyim, *al-Ṭuruq*, 28.
18. Ibn Taymiyyah, *al-Siyāsah al-Shar'iyyah*, 153.
19. al-Qarāfī, *Kitāb al-Furūq* V: 54; Ibn Farḥūn, *Tabṣirah*, I, 131; Ibn Qayyim, *I'lām*, II, 87.
20. Al-Sha'rānī, *al-Mizān*, II, 137; Muḥammad Saleem El-Awa, *Punishment in Islamic Law*, 128.
21. Ibn al-Qayyim, *al-Ṭuruq al-Ḥukmiyyah*, 5; Saḥnūn ibn Sa'īd al-Tanūkhī, *al-Mudawwanah al-Kubrā*, IV, 293. Faḥd al-Suwaylim, *al-Muttaham*, 184.
22. al-Sharbīnī, *Mughnī al-Muḥtāj*, IV, 150; Faḥd al-Suwaylim, *al-Muttaham*, 187–8.
23. A1-Sha'rānī, *Kitāb al-Mizān*, II, 166.
24. Abū Dāwūd, *Sunan*, tr. Aḥmad Hassan, *ḥadīth* no. 3576.
25. A1-Sha'rānī, *al-Mizān*, II, 169.
26. Maḥmūd Shalṭūt, *al-Islām:* 327; see also A1-Sha'rānī, *al-Mizān*, II, 125.
27. Cf. Muḥammad al-Bahī, *al-Dīn wa al-Dawlah*, 394.
28. Maḥmūd Shalṭūt, *al-Islām*, 327.
29. Ibn Ḥazm, *al-Muḥallā*, II, 55.
30. Maḥmūd Shalṭūt, *al-Islām*, 327.
31. 'Abd al-Qādir 'Awdah, *al-Tashrī' al-Jinā'ī al-Islāmī* I, 115. The Arabic version of the maxim reads: *lā ḥukm li af'āl al-'uqalā' qabl wurūd al-naṣṣ.*
32. al-Ghazālī, *al-Mustaṣfā*, I, 63; Al-Āmidī, *al-Iḥkām*, I, 130.
33. Khallāf, *'Ilm Uṣūl al-Fiqh*, 173.
34. Cf. 'Awdah, *Tashrī'*, I, 117.
35. Ibid., I, 115.
36. 1bid., I, 133.
37. Khallāf, *'Ilm Uṣūl al-Fiqh*, 98.
38. Abū Zahrah, *al-Jarīmah*, 185.
39. Muslim, *Ṣaḥīḥ Muslim*, Kitāb al-Imān, Bāb al-Islām yahdim mā qablah wa kadhā al-hijrah wa al-hajj; Abū Zahrah, *al-Jarīmah*, 343.
40. Ibid., 323; al-Sāleḥ, 'The Right of the Individual', 63.
41. Ibid., 60.
42. Abū Zahrah, *al-Jarīmah*, 209.
43. Al-Māwardī explains that some jurists, like Abū 'Abd Allāh al-Zubayr al-Shāfi'ī, have stated a maximum limit of one month's detention for purposes of investigation. Others have suggested different time limits, but the best view is that the Imām may specify the limit as he deems fit. See Māwardī, *al-Aḥkām*, 192; 'Awdah, *al-Tashrī'*, I, 150.
44. Abū Zahrah, *al-Jarīmah*, 208; 'Awdah, *al-Tashrī'*, I. 308.
45. See for details Ibn al-Qayyim, *al-Ṭuruq*, 124; see also Māwardī, *al-Aḥkām*, 205.

46. M. H. Kamali, *Punishment*, Kuala Lumpur: tr. Ilmiah Publishers, 2004. See also idem, *Islamic Law in Malaysia*, 135 f.
47. See for details Kamali, *Punishment*, ch.3, 'An Analysis of *ḥadd* in the Qur'ān, sunnah and Fiqh,' at 45–52.
48. All quotations are from al-Sarakhsī, *Kitab al-Mabsūṭ*, vol. xxiii, 183. See for discussion also Mallat, *Islam and Public Law*, 3–6.

10

DEMOCRACY, FUNDAMENTAL RIGHTS AND THE *SHARĪ'AH*

This chapter is presented in six sections that look into the various aspects of harmony and divergence between democracy, fundamental rights and the *Sharī'ah.* We begin with an overview of justice and rights from the *Sharī'ah* perspective and discuss some of the Orientalist viewpoints concerning them. This is followed in the next sections, by a discussion of rights and liberties and the secularist view. Democracy is the subject of another section where attention is drawn to the growing support for it among Islamic parties and movements in recent years. We then discuss civil society in some detail before ending the chapter with a conclusion and recommendations.

AN OVERVIEW OF JUSTICE

We begin with a brief examination of justice as a matrix of rights and duties in Islam and then proceed to address the Orientalist claim that Islam does not recognize any rights, fundamental or otherwise, for the individual. This is followed by a discussion of the source evidence on freedom, and then we raise the question whether all of this should be secularized and divorced, as some commentators suggest, from the religious tradition and context.

Justice is generally understood to mean 'putting everything in its rightful place', and in the context of *Sharī'ah* as 'giving everyone his or her entitlement'. Islam's unqualified commitment to impartial justice is manifested in numerous places in the Qur'ān. We also note that the Qur'ānic conception of justice is neither rigid nor rule-bound but open to a variety of considerations. This can be seen from the juxtaposition in various places in the text of such concepts as *ma'rūf* (decent, fair, customary) and *iḥsān* (equity, the doing of good) next to *'adl* (justice). The Qur'ān and Sunnah also integrate intuitive insight (*firāsah*) and considerations of a just policy (*siyāsah shar'iyyah*) into its vision of justice. Moreover, the *Sharī'ah* validates *ijtihād bi'l-ra'y* (opinion-based legal judgement) as a basis of adjudication in the absence of a clear text. When the judge adjudicates on the basis of *ijtihād*, he relies not only on his understanding of *Sharī'ah* but also his conscience, insight and experience. This is equivalent to saying that equity and fairness constitute important ingredients of both *ijtihād* and *'adl* in Islam. Justice is primarily administered under the rule of law, the *Sharī'ah*, and everyone is accountable by its standards. This is integrated in the Qur'ānic conception of a law-abiding community, the *ummah*. A certain disagreement has arisen, however, over the accountability of the head of state and his subservience to the rule of law. Whereas the Shī'ites maintain the idea of rule by a rightly guided and infallible Imām, understood to be a descendant of the Prophet, the Sunnis maintain that the community need not be headed by a descendent of the Prophet as long as it is governed by the law. The Shī'ite position was also adjusted somewhat by the late Ayatollah Khomeini's idea of the *vilayat-e faqih* (rule of jurisconsult) which brought the Shī'ite theory close to the Sunni position by holding that the jurist who abides by the *Sharī'ah* effectively succeeds the infallible Imām.

Corrective or retributive justice consists largely of a balanced implementation of rights and obligations. It is the role of the courts and enforcement agencies to ensure redress and judicial relief whenever this balance is disturbed.[1] Surely justice cannot consist only of obligations without the recognition of rights as their necessary correlatives, yet this is precisely what Western Islamologists have asserted about Islam. To quote Hamilton Gibb, 'the Islamic theory of government gives the citizen as such no place or function except as taxpayer and submissive subject', and according to Schacht, 'Islamic law is a system of duties.'[2] Henry Siegman categorically stated that 'no such abstractions as individual rights could have existed in Islam'.[3] Western critics of Islam have maintained similarly negative positions over the prospects of democracy, civil society and constitutional government in Islam, subjects which will be elaborated below.

Exaggerated claims have also been made by Muslim fundamentalists that have bearings on Islam's perspective on justice and government under the rule of law. These are some of the issues we address in the following pages, yet it will be noted that the main realm of abuse in many contemporary Muslim countries is not so much judicially ordered justice, but outside this sphere: abuse of executive power, abridgement of rights and liberties, and violence by both governments and Islamic fundamentalists.

RIGHTS AND LIBERTIES

Notwithstanding a lack of consensus over the basic definition of 'right' in the Islamic discourse, the word '*ḥaqq*' is often said to convey a basic meaning regardless of definitions. *Ḥaqq* (right) in the Qur'ān occurrs in several places and carries a variety of meanings, which include justice, right as opposed to falsehood, a legal claim, an obligation, something that is proven and an assigned portion. The many meanings of *ḥaqq* in the Qur'ān may be said to be a cause sometimes of ambiguity, even misunderstanding. For instance the shared meaning of *ḥaqq* between a right and an obligation has persuaded Western Islamologists to draw, as already noted, the unwarranted conclusion that Islam recognizes only obligations but no right inhering in the individual. This is tantamount to turning a blind eye to the affirmative stance of the Qur'ān and Sunnah on the rights of the individual, including his right to life, right to justice, right to equality, right of ownership, right to sustenance and support within the family, parental rights, right of inheritance and so forth.

Islam's commitment to justice and its advocacy of human dignity could not be sustained without the recognition of rights. It is not our purpose, however, to engage in technical details but to identify the main contours of the debate.[4] We may add in passing, nevertheless, that Islam's perspective on rights and liberties is somewhat different from that of constitutional law and democracy and their underlying Western postulates. Islam, like other great religions, is primarily concerned with human relations. In ordinary life, people do not live primarily in terms of rights against others but in terms of mutual relationships involving love, compassion, self-preservation and self-sacrifice in pursuit of happiness and peace for themselves and their loved ones. The great religious traditions teach people, with good reason, that such things are not a matter of course nor are they always a question of rights. This would partially explain why most religions tend to emphasize moral virtue, obligation, love and sacrifice even more than the individual's rights and claims.

Other differences between the Islamic and Western conceptions of right and duty may be summarized in four points. First, rights and obligations in Islam are inter-related and reciprocal and there is a greater emphasis on obligation that is indicative of the moralist leanings of *Sharī'ah.* Western jurisprudence tends to emphasize rights in tandem with its stronger individualist leanings. The *Sharī'ah* discourse on rights and liberties bears on the other hand the imprints of the Qur'ānic terminology which is premised on a clear distinction between *ḥaqq* and *wājib* (right and obligation) respectively. The difference of terminology is even more striking in reference to freedom, where the concept is expressed both in the Qur'ān and in the *fiqh* literature in such terms as permissibility (*ibāḥah, mubāḥ*), absence of liability (*barā'ah al-dhimmah*) and other similar terms as elaborated below. The renowned scale of five values in *Sharī'ah* (*al-aḥkām al-khamsah*) which begins with *wājib* (duty, obligation) and ends with *ḥarām* (prohibition) consists of three intermediate categories of recommendable (*mandūb*), permissible (*mubāḥ*), and reprehensible (*makrūh*). The intermediate categories consist essentially of options that offer scope for personal freedom. The scope of liberty is thus much wider than that of *wājib* and *ḥarām*.

Another peculiarity of the *Sharī'ah* discourse on rights and duties is that *Sharī'ah* speaks mainly of *ḥukm* (ruling, pl. *aḥkām*), which subsumes both rights and obligations. Even the permissible (*mubāḥ*) is included under the *aḥkām* due to the pervasive influence of *ḥukm* in the *Sharī'ah*, which often subsumes the permissible options. This language and terminology of the *aḥkām* is plausibly equated in the Orientalist discourse with duties and the conclusion that Islam only provides for duties and no rights. This conclusion evidently pays more attention to linguistic analysis and style at the expense of meaning and substance. The fact that the Qur'ān does not speak in the language of a twentieth-century constitution is taken to mean a negative position on freedom. A closer examination of the text leads us to different conclusions over the reality of freedom in Islam.

The Qur'ān is affirmative on religious freedom and pluralism when it declares that

> there shall be no compulsion in religion. (2:256)
>
> لا إكْرَاهَ فِي الدِّين.

This is endorsed in a number of other places in the holy Book to substantiate freedom of religion. This can be seen, for example, in the Prophet Muhammad's assignment in respect of *da'wah* (call to the faith) as in the following verses:

> If God had willed, everyone on the face of the earth would have been believers. Are you then compelling the people to become believers? (10:99)
>
> وَلَوْ شَاء رَبُّكَ لآمَنَ مَن فِي الأَرْضِ كُلُّهُمْ جَمِيعًا أَفَأَنتَ تُكْرِهُ النَّاسَ حَتَّى يَكُونُوا مُؤْمِنِينَ.
>
> Let whosoever wills – believe, and whosoever wills – disbelieve. (18:29)
>
> فَمَن شَاء فَلْيُؤْمِن وَمَن شَاء فَلْيَكْفُرْ.
>
> And you are not to compel the people, so remind by means of the Qur'ān those who take heed. (50:45)
>
> وَمَا أَنتَ عَلَيْهِم بِجَبَّارٍ فَذَكِّرْ بِالْقُرْآنِ مَن يَخَافُ وَعِيدِ.
>
> say to the unbelievers: unto you, your religion, and unto me, my religion. (109:6)
>
> لَكُمْ دِينُكُمْ وَلِيَ دِين.

The Qur'ān thus maintains that faith must be through conviction and that faith which is induced by compulsion is meaningless. Further on religious pluralism, the Qur'ān has, in more than one place, characterized itself as 'an affirmation of the previous revelations and scriptures' that were revealed to other great Prophets preceding Muḥammad (5:44; 5:48; 3:84).

The Qur'ānic principle of *ḥisbah*, that is, promotion of good and prevention of evil (*amr bi'l ma'rūf wa nahy 'an al-munkar*), takes for granted the basic freedom of the individual to speak out, to act, or remain silent, in respect of a good cause, or against evil (3:104; 3:110; 22:41). The Prophet also substantiated this principle in several *ḥadīths*. The detailed guidelines that were subsequently provided in the works of *fiqh* on *ḥisbah* are designed on the whole to regulate the exercise of this freedom. In a similar vein, the Qur'ānic principle of *shūrā* (consultation) (3:159; 42:38) in community affairs, and its parallel principle of *naṣīḥah* (sincere advice) (9:91; 7:68) which grants the individual the freedom to advise, even criticize, another person, including a government leader, also proceeds from the affirmative stance that the Qur'ān takes on freedom of expression.[5] The individual is expected to make his own judgement and determine the course of his action and conduct.

The source evidence of *Sharīʿah* is even more explicit on freedom of the individual to criticize government leaders and eventually to disobey an unlawful command they may seek to impose. This is conveyed in the clear text of several *ḥadīths*:

> There is no obedience in transgression. Obedience is due only in righteousness.[6]
>
> لا طاعة فى معصية، إنما الطاعة فى المعروف.
>
> When you see my community afraid of telling a tyrant, 'O Tyrant,' then it is not worth belonging to it any more.[7]
>
> إذا رأيت أمتى تهاب أن تقول للظالم يا ظالم فقد تودع منها.
>
> Tell the truth, even if it be unpleasant.[8]
>
> قل الحقّ ولو كان مرّا.
>
> The best form of jihad is to say a word of truth to an oppressive ruler.[9]
>
> أفضل الجهاد كلمة حق عند سلطان جائر.

The *fiqh* terminology on freedom is once again somewhat different from the familiar clauses of a modern constitution. Yet there is little doubt of the affirmation of freedom as a normative position in Islam. For reasons that will be explained below, instead of using the standard Arabic term *ḥurriyyah* to denote freedom, *fiqh* writers use such other terms as *ibāḥah* (permissibility), *mubāḥ* (permissible), *barā'ah al-aṣliyyah* (original freedom from liability) and *ʿafw*, or *manṭiqat al-ʿafwa* (sphere of forgiveness). The *fiqh* language has in this regard been influenced by the terminology of the Qur'ān which also uses a number of alternative terms for freedom, such as *aḥall Allah lakum* (God has made permissible to you), *la junāḥa ʿalaykum* (there is no blame on you), *lā yanhākum Allah* (God does not forbid you), *lā ithma ʿalaykum* (you commit no sin), *lā yu'akhidhkum Allah* (God does not take you to task), *lā ḥaraj* (no objection), etc., to convey the basic idea of freedom. This is a peculiarity of the Qur'ānic language of God's communication to humans, where grant of permissibility and forgiveness and absence of liability and blame are used as substitutes for *ḥurriyyah*. The manner of expression may be different, but the substance of freedom in all of them is undeniable.

God's affirmation in the Qur'ān that 'We bestowed dignity on the children of Adam' (17:70) وَلَقَدْ كَرَّمْنَا بَنِي آدَمَ is endorsed elsewhere in the text where it is proclaimed that 'God created people in the natural state', which is the state of freedom, followed by the affirmation that this is God's own illustrious will, and

> none may change what God has determined. (30:30)
>
> لَا تَبْدِيلَ لِخَلْقِ اللَّهِ.

In another place the Qur'ān specifies the three major goals of the Prophethood of Muhammad as follows:

> He enjoins them [his followers] good and forbids them evil, and makes lawful to them the good things and prohibits them from that which is impure, and removes from them the burdens and the shackles which were on them before. (7:157)
>
> يَأْمُرُهُم بِالْمَعْرُوفِ وَيَنْهَاهُمْ عَنِ الْمُنكَرِ وَيُحِلُّ لَهُمُ الطَّيِّبَاتِ وَيُحَرِّمُ
> عَلَيْهِمُ الْخَبَائِثَ وَيَضَعُ عَنْهُمْ إِصْرَهُمْ وَالأَغْلاَلَ الَّتِي كَانَتْ عَلَيْهِمْ.

The three paramount goals of Islam that are thus specified are to promote *ḥisbah*, to identify the *ḥalāl* and *ḥarām*, and to free the people from unwarranted restrictions on their freedom.

THE SECULARIST CRITIQUE

The critics of Islamic law, including some modern thinkers among Muslims, have voiced the view that reform of Islamic law and political thought could be achieved through divorcing the 'reverential attitude' towards the text from the sober and rational evaluation of their import.[10]

Three points need to be made before we take a position over this. First, the concepts of right and freedom are relative and changeable as they are influenced by socio-cultural factors and conditions of time and place. Over the course of time, the concept of right may develop or be stretched and altered to fit some new setting and circumstance. This can be said of almost all legal and cultural traditions. The Universal Declaration of Human Rights 1948 is, for instance, a historic document of momentous significance, but it can now be seen to have mirrored the realities and concerns of that time, including the then attendant asymmetry of political power on the global scale.[11]

Our second point is over the universalist dimension of basic human rights which asserts that the concept of 'human rights' is a kind of shared universal, arrived at by different cultural routes but expressing nonetheless a kind of human consensus. For human rights are entitlements which all persons are supposed to possess simply by virtue of being human. These two aspects of human rights, manifesting respectively the reality and the ideal, can sometimes be difficult to compromise, and have often been prone to receiving divergent interpretations.

Third, the inseparable link between the freedom of religion and other fundamental rights and freedoms tend to suggest that freedom of religion could not be sought and implemented in isolation from other freedoms. 'Struggle for one freedom requires struggle for all other freedoms as well, for they are interdependent.' The exercise of religious freedom in Islam has not, as some commentators have noted, reflected the great diversity of convictions that exist around the world. It has been fairly said that no religious community should plead for its own people religious liberty without active respect and reverence for the faith and basic human rights of others.[12]

Our own understanding of the Islamic conceptions of right, freedom and human rights leads us to the conclusion that there are differences between the theistic view of right and freedom when compared to what they mean in a secular context, but we also note that taking a totally secular approach to them is not advisable in the Islamic context. We believe that human rights and democratic values would benefit if religious values are also taken into consideration.

Whereas the Islamic fundamentalists tend to be dogmatic and exceptionalist, the majority of Muslim observers tend to be inclusive rather than exclusive, universal rather than sectarian and thus receptive, within certain limits, to other viewpoints; they have also spoken affirmatively of the dialogue of civilizations.

For the religious reformers to carry forward their struggle for democracy and human rights, they should be seen as authentic articulators of change espousing an alternative from within rather than without the tradition. Yet they have to prove to the people that they have the knowledge, the ability and the skill to address their problems. Further details on the wider reaches of the secularist debate concerning Islam, and my own responses to them, appear in a separate section in chapter 13 below.

ISLAMIC PARTIES AND MOVEMENTS: GROWING SUPPORT FOR DEMOCRACY

Although Islamic fundamentalists are divided into numerous subgroups which subscribe to different views and philosophies, the radical factions among them have embraced controversial views on aspects of law and government, democracy and basic rights. The proponents of Syed Quṭb (d. 1966) and the *jihadist* groups equated, for instance, Egyptian society to *jāhiliyyah* (Age of Ignorance), accused it of infidelity and embarked on ruthless assassinations of government leaders. These were small and marginalized groups which have, however, evoked the widest media attention within their own countries and beyond.

Islamic fundamentalism emerged after a series of failures of Western-style constitutionalism of the so-called Westminster model that proved not quite workable in Muslim countries. Many Arab countries also tried socialism, Arab nationalism, Marxism and revolution that were ushered in mainly by military juntas, but instead of yielding desirable results and good governance, they brought about dictatorships, dissatisfaction, even disillusion of the masses with their rulers. Other factors that played a role are military defeat in the 1967 Arab/Israeli war, socio-economic dislocation and poverty. The masses, in frustration, turned to fundamentalism as a panacea for society's failings and economic ills.

Islamic fundamentalism was basically home-grown in Arab societies and its protest was mainly focused on the domestic policies of oppressive governments, especially following the torture and execution of Syed Quṭb under Nasser in 1966; the emergence of Baʿthist regimes and one-party systems in Syria and Iraq, as well as clashes between the state and fundamentalists in Algeria. Sudan and Tunisia were also engulfed in similar confrontations that revolved around oppressive government policies. Quṭb's ideas were taken as core ideology by Jama'at al-Muslimin, known as al-Takfīr wa'l-Hijrah, and Ḥizb al-Taḥrīr. Quṭb maintained that existing Arab states were really living in an Age of Ignorance, the idolatry from which the Prophet was sent to deliver his people. The rulers were aping idolatry manifested in both the Western and the communist worlds, the essence of which was to deny the sovereignty of God and confer it on human institutions. This idolatry infected everything: law and government, culture, art, literature, personal relations and so forth.

Whereas at the turn of the twentieth century leading thinkers such as Jamāl al-Dīn al-Afghāni, Muḥammad 'Abduh and Muhammad Iqbal recognized what was positive in both Western thought and Islamic traditions of their time, radical fundamentalism departed from the moderate stance of these thinkers due partly to the course of political events. Ataturk ended the Ottoman caliphate in Turkey in 1924 under the influence of Western secularism, which was also behind the developments in Egypt under Nasser in the 1950s, and Iran under Reza Shah Pahlavi (d. 1941) followed by his son Mohammad Reza (d. 1979). By this time the Cold War between the United States and Soviet Union had polarized world politics. Both sides preferred to install in office a leader whom they could control. Unfortunately the United States did not support democratization in the Muslim world during the latter part of the twentieth century. Western-influenced dictators suppressed traditional Islamic thought and religion, which also shaped the course of Islamic fundamentalism. To the fundamentalist, political freedom increasingly appeared to consist of opposing Western influence and reclaiming Islamic tradition and culture. Had the United States opposed dictators in the Muslim world, the linkage between Western influence and political oppression might not have materialized and the case of radical fundamentalism would have been weakened.[13]

The more moderate fundamentalist trends, the followers of Ḥasan al-Bannā (assassinated in 1949) and his Muslim Brotherhood, highlighted corruption, absence of democratic institutions and civil society as root causes of violence and protest within Arab societies. Al-Bannā accepted the Islamic state as the basic framework of political organization but maintained nevertheless that Islam allowed for multiple adaptations of its own stipulations. The *Sharīʿah* should be implemented, but implemented so that personal rights and liberties and people's authority over the government is maintained. Constitutional mandates on separation of powers, consultative government, and political and interpretative pluralism are acceptable to Islam. Bannā also maintained that mere religiosity without active commitment to the social and political will of society was aimless and misleading. Thus the legitimacy of the state stemmed from adherence to the mores and aspirations of society and execution of the social will.[14] Whereas radical fundamentalists resisted co-operation and dialogue with the Arab regimes and the West in general, moderate fundamentalism, which is often erroneously lumped with the radical trends, is on the whole open to dialogue and speaks affirmatively of basic rights and liberties, civil society, and pluralism.

The post-2001 election results in many Muslim countries show that moderate Islamic parties and movements have scored impressive results in electoral politics. Elections held in Pakistan (2001), Turkey (2002), Bahrain (2002), Morocco, Jordan (2003) and Indonesia (2004) manifest the increased presence of pro-democratization Islamic parties in unprecedented numbers, confirming the saliency of Islam in Muslim politics in the twenty-first century. The Hamas electoral victory in Palestine (2005) also complies with the general trend – although different in some respects. Islamic candidates and Muslim parties increased their influence tenfold in Pakistan, sixfold in Indonesia, and fourfold in Morocco. In Turkey, the Justice and Development Party came to power, and in Bahrain, Islamic candidates won nineteen out of forty parliamentary seats. In Indonesia the Justice and Development Party won forty-five out of 550 seats in parliament, a sixfold increase on the seven seats it won in the 1999 election. In Morocco, the Justice and Development Party won forty-two out of 325 seats in Parliament which represents a more than four-fold increase compared with the 1997 election. In Jordan the Islamic Action Front won seventeen out of 150 parliamentary seats in the 2003 election.

A slightly different picture emerges in Malaysia where the Islamic Party of Malaysia (PAS) lost ground in the 2004 election, reducing its presence in the Federal Parliament from the twenty-seven seats it won in the 1999 election to a mere six seats in 2004. This is explained largely by the change of leadership from Dr Mahathir to Abdullah Ahmad Badawi who presented a more conciliatory stance on Islam and often spoke in favour of integrating the best values of Islam in government. Abdullah Badawi's major policy statement and programme, entitled Islam Hadhari (civilizational Islam), in 2004 not only won him a landslide election victory but is also accountable for the PAS poor election results. This picture confirms nevertheless the general trend that the Muslim electorate support moderate parties and leaders who stand for good governance and democracy.

The reasons to explain these election results tend to vary in each country, but generally they reflect the failure of the governments in power and are heavily influenced sometimes by the course of international events. In the case of Pakistan, for example, the votes for Islamic parties in the 2001 election was as much an indicator of dissent against President General Musharraf's involvement with the US war in Afghanistan as it was a sign of opposition to his gutting of the nation's constitution and encroachment of the military in politics. Other reasons cited for the enhanced voting results for Islamic parties include support for democracy and greater openness of Islamic parties themselves to work with other secular parties to achieve shared goals. Islamic parties have also become more service-oriented and pay greater attention to people's welfare needs, and they are, moreover, relatively clean of corruption. They have often been outspoken in their critique of corrupt leaders, regional economic imbalances, and discontent with the status quo and dictatorship. The leadership of most Islamic movements continues to be lay rather than clergy; they are graduates of modern educational streams in science and engineering rather than madrasahs and religious disciplines. With the exception of Turkey where the Justice and Development (Islamic) party is in power, all the rest of Islamic parties constitute opposition movements.[15]

In a 2004 study of Islamic parties in Egypt (Muslim Brotherhood and Wasat Party), Jordan (Islamic Action Front and Wasat Party), Kuwait (Islamic Constitutional Movement) and Turkey (Justice and Development Party), it was found that Islamic parties represented a wide array of positions on strategic political issues and interpretations of Islam. There is near-consensus among mainstream Islamic leaders in key Arab countries and Turkey on the value of democratic participation. The reformist or *iṣlāḥī* trend among the leading Islamic parties in the key Arab countries has pushed for participation within their respective political systems, greater transparency and internal democracy. On *Sharīʻah*-related issues, there is greater willingness to promote the practice of *ijtihād* and reinterpretation of Islamic law to fit current circumstances. It was cautioned that an undifferentiated approach to Islamic parties that is commonly taken in most of the literature that lumps all Islamic fundamentalists together is a common but indefensible misperception.[16]

Commentators have recorded the view that participation in elections by itself is not a proof of the Islamic parties' attitude to liberalizing their party platform and agenda. Evidence is still lacking to show the extent of their openness to internal democracy, greater transparency and readiness to adjust over the role of *Sharīʻah* and gender equality. Yet the positions tend to vary from country to country. In response to the question whether the Islamic movements support the full range of civil and political rights for all citizens alike, the position tends to vary in countries such as Turkey, Indonesia, Jordan and Egypt, which are relatively more open compared to the rest of the Arab world, especially the Gulf countries. Many tend to subject women's role to conventional *Sharīʻah* interpretations, reject the liberal ethos of the West, and resist even internal reform and *ijtihād* within the *Sharīʻah*.

The extent of receptivity to adjustment over the role of *Sharīʻah* on gender issues tends to depend on four variables as follows:

1) Whether parties can go it alone or must engage in some form of coalition;
2) whether such coalition enhances receptivity to new ideas;
3) whether new ideas can be justified within the terms of their own agenda; and
4) whether coalition would marginalize internal critics who oppose beneficial change.

Unlike Turkey, Indonesia and Egypt where Islamic parties compete for power with an array of secular parties and movements, in the Arab world, Islamic parties operate in a system where non-Islamic parties have no significant presence or role. This would suggest that the Islamic parties have fewer incentives to moderate their politics.

Bahrain's parliament of eighty seats is half elected, and nineteen out of forty seats were won by Islamic candidates from Sunni and Shīʻite parties in the 2002 election. It is the only Gulf country where women are allowed to vote and run for office. However, no women were elected in the 2002 election. In Egypt, Kuwait and Jordan, Islamic parties have sometimes joined forces with secular parties to voice opposition to government policies but have compromised little on gender-related issues.[17] In the Arab world, there is political liberalization rather than democracy. Political parties, including Islamic parties, seek patrons within the state and participation in politics resembles lobbying more than it does direct representation of political interests. The state monopoly of political power prevents development of democratic systems. Islamic parties could win elections in these countries and impose their agendas without necessarily enhancing democratic rights and liberties.

Part of the explanation of the Islamic parties' support for democracy and pluralism, and their increased participation in electoral politics, is that they view themselves to be the main beneficiaries of the democratic process. Yet Islamic parties in Saudi Arabia and the Gulf region tended to be more selective in their commitment to democratic values than Islamic parties elsewhere. But even within the Gulf region there are shades of differences in attachment to democratic rights and liberties among Islamic parties. For instance, it was reported in May 2005 that the government of Kuwait named two women as members of its municipal council (a fairly low-profile body one might say) for the first time in the history of the Gulf Emirate. But even so, one of those two women, Fatima al-Sabah, was a member of the ruling family.[18]

Most Islamic parties have been gradually gaining supporters for years as secular parties have failed to solve grinding economic and social problems. But their sudden gain in votes in recent elections in Pakistan, Bahrain, Turkey and also Morocco is being viewed as a sign that the voters want to assert pride in their faith to the outside world.[19]

Radical fundamentalists are in a minority and tend to enjoy little support in electoral politics. Yet 11 September, the US occupation of Iraq and its deteriorating relations with Iran and Syria as well as its manner of friendship with Egypt, Saudi Arabia and Pakistan provided the Islamic militants with fresh incentives. Radical fundamentalists theoretically uphold the idea of a representative and accountable government that assumed power through consultation (*shūrā*), homage (*bay'ah*) and consensus (*ijmā'*), but tend to make its legitimacy contingent on abstract notions of adherence to the *Sharī'ah.* In so far as the government obeys the *Sharī'ah*, it cannot be legitimately toppled, and by this the original contract based on *shūrā* and *bay'ah* becomes shrouded in ambiguity. The public will manifested in these concepts represents the divine will, and therefore individuals or groups cannot stand against it. For these radical Muslims the freedom of the individual and his rights are not important and are secondary to the community, which is, in fact, managed and controlled by the state. The tendency thus develops that the individual is deemed to be either with or against the community. Minorities, special interest groups and private organizations are subjected to communal interests, which are determined by the state. Radical Muslims thus begin with the rights of the individual, but end up by suppressing them under totalitarian rule that can take shelter under the concept of general/divine will and the *Sharīʻah*.

For moderate Muslim thinkers, Islam's exhortation to justice does not preclude people's interpretations of it. On the subject of women's rights, for example, it is suggested that women's isolation from public life has been due to backward customary impositions on the Qur'ānic discourse. Thus what is needed is to restore women's originally independent status in the Qur'ān, and provide a social context where women can exercise their freedom and independence. It is then added that although pluralism is allowed in Islam, it would be conducted within a consensual context of a set of principles that lead to enhancement of disabled groups. Elections are not only permitted but considered as a form of testimony (*shahādah*) to the suitability of candidates for leadership. Political parties and associations are permitted, and Islam stands for consultative and constitutional government with limited powers subjected to the rule of law. Basic rights and freedoms must be protected and government is accountable to the people.[20]

ISLAM AND CIVIL SOCIETY

If one were to believe Ernest Gellner and Ellie Keddouri, then the Muslim world has little hope of democratization if it clings to its traditions. This is due, they maintain, to the absence of civil society in the Islamic world, the pervasive impact of clientism, 'government by network' in Muslim politics, and the absence of 'intellectual pluralism'. As a result, the Muslim world 'exemplifies a social order which lacks capacity to provide political countervailing institutions and association'.[21] Keddouri similarly wrote that 'the idea of representation, of elections, of popular suffrage, of political institutions being regulated by law passed by a parliamentary assembly, of these laws being guarded and upheld by an independent judiciary, the idea of the secularity of the state, of society being composed of a multitude of self-activating, autonomous groups, and associations – all these are profoundly alien to the Muslim political tradition'.[22]

Gellner and Keddouri are both misleading and oblivious of a number of important principles of Islam as well as the historical realities of Muslim societies. Contrary to these assertions, the whole history of Islam has been of a vibrant civil society which defied state control, especially in the intellectual sphere. The scholastic orientations of juristic thought, for example, have basically developed outside the state machinery. Civil society by definition consists of institutions which are of a voluntary nature and operate independently from the operations of political power. There is some truth in the claim that the Muslim *ummah*, as a self-defined religious community, is one that is, in theory at least, committed to 'an uncompromised devotion to virtue'. Gellner, who himself made this observation, has, interestingly enough, also unwittingly contradicted his earlier claim to absence of pluralism in Muslim communities by giving many examples of diverse sects and movements within the fabric of *ummah*.[23] A closer look at Muslim societies, past and present, tends to confirm that whatever their other problems, one of their distinguishing marks is their singular ability to safeguard the basic orientation of society against state encroachment and control, be it foreign or local. It seems that government has operated on the periphery of Muslim ethos and culture and has been unable to penetrate the core of Muslim identity. 'The truth is', as one of Gellner's critics observed, 'that Muslim societies do have the capacity to develop and sustain structures to defend freedoms against oppressive state mechanisms.'[24] Muslim commentators themselves have identified the absence of political and social freedom and the tyranny of political systems as main causes of the failure of democracy and constitutionalism in the Muslim world – rather than any inherent disabilities of these societies. Official incompetence and corrupt dictatorship as well as foreign factors rather than intrinsic inhibitions of Muslim religion and culture are accountable for the failure of democracy. It is further added in this connection, 'even a cursory look at the Arab world will show how much the Arab people, including the majority of fundamentalists, are interested in democratization and the construction of civil societies'.[25] According to another observer, 'there is a general agreement among the mainstream Islamists that democracy is the spirit of the Islamic governmental system, even though they reject the philosophical assumption of western democracy – that is, the sovereignty of the people'.[26] But even on the subject of sovereignty, according to a minority Muslim opinion, effective sovereignty belongs to the people. The advocates of this view maintain that attribution of sovereignty to God is an article of the Muslim faith and that the power to rule effectively belongs to the *ummah*. Some majority Muslim countries, such as Malaysia and Indonesia, may be said to have functioning democracies, though not without weaknesses. Malaysia has held eleven successful elections since independence in 1957 and most of them were free of rigging, fraud and serious distortion. This is by no means a negligible record. Islam also remains a living force in society, and one sees little convincing evidence of an inherent conflict between Islam and democracy in these countries.

The Qur'ānic principle of *ḥisbah*, to enjoin good and prevent evil, is primarily addressed to the individual and has been shouldered mainly by civil groups, not the state. *Ḥisbah* takes for granted the individual's right to participate in public debates, give an opinion, be actively involved and criticize government policy.[27] The parallel Qur'ānic concept of *naṣīḥah*, as also mentioned earlier, encourages individual initiative in advising government leaders and alerting them to error and weakness in their policies. The principle of *shūrā* is similarly premised on the participation of individuals and groups in decision-making in community affairs. The difference between *naṣīḥah* and *shūrā* is that a counsel within the rubric of *shūrā* is usually solicited before it is given, whereas neither the *ḥisbah* nor *naṣīḥah* depend on that requirement.

The Islamic concept of *farḍ kifāyah*, a duty that is incumbent on society as a whole, in contradistinction to *farḍ 'ayn*, which is addressed to every individual, is particularly conducive to the notion of civil society. To serve as a witness in the cause of justice, or as a judge for that matter, to carry out *ijtihād* or express an opinion and *fatwā* on issues of public concern, to serve as supervisor of *waqf* (charitable endowment) property, or take care of the orphans, etc. – all partake in *farḍ kifāyah*. Thus it is not right for one who can, as a witness, help the cause of justice but holds back for mere apprehension, even if piously motivated, that he may make an error and put someone in hardship as a result. On the contrary, the duty of *farḍ kifāyah* requires a proactive attitude to the advancement of public good in association primarily with other individuals and groups.

The *fiqh* schools and *madhhabs* which have survived to this day are civil society associations formed by the '*ulamā*' community following the intellectual contributions of leading imāms supported by their prominent disciples. The fact that the schools of law bear to this day the names of their individual founders, the Ḥanafi, Shāfi'ī, Māliki,

Ḥanbali, Ja'fari and so forth, is testimony to their civilian character away from government control. The official adoption of one or other of these *madhhabs* by states and constitutions is basically a latent development that featured under the Ottomans. The civilian aspect of these non-governmental associations was so accentuated as to become simultaneously a blessing and a problem, as I have discussed elsewhere. Producing legal opinions to address new and controversial issues was not the prerogative of the state but that of the private scholars who organized themselves in terms of scholastic and doctrinal orientations. The '*ulamā*''s real goal was not to pressurize governments, but to provide law and order that enabled the people to exercise their rights under the *Sharī'ah*. Since their legitimacy was grounded in civil society and not in formal governmental institutions, the influence of the '*ulamā*' was moral and therefore beyond the coercive power of the state. Further to illustrate this anti-statist tendency among the '*ulamā*', we may refer to the idea of general consensus (*ijmā'*), which is the only formula of making binding law known to the *Sharī'ah*, next to the Qur'ān and Sunnah, and it is conspicuously non-statist.[28]

The Sufi orders embodied yet another powerful civil society movement that has remained influential in almost every period of Islamic history. The Sufi masters were venerated by their followers as spiritual guides and leaders. The tenacity of the master-disciple relationship and associational network of Sufi orders often vested them with considerable influence. Ruling authorities were wary of the Sufi orders because of their autonomy and independent action. Research on sainthood and Sufism in fifteenth- and sixteenth-century Morocco, for instance, indicates that they often set limits to the abuse of authority. In their teachings, the Sufi movements emphasized the spiritual essence of the faith far beyond the narrower stipulations of law-based religion and scholarship. Sufism was critical of single-minded attachment to money, power and sacrifice of values in their pursuit and instead emphasized the spiritual impulse of Islam. The reassertion of Sufism in the 1980s, like those of other Islamic orders and associations, also signified renewed interest for collective action independent of both radical fundamentalists and the state.

Another important traditional institution of note is that of *waqf* (pl. *awqāf* – charitable endowment). It has often been argued that the rise of civil society in Europe was to a large extent conditioned by economic factors, most importantly the higher income levels and existence of surplus that empowered citizens to create non-governmental institutions. The institution of *waqf* has similarly played a distinctive economic role in fostering civil society in Muslim lands. It is instructive to note, for instance, that by the time of Muhammad Ali's death in the first half of twentieth century, the *awqāf* endowments in Egypt were providing 50 per cent of educational expenditure.

Guilds and merchants associations (*aṣnāf*) were also active among craftsmen and traders for most of Islamic history. They organized themselves around their professional interests and their leaders served as points of contact between their respective groups and the government authorities. The guilds often applied strict hierarchy and rules, from initiation in the craft through various stages until craftsmanship was attained. Guilds of merchants and craftsmen, although recognized by the Ottoman administration, operated in an autonomous manner, punishing infractions by their members, defining acceptable practices and settling disputes.[29]

And lastly, civil society associations also flourished among non-Muslim minorities in Muslim countries. The leaders of religious minorities represented their own communities and played much the same role as Muslim scholars and ʻ*ulamā*' did on behalf of the Muslims generally. Christian and Jewish minorities were permitted to observe their religious practices, personal laws and customs. Even when the Ottoman Empire codified the *Sharīʻah* according to the recognized four schools of law, the Ḥanafi school of law, which prevailed under the Ottomans, considered People of the Book (*Ahl al-Kitāb*) a genuine part of the mainstream community.[30]

The civil society role of guilds and the religious movements began to deteriorate by the late nineteenth century, and was diminished even further by the 1920s with the emergence of modern state laws and trade unions. As Islamic markets increasingly became part of international markets, traditional markets and crafts were weakened along with the civil society structures they had created. The new structures that replaced them have been unable either to create a true civil society or replicate the independent role played by the crafts, Sufis and ʻ*ulamā*'.

CONCLUSION AND RECOMMENDATIONS

We need to take a long-term view of the possible solutions to problems discussed in this chapter and I propose to address this in the following paragraphs.

1) To stand for moderation and balance (*wasaṭiyyah*, *tawassuṭ*, *i'tidāl*) is a defining element of the Qur'ānic vision of Muslim community, which is described as *ummatan wasaṭan* (2:143), a justly balanced nation that shuns extremism and over-indulgence even in things which might otherwise be praiseworthy and desirable. Moderation also signifies the ideals of an Islamic personality and civilization, for in it lies the essence of all virtues (*faḍā'il*) that Islam promotes. Moderation means avoidance of extremes consisting either of laxity and neglect (*tafrīṭ*, *taqṣīr*) or exaggeration and excess (*ifrāṭ*, *ghuluw*).[31] A perusal of the source evidence shows that moderation is unqualified and multidimensional and it permeates all aspects of Islam, including personal conduct, law, morality and culture, even matters of worship. There are reports in the *ḥadīth* literature that the Prophet discouraged extremism even in acts of devotion (*'ibadāt*) and instructed his community to 'give everything its rightful measure'. If extremism in prayer and *'ibadāh* is discouraged, that advice could by analogy be extended to martyrdom and *jihād.* The judge is advised, in the clear term of *ḥadīth*, not to be too eager in the administration of penalties, and if there be occasion that he cannot avoid a measure of doubt, then it is better for him to make an error on the side of forgiveness than on the side of severity and harshness. Common sense tells us that severity and extremism do not yield good results, rather it is rationality, enlightenment, good planning, consultation and perseverance that constitute important components of *wasaṭiyyah*.

A more detailed discussion of the evidence on *wasaṭiyyah* and its wider implications is attempted in a separate section in chapter 13 below.

2) Sincere advice and consultation (*naṣīḥah*, *shūrā*) that originate in knowledge and sincerity is meant to be an integral part of Islamic ethos at almost all levels, within the family, in the workplace, and the society at large. The Qur'ān also provides that 'the words of thy Lord find fulfilment in truth and justice' (*wa tammat kalimatu rabbika ṣidqan wa 'adlā*) (6:115). Then commitment to truth and justice, avoidance of rash judgements, and remaining patient in the face of adversity must take a high priority in Islamic values.

Yet at times of conflict and situations when one is exposed to divergent voices, the individual may find it hard to determine the sense of truth, balance and justice in all of them. This has now become a problem that Muslim societies face almost everywhere. Questions also arise as to the relevance of the divergent and self-assertive advice to the prevailing conditions and circumstances of the generation, the youth and the society at large. One would expect the media and organized education to provide the needed guidance on matters of concern to the community. Media and education planners should, perhaps, take more specific measures to identify clear agenda on civic education in their programmes. The schools may consider introducing a subject on civic education that provide perspectives, *inter alia*, on the ethical teachings of Islam, on *naṣīḥah*, moderation (*wasaṭiyyah*), the meaning of *jihād*, civil society matters and the crucial importance of peace for economic development that informs and sensitizes the people on what it takes to be a good citizen. Violence and senseless destruction have taken a heavy toll on Muslim societies. The twenty-three years of war in Afghanistan, for example, has pushed the country back by about a century and the people will continue to suffer from the aftermath of that devastating episode for years to come.

3) The international dimension of extremism is not difficult to see. Extremism has become globalized not only in the Muslim lands but also in the West. Aggressive policies and unbridled militarism over Palestine and Iraq should stop pushing Muslims into extremism. This can also be said of oppressive totalitarian governments in the Muslim lands. Violence and tyranny cannot be expected to provide solutions; they are the problem. Obviously there is a disconnection between the West and Islam whereby misunderstanding finds new grounds on both sides. Suicide bombing is an extremely disturbing and totally unprecedented phenomenon. No one in the fourteen centuries of Islam has included it in the meaning of martyrdom or *jihād*. It is wrong to violate innocent life whatever the rest of the argument may be. But I also see that anyone who resorts to suicide bombing does so in absolute despair, loss of faith in humanity and basic collapse of common reason. The crimes of 11 September 2001 were crimes of political protest, they were not something inexplicable or *sui generis*. They represented a final collapse of the centuries-old cosmopolitan conversation with Islam.

I have attempted a more detailed discussion of suicide bombing in a separate section in chapter 13 below.

4) With reference to justice and basic rights, it will be noted that the traditional *fiqh* in the areas of *al-aḥkām al-sulṭāniyyah* (principles

of government) and *siyāsah shar'iyyah* (*Sharī'ah*-oriented policy) has fallen short of reflecting the Qur'ān's comprehensive conception of justice in the sphere particularly of rights and liberties. We see this in Abū'l-Ḥassan al-Māwardi (d. 1058) as well as Abū Ya'lā al-Farrā (d. 1066), both distinguished authors of books bearing the title *al-Aḥkām al-Sulṭāniyyah*, which devote extensive chapters to caliphate, powers and duties of the caliph, the judiciary, taxation, criminal law and so forth, but none on consultative governance or the basic rights of the people. The distinguished authors of these works seem to have taken the realities of the Abbasid state as their basic framework of analysis and thus tended to vindicate the existing *status quo*. This was a structural weakness that set a pattern and the protracted era of *taqlīd*-oriented and imitative scholarship did little to change it.

Modern writings of Arabic origin under *niẓām al-ḥukm fi 'l-Islām* (system of rule in Islam) and *ḥuqūq al-Insān fi 'l-Islām* (human rights in Islam) are considerably more attentive to the rights of citizens *vis-à-vis* the coercive power of state. Yet here too the approach tends to be piecemeal and issue oriented, penetrating certain issues and leaving out others. With regard to freedom of religion, for example, many of the modern works speak of freedom of religion yet continue to reproduce conventional positions on conversion and apostasy. This is admittedly a sensitive issue, but one can hardly afford to take a divided approach on the freedom of conscience. To say that Islam recognizes freedom of religion but also validates the death penalty for even non-hostile renunciation of faith amounts to contradiction in terms. I do not propose to engage in details over this as I have attempted this elsewhere and the issue has also become complex.[32] Yet it may briefly be said that the Qur'ān assigns no punishment for apostasy even though it refers to the subject on over twenty occasions. The death penalty for apostasy occurs only in a solitary (*aḥād*) *ḥadīth*, which I believe consists of temporary legislation (*tashrī' zamani*) that has somehow remained with us to this day, and in the course of time it was presented as a permanent law.

The nascent Muslim community of Madinah during the time of the Prophet was engaged in continuous war with the pagans of Arabia that led to no less than eighty military engagements – and the Prophet personally participated in twenty-seven. There were no neutral grounds under those conditions, hence a person who renounced Islam would flee Madinah and defect to the Quraysh of Makkah and fight the Muslims. Historical accounts indicate that several individuals renounced Islam in Madinah and virtually every one of them joined the enemy forces in Makkah. Hence the *ḥadīth* that 'one who changes his religion shall be killed'. Apostasy combined high treason and active hostility with the Muslim community at a most sensitive point in time. It follows then that apostasy which is not espoused with hostility and treason, and one that emanates in conviction, will always be seen as patently misguided and blameworthy but it is, nevertheless, not a criminal offence.

5) Neither al-Māwardi nor al-Farrā have attempted to translate the Qur'ānic verses on *shūrā* into workable formulas, and there is once again a consistent line of neglect on an important principle of governance. We may extend this analysis, at least partially, also to general consensus (*ijmā'*), another important principle of democratic substance in Islam. *Ijmā'* has been discussed in much detail in almost every manual of the sources of law (*uṣūl al-fiqh*). Yet *ijmā'*, which was to consist, according to Imām al-Shāfi'ī and many others, of general consensus of the Muslim community at large, was increasingly subjected to technicality and difficult conditions, so much so that *ijmā'* lost its popular anchor altogether. The renowned rift between the '*ulamā*' and the ruling authorities that started with the change of *khilāfah* to *mulk* (monarchy) and the '*ulamā*''s objection to Mu'āwiyah's manipulation of *bay'ah* (pledge of allegiance) need not be recounted here. It does not take a strained analysis to see that justice, *shūrā*, *ijmā'*, *ikhtilāf*, *bay'ah* and *maṣlaḥah* (public interest) do provide the basic framework of an Islamic democracy. But it seems that despotism encouraged imitative scholarship (*taqlīd*) and suppressed healthy growth of political thought.

6) Notwithstanding certain reservations, some Muslim commentators have noted the Islamic credentials of formal constitutions in present-day Muslim countries; these constitutions, on the whole, pay greater attention to basic rights and liberties, the foundations of accountable and representative government, and as such tend to be in greater harmony with the basic principles of Islam.[33] Most of these constitutions have also been adopted by representative assemblies and they become a part therefore of the ordinances of the *ulū'l-amr* (*aḥkām ulū al-amr*) which merit obedience.

In response to the question whether a formal constitution was

Islamic, and whether any objectionable elements therein invalidated the whole of a constitution, Muḥammad Rashīd Riḍā (d. 1935) issued a *fatwā* that may be summarized as follows: If a constitution seeks to establish a good government, defines the limits of power and ascertains criteria of accountability, then it would be in harmony with Islam. Should there be an instance of disagreement with any of the principles of Islam, only that element should be addressed and amended. For after all many of the great works of *fiqh* also contain errors, but this does not invalidate the whole of the endeavour or manual in which such an error might have occurred.[34]

I end this chapter by recounting an encounter I recently had with the '*ulamā*' of Afghanistan. In my capacity as member of the Constitutional Review Committee (CRC) of Afghanistan, I had occasion to meet, in the presence of my other colleagues, with a delegation of fifteen '*ulamā*' of Afghanistan at the CRC head office in Kabul (August 2003). One of the leading spokesmen of this group drew a distinction between a constitution and Islam intimating that these were two different preoccupations and agendas, with a view obviously that the one was alien to the other. I personally took exception to this divisive perception and advanced in the comments I made then a Qur'ān-based explanation premised on *āyat al-umarā'* (4:58–9) wherein the text enjoined the believers to 'obey God, obey the Messenger, and the *uli 'l-amr* from among you'. I added that the constitution we were preparing sought to articulate the principles of a just government, and that it also proclaimed Afghanistan an 'Islamic republic'. It thus became a part of the ordinances of the *ulū 'l-amr* and was by no means an outsider to Islam.

7) Islamic criminal law is remarkably flexible in almost all of its parts except for the so-called *ḥudūd* offences which are deemed to be inflexible, but which I have already explained. The whole of criminal law remains open to the exercise of *Sharī'ah*-oriented policy (*siyāsah shar'iyyah*), and the discretionary punishment of *ta'zīr*. Punishments (*'uqūbāt*) in Islamic law fall under the general heading of *mu'āmalāt*, that sphere of the law which is concerned with social affairs and transactions. Unlike devotional matters (*'ibadāt*) which are regulated by the text, the *mu'āmalāt* are open to considerations of public interest and legal reasoning (*ijtihād*). In almost every area of *mu'āmalāt*, be it commercial law, constitutional law, taxation or international relations the *Sharī'ah* lays down some basic rules and

leaves the rest to be regulated by human legislation based on *ijmāʿ*, *shūrā*, *maṣlaḥah* and *ijtihād*. In this way the *Sharīʿah* itself leaves room for development of laws based on the ordinances of legitimate government and the *uli'l-amr*. As such the *Sharīʿah* consists only partially of divine law. By far the larger part of the rich legacy of *fiqh* we have with us is basically a juristic construct that has evolved abreast the changing conditions of time and place. It is a requirement of *ijtihād* and statutory legislation premised on the ordinances of *ulu'l-amr* to integrate not only the basic values of Islam but also the mores and customs (*ʿurf*) of society. In their broad outline and objectives constitutionalism and democracy are also, in the present writer's opinion, in basic harmony with the goals and purposes of *Sharīʿah* (*maqāṣid al-Sharīʿah*). It thus remains to be said that Muslim leaders, religious scholars and '*ulamā*' should integrate them into their scholarly engagements and *ijtihād*. If there are adjustments that need to be made, these should be identified and addressed, but the attitude of circumspection and denial needs to be carefully evaluated and changed.

NOTES

1. See for details Kamali, *Freedom, Equality, and Justice*, Ch. 3, on justice, 103–55, including a brief discussion of *Siyāsah Sharʿiyyah*. For a more detailed treatment of *Siyāsah Sharʿiyyah*, see Kamali, '*Siyāsah Sharʿiyyah*', 59–81. A fuller treatment of equity in *Sharīʿah* can be found in Kamali, *Equity and Fairness*.
2. Gibb, 'Constitutional Organization', 14; Schacht, 'Law and Justice', 541.
3. Henry Siegman, 'The State and Individual', 23.
4. For further details on *ḥaqq*, see Kamali, 'Fundamental Rights and Liberties', 340–67; idem., *Freedom of Expression*, 16–24 and passim.
5. There is a section each on *ḥisbah*, *naṣīḥah* and *shūrā* in Kamali, *Freedom of Expression*, 34–45.
6. Tabrīzī, *Mishkāt*,Vol. II, *ḥadīth* no. 3665.
7. Suyuti, *al-Jāmiʿ al-Ṣaghīr*, I, 41.
8. Aḥmad bin Ḥanbal, *Musnad*, Vol. II, *ḥadīth* 27.
9. Ibn Majāh, *Sunan*, *ḥadīth* no. 4011.
10. See for example Muhammad Arkoun, *Min al-Ijtihād*, 82–6.
11. Cf. John Clayton, 'Religions and Rights', 260–1.
12. Cf. D.M. Paton, ed., *Breaking Barriers*, 106, par. 34. See also Gerald D. Gort, 'The Christian Ecumenical Reception', 211.
13. Cf. Feisal Abdul Rauf, *What's right with Islam*, 204–5.
14. For a summary of al-Bannā's views, see Moussalli, 'Modern Islamic Fundamentalist Discourse', 102 f.

15. Cf. John Esposito, 'Beyond the Headlines: The Prosperous Justice Party', 31.
16. Judy Barsalou, 'Islamists and the Ballot Box', 1–3.
17. Cf. Barsalou, 3–5.
18. *Newsheet*, 17, no. 3 (August 2005), Shirkat Gah, Islamabad, 4.
19. Cf. M.H. Lakdawala, 'It's Time for Justice and Reforms', 2.
20. Cf. Ḥasan al-Turābi, *Tajdīd al-Fikr al-Islāmi*, 34–7; Yūsuf al-Qaraḍāwi, *Min Fiqh al-Dawlah*; M. Saleem El-Awwa, *al-Fiqh al-Islām*; Rashīd al-Ghanouchi, *Ḥuqūq al-Muwāṭanah*.
21. Gellner, *Conditions of Liberty*, 26.
22. Keddouri, *Democracy*, 5–6.
23. See Gellner, *Conditions of Liberty*, 15–24, 69.
24. Abdelwahab el-Affendi, 'Rationality of Politics', 167.
25. Ahmad Moussali, 'Modern Islamic Fundamentalist Discourse', 79.
26. Timothy Sisk, *Islam and Democracy*, 23.
27. Ṭar q al-Bishri, 'Mu'assasāt al-Dawlah', 41–2.
28. The '*ulamā*' defined *ijmā'* as a 'unanimous agreement of the *mujtahids* of the Muslim community of any period following the demise of the Prophet on any matter'. As such, the '*ulamā*' dominated *ijmā'* to the extent of excluding even a reference to, let alone ensure participation of, the government in power. See for details the chapter on *ijmā'* in Kamali, *Principles of Islamic Jurisprudence*, 228–64.
29. Cf. Moussalli, 'Modern Islamic Fundamentalist Discourses', 86–7.
30. Cf. Wajīh Kawtharāni, *al-Sultah wa'l-Mujtama'*, 35–8.
31. Ibn 'Ashur, *Uṣul Niẓām al-Ijtimā'i*, 26.
32. For a detailed treatment of apostasy (*riddah*) see Kamali, *Freedom of Expression*, 212–250.
33. Cf. Kamali, 'The Ruler and Ruled in Islam', xxv–xxxviii.
34. *Fatāwa Imām Muḥammad Rashīd Riḍā*, comp. Ṣalāḥ al-Dīn Manaḥḥid and Yūsuf Khuri, III, 805–8.

11

BEYOND THE *SHARĪ'AH*: AN ANALYSIS OF *SHARĪ'AH*-ORIENTED POLICY (*SIYĀSAH SHAR'IYYAH*)

Siyāsah shar'iyyah or *Sharī'ah*-oriented policy is generally seen as an instrument of flexibility and pragmatism in *Sharī'ah*, designed to serve the cause of justice and good government, especially when the rules of *Sharī'ah* fall short of addressing certain situations or developments. As the term suggests, the policy measures that are taken in the name of *siyāsah shar'iyyah* must be *Sharī'ah*-compliant, as the purpose is generally to facilitate rather than circumvent the implementation of *Sharī'ah*. Rules of procedure, policy decisions, legislative and administrative measures that are laid down and taken for the purpose would thus fall within the ambit of *siyāsah shar'iyyah*.

Although some commentators have attempted to confine *siyāsah shar'iyyah* to administrative measures while others have singled out criminal procedure and punishment as the main areas of its application, our analysis shows that it is not confined to either. There is also a view that *siyāsah* only applies outside the substantive *Sharī'ah* whereas according to an opposite view *Sharī'ah* and *siyāsah* go hand in hand and that the *Sharī'ah* is deficient without *siyāsah*. I shall elaborate some of these views in the following pages and advocate the hypothesis that no unnecessary restrictions should be imposed on the scope and subject matter of *siyāsah shar'iyyah*.

The first part of this chapter explores the basic idea of *siyāsah shar'iyyah* by drawing on a selection of opinion of those who have contributed to this theme, including Ibn Taymiyyah (d. 1328) and his disciple Ibn Qayyim al-Jawziyyah (d. 1356), Ibn Farḥūn (d. 1401), and more recently 'Abd al-Wahhāb Khallāf (d. c.1955) and

Ali Jād al-Ḥāq among others, while the second part addresses the application of *siyāsah sharʿiyyah* in Malaysia.

DEFINITION AND SCOPE

Siyāsah sharʿiyyah means government in accordance with the goals and objectives of *Sharīʿah* and in its widest sense applies to all government policies, be it in areas where the *Sharīʿah* provides explicit guidelines or otherwise.[1]

Ibn Qayyim al-Jawziyyah quoted Ibn ʿAqīl (d. 1119) to the effect that *siyāsah* is 'that action through which the people are brought closer to prosperity'. Elaborating on this, Ibn Qayyim characterized *siyāsah sharʿiyyah* as 'any measure which brings the people nearer to beneficence (*ṣalāḥ*) and moves them further away from corruption (*fasād*) even though the measure in question has not been approved by the Prophet, peace be on him, nor regulated by a revelation. Anyone who says that there is no *siyāsah sharʿiyyah* where the *Sharīʿah* itself is silent is wrong and has misunderstood the Companions.'[2] Ibn Qayyim divided *siyāsah* into two types: oppressive policy (*siyāsah ẓālimah*) which the *Sharīʿah* forbids, and just policy (*siyāsah ʿādilah*) which serves the cause of justice, even if it may at times depart from the letter of an injunction in favour of its spirit. Since justice and good government are the principal goals of *siyāsah ʿādilah*, measures that are taken in pursuit of it are bound to be in harmony with the *Sharīʿah*. Whereas *siyāsah ẓālimah* pursues self-interest and prejudice of rulers to the detriment of the community at large, *siyāsah ʿādilah* is based on moderation which shuns both harshness and laxity and does not sacrifice public interest for the indulgent desires of the few.[3]

Ibn Taymiyyah's[4] concept of a just *siyāsah* is based on the Qur'ānic injunction of *amānāt*, that is, the faithful fulfilment of trusts (4:58). His book *Al-Siyāsah al-Sharʿiyyah* is, in fact, a commentary, as he wrote on the very first page, on this Qur'ānic verse. Government as a whole is a trust in Islam and the bearer of a duty to hand over the trust to those who are entitled to it. Two specific themes that feature prominently in Ibn Taymiyyah's elaboration of *amānāt* in this verse are selection and appointment of government officials, and equitable distribution of wealth in the community. When a leader appoints to public office a person on grounds of friendship and personal favour in disregard of his competence and trustworthiness he would have betrayed his *amānah*. It is also a duty of the leader to depose dishonest and corrupt officials and those who are incompetent. The quality of *amānah* in leaders refers in turn to three attributes: fear of God, refusal to neglect His injunctions for a small price, and lack of fear of men – as in the Qur'ānic verse:

> so fear not people but fear Me, and take not a small price for My messages. (5:44)
>
> فلاَ تَخْشَوُاْ النَّاسَ وَاخْشَوْنِ وَلاَ تَشْتَرُواْ بِآيَاتِي ثَمَنًا قَلِيلاً.

Trusteeship confers on the trustees a measure of discretion to fulfil their trust as best as they can. Just as the form and organization of government are not articulated in Islamic law, so is the case with *siyāsah shar'iyyah*. The *Sharīʻah* only provides broad guidelines for a just polity and leaves its detailed formulation to the discretion of the *ūlu al-amr*.

Ibn Taymiyyah called attention to the *Sharīʻah* on the one hand and tried to widen the scope of *Sharīʻah* on the other. His basic idea was this: government decisions are not always based on legal text and principle. Legal text as well as political and economic considerations, custom and even exceptional conditions all play a role and constitute the premises of decision-making. *Siyāsah shar'iyyah* aims at securing benefit for the people and efficient management of their affairs, even if the measures so taken are not stipulated in the text. A government that seeks to establish justice and secures people's welfare would have automatically followed the *Sharīʻah*. *Siyāsah shar'iyyah* thus denotes administration of public affairs in an Islamic polity with the aim of realizing the interests of the people and preventing them against mischief, in harmony with the general principles of *Sharīʻah*. This may entail adopting policies, taking measures, and enacting laws in all spheres of government.[5] It is a principle of public law 'which enhances and enlarges the power and capacity of the state to promote the people's welfare by keeping law and life in a near perfect equilibrium'. Outside the scope of *Sharīʻah*, it also enables the state to change the operative rules, law and policy as the conditions of the society may demand.[6] It is sufficient if the measures taken by way of *siyāsah* are in harmony with the spirit and purpose of the *Sharīʻah* and taken in order to 'establish and preserve a well-ordered society', there being no requirement to find a specific ruling or precedent in its support.[7]

Ibn Qayyim attributed to Imām al-Shāfi'ī (d. 819) the position that *siyāsah* was permissible only when it was in accordance with the *Sharī'ah*. Ibn Qayyim qualified this by saying that conformity to the *Sharī'ah* only meant conformity to that on which the *Sharī'ah* was explicit. Ibn Qayyim added that *siyāsah* comprises particular rules and decisions that are derived from consideration of overall benefits (*al-siyāsāt al-juz'iyyah al-tābi'ah li'l-maṣāliḥ*) and so they are circumstantial and changeable with the change of circumstances. The explicit rulings of *Sharī'ah* were in contrast not so changeable.

It thus appears that Ibn Qayyim distinguished the explicit rules of *Sharī'ah*, which were basically permanent, from the supplementary and *ad hoc* decisions of government. He maintained that all Muslim rulers, beginning with the Prophet, peace be on him, and the Companions, made *ad hoc* decisions based on considerations of welfare. Thus it was important not to confuse *siyāsah* with the explicit *Sharī'ah*, as that would unduly bind and restrict the powers of Islamic government to the explicit rulings of *Sharī'ah*. Instead Muslim rulers were not only free but were obliged to act in pursuit of benefits that the *Sharī'ah* had not specified or regulated.[8]

In his lengthy discussion on *siyāsah*, the Māliki jurist, Ibn Farḥūn, maintains that *siyāsah* is not *ad hoc* but normative; it is a part of the positive law as its legitimacy is grounded directly in the Qur'ān, the life of the Prophet and the precedent of his Companions. In contrast to Ibn Qayyim, Ibn Farḥūn did not restrict *siyāsah* to a welfare-based rule of *ad hoc* nature, but maintained that in every area of the substantive *Sharī'ah*, including the *ḥudūd*, *qiṣāṣ* and *ta'zīr*, *siyāsah* played a necessary and complementary role.[9] Ibn Farḥūn thus took the view that *siyāsah* was a part of the *Sharī'ah* and that its normativity was established in the Qur'ān and Sunnah, especially those of the Qur'ānic verses and *aḥād th* that enjoined justice, removal of hardship and *maṣlaḥah* as well as the ones on promotion of good and prevention of evil. Ibn Farḥūn added that Māliki law had, in fact, integrated *siyāsah* into the body of its positive law. For example, the Mālikis hold that a traveller whose journey is itself an act of disobedience to God, such as a highway robber, loses his right to perform prayer by dry ablution (*tayammum*) instead of water. This ruling was based on *siyāsah* and the notion that disobedience cannot invoke any concession (*rukhṣah*).[10] Another example he gave concerns bankruptcy proceedings: when the judge suspects that the person who claims bankruptcy has hidden away certain assets, he is empowered to imprison him so that he will reveal the location of his property.[11]

Essential harmony with the spirit of the *Sharīʻah* may at times even justify a certain departure from its letter. This may be illustrated by many of the policy decisions of ʻUmar b. al-Khaṭṭāb. In one such decision, the caliph discontinued the share of the pagan friends of Islam (*muʻallafat al-qulūb* – persons of influence whose support was important for the victory of Islam) in *zakah* (poor tax) revenues, and in another case he refused to assign the fertile lands of Iraq as war booty (*ghanīmah*) to the warriors. The Qur'ān had clearly entitled the *muʻallafah* to a share in *zakah* revenues (9:6) and also the warriors to *ghanīmah* (8:45). In both cases the caliph discontinued the entitlements essentially on policy grounds. Concerning his first decision he went on record to say that 'Allah has exalted Islam and it is no longer in need of their favour', and regarding the second, he explained that he did not want to see the leading Companions be turned into landowners that may eventually divert their attention away from *jihād*.[12] In yet another policy decision, the caliph ʻUmar held that triple divorce was legally binding and those who pronounced it were liable to face the consequences of their conduct. This was his ruling not withstanding the Qur'ānic decaration that

> *ṭalāq* is only twice (2:229)
>
> الطّلاقُ مرّتَان.

and the fact that during the time of the Prophet and that of the caliph Abū Bakr, a triple repudiation uttered in a single pronouncement incurred only one *ṭalāq*. In taking this policy measure, which then became standard law, the caliph wanted to prevent abuse of women, as due to the change of circumstances, men would pronounce triple *ṭalāq* and then leave their estranged wives in a state of suspense.[13] Change of circumstances also led the caliph ʻUmar to impose *zakah* on horses despite the fact that the Prophet had exempted these animals, due to their vital role in *jihād*, from the payment of *zakah*. On this point, it is interesting to note that the caliph ʻUmar b. ʻAbd al-ʻAzīz (d. 719), in an effort to revive the early Sunnah, once again abolished the *zakah* on horses.[14]

It is similarly reported that the third caliph, ʻUthmān b. ʻAffān, validated the right to inheritance of a woman whose husband had divorced her in order to be disinherited. The husband's exercise of his right to *ṭalāq* was thus deemed prejudicial and therefore obstructed on the grounds, it would seem, of just *siyāsah*.

Ibn Farḥūn has identified the following decision of the fourth caliph, 'Ali b. Abū Ṭālib, as an example of *siyāsah shar'iyyah*.

A man complained to the caliph that his father set off with a group of men on a journey but failed to return with them. When the son asked them about his father, they told him he had died. He then asked them about his father's property, in reply to which they claimed he had died leaving nothing. This was despite the son's claim that his father had set off with a substantial amount of capital for trade. The son subsequently sued them before the judge Shurayḥ Ibn al-Ḥārith, who administered an oath to them and released them when they denied the claim. When the caliph 'Ali heard this story, he began a prompt investigation which involved questioning the individuals separately and jailing them alternatively, a policy which led the men to confess that they had killed the man's father. Upon receiving their confession, the caliph required them to pay restitution to the son for his father's property. Then he allowed the son to retaliate against the murderers.[15] *Siyāsah* as illustrated in this example is closely related to *firāsah*, that is, the personal insight and intuitive judgement of the ruler and judge. It is intuitive as it is often grounded, not so much in evidence, as in the personal acumen, general knowledge and experience of a leader. It is reported that when a person requested the eminent jurist Iyās b. Mu'awiyah (d. 740) to teach him the science of adjudication, he was told by the latter that 'the science of adjudication is beyond teaching as it is understanding personified'.[16]

The word *tadbīr* (good management) is often used side by side with *siyāsah* in both the Arabic and Persian languages. When they are used together, they clearly connote conducting the business of government with wisdom and efficiency that relies more on discretionary power rather than the specific rulings of *Sharī'ah*.[17] In Ibn Qayyim's assessment, in their efforts to protect the people against criminality and aggression, the most capable of rulers have exercised intuitive judgement (*firāsah*) and taken decisions on the basis of clues and circumstantial evidence (*amārāt*).[18]

The decisions of Caliph 'Umar seem to stand in a class of their own and tend to represent the upper limits of *siyāsah*. No other leader would appear to have surpassed the calibre and boldness of 'Umar's decisions in that they actually went against the clear text of the Qur'ān. Many commentators have discussed and analysed them but no one has actually disputed the propriety and aptitude of those decisions.

A HISTORICAL SKETCH

As already indicated, early opinion among Muslim scholars was divided between two positions on *siyāsah*, one of which regarded *siyāsah* as distinct and separate from the religious law and *Sharī'ah* but not necessarily contrasting or contradictory to it. The second view overruled such a distinction and maintained that *siyāsah* and *Sharī'ah* went hand in hand with one another. In his *Risālah fi 'l-Ṣaḥābah*, 'Abd Allah Ibn al-Muqaffa' (d. 757) saw the religious and political functions of the caliph as complementary rather than contradictory or contrasting. Ibn al-Muqaffa' saw the legal and administrative practices of the Umayyad and early Abbasid periods as inconsistent and frequently in contrast with the authentic Sunnah of the Prophet. Hence in his view, it was the caliph's duty to standardize and codify the existing usage and exercise his own discretion to introduce new regulations on political, administrative, financial and military matters when none were available in the existing precedent. He maintained that subsequent caliphs could review and revise such regulations, but none had the power to abrogate the major principles of *Sharī'ah*. This was for Ibn al-Muqaffa' the meaning of the *ḥadīth* that 'there was no obedience in transgression'.[19] Writing a little later, Abū 'Uthmān 'Amr b. Baḥr al-Jāḥiz regarded *siyāsah* as distinct from religion but not contrasting with it: *siyāsah* for him was concerned with the affairs of this world, religion with those of the next. The tenth-century writer Abū Ḥayyān al-Tawḥīdi differed with al-Jāḥiẓ and wrote that religion and government (*dīn wa siyāsah*) are complementary, each requiring the other: *Sharī'ah* is the government of mankind by God, *siyāsah* is the government of mankind by man. *Sharī'ah* without *siyāsah* is deficient, *siyāsah* devoid of *Sharī'ah* is also deficient.[20]

In the classical Persian work of Niẓām al-Mulk in the twelfth century, known as *Siyāsatnāma*, usually translated as 'the book of politics', *siyāsah* is equated with statecraft which recognized no clear lines of distinction between *siyāsah* and *Sharī'ah*. This was in line with the general tendency in Persian scholarship which tended to treat *siyāsah* and *Sharī'ah* as an extension of one another, whereas the

Arab writers were more inclined to draw a distinction between the two. Ibn Taymiyyah tried to merge the two by using the composite term *siyāsah shar'iyyah* and wrote his renowned work with this title. Modern writers have generally adopted Ibn Taymiyyah's integrationist approach and have tended to depart from the restrictions that some have tried to impose on *siyāsah*.

Yet in the Arabic-speaking countries the older meaning of *siyāsah* persisted. This can be seen, for instance, in the views of the renowned Ibn Khaldūn (d. 1406) who spoke of two types of *siyāsah*, namely *siyāsah 'aqliyyah* (rational policy) and *siyāsah dīniyyah* (religious policy). Rational *siyāsah* is introduced by wise rulers whereas *siyāsah dīniyyah* follows the revealed text.[21] Writing in the fifteenth century, al-Maqrizī distinguished between *Sharī'ah* and *siyāsah* jurisdictions. In Egypt and Turkey, he said, since the coming of the Turks (i.e. the Mamlūks), rulers have recognized two kinds of jurisdictions, *Sharī'ah* and *siyāsah*. For the latter, there were separate courts in the Mamlūk sultanate and separate judges administering different jurisdictions. In Ottoman usage, *siyaset* (without the adage '*shar'iyyah*') occurred almost exclusively in the sense of punishment for offences against the state, and a ground sometimes of summary executions.[22] The present writer concurs with the integrationist view of *siyāsah shar'iyyah* and maintains that *Sharī'ah* and *siyāsah* cannot be meaningfully separated totally, although the unity between them would appear to be more of a goal-oriented unity that upholds the *maṣlaḥah* (benefit) of the people, and the objectives or *maqāṣid* of *Sharī'ah* through policy measures. Since the *maṣlaḥah* and *maqāṣid* are not confined to temporal affairs only, it would follow that *siyāsah shar'iyyah* also extends to both temporal and religious matters.

THE FALL OF THE OTTOMAN CALIPHATE

The purpose of *Sharī'ah* from a rational viewpoint is to enable man to lead a good and comfortable life in society without infringing other people's rights. It is to construct a society where people can live together peacefully in this world and pursue correct guidance that lead them to felicity in the next. Following the demise of the Prophet, the *Sharī'ah* was operating in an Islamic environment. Islam also witnessed great progress, and in the next six hundred years at least, the

Sharī'ah was operating in an essentially Islamic society, but it witnessed a great deal of diversity within itself. There were two concepts emerging that contributed to continuity of the *Sharī'ah*. One was the concept of *ijmā'* which meant that God Most High guided the Muslim community through consensus of the learned and it was thus protected against misguidance and error. For Shī'ite Islam, the same role was assumed by the Imām, or leader from the family of the Prophet, who provides the assurance that the community was protected against losing its sense of direction. The result of these different approaches did not differ a great deal in that vast areas of Islamic law are in fact in common in both of its Sunni and Shī'ite branches. For Sunni Islam, the caliphate also played an important role for the stability of the legal system over many centuries. Whether the caliph had effective power or not, he still provided a focus for continuity within the Sunni legal structure. For Shī'ite Islam, this role was played by the presumed presence of the twelfth Imām, which may also explain perhaps the continued growth, in many ways, of Shī'ite jurisprudence. However, with the collapse of the caliphate in 1924 and the emergence of non-Muslim hostile superpowers, the Sunni legal structure was exposed to tremendous stress, which has continued to this day.[23] It has brought about the fragmentation of the Islamic world and the emergence in Muslim countries of statutory legislation, a kind of secular Islamic law that is not entirely based on the *Sharī'ah* nor has it completely renounced it. Turkey itself has ironically renounced the *Sharī'ah* as it presumably could not absorb the shock that had erupted in its midst.

The onset of colonialism exacerbated the situation by setting aside the *Sharī'ah*, marginalizing and replacing it with statutory laws of non-Islamic origin. These developments brought in their wake a great deal of disenchantment and social and political upheaval that the Muslim world has still not come to terms with, and a state of tension has prevailed. The Islamic resurgence of the late twentieth century was a violent outburst and rejection of the colonial legacy that had increasingly alienated Muslims from their own heritage, and *Sharī'ah* was an important part of that heritage.

Yet even this was not the first shock the Muslim world and its caliphate had experienced. A trauma of almost equal proportions was the Mongol invasion of Baghdad in the thirteenth century which set in motion the decline of the caliphate of Baghdad and its surrender to military commanders and emirs. Ibn Taymiyyah's reaction to these events was one of disillusionment with the caliphate which, he said, had only lasted for three decades and had long since been replaced by monarchy (*mulk*). What was important to him was to follow the *Sharīʻah*, hence his idea of *siyāsah sharʻiyyah*.

Reflecting on the state of *Sharīʻah* in his time, ʻIzz al-Din ʻAbd al-Salām al-Sulami (d. 1280) maintained that the new varieties of acts that violated religious and legal precepts by nefarious and shameless ways had proliferated and the scale of disputes had expanded likewise. The spread of corruption and multiplicity of disputes among people called for new laws and measures to protect society against their evil. The new measures should not, however, infringe the spirit of the basic principles of *Sharīʻah*. Taq Am n who quoted al-Sulami also underscored the proportion and complexity of the mischief that society has continued to face ever since. This has widened ʻthe gulf between the legal needs of the society and the pre-existing legal precepts. Therefore all those pre-existing principles which prescribe for the removal of hardship and loss shall be violated if no steps are taken to bridge the gulf between law and life.ʼ[24]

RECENT CONTRIBUTORS

Fuʼād Aḥmad has quoted the then shaykh of al-Azhar, ʻAli Jād al-Ḥaqq, to the effect that a government which administers the affairs of Muslim community may be identified as a *Sharīʻah*-based polity (*siyāsah sharʻiyyah*) if it fulfils two conditions: 1) that it complies with the goals and objectives (*maqāṣid*) of *Sharīʻah* and upholds those of its basic principles and postulates that command permanent validity and are not liable to change with the change of circumstances; and 2) that it does not fall into a genuine conflict with a specific ruling of the Qurʼān, the Sunnah, or that which is upheld by the general consensus of Muslims.[25]

With reference to legislation, ʻAbd al-Wahhāb Khallāf emphasized that *siyāsah sharʻiyyah* should aim at opening the doors of mercy and beneficence to the people and select from the rich legacy of the *ʻulamāʼ* that which helps to relieve the people from severity and hardship. Statutory legislation that seeks to prevent corruption and facilitate benefit is bound to be in harmony with the principles of *Sharīʻah* even if it disagrees with the views of the *mujtahidūn* of the past. Khallāf goes on to quote Shihāb al-Dīn al-Qarāfī (d. 1285) to the effect that nothing could be found in the *Sharī'ah* against taking measures, in any area of government, that seek to eliminate corruption and facilitate benefit to the community.[26]

Another prominent professor of al-Azhar and author of a book on *siyāsah shar'iyyah*, 'Abd al-Raḥmān Tāj, went on record to say concerning legislation based on *siyāsah shar'iyyah* that an apparent discrepancy (*mukhālafah ẓāhirah*) in one or the other proofs of the *Sharī'ah* should not defer the introduction of an otherwise beneficial law. He emphasized that a negative judgement should not be passed on such legislation. Unless one tries 'to understand the purpose and spirit of the proof in question, and verifies as to whether it contemplated a particular and temporary situation or whether it laid down a general law [*tashrī' 'āmm*]. Only the latter type of proof is binding and must be observed in the formulation of laws and measures taken in pursuit of *siyāsah shar'iyyah.*'[27] For example, it would not be contrary to *Sharī'ah* if we were to enact a law that would require soldiers to deliver to the government the belongings of their victims which they have taken in the battlefield. Such a law may appear to conflict with the *ḥadīth*

> whoever kills an enemy in the battle may take his belongings
> من قتل قتيلا فله سلبه.

but the conflict in question would be apparent, not real, simply because this *ḥadīth* did not enact a general law. Rather, it was a policy decision which addressed the circumstances of its time, and it is therefore changeable in accordance with *maṣlaḥah*. The government may similarly introduce new laws and policies in the spheres of military strategy and fiscal and foreign policy even if they differ with the positions that were adopted in early Islam. This is because the instructions contained in *ḥadīth* on these matters do not on the whole constitute general law.[28]

Tāj has also drawn attention to the special relevance of the *Sharī'ah* doctrine of *sadd al-dharā'i'*, or blocking the means, to *siyāsah shar'iyyah*. The *Sharī'ah* doctrine of *sadd al-dharā'i'* authorizes the ruler to obstruct the means that lead to criminality and corruption. The authorities may thus 'forbid what is permissible (*mubāḥ*) if the (*mubāḥ*) in question is widely used as a means to transgression and evil'. When the authorities observe, for example, that something which was once lawful has subsequently been turned into a mischief, they may exercise discretion and ban it if this is deemed to be the only way by which to protect the public interest.[29]

SIYĀSAH SHAR'IYYAH IN MALAYSIA

Having expounded the theoretical dimensions of *siyāsah shar'iyyah*, we may now attempt to establish its relevance and application in Malaysia by taking stock of actual developments of relevance to *siyāsah shar'iyyah*, especially in recent decades. This is a question to a large extent of examining the evidence, which I shall presently attempt, but I pose a question as to why *siyāsah shar'iyyah* is deemed to be a relevant, or an appropriate, option for Malaysia. To respond to this question we refer mainly to the pluralist make-up of Malaysian society and government which has, in turn, generated a persistent demand for politics of accommodation and inclusiveness that is widely regarded as a matter of necessity for Malaysia. Balancing the needs and interests of its multi religious and multi-ethnic population has always been at once a most crucial and also challenging aspect of the Malaysian political system.

Of the twenty-six million population of Malaysia about 58.4 per cent are Malay and Indian Muslims, while non-Muslims account for over 40 per cent consisting mainly of Buddhists, Christians, Hindus, Confucians and others. There are no less than 178 ethnic groups in Malaysia. The aboriginals of west Malaysia have animistic beliefs although many Dayaks, Ibans and Kadazans of east Malaysia have converted to Catholicism.[30] Very little of any political significance that goes on in Malaysia 'is not influenced by the ethnic and religious diversity' that is found among its diverse population.[31] The pluralist character of Malaysian government is also evident in that more than one-third of the Malaysian parliament and its federal cabinet are non-Malay and non-Muslim at any given time and there is considerable non-Malay participation in the public services and government agencies.[32]

The next most important reality of Malaysian life is evidently Islam. It is almost unthinkable for the Malays to be anything but Muslim and they expect their government to protect that identify. The Federal Constitution (Art. 16b) defines a Malay as one 'who professes the Muslim religion, habitually speaks the Malay language and conforms to Malay customs'. The UMNO Constitution 1960 also includes in its statement of objectives 'to promote, uphold, and safeguard Islam in Malaysia'. All state constitutions in the Malay states (nine out of the thirteen states) prescribe that the ruler of the state must be a Muslim. Some even require the same of the Chief Minister and State Secretary. Except for Sarawak, Islam is the official religion in all states of Malaysia. One of the five principles of Rukun Negara (national ideology) is belief in God as a cardinal principle of state policy. This relatively strong Malay identification with Islam demanded an affirmative stance towards Islam, leading in turn to what was subsequently known as the Islamization policy. There has been no formal announcement of such a policy by the government of Malaysia and many have even doubted its existence, but affirmative evidence given in its support consists of a series of piecemeal developments including the introduction of laws, policies and institutions that followed a common trend of enhancing the presence of Islam in the various areas of public life. 'There is a mixed picture', as I wrote a few years ago, 'which offers some basis for an Islamic identity in the constitution and government policy and some basis also for secular orientation of law and government in Malaysia.'[33]

Malaysia has obviously taken an affirmative stance on the implementation of *Sharīʻah* in the sphere of matrimonial law, divorce, guardianship, maintenance, child custody, inheritance, etc., for its Muslim citizens, and the pattern here is well entrenched. The law also provides for a structure of *Sharīʻah* courts, State Councils of Muslim Religion, Fatwa Committees, the Islamic Centre and the Islamic Religious Affairs Department. The International Islamic University Malaysia (IIUM), the International Institute of Islamic Thought and Civilization (ISTAC) and the Institute of Islamic Understanding Malaysia (IKIM) were established in 1983, 1987 and 1991 respectively. There are also other research institutes that take interest in Islam. The Syariah Courts exercise exclusive jurisdiction on Islamic and *Sharīʻah*-related matters. The Administration of Islamic Law Enactments in the various states penalize offences against Islam and deviationist teachings. Article 121A of the Federal Constitution protects the Syariah Court against interference by the civil courts.

Various other projects were undertaken to enhance the Islamic dimension of Malaysian public life. PERKIM was established in 1960 to promote *daʻwah* (Islamic call) activity and welfare of converts to Islam. The national Qur'ān reading competition was held in 1966 and has continued annually ever since. The prayer call and Islamic programmes are aired over radio and television. Radio and television broadcasts devote considerable time to Islamic programmes. Islamic salutation and prayers are offered at most government functions, and Islamic dress form has increasingly become mainstream. In many government departments, Qur'ānic verses and quotations decorate important venues and Qur'ānic verses are read to mark the beginning and end of public functions.[34]

One of the early Islamic institutions to be established since independence was Tabung Haji, Pilgrims Management and Fund Board, which also combined saving schemes and accounts for Muslim Pilgrims. Amanah Ikhtiar Malaysia became active in extending *qarḍ ḥasan* (interest-free loans) for business and welfare purposes to needy individuals and families. Malaysia has taken significant strides, since the early 1980s, to revive the Islamic law of transactions (*muʻāmalāt*) through the introduction of Islamic banking, *takaful* Islamic insurance, and the development of an Islamic capital market.

Islamic banking and insurance in Malaysia have moved at an impressively rapid pace and Malaysian specialists often speak of Malaysia as a leading influence on a global scale in the sphere of Islamic banking and finance. In a highly competitive market, Islamic banking products and diversification of trading and investment vehicles in Malaysian institutions have reached a level of sophistication that is decidedly impressive. Since 1993 Islamic banking windows have also been opened in conventional banks.[35] Under section 2 of the Islamic Banking Act 1983, 'Islamic banking business' means banking business 'whose aims and objectives do not involve any element which is not approved by the religion of Islam'. Section 3 provides for a *Sharīʻah* Advisory Council to advise Bank Islam Malaysia Berhad in its banking business to ensure conformity with the *Sharīʻah*.

These and other similar laws, including the Islamic family reform laws, in Malaysia were formulated 'within the general framework of *siyāsah sharʻiyyah*, or *Sharīʻah*-oriented policy, that encouraged adoption of judicious measures aimed at securing benefit for the people and were not contrary to the *Sharīʻah*'.[36] Many of them were in fact based on the substantive *Sharīʻah* and articulated the generally accepted doctrines of the existing *madhāhib*, especially that of the Shāfiʻī school of law. Laws that extended the scope of the existing legislation and were *Sharīʻah*-compliant also fell within the ambit of *siyāsah sharʻiyyah*, and the process seems to be continuing. Whereas some of the laws, such as the ones on marriage, divorce and religious offences are binding on Muslims, the *Sharī'ah*-based modes of transactions in the Islamic banks and institutions are not imposed on anyone as they only offer an alternative and are equally open to non-Muslims.

In the sphere of Islamic education and learning of *Sharī'ah*-based disciplines, Malaysia has retained its traditional madrasa teaching institutions, some of which have been upgraded in recent years, and saw interesting developments including, in one or two cases, academic liaison with the Azhar University. The International Islamic University Malaysia has consistently expanded its programmes over the two decades or so of its operation and offers courses and degree programmes in Arabic and *Sharī'ah*-based disciplines related to the training of prospective *qadis*, *muftis* and teachers. As of 1997 the Ministry of Education has also made the teaching of Islamic civilization a compulsory subject in the national schools. There are in the meantime numerous Chinese and Indian schools in Malaysia which cater for the educational needs of their respective communities and religion.

The Federal Constitution 1957 declared Islam as the official religion of Malaysia but provided that all other religions may be peacefully practiced in the country (Art. 3.1). The implication is that the state may promote Islam, establish and maintain Islamic institutions and incur expenditure for the purpose. Although some historical evidence exists to identify the Malaysian government as a secular polity,[37] the word 'secular' does not occur anywhere in the Federal Constitution. References to 'Islam' occur, on the other hand, in twenty-four places[38] and to Syariah on three occasions.[39] Other Islamic words such as *mufti*, *kādi* and *kādi besār* also occur in the text.

An unprecedented development was the former Prime Minister Dr Mahathir's announcement on 29 September 2001 that 'Malaysia is an Islamic country'. The Barisan Nasional supreme council meeting of 5 October 2001 endorsed the Prime Minister's declaration. Dr Mahathir also spoke on the matter on subsequent occasions, and although there were rumours he might amend or retract his earlier statement, he did not. Instead he went on record to say: 'Actually Malaysia is already an Islamic country, the state religion is Islam and Muslims can practice their religion.'[40] On another occasion, Dr Mahathir said: 'The majority of people in this country are Muslims. Muslims are in power. The power held by Muslims is not to oppress non-Muslims. Instead where Muslims are in power, they must rule fairly.'[41]

Dr Mahathir's successor, the present Prime Minister, Abdullah Ahmad Badawi, comes from a religious family and is generally known for his interest in Islam and his pro-Islam policies. He has made several statements to encourage further development of the Islamic banking sector in Malaysia and has also taken an affirmative stand on the development of Islamic education and institutions of learning in the country. His moderate stance on religion and continued support for inclusiveness and participation of non-Muslims in government has invoked voices of support for his policies from both Muslim and non-Muslim quarters of the Malaysian public ever since he took office on 31 October 2003.

Abdullah Badawi introduced a fresh emphasis on Islamic values in governance under the rubric of Islam *ḥadhāri*, or civilizational Islam. This he did following his landslide election victory in the March 2004 election. The precise definition and understanding of Islam *ḥadhāri* has been the focus of media attention ever since, but the coalition goverment that consists mainly of the Malay, Chinese and Indian component parties have adopted Islam *ḥadhāri* in their election manifesto and it became a goverment policy programme. The concept has stimulated extensive civil society discourse on its priorities and values. It is not my purpose to enter into detail but merely to underscore the changes Malaysia is experiencing in its policy formulations concerning Islam and other religions. In his maiden speech on the subject at the fifty-fifth UMNO General Assembly on 23 September 2004, the Prime Minister laid stress on the broader civilizational appeal of Islam to Malaysians of all faiths, and spelled out the ten principles of Islam *ḥadhāri* as follows: 1) faith and piety in Allah; 2) a just and trustworthy goverment; 3) a free independent people; 4) mastery of knowledge; 5) balanced and comprehensive economic development; 6) a good quality of life; 7) protection of the rights of minority groups and women; 8) cultural and moral integrity; 9) safeguarding the environment; and 10) strong defence capabilities.

The Prime Minister explained that these principles have been formulated to ensure that their implementation did not cause anxiety among any ethnic or religious group in Malaysia. They are also meant to empower Muslims to face the global challenges of today. Abdullah Badawi characterized Islam *ḥadhāri* as 'an approach that emphasizes development, consistent with the tenets of Islam, and focuses on enhancing the quality of life'. This is to be achieved, he added, via the mastery of knowledge and the development of the nation, the implementation of a dynamic economic, trading and financial system, integrated and balanced development that creates a knowledgeable and pious people who hold noble values and are honest, trustworthy, and prepared to take on global challenges.

In his speech, the Prime Minister chose to use 'Islam *ḥadhāri*' instead of the more familiar term '*ḥaḍārah Islam*' or '*ḥaḍārah Islamiyyah*' (Islamic civilization) to imply a certain focus on the broader values of Islam of relevance to Malaysia as it is at present and not so much as it was in historical times. This usage is also concerned with Islamic values of interest and relevance to other civilizations, religions and cultures. The term may also be said to be suggestive of a positive response to the cultural dimension of globalization which is more closely akin to the value structure of Western civilization and its scientific and technological achievements. It is expressive of the concern as to how Muslims can have a constructive engagement with modernity, people's well-being and a democratic and welfare-oriented goverment. Since '*ḥaḍārah Islamiyyah*' (Islamic civilization) was seen to be more focused on historical Islam, which now stands in a different set of relationships from the supremacy it once enjoyed in earlier times, the new expression seeks to focus on the present structure of values and relationships with modernity as well as a progressive outlook on prosperity and economic development.

CONCLUSION

The Mongol invasion of Baghdad in the mid-thirteenth century and the aftermath of that momentous event prompted Ibn Taymiyyah to propose *siyāsah shar'iyyah* as a more pragmatic alternative to the embattled caliphate of Baghdad. He considered the caliphate as an historical phenomenon rather than a *Sharī'ah* requirement. The Madinan Rightly Guided caliphate had hitherto been widely regarded as a model of Islamic polity and state. Writers on Islamic government in the genre of *aḥkam sulṭāniyyah* (principles of government) included al-Māwardī (d. 1050) and Abū Ya'lā al-Farra who wrote at a time when the military rulers of Baghdad had taken over much of the effective powers of the caliph. This is why al-Māwardī's work has invoked some criticism that it sought to endorse the then prevailing status quo.

Ibn Taymiyyah, who saw the Mongol invasion of Baghdad (1258), looked for an alternative approach to caliphate as he had become somewhat critical of the existing literature on the subject. He thought it impractical for scholars to continue focusing on a precedent which had been absent for centuries. Ibn Taymiyyah wrote that caliphate was not a *Sharīʿah* requirement and what had remained of it was also defective. He spoke of two types of *khilāfah*, namely *khilāfah kāmilah* (perfect caliphate) which was short-lived and only lasted thirty years, and *khilāfah nāqiṣah*, or deficient caliphate which had prevailed ever since. The monarchical system (*mulk*) that toppled and replaced the early caliphate followed a different course altogether. What was important, Ibn Taymiyyah maintained, was to have a system of government that upheld the *Sharīʿah* and ruled in accordance with its basic principles regardless of the form it might take. This was how he saw *siyāsah sharʿiyyah* as an alternative to caliphate, and wrote his renowned treatise bearing the generic title *Al-Siyāsah al-Sharʿiyyah fi Islāḥ al-Rāʿi waʾl-Ruʿiyyah.*

History does not repeat itself in any degree of accuracy, yet there is a certain resemblance in these patterns of events. The idea of *dawlah Islāmiyyah* (Islamic state) which came into the picture following the abolition of the caliphate in 1924 was also conceived as an alternative to caliphate.[42] Within the few decades that followed the collapse of caliphate, European colonialism engulfed almost the whole of the Muslim world and thus intensified the disillusionment that was caused by the collapse of Ottoman caliphate. Although *dawlah Islāmiyyah* has been with us for about a century, it seems to have had a checkered history, as no consensus has yet emerged over the definition and basic requirement of an Islamic state. Somewhat like the caliphate, *dawlah Islāmiyyah* also lacked a textual basis in the *Sharīʿah*, but unlike the former, for which a precedent had existed, *dawlah Islāmiyyah* lacked even that, and controversy over it has persisted even in Iran and Pakistan (and more recently Afghanistan) which have formally embraced the idea. The history of state and goverment in Islam has known a variety of nomenclatures, including caliphate, imamate, sultanate and emirate, which, however, did not include *dawlah Islāmiyyah.* Was this an accidental exclusion, or indicative perhaps of an understanding that religion and state, although related entities and concepts, were not necessarily an extension of one another?

Maybe there is an occasion for further reflection on this and reason for us to take the more pragmatic *siyāsah sharʻiyyah* as an alternative to *dawlah Islamīyyah*. The difference between the two ideas may not be very wide bearing in mind that *siyāsah sharʻiyyah* is flexible enough to encapsulate much of what is known about *dawlah Islamīyyah*. And yet *siyāsah sharʻiyyah* is a substantive idea rather than a form of government and it can as such accommodate diversity within its bounds. One can think of a number of contemporary Muslim countries that have hitherto shifted away from the idea of *dawlah Islamīyyah* but may find *siyāsah sharʻiyyah* an easier proposition to take.

In saying this I also draw attention to a certain intellectual bipolarity that dominated the Islamic scholarship of the twentieth century. The Muslim world has been offered two opposing options, either of an Islamic or of a secular state, neither of which has been representative of the realities of the Muslim world in the post-colonial period. The Islamic state idea has almost been monopolized by the hardline conservatives who generally maintained a dogmatic stance over it and hardly considered the idea that politics and statecraft cannot be too closely bound by dogma away from the mundane realities of life. One is inclined to think that most present-day Muslim countries would be likely to fall somewhere between the two propositions, and *siyāsah sharʻiyyah* would seem to provide the intermediate option.

I may conclude by saying that a great deal of what Malaysia has done in order to establish a good government that is committed to justice and seeking to realize *maṣlaḥah* for the people as well as protect them against corruption fall within the ambit of *siyāsah sharʻiyyah*. Then it remains to be said that Malaysia is a *Sharīʻah*-oriented polity, or else that *siyāsah sharʻiyyah* has a visible place in the politics and administration of Malaysia. I also hope that Malaysia succeeds in making its system of government even more appealing to its own citizens and to those outside Malaysia who view the Malaysian experience of government as in many ways worthy of emulation. I believe Malaysia's appeal has a great deal to do with its politics of moderation and its effort to accommodate the varied interests of its multi-religious and multiracial society, which in this case has evidently proved to be a positive influence and an incentive to greater toleration and refinement.

The introduction of Islam *ḥadharī* represents an interesting development in Malaysia as the whole idea seeks to combine Islamic values and objectives with government policy. Islam *ḥadharī* is essentially focused on a welfare programme for all the citizens of Malaysia and merits attention by all its citizens. On the whole, Islam *ḥadharī* does not seek to change the pattern of continuity and Malaysia's politics of accommodation, yet it does articulate the role of Islam in goverment policy with greater clarity than the 'Islamization policy' that preceded Islam *ḥadharī*.

NOTES

1. Cf. M. H. Kamali, '*Siyasa Shar'iyya* or the Policies of Islamic Government', 59–81 at 60.
2. Ibn Qayyim al-Jawizyyah, *al-Ṭuruq al-Ḥukmiyyah fi'-l-Siyāsah al-Shar'iyyah*. Cairo: al- Mu'assasah al-'Arabiyyah li'l-Ṭabā'ah, 1380/1961, 16.
3. Ibn Qayyim, *al-Ṭuruq al-Ḥukmiyyah*, 16.
4. Ibn Taymiyyah, *al-Siyāsah al-Shar'iyyah*, 6–13.
5. Idem, 5.
6. Cf. Khallāf, *al-Siyāsah*, 3.
7. Taqi Amini, *Time Changes and Islamic Law*, 29.
8. Ibn Qayyim, *al-Ṭuruq al-Ḥukmiyyah*, 17–18.
9. Ibn Farḥūn, *Tabṣirat al-Ḥukkām*, II, 138–9.
10. Idem, II, 188.
11. Idem, II, 204.
12. Cf. 'Abd al-Raḥmān Tāj, *al-Siyāsah al-Shari'iyyah wa al-Fiqh al-Islāmī*, 28.
13. Cf. Khallāf, *al-Siyāsah*, 8–9.
14. For an interesting discussion of these policy changes on *zakah* and how *siyāsah shari'iyyah* can be utilized to address modern legal issues see I. K. A. Howard 'Muslim Legal Approaches to Modern Problems', *Islam 21*, issue 8 (April 2001), 2–3.
15. Ibn Farḥūn, *Tabṣirat al-Ḥukkām*, II, 144–5.
16. Ibn Qayyim, *al-Ṭuruq al-Ḥukmiyyah*, 34.
17. Cf. Lewis, 'Siyasa,' in Green ed., *Islamic Humanism*,7.
18. Ibn Qayyim, *al-Ṭuruq al-Ḥukmiyyah*, 28.
19. Ibn al-Muqaffa' as quoted in Bernard Lewis 'Siyasa', 6–7.
20. Abū Ḥayyān al-Tawḥīdi, *Kitāb al-Imtā' wa'l-Mu'ānasah*, II, 32.
21. Ibn Khaldūn, *Muqaddimah*, 337.
22. Cf. Lewis, 'Siyasa', 9–11.
23. Cf. Howard 'Muslim Legal Approaches', *Islam 21*, 8.
24. Amīnī, *Time Changes*, 43.
25. Fu'ād 'Abd al-Mun'im Aḥmad, *Uṣūl Niẓām al-Ḥukm fi'l-Islām*, 14, referring to Jād al-Ḥaqq's Centennial Lecture on the dawn of the fifteenth century hijrah.
26. Khallāf, *al-Siyāsah*, 14–16.
27. 'Abd al-Raḥmān Tāj, *al-Siyāsah al-Shar'iyyah*, 21.
28. Idem, 21–2.

29. Idem, 71–2.
30. *Statistics Malaysia*, January 1997, 5.
31. Von Der Mehden, 'Islamic Resurgence', in Esposito (ed.), *Islam and Development*, 56.
32. Cf. Chandra Muzaffar, 'Tolerance in the Malaysian Political Scene', 143.
33. Kamali, *Islamic Law in Malaysia*, 20.
34. Cf. Shad Saleem Faruqi, 'Concept of an Islamic State', 8–9.
35. See for details Kamali, *Islamic Law in Malaysia*, 237–74.
36. Idem, 12.
37. Cf. Faruqi, 6.
38. Cf. Arts 3 (1) through to 3(5), 11(4), 12(2), 34(1), 150(6A), 160(2) Fourth schedule and Ninth schedule, List II, Item I.
39. Arts 121(1A), 145(3), 9th schedule, List II, Item 1.
40. Mahathir Mohamad, 'Ulama have distorted Islam', speech delivered at the World Economic Forum Special on 'The Role of Islam in the Modern State' in New York. *New Straits Times*, 4 February 2002.
41. *New Straits Times*, 30 September 2001.
42. Cf. Hamid Enayat, *Modern Islamic Political Thought*, 69. The phrase '*dawla Islamiyya*' was probably first used by Muḥammad Rashīd Ridā.

12

ADAPTATION AND REFORM

For an adequate treatment of recent developments in Islamic law, its writing styles, its teaching methods, codification and research as well as some notable reforms we need to take a glance at the six phases that legal historians have distinguished in the development of Islamic law from its early origins to the present time. This chapter is thus presented in two sections, the first of which briefly addresses the first five phases with a view to establish the context that would then take us to the early twentieth century. The second section expounds the last phase, focusing mainly on twentieth century developments in fuller details.

THE FIRST FIVE PHASES OF *FIQH*

In its initial phase, that is the Prophetic period (c. 610–32), the Qur'ān was revealed and the Prophet explained and reinforced it through his own teaching and Sunnah. There was a general preoccupation with the Qur'ān and the emphasis was not as much on law as on the dogma and morality of Islam. The legal rulings of the Qur'ān which were mainly revealed during the second decade of the Prophetic mission in Madinah were on the whole issue-oriented and practical. There was basically no need for speculative legal reasoning or *ijtihād*, since the Prophet himself could provide definitive rulings on issues as and when they arose.

The second period, the era of the Companions (c. 632–61), is one of interpretation and supplementation of the textual subject matter of *Sharī'ah*, and it is in this period that *fiqh* and *ijtihād* find their historical origins. The Companions of the Prophet took a rational approach towards the text and message of the Qur'ān and Sunnah. Their understanding and interpretation of the text was not confined to the meaning of words but also included its underlying rationale, effective cause and purpose. Interpretation by the Companions is generally considered authoritative not only because they were the direct recipients of Prophetic teachings but also because of the latitude they exhibited in the understanding of the text. They are known for their frequent recourse to personal reasoning and consultation in the determination of issues. Notwithstanding the rapid pace of developments and their ensuing preoccupation with political and military matters, the Companions attended to the development of *Sharī'ah*. The first four caliphs, Abū Bakr, 'Umar b. al-Khaṭṭāb, 'Uthmān Ibn 'Affān and 'Ali Ibn Abū Ṭālib, collectively known as the Rightly Guided Caliphs (Khulafā' Rāshidūn), inspired the community's trust in their leadership, which is why their collective decision, as well as individual opinion and verdict, is generally held to be authoritative and reflective, in many ways, of the teachings of the Prophet.

The third phase of *fiqh*, known as the era of the Successors (*tābi'ūn*), began with the coming into power of the Umayyads and ended with the ending of that dynasty (661–750). Due to the territorial expansion of the Umayyad state, new issues arose which stimulated significant developments in *fiqh*. This period is marked by the emergence of two schools of legal thought which left a lasting impact on subsequent developments of *fiqh*. These were the Traditionists (*Ahl al-Ḥadīth*) who were centred mainly in Makkah and Madinah in the Hijaz, and the Rationalists (*Ahl al-Ra'y*) who were active in the Iraqi cities of Kufa and Basra. Whereas the former relied mainly on textual authority and were averse to the use of personal opinion (*ra'y*), the latter were inclined, in the absence of a clear text, towards a more liberal use of personal reasoning. The Traditionists were opposed to taking an inquisitive approach to the understanding of the text, but the Rationalists maintained that the rules of *Sharī'ah*, outside the sphere of devotional matters, pursued certain objectives and were founded in effective causes that provided the jurist and *mujtahid* with guidelines for further enquiry and research. The secession of the Shī'ites from the main body of the Muslims, the Sunnis, which took place as a result of disagreement over political leadership, later led to the emergence of the Shī'ite school of law during this period. The

Shīʿites maintained that ʿAli, the cousin and son-in-law of the Prophet, was the rightful caliph and leader but that his predecessors, Abū Bakr, ʿUmar and ʿUthmān, denied him that right. The Shīʿite school advocates doctrines that are significantly different from those of their Sunni counterparts.

The next two centuries (c. 750–950), known as the era of independent reasoning (*ijtihād*), marked the fourth phase in the history of *fiqh*. It saw major developments which were later manifested in the emergence of the schools of law, namely the Ḥanafi, Māliki, Shāfiʿī, and Ḥanbali, that have survived to this day.

The Ḥanafi school, named after Abū Ḥanīfah Nuʿmān Ibn Thābit (d. 767), has the largest following of all the surviving schools, owing partly to its official adoption by the Ottoman Turks in the early sixteenth century. Abū Ḥanīfah advocated analogy (*qiyās*), which gained general acceptance over time, but his extensive and relatively liberal use of personal opinion (*ra'y*) and juristic preference (*istiḥsān*) were criticized by the Traditionists. The Ḥanafi school has to this day retained its relatively liberal stance.

The Māliki school, founded by Mālik Ibn Anas al-Aṣbaḥ (d. 795), led the Traditionist movement in Makkah and Madinah and advocated the notion of the Madinese consensus (*ijmāʿ*) as the only authoritative *ijmāʿ*. Despite its Traditionist leanings, however, the Māliki school has embraced a number of important doctrines that are inherently versatile, and its jurisprudence is in many ways more open than that of the other schools. It is the only school, for instance, that has accepted almost all the subsidiary sources and proofs of *Sharīʿah* regarding which the other schools have remained selective, accepting some and rejecting or expressing reservations over others.

Muḥammad ibn Idrīs al-Shāfiʿī (d. 819) was also a leading figure in the Traditionist camp, but he tried to reconcile the various trends and strike a middle course between the Traditionists and Rationalists. Al-Shāfiʿī's major contribution is also seen in his articulation of the broad outline of the legal theory of the sources, the *uṣūl al-fiqh*. He spent the last five years of his life in Egypt and found the customs of Egyptian society so very different from those of Iraq that he changed many of his legal verdicts as a result. These changes were extensive enough to lead his followers to the conclusion that he actually founded two schools, known as the Old School and the New School.

Even al-Shāfiʿī's degree of emphasis on tradition and his strong advocacy of the Sunnah did not satisfy the uncompromising

Traditionists, who preferred not to rely on human reason and chose to base their doctrines, as much as possible, on the Qur'ān and *ḥadīth*. This was the avowed purpose of the two new schools which emerged in the ninth century. The first and the only successful one of these was the Ḥanbali school, founded by Aḥmad Ibn Ḥanbal (d. 855). The other was the Ẓāhir school of Dāwūd ibn 'Ali al-Ẓāhir (d. 885), which is now extinct. Ibn Ḥanbal's followers were also declining until the eighteenth century when the Wahhabiyyah puritanical movement in the Arabian peninsula gave it a fresh impetus.

The last of the five phases in the formative history of *fiqh* began around the mid-tenth century. It was generally one of institutionalization of the dominant schools, with emphasis not so much on new developments as on following existing precedent (*taqlīd*). The '*ulamā*' in this period generally occupied themselves with elaboration and commentaries on the works of their predecessors. By far the longest in the history of *fiqh*, this period lasted for about nine centuries and witnessed the downfall of the Abbasid and Ottoman empires, expansion in the military and political powers of the West, industrial revolution and colonial domination of Muslim lands by European powers. The colonial powers propagated their own doctrines and legal codes in almost every area of the law in their dominions. *Fiqh*, as a result, lost touch with social reality and underwent a sustained period of stagnation.

THE CURRENT PHASE OF DEVELOPMENTS IN *FIQH*

The current phase in the history of *fiqh* began at around the turn of the twentieth century. It is marked by a lesser emphasis on precedent and greater emphasis on original thinking and *ijtihād*, and the quest to make the *Sharī'ah* once again relevant to the social reality and experience of contemporary Muslims. The revivification of *fiqh* and its necessary adjustment to respond to the prevailing needs of society is seen as an important component of developments of this period.

Following World War 2, the collapse of colonialism, the rise of nationalism and independence movements, Islamic revivalism in the Arab world, North Africa and elsewhere began with a demand by the Muslim masses to revive the *Sharī'ah* in the spheres of law and government. There were also those who opposed this voice and called instead for continuation of the colonial legacy, ideas and institutions. This latter group emphasized that the Muslim world did not possess a self-contained *Sharīʻah* – based civil code or a constitutional model to provide a ready recourse for government leaders, judges and teachers and those who wished to revive the *fiqh* heritage.

The first group was supported by the masses and the prevailing public sentiment whereas the second consisted mainly of Western-educated government leaders and advocates of modernization and secularism. Amidst this, many newly independent Arab countries in the Muslim world introduced new constitutions which basically originated in European thought but offered a partial response to public opinion through the incorporation of clauses that declared Islam as the state religion, *Sharīʻah* as a source, and in some cases, the source, of statutory legislation.

Codification and Reform of Islamic Law

Muslim countries have on the whole seen it as necessary and advantageous to codify their applied *Sharīʻah* laws for the following reasons:

1) the law embodied in the classical books of *fiqh* does not contain all the provisions relevant to the needs of present-day society which are more complex and diverse;
2) exclusive reliance on a particular school of *fiqh* is likely to cause rigidity and hinder objectivity and growth; and
3) in countries such as Pakistan, Malaysia and Sudan the positivist approach of Western law has largely been integrated into legal and judicial practice, and codification is a necessary part of that approach. This is seen to be a pragmatic approach that allows the judges and jurists to refer to classical *fiqh* while interpreting the codified laws.[1]

The demand for codification of law, especially with reference to the formulation of a *Sharīʻah*-based civil code, grew stronger with the course of events, and working groups of *Sharīʻah* and modern law experts began to be engaged in Syria and Egypt. The renowned Egyptian jurist and minister, ʻAbd al-Razzāq al-Sanhūrī (d. 1971), featured prominently in these early efforts. Sanhūrī's assistance was sought by his own country and also Syria and Iraq, mainly due to his harmonizing tendency to incorporate salient aspects of Western jurisprudence into his Islamic revivalist projects. Sanhūrī's influence in Egypt led to some concrete results especially regarding the prohibition, for example, of consumption of alcohol in public places, and also certain provisions concerning women's participation in public services and professions. Sanhūrī also retained a great deal of the French Civil code but departed from some of its theoretical postulates in the spheres, for example, of contracts, evidence and court procedure. The French approach was marked by its emphasis on externality and appearance at the expense sometimes of conscionability and fairness. Whereas the *Sharī'ah* tends to be society-oriented, Western law bears the imprint of individualism. When a legal system is founded on individualist values, the system will pay less attention to conscionability, and unforeseen events that may call for suspension and review of a contractual agreement. The Egyptian Civil Code of 1949 thus tends to be more socialist in its spirit, thanks to Sanhūrī's influence, despite its grounding in the French precedent.[2] Yet Sanhūrī's approach remained a predominantly mixed approach, which has largely become a part of the Egyptian legal heritage to this day. Only in the closing decades of the twentieth century in the sphere mainly of commercial law and Islamic banking, Egypt has relied on predominantly *Sharī'ah* sources in the formulation of its laws.

An early Syrian initiative to enact an Islamic civil code was thwarted, however, by a military coup that made Syria revert to the prevailing Egyptian civil law model which bore the imprint of the French influence. Yet the demand for a return to *Sharī'ah* grew stronger in the Arab world, so much so that it marked a turning point in the style and substance of statutory legislation in the Middle East in the succeeding decades.

In the background of all this lay the Ottoman *Mejelle* of 1876 that marked an early attempt by the Turkish government and '*ulamā*' to codify and make easily accessible the Ḥanafi *fiqh* of civil transactions (*mu'āmalāt*). After some seven years of preparation the *Mejelle* was completed in 1851 with articles consisting of an introduction and sixteen chapters. The *Mejelle* did not cover the area of family law, which is why it was followed in 1917 by the promulgation in Turkey of the Law of Family Rights. This law utilized the resources not only of Ḥanafi *fiqh* but also of the other three Sunni schools more widely than the *Mejelle*, marking in effect a departure from the scholastic particularity of adherence to a single *madhhab* in the country. Although Turkey herself eventually abandoned these laws, the works remained in use in other Muslim countries and influenced subsequent legislation in the Arab Middle East.

The new trend towards openness had influenced Egypt even earlier. The 1929 Egyptian Law (no. 25) of Personal Status drew not only from the juristic legacy of the four major schools of *fiqh* but also from the opinions of individual jurists when this was deemed to be more conducive to public interest. The Syrian Law of Personal Status 1953 took a step further in this direction and not only relied on the resources of the leading schools but formulated new rules which had no precedent in the existing *fiqh*. The Syrian legislation also marked a new beginning for *ijtihād* through statutory legislation, as it departed from the traditional pattern of *fiqh*-based *ijtihād* which was the concern primarily of private jurists and *mujtahids*. This neo-*ijtihādi* approach to legislation was followed in the same decade by similar attempts in Morocco, Tunisia, Iraq and Pakistan where statutory reforms were introduced in the traditionally *Sharī'ah*-dominated laws of marriage, polygamy, divorce and inheritance. The new reforms were often based on novel interpretations of the Qur'ān and were generally expressive of the desire to retain the Islamic identity of their laws but also to revise and reform them in light of prevailing social conditions. These early precursors of reformist legislation were, however, generally confined to the traditionally *Sharī'ah*-dominated field of matrimonial law and inheritance.

The desire to formulate a more comprehensive *Sharī'ah*-based civil code was accentuated by a call for collective *ijtihād* that was marked by a) recourse to the wider resources of *fiqh* in all of its diverse schools and *madhhabs*, itself a contrast to the Ottoman *Mejelle* that singled out the Ḥanafi school to the near total exclusion of all other schools; and b) direct recourse to the sources of *Sharī'ah* and its goals and objectives (*maqāsid al- Sharī'ah*) as aids to *ijtihād*. The fresh emphasis on the wider resources of *fiqh* was to address new issues in the fields especially of civil transactions (*mu'āmalāt*) and commercial contracts, companies and partnerships, insurance and the like. The new emphasis on *ijtihād* was the most explicit yet to mark the reopening, as it were, of the door of *ijtihād*, following the so-called closure of the door of *ijtihād* after many long centuries.

Developments in Syria, Iraq and Jordan prompted a more consolidated attempt, particularly in Jordan, to formulate a civil code that was based on the *fiqh* sources in their wider reaches, drawn not only from the established schools but also modern opinion and *ijtihād*-oriented developments. In 1976 Jordan completed and promulgated a civil code which replaced the hitherto entrenched Ottoman *Mejelle* and the code has remained in force ever since. The Jordanian code is now widely seen as a model that combines and balances diverse influences in modern thought and the established schools of law. The UAE adopted it and issued a civil code on its basis, as did the republic of Sudan in the early 1980s. One of the interesting features of the Jordanian Code of 1976 is that its various articles are frequently followed by explanatory notes that indicate the sources from where these detailed contents were drawn. Efforts are also under way at present for the formulation of a unified civil code for all the Arab countries.

Another dimension of codification and reform in Muslim countries has been to purge the applied *Sharī'ah* codes of the unacceptable content that contravened Islamic principles. In Pakistan, the Council of Islamic Ideology has been engaged in the identification of laws that were deemed un-Islamic in the applied laws of Pakistan, including laws it had inherited from the British colonial period. After some five years and examination of hundreds of statutes, it was found that certain provisions in about 10 per cent of the laws needed to be changed. A new Federal *Sharī'ah* Court was established as part of the Supreme Court of Pakistan in 1980 with powers to strike down or amend laws and statutes it found contrary to the injunctions of Qur'ān and *ḥadīth*. About one hundred statutes were referred to the FSC over the years, including, for example, property and inheritance laws that restricted women's share of inheritance in landed property, and also laws that introduced restricted ownership, as well as laws that decriminalized consensual adultery, changes in the laws of evidence and so forth.

The Sudan experience of codification-cum-Islamization of laws resembled that of Pakistan in its attempt to purge the applied Islamic laws from the colonial legacy of British laws, yet it differed in its approach to doing this. Whereas Pakistan took a gradual approach to making its laws *Sharī'ah*-compliant, Sudan adopted the faster approach of introducing statutory codes without proper case-by-case scrutiny. This was the main reason why the Sudan Penal Code 1983, which introduced Islamic penal laws of *ḥudūd* and *qiṣāṣ* etc., were met with resistance. The Sudan Civil Law 1984 on the other hand only focused on certain aspects of the laws of property and transactions and made them *Sharī'ah*-compliant while leaving intact the bulk of the civil laws of British origin. Some of the provisions of the Civil Law were also taken from the renowned Ottoman *Mejelle*.

On a general note, in cases of absence of necessary laws in the *fiqh* sources, the tendency prevailed in post-colonial Muslim countries to retain or utilize Western laws which did not contravene any of the principles of *Sharī'ah*, on the assumption that the basic norm of *Sharī'ah* regarding such laws was permissibility (*al-ibāḥah*). One of the widely known maxims of Islamic law proclaims permissibility as the norm in all matters (*al-aṣlu fi'l-ashyā' al-ibāḥah*) unless expressly forbidden by the clear text or general consensus (*ijmā'*). Acts and transactions, even those which originate in non-Islamic sources, are covered by this maxim of Islamic law. Instances of this practical norm of *Sharī'ah* thus included adoption of administrative and judicial procedures of Western origin which were not contrary to *Sharī'ah* and yet facilitated the objectives of justice and good government. The scope of permissibility and *ibāḥah* also extended to adoption of Western laws and regulations in the sphere of industrial relations, new developments in commerce and economic affairs.[3] Yet the renowned Sudanese Islamic scholar, Ḥasan al-Turābi had a word of caution concerning such laws: 'What we import and adopt from external sources must be verified and its compatibility with our character and heritage must be ascertained first.'[4] 'Aṭiyyah has voiced a similar sentiment saying that we ought to confine borrowing from other legal traditions to the sphere of civil transactions (*mu'āmalāt*) alone.[5]

Fiqh *Encyclopedias*

Notwithstanding their many advantages such as pragmatism, better classification and access, the new *Sharī'ah* law reforms were decidedly selective in that they confined the applied aspects of *fiqh* to matters mainly of personal law which consequently isolated the wider legacy of *fiqh* in the other areas of *mu'āmalāt*. The new codes had also a restrictive effect in that they confined judges and practitioners to specific provisions and minimized the need for them to maintain regular contact with the sources. They had the effect of pushing the source materials of *fiqh* and its methodology further into the background so that their relevance to the applied laws of the land became even less visible than before. The need was consequently felt for new measures to consolidate the rich legacy of *fiqh* into convenient collections which would stimulate scholarly interest in *fiqh* and respond to the needs and interests of both the legal profession and academic research. Hence the call by the Organization of Islamic Conference (OIC) for the compilation of a comprehensive encyclopedia of *fiqh*, following which several projects were taken up towards that end. The University of Damascus began a project in 1956, and the governments of Egypt and Kuwait started their own projects in 1951 and 1971 respectively. The Egyptian project came to an abrupt close within a few years. The Kuwait encyclopedia of Islamic Law (*al-Mawsū'ah al-Fiqhiyyah*) has reached forty-five volumes and is nearing completion.

These and other similar encyclopedic compilations have on the whole departed from the scholastic exclusivism of the traditional writings by treating all the major schools of *fiqh* (the four Sunni schools plus Shī'ah-Ja'farī, Zaydī, Ibāḍī and Ẓāhirī) strictly on the merit of their contribution and the information compiled is relatively free of sectarian bias. Yet by their terms of reference, the encyclopedia collections were designed to consolidate rather than reform the existing *fiqh* and this has meant that the compilers were not in a position to address new issues at the level of *ijtihād*. They have undoubtedly provided valuable resource materials but they consist basically of uncritical expositions of the scholastic heritage of *fiqh*. The need was then felt to supplement and enrich the scope of these endeavours by further developments in collective *ijtihād* over new issues.

Islamic Law Academies

Collective *ijtihād* was to constitute the principal method of arriving at consultative decisions. An Islamic *Fiqh* Academy (*Majma' al-Fiqh al-Islāmi*) was thought to be one way of implementing the idea of collective *ijtihād*. This was to consist of a number of prominent Muslim jurists to be selected from various Islamic countries. The Academy was to have permanent headquarters but to convene periodically to deliberate topical issues of concern to Muslims in the light of the *Sharī'ah* objectives and principles. Several conferences were held to deliberate over this and other issues in Damascus, Cairo and Casablanca in 1961, and some years later in Riyadh in 1976. The first *Fiqh* Academy to be opened was the Islamic Research Academy (*Majma' al-Buḥūth al-Islāmi*) of Al-Azhar in 1961. The Muslim League subsequently inaugurated its own *Fiqh* Academy in Makkah and held its first session in 1978. Then the Organization of Islamic Conference created another *Fiqh* Academy in Jeddah and convened its first session in 1984. This Academy has a member from every Muslim country that is represented in the OIC and that includes virtually all Muslim countries, of which there are fifty-seven altogether. India and Pakistan too organized their own *Fiqh* and *Sharīʻah* academies and there are a number of international research institutes that undertake research in Islamic legal themes. King Abdulaziz University in Jeddah, for instance, established its International Centre for Islamic Economic Research.

The OIC and the Muslim League *Fiqh* academies have permanent headquarters and hold annual sessions that deliberate topical issues from the perspective of Islamic law. Wide-ranging issues including artificial insemination, test-tube babies, organ transplant, prayer times in places near Antarctica, expropriation of private property for public purposes, intellectual property rights, issues of concern to marriage and divorce, Islamic banking and finance and so forth have been submitted from time to time to the academies and *fatwās* issued following academy deliberations. All of these manifested the practice of collective and consultative *ijtihād*. One of the distinctive features of collective *ijtihād* is that expert opinion from specialists in other disciplines, such as science and medicine, economics and finance is solicited whenever it is deemed necessary and conducive to *ijtihād*. The *fiqh* academies have, on numerous occasions, practised this and frequently taken into consideration the expert advice they obtained.

Whereas the *fiqh* academies mentioned so far were formed at the initiative basically of international organizations and private individuals, Pakistan gave it a constitutional mandate by forming an Islamic Ideology Council as the government's initiative. Malaysia's National *Fatwā* Council is also a statutory body and so are the Muftis and their *fatwā* committees that are currently operative in the various states of Malaysia excluding Sabah, Sarawak and Penang, as non-Muslims constitute the majority population of these states. India has an Islamic *Fiqh* Academy based in New Delhi which operates at the national level established at the initiative of the Muslim community organizations of India. These are all engaged in *fatwā*-related activities and organize national and international seminars and conventions on *fiqh*-related issues from time to time.

A more recent development of interest is the introduction of *Sharīʻah* advisory committees in major banks and financial institutions with the task mainly of ensuring due compliance with the *Sharī'ah* in banking operations. These committees are also engaged in *ijtihād* and *fatwā*-related activities which contribute to the growth of the *fiqh* of *mu'āmalāt*. The Central Bank of Malaysia (Bank Negara) has a Syariah Advisory Committee that is the most prominent and there is a tendency now for the smaller Syariah Committees to follow decisions and *fatwās* issued by the Bank Negara Syariah Committee.

Teaching and Research

Another dimension of the *fiqh* reform movement that emerged in the latter part of twentieth century was a certain change in the style and format of teaching of Islamic law. New methods of teaching and scholarship marked the emergence of self-contained Islamic universities. This was due to an awareness that scholarship of the earlier periods produced poorly classified works and their teaching methods were not always suitable for modern institutions of higher learning. *Fiqh* scholars in *Sharī'ah* faculties began to address the needs of students at undergraduate and higher levels of competence. Methods of instruction to masters and doctoral students were separately considered. Research-oriented scholarship in doctoral programmes took into consideration expertise not only in the traditional subjects but also relatively new areas such as the Islamic law of obligations, Islamic constitutional law (*al-fiqh al-dusturi*), Islamic economics, Islamic banking and finance, human rights studies and so forth. Students and candidates have to go through progressive stages of accomplishment and follow the stipulated course structure and requirements that did not obtain in the earlier methods of *fiqh* teachings. The scope of *fiqh* teaching has also been widened and extended to comparative studies not only of the various schools and *madhhabs* but also of other legal traditions including common law and European laws. Greater attention is being paid now to individual scholarly works outside the established *madhhabs* and those that preceded the formation of the *madhhabs*, including prominent jurists of the eighth century, such as Abū 'Amr al-Awza'ī, Layth b. Sa'd, Ibn Shubrumah, Sufyān al-Thawrī, Ibn Abī Laylā, Ḥasan al-Basrī and many others whose contributions lay in the margins of scholastic *fiqh* and they now constitute fresh areas of comparative *fiqh* studies. I have discussed the decline of traditional madrasah education in the Muslim countries in a separate section in the next chapter.

Teaching of Islamic law in Western universities continues to be, on the whole, theoretical, dominated by academic and comparative interests and continues to be over-critical in line with Orientalist viewpoints. One is inclined to note that some adjustment and balance was returning to the over-critical tone of Orientalism in recent decades, but the events of 11 September 2001 and their aftermath have probably set back any gains that might have been made. British and American law schools that include Middle Eastern and oriental studies usually teach Islamic law as an elective course. Since Islamic law is not an applied discipline in the West, its teaching programmes do not cater for the needs of the legal profession. If one area can be mentioned where treatment and coverage of Islamic law is now dominated by its applied concerns almost everywhere, it is Islamic banking and finance. An impressive range of courses and programmes are now available on Islamic commercial law, Islamic law of contract and modes of *Sharī'ah*-compliant banking transactions.

Scholarship and research in Western universities on Islamic law also tend to follow its teaching patterns although postgraduate research in the West now extends to almost all areas and branches of Islamic law. It is of interest to note that the theoretical orientations of teaching and research in Islamic law can also be said to be true for Muslim countries and universities. *Sharī'ah* scholars are notorious for their theoretical orientation to the teaching of Islamic law and for their detachment from the more pragmatic concerns of practitioners and judges.

Whereas the civil law subjects that are usually taught in Muslim countries tend to cover the relevant case law and court decisions, *Sharī'ah* textbooks and course coverage of Islamic law tend to lack this dimension – although this too is now beginning to change. Leading universities in the Middle East and Gulf countries offer substantive courses in Islamic law, and full degree programmes in *Sharī'ah* in their Islamic universities. Many universities in Asia also offer Islamic law as a subject in their law programmes. The contents vary from an introduction to Islamic law to more specific courses like Islamic jurisprudence (*uṣūl al-fiqh*), family law, commercial transactions and criminal law. Universities in Malaysia offer degrees in Islamic law as well as combinations with Islamic studies, economics, political science, sociology and psychology. This seems to be the practice also in Thailand, the Philippines, Brunei, India and other Asian countries, although in India, Islamic law is often a compulsory subject in undergraduate law degrees.

Islamic law studies in Muslim countries have gained prominence partly due to the demands of the legal profession. Law firms in Malaysia, for example, have started setting up Islamic law units to deal with the growing demand in this area. University graduates with a good grounding in Islamic law are much sought after as they can represent clients in both the civil courts and *Sharīʿah* courts. In Malaysia, Singapore and Thailand which apply a dual legal system, judges and personnel who specialize in Islamic law are now in greater demand.

Islamic personal law in the areas especially of marriage, divorce, guardianship, inheritance and bequest has remained to be the applied law of Muslim countries almost everywhere. Teaching and research in the field of personal law has been less theoretical than some of its other branches and has consequently remained in touch with developments in case law, especially in countries that apply the common law tradition of judicial precedent. This is the case, for example, in Malaysia, the Sudan, Pakistan and Bangladesh, although there is another factor which is now influencing the position of Islamic law in Sudan and Pakistan. This is the phenomena of Islamization and the Islamic state which has extended the application of Islamic law throughout the legal system. Yet in certain areas, such as the Islamic criminal law and *ḥudūd* penalties, experience in Pakistan, for example, has been less than successful, which is why it has started actually folding back the *ḥudūd* laws it had introduced in the late 1970s.

The fresh openings in Islamic law also marked a departure from the *taqlīd*-based environment of exclusivity on the part of the followers and protagonists of the leading schools. A certain balance and reverential perspective has gained ground and has nurtured respect for all the schools and scholars of *fiqh* and their followers. Government leaders and parliamentarians have consequently been enabled to select from a wider range of scholastic contributions views and interpretations that are most suitable for legislation and enforcement.

These developments have on the whole improved the prospects for Islamic law to play a more prominent role in statutory legislation and court decisions. Islamic family law reforms of the mid-twentieth century ushered in significant changes in the laws of many Muslim countries and led to the introduction of new laws and codes that incorporated reforms of the matrimonial law. There is now a stronger nexus between the contemporary *fiqh* and statutory legislation. Research scholars in *Sharīʿah* and modern laws are now inclined to be more in tune with the needs of contemporary students and the concerns also of their countries and universities. This is manifested to some extent by the statutory requirements in many countries whereby candidates for *Sharī'ah* judicial posts are assigned to obtain parallel qualifications in modern legal disciplines.

The new *fatwā* collections, often in several volumes, written by prominent twentieth-century Muslim jurists and *'ulamā'*, including Muḥammad Rashīd Riḍā, Maḥmūd Shaltūt, 'Ali Jād al-Ḥaq, Muḥammad al-Ṭantawi, Muḥammad Abū Zahrah, Yūsūf al-Qaraḍāwi and many others have made a significant contribution to the discipline. This can also be said of the multi-volume collections of *fatwās* published by the Islamic Law Academies in recent decades, all of which have added to the academic substance of the *fiqh* reforms and its adaptations to the prevailing conditions of contemporary Muslim socities.

This account would be less than adequate without mentioning, however briefly, the landmark decisions of prominent courts and judges in a number of Muslim countries including Pakistan, Egypt, Malaysia and Sudan. For instance, the Supreme Court of Pakistan decision in the well-known case of *Khurshid Bibi v Muhammad Amin* in 1967 on the subject of *khul'* divorce effectively declared *khul'* as a form of divorce that can take place at the initiative of the wife. This could be cited as an instance of judicial *ijtihād*, which was also based on a novel interpretation of a Qur'ānic passage on the subject. Pakistan has established a Federal *Sharī'ah* Court (FSC) which is the highest tribunal of *Sharī'ah* as a separate bench of the Supreme Court of that country. The landmark FSC decision in 1999 on the elimination of usury (*ribā*) from the banks and financial institutions of Pakistan is another example of its contribution to *Sharī'ah* law reform.

I conclude this account by giving just one example of scholarly views and contributions to the on-going efforts in *ijtihād* and refer to Yūsūf al-Qaraḍāwi's view which validates air travel by women without the company of their male relatives. Women were not permitted to travel alone, according to the rules of *fiqh* that were formulated in pre-modern times. Al-Qaraḍāwi's conclusion is based on the analysis that the initial ruling was intended to ensure the physical and moral safety (*al-ṭama'nīnah*) of the women concerned, and that modern air travel fulfils this requirement. The learned author has supported his view by an analysis of the relevant *ḥadīths* on the subject and has arrived at a ruling which is better suited to contemporary conditions.

NOTES

1. Cf. Tazilur Rahman, *Islamization of Pakistan Law*, 7; see also Fikret Karcic, 'Applying the *Sharī'ah*', 223 f.
2. Cf. Amr Shakalany, 'Between Identity and Redistribution,' 20f.
3. Cf. 'Aṭiyyah, *al-Wāqi' wa'l Mithāl*, 210–11; Tawfīq al-Shawi, *Taṭbīq al-Sharī'ah al-Islāmiyyah*, 54–55.
4. Ḥasan al-Turābi, *Qaḍāya al-Tajdīd*, 204.
5. 'Aṭiyyah, *Tajdīd al-Fiqh al-Islāmi,* 41.

13

REFLECTIONS ON SOME CHALLENGING ISSUES

This chapter addresses five subjects which have been the focus of public debate in recent years and what I have presented concerning them basically consists of my own synoptic responses rather than attempting an in-depth analysis. The five topics to be discussed, each in a separate section, are secularism and the secularist debate among contemporary Muslims, to be followed by a discussion of the gender equality issues, and the decline of madrasahs. Suicide bombing is presented in section four. The last section highlights an important yet somewhat neglected Qur'ānic principle of moderation and balance (*wasaṭiyya, i'tidāl*) which has a bearing on many other issues of concern to contemporary Muslim societies. I begin with the secularist debate concerning Islam as it tends to underline much of what is said in the rest of the chapter.

THE SECULARIST DISCOURSE

Secularism (Arabic: *'alamaniyya, dunyawiyya*) means that which is worldly and temporal. It is a concept that came to the Muslim world in the company of other related terms such as modernity and westernization in the context of colonialism. Although secularism is usually taken to imply the liberation of politics from religion, it has been employed in various ways to marginalize Islam and exclude it from restructuring society during both the colonial and post-colonial periods. Secularism proclaims the independence of 'secular truth' which is experimental and temporal, thereby excluding metaphysical and non-experimental aspects of knowledge.

The historical roots of secularism are intertwined with Church and State relations in Christian Europe and find an uneasy locale in the Islamic tradition. Political theorists and historians are generally in agreement on the European origins of secularism and many Muslim commentators have also held that the concept cannot be adequately comprehended outside Europe's evolution and its Christian reform movements. One of the differences of note in this context, as Muhammad 'Abduh (d. 1905) and also Muhammad al-Bahiy (d. 1982) pointed out, is the absence in the Islamic tradition of anything equivalent to the Christian Church or the powers exercised by the Pope and Vatican. The proposed separation of Church and State which constitutes the main context of secularism in Europe cannot thus easily fit in with the principles of Islamic governance.[1]

The prevailing Western view maintains that mixing religion and politics is bound to corrupt both. The quest for integration of religion and politics in Islam, on the other hand, proceeds from the basic postulate of unity (*tawḥīd*) to mean that what is right and wrong is not a matter simply of personal morality and practice but should also guide law and government policy. Corruption from the Islamic viewpoint comes from severing the connection between eternal truths and public affairs, and for much of Islamic history this view has generally taken a legal form. I record here the view held by many Western observers, including Nathan J. Brown, who noted in one of his conference papers (2007) that liberal polities in the West do not exclude religion totally from public life, but devise a variety of formulas to institute some degree of separation. Yet there is considerable variation in implementing that separation. Many Europeans are not quite in tune with the consistency with which American political leaders speak of their personal faith and belief in God. Many Americans are also puzzled by the degree to which a number of European states offer financial support and legal protection to some religions, yet manage to run matters of Muslim women's dress into protracted political crises.

Some of the postulates of secularism also do not relate well to the Islamic tradition. For instance, while the advocates of secularism subscribe to the view that the hold of religion on society is bound to diminish over time, Islam's influence has, on the contrary, increased over the last hundred years or so. Muslim scholars, including Azzam

Tamimi, Rachid al-Ghannouchi and Muhammad Mahdi Shams al-Din, acknowledge that in the European context, secularism has helped to tame Christian fundamentalism and nurture the values of civility and power-sharing, yet the attempted secularization of the twentieth century Muslim world has produced dictatorship, state-enforced religion, violation of human rights, and the weakening or outright destruction of civil society.[2]

The secularist discourse concerning Islam and the *Sharī'ah* is wide ranging and raises methodological questions as to whether the legal theory of *Sharī'ah* (i.e. the *uṣūl al-fiqh*) and *ijtihād* are adequate to respond to contemporary challenges. Issues debated also include the methods of Qur'ān hermeneutics, relationship between revelation and reason, Islam and science, challenges posed by the human rights discourse, pluralism, religion and state, and gender equality issues. The outer ranges of this discourse also extends to the historicity of the Qur'ān, the nature and finality of prophethood in Islam and so forth. I do not propose to engage in detail beyond making a few points, but I begin by saying that the secularist discourse is not monolithic, as there are shades of differences in the approaches taken towards issues. Some of the advocates of secularism do not confine their proposals for change to the internal resources and mechanisms of *Sharī'ah* and take rationality as the principal framework of their discourse. Yet the majority of commentators from the secularist camp tend to seek support for their reform proposals from within the tradition, although occasional departures on selected issues are also noted.

Piecemeal reform measures that have been introduced in the Muslim world may only partially relate to certain aspects of secularism. Whereas most of the twentieth century reforms that have taken place in Islamic personal law, for example, utilize the internal resources of *Sharī'ah*, we are equally familiar with the history of statutory legislation, royal edicts and administrative decrees throughout the Muslim world to bring changes that did not claim their origins in the *Sharī'ah* nor in any theological doctrine. This may in some ways relate to secularism in the sense that the laws and administrative decrees so introduced were not always based on any religious or *Sharī'ah* premises. I also refer here to what I have discussed in a previous chapter, namely the Islamic public law doctrine of *siyāsah shar'iyyah*, or *Sharī'ah*-oriented policy, which is cognizant of the need for decision making on matters that are not covered by the established *Sharī'ah* or which belong to the discretionary authority of legitimate leadership. Administrative decrees that do not conflict with the principles of Islam and promote good governance may thus fall within the ambit of this doctrine. For all the theoretical importance of Islamic law and the recent rise of Islamic revivalism, most states in the Muslim world, including those who hold a strong claim to Islamic legitimacy, base their legal systems on civil law. Most of the states in the Arab world and South-East Asia have restricted the application of Islamic law to personal status matters (marriage, divorce, child custory, inheritance, etc.) and even there they have introduced wide-ranging legal reforms that few classical jurists would recognize. Notwithstanding significant differences in the approaches Muslim states have taken towards religion and state (compare Saudi Arabia with Turkey, and Morocco with Iran!) the fact remains that throughout the Muslim world today, and for much of its long history of governance, power has been in the hands of individuals who are primarily politicians, not religious leaders or '*ulamā*'.

I may not share some of the ideological underpinnings of secularism, as I am of the view that a Western-style separation of religion and politics would have little utility for much of the Muslim world and would, in any case, most likely be met with resistance, yet I am inclined to look at its contents from a rationalist perspective and take the view that Muslims can benefit by taking up some of the challenges of the secularist discourse in so far as they relate to human welfare, human rights, equality and justice. This also brings to mind a principle of the *Sharī'ah* itself to the effect that the rules of *Sharī'ah* may change in response to the exigencies of time and circumstance. Secularist proposals that seek to widen the scope of human rights and commitment to people's welfare can, I believe, mostly be supported by authoritative evidence in the Qur'ān and Sunnah on human dignity, considerations of public interest (*maslaḥah*), the goals and purposes (*maqāsid*) of *Sharī'ah*, equality and justice.

I have also advanced an aspect of this discussion in my existing works to say that there is a side to the *Sharī'ah*, not commonly known, that is essentially civilian and secularist in character – if secularism poses a certain demand for legal positivism that does not refer resolution of juristic problems to theological principles. I have explained, for example, that political leadership in Islam is essentially civilian, elective and consultative. The *Sharī'ah* blueprint on justice, trial procedures and evidence is also civilian in character and responsive, for the most part, to the demands of positivism. We also note that the

Sharī'ah itself draws a distinction between juridical obligations and religious obligations (*wajib qaḍā'i, wajib dini*) and takes the latter out of the jurisdiction of the courts of justice. Note also the renowned scale of five values, from the obligatory, to the recommended, to permissible, reprehensible and the forbidden, in which only the first and the last are enforceable in the courts of justice, whereas the three intermediate value points consist largely of persuasive advice and fall within the sphere of personal freedom. One can add to this line of discussion but the point I propose to make is that it is inaccurate to say that the *Sharī'ah* is a religious law pure and simple and that it has no room for some of the positivist aspects of secularism.[3]

Commentators in the human rights discourse have often called for a departure from the strictures of the scholastic legacy of the *madhāhib* in the direction of greater openness and receptivity towards human rights principles. This is basically acceptable and so is the suggestion of revising the methodology of Qur'ān hermeneutics and *ijtihād* to open up prospects of meeting legitimate demands for socio-legal reform. The international human rights law merits our attention, not just in terms of generalities, but the unequivocal support and commitment of political leaders, *Sharī'ah* scholars and '*ulamā*' in the Muslim world. This is a momentous challenge and meeting it would require long-term commitment, sustained engagement and mobilization of available resources as the prevailing conditions of society may permit. If justice, human dignity and human welfare are the expressed goals of the *Sharī'ah*, then it should be possible to open the horizons of innovative thought and *ijtihād* to accommodate them.

Elsewhere in my previous writings, and in chapter 8 of the present volume, I have taken up the question of the changes that need to be carried out in the legal theory of *ijtihād* and have put forward some specific proposals for that purpose.[4] I have also noted in my discussion of the goals and purposes (i.e. *maqāṣid*) of *Sharī'ah* in this volume a growing awareness many commentators have shown concerning the limitations of the legal theory of *uṣūl al-fiqh*, which is somewhat over-burdened with technicality and literalism. For one thing, the *uṣūl* theory was constructed at a time when parliamentary legislation was unknown and it is therefore not very well suited to accommodate this rather overwhelming new development. This has given rise to a body of opinion whereby Muslim jurists and commentators pay more attention to the *maqāṣid al-Sharī'ah*, which is, on the whole, more versatile and less hampered by technicality and can be utilized as a supplementary, even as an alternative, framework for *ijtihād*.

ISSUES IN GENDER EQUALITY AND JUSTICE

An adequate coverage of gender equality issues would fall beyond the scope of this chapter and what I am presenting is, in any case, based on my own somewhat synoptic responses to the issues raised. I may begin by saying that *Sharī'ah* law reform in this area has, for a variety of reasons, lagged behind and has been rather slow to provide adequate responses to the challenges of modern society. Numerous factors come into the picture, some of which are not peculiar to Islamic law and society but constitute challenges of civilizational concern on a global scale. The patriarchal character of human society has generally meant that male dominance infiltrated law and religion as it did the custom and culture of societies in all parts of the globe. In Muslim societies factors such as poverty, low levels of female education and employment and prevalence of tribalism still constitute formidable challenges to gender equality and justice at the dawn of the twenty-first century.

Many Muslim countries have introduced egalitarian laws and constitutions in the post-colonial period which have, however, had a limited effect on curbing entrenched prejudicial practices concerning women's rights. Muslim countries are not a monolithic entity and their problems often need to be read in the context of their own set of conditions in every country and region. Law reform on women's rights in South-East Asia and North Africa has been relatively more successful than other regions of the Muslim world. Then there are more specific problems that have adversely affected the healthy growth of Islamic law including, for example, the imitative tradition of scholarship (i.e. *taqlīd*) and the consequent decline of juridical construction (*ijtihād*) to keep the *Sharī'ah* abreast of social reality. These problems have been with us for centuries and the clarion call by Jamāl al-Dīn al-Afghāni (d. 1898), his disciple, Muḥammad 'Abduh (d. 1905), and Muḥammad Rashīd Riḍā (d. 1935) at the dawn of the twentieth century for the revival of innovative thinking and *ijtihād* helped to raise awareness of the challenges but on the whole generated limited results with regard to the revival of *ijtihād*. Some exceptions apart, Muslim jurists continued, on the whole, to look back for solutions to current problems in the hallowed works of the learned imams and jurists of the past. Due to the prevalence of entrenched patriarchal custom in many parts of Asia, Africa and the Middle East, matrimonial law and inheritance remained the most challenging areas of concern for women's rights. Conservative Muslim mentality and the '*ulamā*' attitude to issues of gender equality and justice also wavered between partial admission and outright denial which has only added to the nature and size of the challenge. One can hardly speak of reform to someone who denies that gender equality is an issue in *Sharī'ah* and that the challenge is only imaginary and non-existent.

I have addressed elsewhere some of the more detailed juridical issues of gender equality and my purpose here basically is not to enter into detail but merely to develop a perspective on issues and give my own views on the challenges before us. This I have discussed in the following paragraphs.

1) It is submitted at the outset that issues of equal rights for women should be addressed from within the tradition and the prevailing conditions of each society. One should avoid the tendency of putting an Islamic veneer on some foreign ideas which may be altogether unfamiliar to the Muslim law and culture. Muslims should also find their own realistic solutions and should not allow the real challenges to get entangled in the heated exchanges of secularist, religious and ultra-conservative debates. To correct the imbalances of history naturally takes time and reflection over the newly emerging issues. Gender equality and justice are undoubtedly long-term engagements. Windows of opportunity present themselves from time to time and prudent government leaders should be alert to utilizing them for society's benefit. Juridical issues of concern to *Sharī'ah* should also be addressed, as far as possible, through imaginative *ijtihād* that is informed by the broader guidelines of the Qur'ān and Sunnah on human dignity, equality and justice. We say this because scholastic Islamic jurisprudence on women's rights has been influenced by medieval social values that also found their way into Qur'ān hermeneutics and juristic interpretations of the schools of Islamic law. To say, for example, that the *diyya* (blood money for manslaughter) for a woman is half that of a man simply overturns the broader Qur'ānic principles on the sanctity of life, on just retaliation (*qiṣāṣ*), and its unqualified and gender-blind proclamation on human dignity.

2) With regard to women's participation in government, we can maintain equality at all levels with the exception perhaps of cases where equality may not be advisable on grounds of judicious policy (*siyāsah shar'iyyah*), such as police and military duties in a male-dominated environment, or going against the prevailing culture and custom of society. While observance of dominant culture is prudent, yet cultural constraints should be viewed as *ad hoc* and temporary and be included in the long-term campaign for gender equality. My observation on this point is informed by my personal experience of involvement in the gender-equality campaign in Afghanistan since 2003 and the advice of caution I take is not to risk agitation and protest that can be overwhelming in its negative sweep and can easily render the purpose one fights for even more remote. Gender justice and equality issues should be approached in the true spirit of moderation (*wasaṭiyya, i'tidāl*), itself a Qur'ānic designation and assignment of the *ummah*, and seek solutions that strike the middle ground between idealism and reality and between traditional and modern social values. It may be necessary under certain conditions to design a two- or even a three-phased approach to equality issues, beginning with the least challenging and proceed towards the more sensitive areas of reform. What is important is follow-up effort and measurable implementation over time. One should avoid the temptation to introduce prescriptive reforms that remain largely unimplemented. I would like also to add that even in Afghanistan, probably one of the most conservative of all Muslim countries on gender-equality matters, I note a growing awareness of, and support for, female education, the importance of women's participation in government as well as growing support for the human rights principle. Such may be the windows of opportunity that prudent political leaders can utilize for people's benefit. What I have said of Afghanistan may not be, of course, as relevant for other countries who may have already gone through their own experiences and campaign for gender equality and can afford to aspire to higher levels of refinement.

The only exception of note in Islamic law with regard to women's participation in government concerns the position of the head of state, which is reserved for men; this seems to be based on a presumptive consensus (*ijmā'*), there being no clear authority in the sources to prevent equality even at this level. Our conclusions on this should also be informed by such developments as the prevalence of constitutional checks and balances and separation of powers in modern constitutions, which have altogether altered the material attributes of leadership. Whereas Islamic jurisprudence justified its ruling on this by reference to the position, in earlier times, of the head of state as leader in *jihād*, it is doubtful whether the logic of that conclusion can be sustained now due to material changes in the nature of leadership and warfare. It would seem patently inadvisable now for the head of state to lead the army into the battlefield in present circumstances.[5] The rules of Islamic jurisprudence also hold that a substantial change in the effective cause and rationale (*'illah*) of a ruling should be followed by a corresponding change and a suitable ruling through *ijtihād*.

3) With regard to women's qualification for appointment to judicial posts, the correct interpretation is that of the Qur'ān commentator Ibn Jarīr al-Ṭabarī (d. 923) who held, contrary to the prevailing position of the majority, that women are fully qualified for employment to judicial posts. Except for the Ḥanafi School which qualified women to be judges in all disputes outside the prescribed penalties and retaliation cases (*ḥudūd* and *qiṣāṣ*), the majority of the leading schools passed negative judgements on this, based on a specious analogy drawn with the position of the head of state. Al-Ṭabarī was right to regard this a discrepant analogy (*qiyās ma' al-fāriq*) and say that women judges do not necessarily lead the *jihād*. The principal task of a judge is to comprehend and implement the *Sharī'ah*, and men and women stand on the same footing in this regard.[6]

My recent experience of developments in Afghanistan shows that women can themselves significantly promote their position once they are granted the opportunity to do so. In this case, affirmative action measures that were taken under the 2004 constitution of Afghanistan brought about a significant change in the direction of equality. Articles 83 and 84 of this constitution imposed a quota system in favour of women's election to Parliament by stipulating that at least two MPs in the Lower House (Wolesi Jirga) from each of the thirty-four provinces must be women. A similar quota was imposed regarding the Upper House (Meshrano Jirga) ensuring the election and appointment of about one-sixth of its total membership for women. These quotas were followed in the September 2005 elections which brought a significant number of women to the Afghan Parliament.[7] To compare their presence now (sixty-eight and twenty-three in each of the two Houses respectively) with the mere five women that found their way to Parliament in the 1965 election (the last in Afghanistan before the Soviet invasion and civil war) is a milestone of change for the prospects of women's empowerment in that country. I believe that similar quotas should be followed in the executive and the judiciary branches of the Afghan government. Yet the realities of that country and the receding confidence of Karzai's government in its own standing proved so compelling that President Karzai, himself a pro-equality figure by his track record, reduced the numbers of women Cabinet members from three to just one, after his election victory in the September 2004 election. There is no woman Supreme Court Judge among the nine Judges the President appointed in July–August 2006.

4) With regard to women's partial disability to act as witnesses in the courts of justice, my enquiry into this led me to the conclusion that there is no clear textual mandate on this in the Qur'ān or authenticated *ḥadīth*.[8] In view of the unwavering commitment these sources provide on truth and justice, it would seem only natural to proceed from this position and say that all avenues that vindicate the truth and serve the cause of justice must be left open. If allowing women to give credible testimony in the quest for justice, especially in critical situations where a woman holds vital testimony, one sees no reason to impose a prior restriction on her ability to give it. The Qur'ānic provision on this occurs in the context of commercial transaction and was informed by the conditions of women at the time. Space does not permit elaboration but when one reads the fuller version of the relevant Qur'ānic verse on this subject (2:283), the text itself encourages witnesses to come forth and not to withhold testimony in the cause of justice.

5) Women enjoy equal rights in *Sharī'ah* in respect of ownership, management of financial affairs, civil transactions and contracts. The Ḥanafi school has extended this position to the contract of marriage, although the majority of other schools have considered marriage an exception and require its solemnization by the legal guardian (*wali*) even of an adult woman. Since Islamic jurisprudence permits selection (*takhayyur*, or *takhyir*) among the leading schools, a position which has been utilized in the statutory legislation in many Muslim countries, then there is basically no *Sharī'ah* issue of concern in this area. Yet patriarchal customary practices, especially among the tribes of Asia and Africa, present obstacles to women's enjoyment of their civil and financial rights. The problem here is essentially not juridical but one of prevalent prejudicial custom and male-dominated family and society. To give an example, the Qur'ān unequivocally entitles female relatives to specified shares in an inheritance, which is,

however, widely denied to them by their male relatives. Prohibitive statutory enactments in many Muslim countries on this and similar other issues have not succeeded in curbing entrenched customary positions. The lesson one learns here is that prescriptive law reform needs to be followed by a wider campaign on awareness raising, education and policy initiatives. Muslim women in rural Asia and Africa are not well aware of their rights either under the *Sharī'ah* or statutory law. Legislation should naturally be continued to lead the way in the campaign for gender equality and economic empowerment of women. In some particularly difficult situations, recourse may be had to affirmative action legislation and quota system, for example, in admission to schools and employment centres, on a temporary basis at least, to promote the objectives of gender equality.

6) Some progress has admittedly been made as a result of the Islamic family law reform movement of the mid-twentieth century, which brought many *ijtihād*-oriented changes of matrimonial law in Muslim countries of the Middle East, Asia and Africa. New civil codes and personal status laws were introduced in the 1950s and 1960s and thereafter which reformed the Islamic law provisions in several areas, including the marriage contract, marriageable age, polygamy, child custody, divorce and testamentary succession. The actual reform measures adopted tended to vary from country to country. Broadly speaking, adult boys and girls were enabled, through the introduction of statutory marriageable age, to contract their own marriage without the intervention of their legal guardian. Polygamy and divorce were both subjected to statutory restrictions and made dependent on obtaining a judicial order. Measures were also introduced on registration formalities as well as the admissible means of proof in matrimonial disputes that were on the whole favourable to women. This phase of family law legislation was an improvement on the earlier experience of certain reforms incorporated in the Ottoman *Mejelle* (1876). Whereas the *Mejelle* legislation was based almost entirely on the Hanafi school of law, the new reforms witnessed cross-fertilization of ideas and some instances of selection (*takhayyur*) within the leading schools of law. The Ḥanafi law of marriage was thus adopted in non-Ḥanafi countries and the Māliki law of divorce was similarly adopted in non-Māliki countries. Some Sunni Muslim countries even adopted provisions of the Shī'ite inheritance law that were favourable to female relatives, and opened also the scope of the law governing bequests in an attempt to ameliorate occasional

imbalances in the strict enforcement of the Qur'ānic laws of inheritance. The husband's power of unilateral divorce (*ṭalāq*) was subjected to court order and divorce became in almost all cases subject to court proceedings. Measures were also taken to extend the *Sharī'ah* provisions on *khul'* divorce that is initiated by the wife in all schools but has wider scope under the Māliki law. The reform measures in some cases vested the final authority on *khul'* divorce also in the court of law. Statutory restrictions on polygamy and divorce actually went beyond the scholastic framework and were based on novel interpretations of relevant passages of the Qur'ān.

As noted earlier, the pace and scope of reform varied from country to country and, significant as they were, they were minimal in the sphere of inheritance and bequest due mainly to the sensitivity of the subject and the Qur'ānic mandate on specific quanities of shares to a number of relatives (mainly of allocation of shares to female relatives: eight out of the total of twelve relatives in the Qur'ānic scheme are female). Seen in its historical context, the Qur'ānic law of succession significantly strengthened the position of women. Muslim jurists across the centuries have also devised additional formulas that can be used to remove possible rigidity that can arise in particular combinations of circumstances in the administration of estates.

Customs and attitudes that still prevail among the Muslim masses may suggest that a piecemeal approach to reform on matrimonial law and inheritance may be preferable to sweeping changes that pose difficulties in implementation. The prospects of a backlash and conservative reaction need to be taken into account even if it means a slow pace for law reform. Democratic and consultative methods, civil society engagement and persuasive media involvement would obviously be needed to ensure receptivity and enforcement.

With regard to the *Sharī'ah* law of inheritance, the conventional argument given in support of the larger share that men get in inheritance compared to women, namely that men are responsible for providing women with maintenance both before and after marriage, as well as some remedial financial provisions that help divorced women, still holds good for the vast majority of women in areas and countries where employment and education opportunities are severely limited for women. The picture is also not always a negative one as Muslim men, in many countries and cultures, tend to be on the whole protective of women in the family. We may, nevertheless, draw attention to one or two points on the subject of inheritance.

As already indicated, bequests can be used to adjust some instances of unequal distribution of shares under the Qur'ānic laws of inheritance. The testator enjoys some flexibility with regard to making a bequest and how he or she may choose to use it. Under the Sunni law of succession, the testator is entitled to make a bequest of up to one third of his or her estate in favour of an outsider, or even a legal heir as under the Shī'ite law. Sunni law also permits making a bequest to a legal heir, who may be suffering disability and need, with the consent of the other surviving heirs, which the Shī'ite law allows even without such consent, provided it does not exceed the limit of one third. This may be used to address the individual circumstances of a disadvantaged relative, or an outsider for that matter, be it a Muslim or non-Muslim, and thus help to meet the needs of particular situations, or indeed of an anticipated imbalance in the distribution of shares. Statutory law in some Muslim countries (Egypt and Tunisia for example) goes so far as to stipulate the obligatory bequest (*waṣiyyah wājibah*) provision for certain predictable situations where, for instance, orphaned grand-children, male or female, are precluded from inheritance by the presence of an uncle, who may be a son. What this means is that even in the absence of a bequest by the testator, a bequest will automatically be presumed to have been made in order to address the stipulated circumstances as and when they arise.

Some instances of obvious imbalance in the distribution of inheritance can also be addressed, I believe, by recourse to the principle of *istiḥsān* (juristic preference), especially in cases where strict enforcement of the existing law leads to unfair results in the distribution of family wealth. In such situations, *istiḥsān* authorizes the judge and the jurist to find an alternative and a preferable solution to the case before them which would realize considerations of equity and fairness. Notwithstanding the existence of valid precedent on this as reviewed below, Muslim jurists and judges have not made an effective use of the resources of *istiḥsān*. Without wishing to enter into details, I may refer here briefly to the renowned case of *al-mushtarakah* (the apportioned) which was decided by the caliph 'Umar b. al-Khaṭṭāb. In this case, a woman was survived by her husband, mother, two germane and two uterine brothers. The Qur'ānic rules of inheritance were strictly applied but the result was such that the two maternal brothers received one-third of the estate and the two full brothers were totally excluded. This is because the former are Qur'ānic sharers (*dhawu'l-furūḍ*) whereas the latter belong to the category of residuaries (*'aṣabah*).The former must take their shares first and what is left is then distributed among the residuaries. The full brothers complained to the caliph and forcefully pleaded with him about the justice of their case. According to reports, the full brothers addressed the caliph in the following terms: suppose our father was a donkey (which is why the case is also known as *al-ḥimāriyyah*), we still shared the same mother with our maternal brothers. The caliph was hesitant to act in the face of the clear Qur'anic mandate, yet he decided on equitable grounds, after a month of consultation with the leading Companions, that all the brothers should share equally in the one-third.

Unfair results of a similar type can occasionally arise, sometimes due to technical reasons, which could be addressed by recourse to *istiḥsān*, and the judges should not hesitate to do so when *istiḥsān* can be invoked to serve the ideals of equitable distribution.[9] To give an example, suppose that a deceased person is survived by a son and a daughter. During the lifetime of his father the son had bad relations with him and did not bother to seek his forgiveness even during the months of his last illness, while the daughter took the responsibility and spent much of her hard-earned income on her father's medical bills before he died. When this happened, however, the son was quick to claim double the share of his sister in inheritance. This would be the kind of case, in my view, where *istiḥsān* can be invoked to remedy the unfair outcome that is anticipated from a strict conformity to the normal rules of inheritance. This is the basic rationale of the doctrine of *istiḥsān*, to remedy unfair results which may arise from a strict application of the existing rules of *Sharī'ah*. Yet to the best of my knowledge, Muslim countries have not introduced enabling legislation that would authorize the judges to apply *istiḥsān* to remedy such situations. *Istiḥsān* admittedly does not seek to introduce new law. It is rather designed so as to address case by case situations where strict implementation of the existing law may lead to unfair results. *Istiḥsān* in this way offers some potential to vindicate the cause of equity and fairness when this might present a compelling case for reconsideration and review. For this to become reality, we need lawmakers, judges and jurists of great professional fortitude to make laws and adjudicate cases that break away with the prevailing mindset of *taqlīd*.

Lastly, some aspects of the Shī'ite law of inheritance that are favourable to female relatives can also be adopted by Sunni jurisdictions under the principle of selection (*takhayyur*) as discussed in an earlier chapter on the *madhāhib*. Some Sunni Muslim countries have already done so as a part of the law reform measures they have introduced. The Shī'ite law principles on enhancing women's entitlements in certain specified circumstances stand on sound foundations on the whole and merit, in my view, an *ijtihād*-oriented option that can be considered under the principle of *takhayyur*.

7) The subject of veiling, or *ḥijāb*, has invoked more attention of late than it merits and has evidently far exceeded its strictly juristic framework. It has become a cultural symbol and a mark of identity, even of protest, for Muslim women living in Europe, against the mostly unwarranted demands for conformity and assimilation to the dominant culture. The situation took a turn for the worse following the former British Foreign Secretary Jack Straw's comments on the veil in September 2006 and the action of the Dutch Immigration Minister, Rita Verdonk, later in November on banning the wearing of the burka and face veil in public. These demands are simply indicative of an over-reaction that goes against Europe's own expressed values, but I do not propose to engage in these issues. I might add, however, that in Muslim countries also veiling is not always practised for pious reasons but also for conformity to male domination, protection against fundamentalist aggression, even protest against Western values.

There is no mandate on veiling in the Qur'ān and Sunnah. The available evidence in these sources shows that during the Prophet's time, women participated in public life, and most of the women Companions did not practise the *ḥijāb*, except for the wives of the Prophet, who began to practise it after the revelation of the Qur'ānic verse (33:59) concerning them. Even after this event, other female Companions did not practise the *ḥijāb*, as they knew that the Qur'ānic directive was addressed to the Prophet's wives only. Women's participation in the life of the community during this time was dignified and social encounters took place at the initiative of men and women as and when the occasion arose.

The Qur'ān advocates modesty and moral decorum and cautions against provocative behaviour, especially in the context of interaction and encounter between the opposite sexes (cf., 7:26, 7:31, 24:30, 24:60 and 33:53). This is the basic message but the text does not specify exactly how modesty is achieved. Modesty is important for the upkeep of moral standards in society, and the Qur'ān has addressed it without any quantitative specifications of the kind that subsequently preoccupied the jurists and cultural trend-setters in different times and places. The Qur'ān reminds believers, men and women alike, to lower their gaze and avoid provocative behaviour. Covering the body parts during worship and social encounter is treated in the *fiqh* writings on *'awrah*, on which the leading schools have also recorded some differring interpretations.

The veil was apparently in use in Sasanian society prior to the advent of Islam, and segregation of the sexes was in evidence in the Christian Middle East and Mediterranean regions at the time of the rise of Islam. During the Prophet's lifetime, as noted earlier, his wives were the only Muslim women required to veil. After his demise and following the Muslim conquests of the adjoining territories, where upper-class women veiled, the veil became a commonplace item of clothing among upper-class Muslim women 'by a process of assimilation that no one has yet ascertained in much detail'.[10] Abu Shaqqah's encyclopedic six-volume work[11] remains the most exhaustive and acclaimed work on its subject to date. The author gives his monumental work the self-explanatory title, *Taḥrīr al-Mar'ah fī 'Aṣr al-Risālah* (liberation of women during the Prophet's era). He has noted that women's participation in public life is established by no less than three hundreds *ḥadīths*, and it becomes, as such, an approved Sunnah of the Prophet.

The practice of the largely custom-driven phenomenon of veiling in many parts of the Muslim world has become a tool of continued male domination so that in some cases a woman is not to be seen outside her marital home; she is not even free to enjoy her recognized rights under the *Sharī'ah*. While the *fiqh* rules entitle married women to leave their homes to visit close relatives, to seek advice from a learned person, for health and safety reasons, and emergency situations, etc., none of these are granted without permission from the husband and male guardian. Islam entitles women to education and dignified work, which are also denied to them, even in parts of the affluent Arab world where opportunities are available. The law in many Muslim countries has yet to address issues of guardianship, which the *fiqh* texts mainly entrust to male relatives without there being convincing evidence in the sources. This raises issues over guardianship of minors and decision-making regarding their schooling and place of residence, especially in the event of strained relations between their parents or divorce, but also issues of nationality and citizenship under statutory law. A woman can hardly pass on her identity under the present law to her minor child, which can in certain situations mean that the child remains stateless with no recognized status under the law.[12] The challenges of gender equality thus remain largely unmet and a shared responsibility exists to respond to them in line with a balanced reading of the normative guidelines of the Qur'ān and Sunnah, and the prevailing conditions of contemporary society.

THE DECLINE OF MADRASAHS

Several historical phases can be detected in the decline of madrasahs. As is well known, the madrasah was initially a mosque-based place for Qur'ān study and basic literacy until it went through its first transformation under the Abbasids (750–1258). With the expansion of the Abbasid empire, Greek rationalism and Persian philosophy entered the Islamic domain and Muslim scholars subsequently sought to amalgamate these influences with their own scholarly engagements in the religious sciences. The Mu'tazilites who led this intellectual trend found favour with the caliphs and became prominent for almost a century (765–846). The educational system of that period reflected the rationalist bent of the age and the madrasah syllabus was revised to include philosophy, mathematics and logic, in addition to Qur'ān and *ḥadīth* studies. The next phase was the emergence of the scientists and philosophers who ushered in the 'golden age' of the Islamic sciences (800–1200), such as al-Bīrūni, al-Khawārizmi, Ibn Sīnā al-Ghazāli, al-Rāzi and Ibn al-Rushd, until the destruction of Baghdad at the hands of the Mongols (c.1258) which marked the end of the Abbasid dynasty. Science and philosophy gained prominence but the former also became the target of much controversy and debate.

The Sufis emerged out of the ashes of the Mongol destruction. The madrasah in turn reflected the spiritual quest of this era and *tazkiyah* (purification of the soul) and ethics acquired new prominence in the madrasah curriculum. This period culminated in the injection of an ethical culture in the Islamic tradition of scholarship under the aegis, for example, of the great Mogul emperors (1526–1707) of India and the consequent proliferation of madrasah education in the Indian subcontinent.

With the subsequent spread of corruption in the body politic Muslim countries and colonialist distortions of the infrastructure of Islamic education, the Salafis (puritans) asserted themselves by placing greater emphasis on positive law and *fiqh* and the emergence as a result of the age of legalism and *fatwā* that began to also influence the educational syllabus of the madrasahs.

This can be seen in the teachings, for example, of Muḥammad 'Abd al-Wahhāb of Arabia (d. 1792) and Dan Fudio (d. 1817) of Nigeria who gave a fresh impetus to conformity and imitation of the *fatwā* and rulings of the schools and jurists of the past. Yet in their urge to purge society, the Salafis indulged in their own excesses and injected rigidity and dry legalism into the educational system of the madrasah. Islamic civilization thus changed focus from *taqwa* (spiritual awareness) to *fatwā* (legal edict), from an emphasis on spirituality to a penchant for legalism that was also embraced by the madrasah. The consequence has been the decline of spirituality and rise of extremism and intolerance in parts of the Islamic world. Then the European ascendancy in the nineteenth century challenged Muslims and resulted in the introduction of the Tanzimat reforms in the Ottoman Empire, which sought to reform not only traditional Islamic education but also law and government generally. But they were short-lived and faded with the disintegration of the Empire in 1924. The Tanzimat were short-lived partly because they confronted traditional values, used coercive methods, and did not enjoy the support of religious leaders and '*ulamā*'.[13]

The decline of madrasahs in modern times began with the colonial interference that scuttled the natural evolution of this institution in the Muslim world, and the decline continued with the spread of government-sponsored education over much of the post-colonial period. Governments were inclined on the whole to withdraw financial support for madrasahs, and in some cases, established a network of religious schools that either rivalled or replaced madrasah education. Politicization of Islam and the events post-9/11 further jeopardized public perceptions of the madrasah system and the sweeping charges levelled against it as a training ground for religious zealots and extremists.

The madrasah decline may be said to be in many ways reflective of the political malaise and poor record of governance in the greater part of the Muslim world today. Madrasahs have been politicized to the extent that they stand to lose support under secularist governments and leaders, and gain it with the success of Islamic political parties and movements. But since the Islamic parties and movements in most Muslim countries usually stand in opposition to the government in power, this makes the madrasahs generally inclined to align themselves with the opposition. The politicization of madrasahs also tends to affect negatively the prospects of government support for cash-strapped madrasahs. All of this is apparently not welcome by the people who regard madrasahs as a part of the educational tradition of Islam. Commenting on the Pondok schools (madrasah as it is known in Malaysia), Nakhaie Ahmad, a former Vice-President of the Islamic Party of Malaysia (PAS), referred to how the PAS tends to influence and politicize the Pondoks, and added 'I hate this type of politics. I study Islam and I know it is unnecessary to go so far to win support. Schools should be free of politics.'[14] It thus appears that the decline of madrasah is due to a large extent to extraneous factors, mostly political in nature, other than the education itself. Yet there are also deficiencies in the madrasah educational system that call for reappraisal and reform – if the madrasah graduates were to be successfully integrated into the larger society. As it is, the marginalized syllabus of the madrasah produces graduates who are not well equipped to compete with better funded modern school and university graduates in the increasingly globalized market economy. Frustrated and disillusioned, the madrasah graduates walk into the arms of the extremists and blame all their misfortunes on the outside world.

The emergence in recent decades of the Islamic University in many Muslim countries has also contributed to the decline of madrasah education, although a parallel, yet a marginal, tendency also obtains, within the madrasah system itself, in favour of adaptation and development of a balanced curriculum of traditional and modern disciplines. The reformist tendency within the madrasah has not, however, become an engaging process due largely to internal resistance on the part of their conservative teachers and *'ulamā'*, isolation from the government, and in some cases also due to the development of a separate government-funded system of religious schools that operate side by side with the madrasahs and enjoy greater financial support from the government.

The method of instruction in the madrasah is characterized by rote learning. The deductive and inductive methods as well as analytical and inquisitive skills of modern education are severely neglected.

These traditional methods need to be changed so that in addition to memorization of Qur'ān and *ḥadīth*, the students also acquire knowledge in natural and historical sciences, computer skills, etc., to enable them to find jobs in a globalized marketplace.

One also notes that the great majority of students who attend the madrasahs are from poorer sections of society. Families that cannot afford the cost of a secular education often bring their children to the madrasah, itself a factor that contributes to the decline of this institution. The madrasahs on the whole provide valuable service in parts of the Muslim world such as the North-West Frontier province of Pakistan, Afghanistan, India and elsewhere in giving their students grounding in the religious sciences which are often diluted or not available in modern schools. The madrasah teachers are often dedicated individuals who are paid very little and they teach basic literacy in the local language, Arabic, Islamic history, and reading and translation of the Qur'ān and *ḥadīth*. Their simplicity, piety and personal touch with the tradition are often valued by their constituencies.

Aggressive militarism of the post 9/11 era and the West's increasingly hostile posture towards Muslims has been a shot in the arm of extremist movements and a cause for much concern, even disillusionment, of the Muslim masses with the West. The perception has grown that the madrasah has provided a breeding ground for 'jihadis and terrorists'. The concerted Western clamp-down in the post-9/11 period on transfer of funds between Muslim countries, institutions and individuals, included within its broad sweep charities and educational grants to madrasahs which reduced to a trickle any transfer of funds to these institutions from its traditional supporters in Saudi Arabia and the Gulf. In the past, the madrasahs had relied extensively on religious endowments (*awqāf*) and donations from within and outside their home countries, but the *awqaf* properties and institutions are also beset with their own set of problems of illiquid assets, lack of fund mobility and investment options, and chronic problems of poor management.[15]

In Malaysia, the Pondok schools, according to one commentator, 'is more than just a school system. It is tied up with the history of Islam in the country and to the growth of Islamic education . . . The sekolah pondok is not a fossil. If you want your children to have Islamic education, the pondok still offers the best option with its environment of religious knowledge and the learning of classical texts.'[16] Yet in Malaysia, over the years, the pondok schools have been outranked by religious schools which provide a mix of both religious and secular disciplines. Due to this development the madrasahs in Malaysia have on the whole been marginalized. According to Nakhaie Ahmad, 'you are supposed to be training an '*ulamā*' class. How can he be effective if he has so little interest in what is happening around him?'[17]

In Indonesia, Islamic boarding schools, known variously as Pesantren, Surau, Daya, or Pondok, have played a significant role not only in education but also in preparing the country's social and political leaders. The issue of terrorism, as one commentator put it, is a recent phenomenon, while Pesantren is as old as the history of Islam in Indonesia: 'Since the Bali bombing of October 12, 2002 which killed 190 people and injured more than 300 others, many foreign analysts have been misled into believing that the schools are a refuge for terrorists.'[18] The *kyai* (religious teacher) is typically described as 'modest and a model to emulate in terms of knowledge, behaviour and leadership. The kyai–student relationship is close, informal and egalitarian. Through continued *sillaturrahmi*, or communication for brotherhood and common humanity, networking is established between the cleric and his disciples and among the disciples . . . All graduates have been taught literacy, honesty, devotion, brotherhood, independence, and mutual help.'[19] In 1989 there were 6631 pesantren in Indonesia teaching 958,670, that is, close to a million male and female students. The madrasahs in the South-East Asian countries, including Malaysia, are on the whole not involved in extremist activities.

Notwithstanding its decline in recent times, the madrasah is very much a part of the fabric of Muslim society and enjoys grassroots support. It also serves a useful purpose in the preservation of traditional values and tends to exert a stabilizing influence in society. Any attempt to reform the madrasah should perhaps be gradual, preserving the stability that this institution provides while enhancing its social usefulness. The changes must also come from within the community and the madrasahs themselves rather than be imposed from outside. A transformation of madrasah, its syllabus and teaching methods cannot take place, however, without substantial investment of funds by government organizations and NGOs to assist in the preparation of reading materials, teacher training and technical skills. This will most likely enable the madrasahs to find their proper role and bearing in the educational system and larger society and help them prevent their graduates becoming easy targets for extremist influences.

SUICIDE BOMBING

Suicide bombing has no precedent in Islamic law and history and it is a new issue, open in that sense to fresh contributions, and it seems that a consensus has not yet been reached over its permissibility, and whether it can be subsumed under martyrdom, from the *Sharī'ah* perspective. Suicide (*intiḥār*) does occur in Islamic law, more specifically in the *ḥadīth* as reviewed below, but it can also be subsumed under the Qur'ānic provision of killing without a just cause. The Qur'ānic dictum on the sanctity of life addresses the believers to

> slay not the life which God has made sacrosanct unless it be in a just cause. (6:151)
>
> وَلاَ تَقْتُلُوا النَّفْسَ الَّتِي حَرَّمَ اللَّهُ إِلاَّ بِالْحَقِّ.

The terms of this address apply to all living creatures but the focus is on human life. This is because life is a God-given gift and not the creation of its bearer, hence the latter does not have the right to destroy it. This is why suicide is forbidden in Islam without any exception whatsoever. It is an offence for which the perpetrator is liable, in the event of an unsuccessful attempt, to a deterrent but discretionary penalty of *ta'zīr*. But even when the attempt succeeds, the person is still liable to an expiation (*kaffārah*) which may be taken from his property, according to the Shāfi'īs and some Ḥanbalis, whereas the Imams Abū Ḥanīfah and Mālik do not make expiation a requirement.

Qur'ānic authority on the prohibition of suicide is found in a prohibitive text which addresses the people:

> And kill yourselves not [*la taqtulu anfusakum*], for God is truly merciful to you. (4:29)
>
> وَلاَ تَقْتُلُوا أَنفُسَكُمْ إِنَّ اللَّهَ كَانَ بِكُمْ رَحِيمًا.

People who are driven to despair are thus reminded to have faith in God's mercy in the hope that they may be relieved of their suffering. Since suicide is prohibited, anyone who tries to facilitate it, or acts as an accomplice, is also liable to a deterrent punishment that may be quantified by the court while taking into consideration the material circumstances of the case. Commentators have, moreover, drawn a five-point conclusion from this verse as follows: 1) the obvious meaning is that suicide is forbidden; 2) the text also stipulates that 'you may not kill one another' nor facilitate suicide; 3) one may not undertake a task which is likely to cause his own death, even if it be in lieu of a religious obligation; 4) no one should deprive himself of the necessities of life to the point of self-destruction; and 5) the text covers cases of self-destruction regardless of the manner in which it is done.

The Qur'ān also forbids courting danger that is most likely to destroy one's life – as in the following verse: 'Throw not yourselves [*la tulqu anfusakum*] into the mouth of danger' (2:195).

The noble Prophet has spoken strongly in condemnation of suicide as in the following *ḥadīth*:

> One who throws himself off a mountain cliff and kills himself, he will be doing the same to himself perpetually in Hell. One who takes poison and kills himself shall be holding the same in his hand permanently taking it in Hell . . . and one who kills himself with a weapon, he will be piercing his body with it perpetually in Hell.[20]

This is confirmed in another *ḥadīth*: 'One who kills himself with something in this life will also be tortured by it on the Day of Resurrection.'[21] Life is accordingly a Divine trust (*amanah*) in the custody of its bearer, who has a duty to safeguard and protect it.

Al-Bukhāri has recorded a *ḥadīth* to the effect that the Prophet looked at a Muslim warrior, in the course of a battle waged to repel the enemy attack on Muslims in Madinah. The man was by all accounts a most devout Muslim and a competent warrior, yet the Prophet said the following concerning him:

> 'One who wants to look at someone from the dwellers of Hell, let him look at this man.' Another man followed him and kept on following him until the fighter was injured, and in a wish to die quickly, he placed the tip of his sword on his chest and leaned over it until it passed through his shoulders and died. When the Prophet was informed of the incident, he said: 'A person may do deeds that seem like the deeds of the people of Paradise, while in fact, he is from the dwellers of Hell. Similarly, a person may do deeds that look like the deeds of the dwellers of Hell while he is, in fact, from the dwellers of Paradise. Verily the deeds of people are judged by their end results.'[22]

The manuals of Islamic law are silent on the issue of suicide bombing, a disturbing phenomenon of our time that became frequent in connection with Israeli–Palestinian conflict, especially when Israel unleashed a new wave of aggression on the street processions of unarmed Palestinian youth in 2000–1. The aftermath of 11 September 2001 and more recently the horrendous violence in Iraq and Afghanistan, added new dimensions to the incidence of suicide bombing among Muslims.

The issue has invoked mixed responses from Muslim commentators, most of whom have denounced this as well as the 11 September attacks, as being contrary to Islamic principles. Others have gone on record to equate suicide bombing with martyrdom and *jihād*. The advocates of suicide bombing included the late Hamas leader, Shaykh Ahmad Yasin (himself a victim of Israeli target bombing) who has been quoted as having said in reference to Israel: 'As long as they target our civilians, we will target their civilians.'[23] In a 1998 interview, Muḥammad al-Ṭanṭāwi, Sheikh of al-Azhar, also validated suicide bombing if the enemy targeted the civilian population, in which case it would fall, according to him, under *jihād* and death for an honourable cause.[24]

In a recent *fatwā*, Sheikh Yūsūf al-Qaraḍāwi also allowed suicide bombing by Palestinians in self-defence and in defence of their homeland against Israeli occupation. 'These are acts of sacrifice' (*'amaliyyat fidā'iyyah*), according to the learned Sheikh, rather than suicide. As for the loss of innocent life as a result, al-Qaraḍāwi considered it as collateral damage and invoked the rule of necessity (*ḍarūrah*) and the legal maxim that 'necessity makes the unlawful lawful – *al-ḍarūrat tub ḥ al-maḥẓūrāt*'. For the non-combatants and innocent bystanders [*al-musālim n wa'l-abriyā'*] are not the intended target but killed unintentionally [*fa-huwa lam yuqsad bi'l-qatl, bal 'an ṭar q al-khatā'*], similar to war casualties, whereby children are sometimes struck by their parents.'[25] In response to another question as to how the learned Sheikh can justify the loss of the innocent life of a person who is not at all involved in military activities, al-Qaraḍāwi basically repeats that he 'gave verdict on the permissibility of the acts of sacrifice against the occupation forces and those who assist them in their atrocities'. Al-Qaraḍāwi adds further that among jurists there are those who say that these non-combatants suffer as a result of their settlement and usurpation of the Palestinian homeland and that they should leave and go back to where they or their parents came from.[26] My review of the much longer text of this *fatwā* sustains the conclusion that al-Qaraḍāwi has confined his *fatwā* only to the Palestinian case, and has on no other occasion validated suicide bombing generally, nor has he subsumed it under martyrdom.

I hold the learned Sheikh Yūsuf al-Qaraḍāwi in high regard for his many enlightening contributions on complex issues of contemporary relevance in *Sharī'ah* and I have extensively quoted him on numerous occasions in this volume. Without wishing also to question his noble intentions, nor our shared condemnation of the extreme brutality of the Israeli aggressors, I have nevertheless reservations over the premise on which this *fatwā* is founded, namely that the innocent bystanders are not the intended target. One might ask then: who is the intended target? Presumably the occupation forces! The occupation forces, the Israeli government, or its military are thus deemed to be the indirect targets. I submit, however, that the crowd which the suicide bomber walks into and blows up is the intended target. The suicide bomber definitely intends to kill those people, and this target is often located outside the military barracks. If this is granted, then it would mean that the *fatwā* we have just reviewed bypasses one of the crucial *Sharī'ah* law principles of *mubāsharah*, that is, the direct cause (as opposed to *tasabbub*, indirect causation).[27] The first party, that is intended, as being the most relevant criterion of determining criminal responsibility under *mubāsharah*. This principle is simply overturned and ignored. A valid *fatwā* must surely be founded on sound and indisputable premises, and I have reservations as to whether this *fatwā* does qualify.

In September 2003, the then Malaysian Prime Minister, Dr Mahathir, denounced Palestinian suicide bombing and said that suicide bombing was unacceptable to Islam. Mahathir, himself a strong supporter of the Palestinians, added that they resorted to suicide bombing because they did not have proper weapons in their fight for an independent homeland. 'Nevertheless, it is wrong to commit suicide bombing' because it causes loss of innocent lives. 'Fighting is one thing, but if you go on board a school bus and kill all the school children, I don't think it is a brave move.'

Dr Mahathir made these remarks in response to a statement of Abdul Hadi Awang, the then leader of the opposition Islamic party of Malaysia, PAS, who had said that Islam permitted suicide bombing in the fight against oppression. He added that his party supported the Palestinian militant group Hamas and considered suicide bombings as acts of martyrdom. Mahathir added in his response to these remarks that the root cause of the Palestinian problem was not religion but territory and unless this issue was resolved it would be difficult to persuade Hamas not to resort to violence.[28]

In November 2003 the Arab states condemned the suicide car bombing in Riyadh that killed seventeen and wounded more than a hundred persons, mainly Arabs. The twenty-two-member Arab League denounced the attack as 'terrorist and criminal', and Saudi Arabia, alongside its five neighbours in the Gulf Cooperation Council, condemned it as 'cowardly and terrorist'.

The Arab League Secretary General, Amar Musa, said such acts 'only aim to destabilize . . . terrify and kill' innocent people. The Egyptian President Husni Mubarak condemned it as a 'criminal act', and the then Foreign Minister of Iran, Kamal Kharazi said 'killing defenceless women and children in the holy month of Ramadan . . . is against Islamic values and human ethics'.[29]

Robert Pape, a political scientist who studied suicide terrorism from 1980 to 2001, made the observation that 'religion is not the force behind suicide terrorism'. He says 'the data shows that there is little connection between suicide terrorism and Islamic fundamentalism, or any religion for that matter', adding that the group responsible for the highest percentage (40 per cent) of all suicide attacks has been the Tamil Tigers in Sri Lanka, who are adamantly opposed to religion. Rather he suggests nearly all suicide terrorist campaigns are 'coherent political or military campaigns' whose common objective is a specific and strategic goal, namely to compel military forces to withdraw from their homeland. 'From Lebanon to Israel to Sri Lanka to Kashmir to Chechnya', the objective was 'to establish or maintain political self-determination'.[30]

Suicide bombing in the name of Islam is therefore a 'sociopolitical phenomenon, not a theological one'. And any long-term solution to the problem must also address the causes that have brought so much pain and hopelessness to many Muslim societies.[31]

It would be simplistic to lump the Palestinian suicide bombing with al-Qaedah terrorist activities. One can hardly deny the genuine suffering of the Palestinian people and legitimacy of their struggle against sustained Israeli brutalities. It would appear equally simplistic, however, to equate suicide bombing with martyrdom and *jihād*. This is because suicide bombing contravenes two fundamental principles of Islam: prohibition against suicide, and deliberate killing of non-combatants. The argument that proceeds over reciprocity and retaliation is also flawed by the involvement of innocent non-combatants in suicide bombing.

Those who have raised the issue of 'collateral damage' in this context have also exaggerated their case, simply because non-combatants are chosen as the direct target of suicide bombing. They are, as such, neither collateral nor incidental. Even if the cause of fighting the Israeli aggression is deemed valid, that would still not justify killing non-combatants.

According to the *ḥadīth*, reviewed above, the Prophet denounced those who deliberately took their own lives even in the course of a defensive war, including suicide by a warrior who suffered from severe wounds. The Muslim fighter who is motivated by the spirit of *jihād* enters the battle, not with the intention of dying, but with the conviction that if he should die, it would be for reasons beyond his control. Martyrdom in Islam does not begin with suicidal intention, let alone the linkage of that intention with the killing of non-combatants.

To justify suicide bombing under the banner of retaliation, or as a form of *jihād*, is therefore questionable, simply because it begins on an erroneous note, which goes against the essence both of just retaliation and justified *jihād*.

MODERATION AND BALANCE (*WASAṬIYYAH, I'TIDĀL*)

A brief review of the source evidence that is offered in the following pages would show that *wasaṭiyyah* is a major theme of the Qur'ān and an important dimension of its worldview. Yet notwithstanding its unquestionable importance, *wasaṭiyya*h is a much neglected aspect of the teachings of Islam. It is an aspect of Islam, however, which holds valid in almost all aspects of life, including civil transactions, customary matters, ethics and acts of devotion (*mu'āmalāt, 'ādāt, akhlāq* and *'ibādāt* respectively). The principal Qur'ānic verse on *wasaṭiyyah* to be reviewed in some detail is as follows:

> Thus We have made of you a community justly balanced that you might be witnesses over the nations and the Messenger a witness over yourselves. (2:143)
>
> وَكَذَٰلِكَ جَعَلْنَاكُمْ أُمَّةً وَسَطًا لِّتَكُونُوا شُهَدَاءَ عَلَى النَّاسِ وَيَكُونَ الرَّسُولُ عَلَيْكُمْ شَهِيدًا

The renowned Qur'ān commentator, Ibn Kathīr (d. 1373) wrote concerning this verse that the Muslim *ummah* qualifies as a witness because of its commitment to moderation and truth – as testimony is not admissible of extremists who transgress the limits of moderation. The *ummah* is a forgiving and just community with the capacity to mediate between people and show forth in its very existence the mercy and justice of God.[32] The verse specifies the manner this *ummah* should relate to other communities and nations, most of whom had their own scriptures and prophets that guided them and showed them the path to deliverance. 'Our Prophet and our *ummah*', wrote another renowned Qur'ān commentator, al-Qurṭubī (d. 1263), 'witness that the previous prophets faithfully fulfilled their missions, and our Prophet testifies also that he faithfully accomplished his mission to us.' Al-Zamakhshari's (d. 1180) commentary on this verse points out that 'the middle or *wasaṭ* is the best choice as it is protected by its peripheries against corruption and collapse'.[33] The Qur'ānic conception of the *ummah* is a community united in faith and the goals and objective of Islam – and unity can best be achieved through moderation and balance.

In another Qur'ānic passage, the Prophet Muhammad received the following instructions:

> And become moderate in thy pace, and lower thy voice. (31:19)
>
> وَاقْصِدْ فِي مَشْيِكَ وَاغْضُضْ مِن صَوْتِكَ.

Abdullah Yusuf Ali regards this as the 'golden mean' and pivotal to Islam's outlook, which describes our relationship to God, to His universe and to our fellow humans. In all things be moderate. Do not go the pace and do not be stationary or slow. Do not be talkative and do not be silent. Do not be loud and do not be timid or half-hearted. Do not be too confident nor let yourself be cowed down.[34]

The Qur'ān also characterizes its own teachings in a way that strikes a close note with *wasaṭiyyah*:

> Verily this Qur'ān guides toward that which is most upright and stable – *bil'llati hiya aqwam*'. (17:9)
>
> إِنَّ هَذَا الْقُرْآنَ يَهْدِي لِلَّتِي هِيَ أَقْوَمُ

Stability and uprightness are best achieved through moderation and balance. It is reported, on the authority of Ibn 'Abbās that the Prophet said in a *ḥadīth*: ‘in all matters the middlemost represents the best choice’ (*khayr al-umūri awsaṭuhā*).[35]

The Holy Book advocates moderation through its guidelines on a variety of other themes, such as bringing ease to the people and removal of hardship from them – as in the verse

> God intends every facility for you and He intends not to put you in hardship. (2:185)
>
> يُرِيدُ اللّهُ بِكُمُ الْيُسْرَ وَلاَ يُرِيدُ بِكُمُ الْعُسْرَ.

Moderation in punishment is also recommended – as in the verse that follows:

> Whoever is aggressive toward you, your response must be proportionate to the aggression inflicted on you. (2:194)
>
> فَمَنِ اعْتَدَى عَلَيْكُمْ فَاعْتَدُواْ عَلَيْهِ بِمِثْلِ مَا اعْتَدَى عَلَيْكُمْ.

The text also proclaims in an objective and unqualified address to the believers that justice must be rendered to every one, even to one’s foes:

> Let not the hatred of a people swerve you away from the path of justice. Be just. For it is closest to righteousness. (5:8)
>
> وَلاَ يَجْرِمَنَّكُمْ شَنَآنُ قَوْمٍ عَلَى أَلاَّ تَعْدِلُواْ اعْدِلُواْ هُوَ أَقْرَبُ
> لِلتَّقْوَى وَاتَّقُواْ اللّهَ.

Islam encourages a sense of essential human fellowship that stands on the twin principles of *ʿadl* and *iḥsān* (justice and being good to others: Q. 16:90). This is endorsed elsewhere in another directive to Muslims ‘to be the agents of good, for God loves those who do good’ (*wa aḥsinū, inna Allaha yuḥibbu al-muḥsinīn*) (2:195). To be good to others naturally includes the manner of one’s speech and address, and Muslims are enjoined to

> speak to the people in good words. (2: 83)
>
> وَقُولُواْ لِلنَّاسِ حُسْناً.

The courteous encounter in one’s dealings with others is also reflected in the manner one propagates Islam, in that it should be through ‘reason and good advice’ (*bi’l-ḥikmat-i wa’l-maw’iẓat al-ḥasanah*) (Q. 16:25). All of this may be seen, in turn, to be a corollary of the unqualified affirmation of human dignity in God's illustrious words that

> We have bestowed dignity on the children of Adam. (17:70)
>
> وَلَقَدْ كَرَّمْنَا بَنِي آدَمَ.

The Prophet Muhammad said in a *ḥadīth* that 'the best of people are the ones who are the most beneficent to them' (*khayr al-nās-i anfa'uhum li'l-nās*), and in another *ḥadīth* he said that

> none of you is a [true] believer unless he loves for his brother that which he loves for himself.[36]
>
> لايؤمن أحدكم حتى يحب لأخيه ما يحب لنفسه.

Islam recognizes two levels of fraternity, namely fraternity in faith (*al-ikhā' al-dini*) and human fraternity (*al-ikhā' al-insāni*), hence the teachings we review are not confined to Muslims alone. Avoidance of suspicion concerning others is yet another dimension of the Qur'ānic vision of *wasaṭiyyah* – as in the verse:

> O believers, avoid indulgence in suspicion, for surely suspicion in most cases is sinful, and spy not (on one another). (49:12)
>
> يَا أَيُّهَا الَّذِينَ آمَنُوا اجْتَنِبُوا كَثِيرًا مِّنَ الظَّنِّ إِنَّ بَعْضَ الظَّنِّ إِثْمٌ وَلَا تَجَسَّسُوا.

The Prophet reiterated this in a renowned *ḥadīth* addressing the Muslims: 'you must avoid suspicion, for suspicion can amount to the worst form of lying', and extended this sense of essential optimism in his other saying that

> thinking well of others partakes in service to God.[37]
>
> حسن الظن من العبادة.

The renowned Tunisian scholar, Muḥammad Ṭāhir Ibn 'Āshūr, went on record that 'in moderation lies the essence of all virtues (*faḍāa'il*) and it is a great protector against indulgence in corruption and caprice'.[38] Yūsūf al-Qaraḍāwi has similarly observed that moderation is the correct path that leads the Muslim *ummah* to its ideals of attaining material and spiritual success: 'It is the divinely ordained moral and humanitarian mission of the Muslim community to pursue all its goals through moderation. I also believe that deviation from the path of moderation brings nothing but destruction and loss.'[39] In his recent book entitled *Isssues in contemporary thought and jurisprudence* (*Qaḍāyā al-Fiqh wa'l-Fikr al-Mu'āṣir*) (2006), 583, Wahbah al-Zuhaili spoke along the same lines when he wrote: '. . . at the root of almost any social problem, there is some form of deviation from the path of moderation. Recourse to moderation is most likely to bring stability and calm that contribute greatly to the well-being of the individual and society . . . For *waṣaṭiyyah* epitomizes the essence of Islam's moral uprightness and virtue.'

One of the manifestations of extremism is an obsessive pursuit of fault-finding in others and making exacting demands of them. The Prophet condemned this in a *ḥadīth* when he urged the Muslims to 'Avoid extremism (*al-ghuluw*), for people before you were led to destruction because of extremism in religion.'[40] In another *ḥadīth*, the Prophet rigorously spoke against the extremists when he said: 'Perished are the hair-splitters, perished are the hair-splitters, perished are the hair-splitters.'[41] The same sentiment is conveyed in the Qur'ānic proclamation that 'God does not burden a soul beyond his capacity' (2:86). The Prophet has, in turn, reiterated this in a renowned *ḥadīth* which addresses the believers: 'Fear God to the extent you can, but you should listen and obey' (*fa'ttaqullaha ma'staṭa'tum, wa'sma'u wa aṭi'u*). It is interesting then to see how the Qur'ān promotes the spirit of moderation in its address to believers in the following verse:

> If you avoid the most heinous of the prohibited conduct (*kabā'ira ma tunhawna 'anhu*), We shall conceal all your sins and admit you to a gate of great honour. (4:31)
>
> إِن تَجْتَنِبُوا كَبَآئِرَ مَا تُنْهَوْنَ عَنْهُ نُكَفِّرْ عَنكُمْ سَيِّئَاتِكُمْ وَنُدْخِلْكُم
> مُّدْخَلاً كَرِيمًا.

Thus it is noted in the relevant commentaries on this verse that avoidance of major sins acts as a concealer on minor ones, an indication that God will forgive the latter. Al-Qaraḍāwi has consequently drawn the conclusion that it is enough in our time to comply with the principal teachings of Islam and avoid the major sins in order to gain the good pleasure of God.[42]

When two of the Prophet's leading Companions, Mu'ādh b. Jabal and Abū Mūsā al-Ash'ari were leaving as judges to the Yemen, the Prophet instructed them to:

> Be gentle to the people and avoid harshness to them; bring them good news and scare them not [with gloomy predicaments].[43]
>
> يسروا ولاتعسروا و بشروا ولاتعسروا.

With regard to the implementation of penalties, the Prophet instructed the judes and rulers to 'Suspend the prescribed punishments (*ḥudud*) as far as you can. For it is better to err in forgiveness than making an error in punishment.'[44]

In a *ḥadīth* narrated by the Prophet's widow, 'Ā'ishah, and recorded by both al-Bukhārī and Muslim, the Prophet said: 'God is gentle and he loves gentleness in all matters' (*In-Allha raf qun yuḥibbu al-rifqa fi'l amr-i kullih*). Then he confirmed this in another *ḥadīth* to say that

> Gentleness fails not to bring beauty in everything, and it is not taken away from anything without causing ugliness.[45]
>
> لايدخل الرفق فىشيئ ولاينزع من شيئ إلا شانه.

Moderation is also recommended in financial matters in more than one place in the Qur'ān but more specifically in its address to the faithful: 'And let not thy hand be chained to thy neck nor stretch it to its utmost reach lest it brings anguish and remorse'(17:29).

Lastly, our discussion of *wasaṭiyyah* and *i'tidāl* would be deficient without a reference to *samāḥah*, that is, inclination towards easiness, which is a prominent feature of the Islamic ethos. *Samāḥah* is defined as 'commendable easiness in matters in which people usually incline toward sternness and severity [*tashdīd*] in such a way that the ease granted does not lead to a mischief or harm'.[46] Textual evidence supporting *samāḥah* is abundant both in the Qur'ān and *ḥadīth*. Suffice it here to draw attention to two Qur'ānic verses and a *ḥadīth* on the subject. The former thus enjoins the believers to

> Take to forgiveness, enjoin good, and turn away from the ignorant. (7:199)
>
> خُذِ الْعَفْوَ وَأْمُرْ بِالْعُرْفِ وَأَعْرِضْ عَنِ الْجَاهِلِينَ.

The text thus advises turning a blind eye, even forgiveness, to unpleasant words one sometimes hears from thoughtless people. Elsewhere in the text, God declares His love for those 'who control their anger and are forgiving toward others'(3:134). The Prophet similarly recommended leniency and *samāḥah* when he said in a *ḥadīth*

> May the mercy of God be on one who is lenient when he sells, lenient when he buys, and lenient when he makes a demand.[47]
>
> رحم الله عبدا سمحا اذا باع، سمحا اذا اشترى، سمحا اذا اقتضى.

A juristic conclusion drawn from these guidelines is that bringing ease to the people and removal of hardship from them is one of the cardinal objectives of *Sharī'ah*. Hence it is not permissible for a *mufti*, judge or jurist to opt for a harsh verdict in cases where an easier alternative can be found. *Wasaṭiyyah* and *samaḥah* are manifested, according to Wahbah al-Zuḥaili, in the balanced attention one pays to one's rights over, and one's obligations towards, others, to the material world and the spiritual world; it also means a balance between forgiveness and resistance, between prodigality and niggardliness, and a resolute aversion to extremism and terrorism in all their manifestations. Zuḥaili added that Islam advocates these values, not only among Muslims themselves, but also in their relations with other communities and nations. Moderation, a balanced temperament and easiness (*wasaṭiyyah, i'tidāl* and *samāḥah)* thus constitute the pillars and sustainers of civilization.[48]

Al-Qaraḍāwi is right to say that Sayyid Quṭb (d. 1966) indulged in extremism by charging with the society of his time disbelief (*kufr)* and ignorance (*jāhiliyyah*) and by declaring aggressive *jihād* against it. Quṭb also went wrong in his derision of tolerance and denunciation of those who advocated gradual renewal and reform. Qaraḍāwi further observed concerning the neo-literalists among the *Salafiyyah* (presumably including the Wahhabis and Muslim Brotherhood) that they rigidified 'Islamic teachings through their dry literalism and giving of undue importance to formalities such as wearing long beards and long clothes for men and women'.[49]

One ought to acknowledge, perhaps, in the same spirit of *wasaṭiyya* and *samaḥah*, that something has gone wrong with the substantive equilibrium of Islamic legal thought concerning the treatment of women. I shall, however, be brief on this issue here as I have already discussed it in a separate section of this chapter. I can hardly do better but to refer once again to Yūsūf al-Qaraḍāwi's insightful remarks: 'It is an obligation of the *ummah*', he wrote, 'to protect the women from the excesses of the Muslim juristic legacy of the past, and those of the modern West, both of which strip women of their essential humanity.'[50] Both need to be corrected through search for balanced and moderate solutions. Qaraḍāwi then calls for the establishment of an Ummatic Foundation for Moderation in Thought and Culture (*Jam'iyyat al-ummah al-wasaṭ fi'l-fikr wa'l-thaqāfah*) to vindicate *wasaṭiyyah* and promote it in the spheres of education, social mores and culture. 'This would be an invaluable gift we can pass on to the next generation of Muslims.'[51] It is of interest to note that Kuwait has already set up an institute known as the Wasaṭiyyah Centre of Kuwait, with the principal assignment to promote moderation and balance in the applied laws and social mores of contemporary Muslims.

I conclude this section by bringing into the picture two additional aspects of the Qur'ānic conception of *wasaṭiyyah*, one of which is concerned with the earth's natural environment, and the other about the Qur'ānic verse under review itself. The reference to natural environment occurs in the following verse in the Qur'ān:

> And the firmament has He raised high and set up therein [the fine] balance in order that you do not transgress the balance. So establish weight with justice and detract not from the [divinely ordained] balance. (55:7–9)
>
> وَالسَّمَاء رَفَعَهَا وَوَضَعَ الْمِيزَانَ أَلَّا تَطْغَوْا فِي الْمِيزَانِ وَأَقِيمُوا الْوَزْنَ
> بِالْقِسْطِ وَلَا تُخْسِرُوا الْمِيزَانَ.

The verse that immediately follows (55:10) explains that the overall purpose of the suggested balance is human welfare and protection of other life forms on earth. In human treatment of the natural world, moderation and balance thus signify the Islamic outlook and approach towards the environment. Note also the wording of the latter portion of the same verse which equates disturbance of the divinely ordained natural balance with transgression and rebellion (*tughyān* – in the phrase: *an la taṭghaw fi'l-mīzān*) that should be avoided.

A brief reference may now be made to what Seyyed Hossein Nasr has observed regarding a certain geo-physical dimension of *wasaṭiyyah* in the Qur'ān when he wrote: 'Just as Islam is one of the "middle ways" so too did its territory come to occupy the "middle belt" of the globe, from the Atlantic to the Pacific. In this region, Islam came into contact with other civilizations, their philosophies and their sciences – so that the Islamic worldview is informed by the outlook and values of other great traditions.'[52]

Lastly, is it a coincidence, one might ask, to note that the principal verse of *wasaṭiyyah* (i.e. 2:143), which we reviewed, occurs in the exact middle of the longest chapter (al-Baqarah) of the Qur'ān, which consists of 286 verses.

NOTES

1. Cf. Riḍwan al-Sayyid, 'al-'Alamaniyya fi'l-'Ālam al-Islāmi', 556 f.
2. Azzam Tamimi quoting R. Ghannouchi and Mahdi Shams al-Din in support of his own conclusions. See ed. Azzam Tamimi and John Esposito (eds), *Islam and Secularism in the Middle East*, 26, 36.
3. Cf. M. H. Kamali, 'Civilian and Democratic Dimensions', *Al-Shajarah*, 125–45. See also Chapter12 above.
4. Cf. Kamali, 'Issues in the Legal Theory', 5–23.
5. For a discussion of the source evidence on women and leadership see Kamali, *Freedom, Equality and Justice in Islam*, 63–5.
6. See for details on this, idem, 66–70
7. The Wolesi Jirga currently consists of a total of 269 members and the Meshrano Jirga of 102 Senators. See for details on developments in Afghanistan, M. H. Kamali, 'Islam and Its *Sharī'ah* in the Afghan Constitution 2004', 23–43; idem, 'Islam and women's rights in the the constitution of Afghanistan 2004', (*International Journal of Middle Eastern Studies*: forthcoming).
8. Cf. Kamali, *Freedom, Equality and Justice in Islam*, 66–9.
9. For further details on this see Kamali, *Equity and Fairness in Islam*, 44 f.
10. Cf. Leila Ahmed, *Women and Gender*, 5.
11. 'Abd al-Ḥalīm Abū Shaqqa, *Taḥrīr al-Mar'ah*.
12. See for a discussion of the source evidence in the Qur'ān and *ḥadīth* on *wilāyah* (guardianship) Kamali, *Islamic Law in Malaysia: Issues and Developments*, Ch. vi 'Issues over Custody and Guardianship', 105–28.
13. Cf. Nazeer Ahmed, 'From Saints to the Taliban: the Transformation of the Madrasah', Conference paper presented in Jakarta, December 2004.
14. Nakhaie Ahmad inteviewed by Joceline Tan in 'Fertile Ground at Pondok schools', *The Star*, Kuala Lumpur, 27 January 2002, Focus, 21.
15. For a glimpse of the *awqaf* financial and managerial problems see M. H. Kamali, *Equity and Fairness in Islam*, 92–101.
16. Joceline Tan, 'Pondok schools need to change', *The Star*, Kuala Lumpur, 28 January 2002, Focus, 22 (comment by Zaidi Hassan).
17. Idem.
18. Comment by A. Chaedar Alwasilah, 'Wrong to malign Islamic boarding schools', *New Straits Times*, Kuala Lumpur, Editorial, 10.
19. Ibid.
20. Al-Tabrīzī, *Mishkāt al-Maṣābiḥ*, II, *ḥadīth* no. 3453.
21. Bukhāri, *Ṣaḥīḥ al-Bukhāri*, *kitāb al-adab, bāb mu yunha 'anhu min al-sibab.*

22. Idem, *kitāb al-riqaq* (book on what affects emotions), *bāb al-a'mālu bil-khawāt m* (the result of deeds depend on the last action).
23. Quoted by Sohail Hashmi, *Washington Post*, 9 June 2002, 38.
24. Ṭanṭāwi's view published in *al-Ḥayāt*, 24 May 1998, also quoted by Muḥammad Tawfiq al-Shāwi, *al Mawsū'a al-'Asriyya fi'l-Fiqh al-Jinā'i* (Islamic criminal law encyclopedia) (2000), III, 93.
25. Press interview dated Tuesday 7 November 2006 posted on www.qaradawi.net, p. 9.
26. Idem, 10.
27. One who directly and intentionally kills another is liable to the capital punishment of just retaliation (*qiṣāṣ*) whereas the indirect participant may be held liable to a lower degree of punishment, depending on the elements of intention and proximity of the intervening act to the expected outcome. See for details Wahbah al-Zuḥaili, *al-Fiqh al-Islāmi*, VI, 235 ff.
28. www.mpppillai.com/bwatch.php.3?op=see&lid=2024.
29. www.utusan.com.my/utusan/content.asp?y=2003&dt=1111&pub=utusan_Express.
30. Robert A. Pape, op-ed article, *New York Times*, 22 September 2003 as quoted in Imam Feisal Abdul Rauf, *What is Right with Islam is What is Right With America*, New York: Harper Collins Publishers, 2005, 146.
31. Rauf, ibid, 149.
32. Ibn Kathīr, *Tafsīr al-Qur'ān al-'Azīm*, I,190.
33. Al-Qurṭubī, *Tafsīr al-Qurtubi*, and al-Zamakhshari, *Tafsīr al-Kashashāf* as quoted in Wahbah al-Zuhaili, *al-Fiqh*, 550.
34. *The Holy Qur'ān, Translation and Commentary* by Abdullah Yusuf Ali, note 3,604.
35. Wahbah al-Zuḥaili, *Qaḍāyā al-Fiqh*, 550, adds that according to another report, this elevated *ḥadīth* is attributed to 'Ali b. Abū Ṭālib but that there is ambiguity in the *sanad* of this *ḥadīth*.
36. Muḥy al-Dīn al-Nawawi, *Riyāḍ al-Ṣāliḥīn*,113, ḥadīth 118.
37. Abū Dawūd, *Sunan Abū Dawud, kitāb al-adab, bāb fi ḥusn al-ẓann*.
38. Ibn 'Āshūr, *Maqāṣid al-Sharī'ah*, 45.
39. Yūsuf al-Qaraḍāwi, 'Min al-Ghuluw', 294.
40. Ibn Ḥanbal, *Musnad Ibn Ḥanbal*, vol. V, *ḥadīth* no. 3655.
41. Muslim, *Mukhtaṣar Ṣaḥīḥ Muslim*, p.481, *ḥadīth* 1824.
42. Qaraḍāwi, 'Min al-Ghuluw', 304.
43. Muslim, *Mukhtaṣar Ṣaḥīḥ Muslim*, p.294, *ḥadīth* no. 1112.
44. Abū Yūsuf, *Kitāb al-Kharāj*, p.164.
45. Muslim, *Mukhtaṣar Ṣaḥīḥ Muslim*, p.474, *ḥadīth* 1783.
46. Ibn 'Āshur, *Maqāṣid al-Sharī'ah*, 269.
47. Ibn Ḥajar al-'Asqalāni, *Jawāhir Ṣaḥīḥ al-Bukhāri*, *ḥadīth* no. 275.
48. Wahbah al-Zuhaili, 'al-Taṭarruf fi'l-Islām', in Mu'assasah al-Bayt, *Mustaqbal al-Islām*, 223–4.
49. Qaraḍāwi, 'Min al-Ghuluw', 297–8.
50. Ibid., 334.
51. Ibid., 294.
52. Seyyed Hossein Nasr, *Science and Civilization in Islam*, 196.

CONCLUSION

This chapter provides a synoptic view of the contents of the present volume in an attempt to recapture its major themes and role in anticipation of what may be in store for the future of Islamic law. This summary and conclusion is presented in four sections as follows.

The first four chapters of this book, on the nature and sources of *Sharī'ah*, characteristics of *Sharī'ah*, the *madhāhib*, and *ikhtilāf* introduced the *Sharī'ah*, its history and resources, its major contributors and the diversity it has nurtured in its own understanding and development. We then proceeded to draw a distinction between *Sharī'ah* and *fiqh* with the purpose mainly to say that Islamic law is man-made as much as it is divine in its composition and development through its long history. Our attempt to introduce the *Sharī'ah* also took us into an exposition of its main themes and classifications under its binary division into devotional matters (*'ibādāt*) and human transactions (*mu'āmalāt*) and the sub-divisions thereof into a number of categories by the various schools that tried to reflect their respective viewpoints and concerns.

The emergence and development of the schools of law was expounded into two phases, the first of which consisted of two camps, namely the partisans of *ḥadīth* and the partisans of *ra'y* (i.e. *Ahl al-Ḥadīth* and *Ahl al-Ra'y*) during the seventh century that was later followed by the formation of a number of other schools. The five leading schools that have survived to this day have each contributed new ideas and doctrines to the methodology and substantive doctrines of Islamic law. The schools of law have left an impressive legacy of lively engagement in the development of *fiqh*, each with its own characteristics and priorities for the formulation and conduct of *ijtihād*. We also explained the major proclivities of these schools, some of which sought a closer adherence to the text of the Qur'ān and *ḥadīth* whereas others allowed more space for speculative thought and juristic reasoning based on personal opinion.

The schools of law have remained with us to this day and they each command a following among world Muslims in almost all continents. It is of interest to note that the twentieth century marked the development of *fiqh*-based parliamentary legislation not only in the sphere of personal law but also in public law fields such as commercial law, evidence and criminal law. For much of the twentieth century many of the newly independent Muslim states also adopted one or other of the leading *madhhabs* as the official *madhhab* in their constitutions and other laws. The selection of an official *madhhab* by the state authorities had a longer history dating back to the sixteenth-century Ottoman state which for the first time adopted the Ḥanafi school of law as the official *madhhab* for purposes of enforcement. The latter part of the twentieth century witnessed, however, a certain weakening of the identification of a *madhhab* in the constitution and state law, so much so that we may soon be seeing a narrowing down of the scope of application or even the end of that practice. The tendency now is to bring the *madhāhib*, Sunni and Shī'i and their sub-divisions, closer to one another in the interest of developing greater uniformity and consensus among them.

Choosing an official *madhhab* for enforcement served the practical purpose of ensuring uniformity in court decisions, a purpose which is still valid. However the scope of that application was narrowed down, in the course of the twentieth century, by two factors, one of which was the introduction of new constitutional clauses in many Muslim countries that selected the rulings of a particular *madhhab* for enforcement only when the existing statutes failed to cover a particular case or issue under court consideration. These constitutions also contained additional clauses which declared the primacy of the constitution and state laws and permitted recourse to the rulings of *Sharī'ah*, or a *madhhab*, only when the statutes were silent on a matter. The constitution thus established the priority of statutory law over the *fiqh* manuals but retained the latter as a supplementary source for purposes of implementation and judicial practice.

The second factor that narrowed down recourse to the resources of an official *madhhab* was a gradual increase in the scope and size of statutory law codes. Over a period of decades many of the newly independent states enacted civil and criminal law codes that provided a comprehensive coverage of their respective fields. Hence the need for recourse to the juristic manuals of the *madhhab* was progressively reduced. The new codes were also generally favoured by judges and practitioners on grounds of easy access, definitive ruling, and also the fact that most of the scholastic manuals were in Arabic. So the statute book gradually replaced the earlier practice of direct recourse to the *fiqh* manuals.

A certain line of distinction is also found in the constitutions of some Muslim countries in respect of recourse to the *Sharī'ah* for purposes either of legislation or adjudication. Legislation that adopts the *Sharī'ah*, or which is based on a fresh interpretation and *ijtihād*, is usually not confined to any particular *madhhab* and can utilize the resources of all the available schools of law, or even of individual jurists outside the established schools. In the event where the constitution requires recourse to the *Sharī'ah* or 'the basic principles of Islam', it would have the widest scope and enable recourse to the rich resources of *Sharī'ah* in all the juristic schools. The second level of constitutional reference to *Sharī'ah* usually involves court decisions, and the concern for uniformity in court decisions necessitates choosing only one *madhhab* to the exclusion of others, but may allow recourse to other *madhhabs* for a specific reason that warrants such a departure.

To give an example, the 1964 constitution of Afghanistan permitted recourse to the 'basic principles of the Ḥanafi jurisprudence of the *Sharī'ah* of Islam' whenever a gap was found in the applied statutory law, be it in court decisions or other government affairs. But then this constitution also permitted recourse to 'the basic principles of the *Sharī'ah* of Islam' for purposes of legislation, and made no reference to any *madhhab* at this level. The 2004 constitution of Afghanistan retained the reference to Ḥanafi law but confined its application to cases under court consideration only and no longer validated the same for other government decisions. This constitution retained, on the other hand, the second provision of the former constitution unchanged, thus enabling recourse to the wider resources of *Sharī'ah* for purposes of legislation. A new feature of the 2004 constitution in this connection was its recognition of the Shī'ite *madhhab*, side by side with that of the Ḥanafi, for purposes of adjudication in the event that both parties to a case were followers of the Shī'ite *madhhab*. This new extension of the *madhhab* provision in the 2004 constitution is likely to have the effect of further narrowing down the application of Ḥanafi *madhhab* in court decisions. Recourse to the Ḥanafi and Shī'ite *madhhabs* is permitted only in the absence of a statutory provision regarding the case under adjudication.

These developments are reflective on the whole of a stronger awareness of the unitarian impulse of Islam as a religion of *tawḥīd*. Although Islam permitted legitimate disagreement in its understanding and practice, the level of divergence and disagreement should ideally not be so wide as to erode the basis of unity in Islam and its *Sharī'ah*. The fact that prominent twentieth-century scholars among the Sunni and Shī'ite schools started to write about one another's contributions marked a departure from the *taqlīd*-dominated legacy that favoured scholastic particularity and isolation. This over-emphasis on scholastic particularity was a latent development that had no clear support in normative precedent and was in contrast to the pattern that prevailed during the classical period. For instance, we note that almost all Imāms of the leading schools went on record to express praise and appreciation for one another and explicitly discouraged blind following of anyone's opinion or *madhhab*, including their own. Then there came a time, centuries later, when the followers of *madhhab* became defenders and partisans of their own schools and Imāms to the extent of claiming exclusivity and righteousness for them. The twentieth century seems to have turned the page and recaptured to some extent the original spirit of unity among the leading schools and *madhhab* of Islam.

The next three chapters of this volume, *ijtihād*, the *maqāṣid* and legal maxims, looked into the inner resources of *Sharī'ah* for development and growth. These are the vehicles for keeping the *Sharī'ah* abreast of the changing needs of society. They also motivated the revivalist trend in *Sharī'ah* which has been the focus of renewed attention in the latter part of the twentieth century. *Ijtihād* consists mainly of interpretation of the broad guidelines of the Qur'ān and Sunnah in conjunction with particular and unprecedented issues. Any qualified *mujtahid* may advance an interpretation of the same issue. Hence *ijtihād* goes hand in hand with the possibility of disagreement (*ikhtilāf*). It seems that in the past *ijtihād* has widened the scope of disagreement among the schools and scholars more than it has advanced unity and consensus among them. For so long as *ijtihād* remains a valid proposition and exercise, disagreement is bound to arise. The fact that *ijtihād* has in the past been entrusted to individual jurists rather than a consultative assembly or council of any kind has contributed to widening the scope of disagreement and the result was an impressive diversity of interpretation and opinion that made consensus over ideas more difficult to obtain.

Twentieth-century scholars proposed the idea of collective and consultative *ijtihād* through representative assemblies and parliaments. Collective *ijtihād* bore greater harmony with the Qur'ānic principle of *shūrā* which was also expected to nurture unity and consensus on a wider scale. This was not meant, of course, to discourage *ijtihād* by individual scholars. *Ijtihād* by individual scholars was to continue, yet there was greater consciousness of the need for unity and consensus among the *ummah*. Consultative and participatory approaches to decision-making and *ijtihād* can also help develop internal credibility in their mechanisms. One can hardly fail to be impressed by the need to pay attention to problems of poverty and disease, and find innovative approaches to capacity-building and also utilizing consensus-based *ijtihād* towards these objectives. Collective *ijtihād* has been practised by the *fatwā* committees and Islamic law academies especially since the closing decades of twentieth century. What we proposed was that collective *ijtihād* should now be recognized as a matter of principle and made a part of the working agenda of representative assemblies and parliaments.

Our selection of themes in the three chapters under discussion also highlighted aspects of the *Sharīʿah* that bore greater affinity and relevance to the concerns of law reform and the future prospects of *Sharīʿah*. Thus we assigned a larger space to the goals and objectives of *Sharīʿah* (i.e. *maqāṣid al-Sharīʿah*) which is a much neglected and yet a dynamic chapter of *Sharīʿah*. It is ironic, however, that this very capacity for dynamism of the *maqāṣid* has, in our view, been the cause, at least partially, of its neglect in the conventional treatment of *uṣūl al-fiqh*. For the *maqāṣid* did not blend well with the heavily textualist approach of the *uṣūl* jurists, who focused on the particularities of words and sentences and stayed clear of developing broad theoretical perspectives. Besides, the *maqāṣid* were not always found in the clear text, and utilizing the *maqāṣid* demanded a level of insight in the understanding of the text that often went beyond its words and sentences. The early juristic writings expatiated on the legal rules and injunctions (*aḥkām*) of Qur'ān and Sunnah concerning issues they encountered but did not go deeper to unveil the fundamental ideas and purposes underlying them.

The *uṣūli* approach basically subsumed the goals and purposes of the *aḥkām* under their effective causes (*'ilal*) at the expense often of deducing general principles, whereas the Qur'ān often explicates the objectives or principles that are the essence of its laws. The notion of *'illah* also remained aloof, in the *uṣūl* methodology, from the occasions of revelation (*asbāb al-nuzūl*) that could be utilized to great advantage in the development of broad principles. For they establish the historical context of the *aḥkām*, how they related to social customs and provided an insight also into the spirit and intention of the original *ḥukm*. The attempt to marginalize the *asbāb al-nuzūl* and their role in interpretation and *tafsīr* was manifested, for example, in the following legal maxim: 'credibility is attached to the generality of the ruling of the text and not to the particularity of its cause' (*sabab*). Early writings on *uṣūl al-fiqh* and the hermeneutics of Qur'ān (*tafsīr*) tended to sideline the *asbāb al-nuzūl* so much so that they hardly feature in the discussions of *'illah* and *qiyās* beyond cursory and inconsequential references that are sometimes made to them.

Colonialism during the nineteenth and twentieth centuries marginalized the *Sharī'ah* in an attempt to convince the Muslims of the inadequacy of their own heritage and *Sharī'ah's* inability to meet their needs in the post-industrial age. European laws replaced the *Sharī'ah* in almost all areas of public law. The Islamic resurgence of the latter part of twentieth century was expressive on the other hand of a desire on the part of the Muslim masses to retain and restore their own heritage, including the *Sharī'ah*, but also to take stock of what needed to be done to make the latter more relevant and resourceful for a system of governance through statutory law and constitution.

Our overview of the theory of *ijtihād* in chapter 8 highlighted the concern for a reappraisal and reform of some aspects thereof, if one were to see *ijtihād* playing a significant role in statutory legislation. We have noted that *ijtihād* has begun playing an increasingly important role in law-making in *Sharī'ah*-related areas, a role which is likely to continue. Our brief survey of the still continuing series of adaptations and reforms of *Sharī'ah* also underlined their importance in paving the way for a bigger role *ijtihād* could play in statutory law and government. It is proposed that the *maqāṣid al-Sharī'ah* should be utilized as a framework for *ijtihād* in all its varieties, especially in respect of issues on which the text may be silent but which can be covered by its broader goals and objectives.

From a historical perspective, we have noted a tendency ever since the time of Imām al-Shāfi'ī that analogy (*qiyās*) spearheaded *ijtihād*, and his emphatic stand on *qiyās* had the effect for a time, at least, of reducing the wider applications of *ijtihād. Qiyās* may have actually served the unintended purpose of restricting *ijtihād* by stressing that it must conform to the specifications of *qiyās*. Our purpose in juxtaposing the *maqāṣid al-Sharī'ah* with *ijtihād* is mainly to relax the scholastic hold on *ijtihād* and also to provide new avenues and prospects for its development. We have called attention to the need to open up the theory of *ijtihād* by reducing its heavy reliance on the methodology of *uṣūl* and *qiyās* in the direction of greater flexibility and resourcefulness. *Ijtihād* should thus encourage innovative thought and legislation not only in *Sharī'ah*-related themes but in such other areas as Islamic economics, sociology and science. Numerous issues of contemporary concern in the spheres of gender equality, constitutional law and democracy, Muslim minority issues, violence in the name of *jihād* and so forth need to be addressed by *ijtihād* that inspires consensus through collective and consultative methods.

Legal maxims of *fiqh* is another area of considerable interest that relate meaningfully to both the *maqāṣid* and *ijtihād*. There is a dearth of literature in English on legal maxims so that the subject has remained totally obscure to the English readers of Islamic law, which is why I have discussed them in some detail. A number of earlier Muslim jurists have, in fact, treated the legal maxims as an extension of the *maqāṣid*, and both were somehow neglected in the conventional coverage of *uṣūl al-fiqh*. Legal maxims provide a bird's-eye view of the vast literary legacy of *fiqh* and deal with their subject-matter in short, epithetical and condensed style and language. They are typically unburdened with details, yet they convey insight that helps, in turn, to stimulate originality and innovative juristic *ijtihād*. Legal maxims became the focus of renewed interest in recent decades and were given a high profile in the Islamic law syllabi of university degree programmes in the Muslim world. The renowned Ottoman *Mejelle* that for the first time codified the Ḥanafī law of civil transactions in about 1850 articles also gave the legal maxims a degree of prominence by placing the ninety-nine most comprehensive legal maxims in its introductory chapter.

The *fiqh* literature has become exceedingly voluminous and it is not a facile task for readers of Islamic law to traverse the entire bulk of the Arabic works in this discipline. Legal maxims help to make that task easier for both beginners and specialists. Beginners are given a convenient entry into the various branches of Islamic law whereas the specialist can be inspired by the strikingly imaginative brevity and style of this branch of the *fiqh* literature.

With regard to *fatwā* and *fatwā*-making procedures, we drew attention to two somewhat conflicting trends that developed in recent decades, the first of these being that many Muslim countries have made *fatwā*-making the exclusive prerogative of official *muftis* and state functionaries. Secondly, a degree of arbitrariness is noted in the works of self-interested individuals and committees that issue ill-considered *fatwās* to advance their narrow and partisan objectives. We are of the view that neither a total ban on open *fatwā*-making nor a completely *laissez-faire* attitude towards it would be advisable. In a broad sense, what we propose for *ijtihād* we also essentially propose for *fatwā*. *Fatwā*-making authority may be entrusted to a competent council of scholars and *muftis* who possess certain qualifications but who also enjoy substantive autonomy in the exercise of their opinion and judgement. However, the authorities may determine the procedures that regulate the issuance of *fatwā*, its registration and gazetting procedures, and the role, if any, that the *fatwā* is supposed to play *vis-à-vis* parliamentary legislation.

The next two chapters namely 'democracy, fundamental rights and the *Sharī'ah*', and '*Sharī'ah* and the rule of law', are concerned with government under the rule of law, the extent of *Sharī'ah's* responsiveness to democracy and how it qualifies the requirements of the principle of legality and due process. Democracy and fundamental rights are the most commonly debated themes of modern governance and also areas where, barring exceptional cases, the recent history of government in the Muslim world has generally been unsatisfactory and problematic. We have raised questions over the *Sharī'ah* positions on fundamental rights and liberties and expounded the basic blueprint it provides on them. The subject is not devoid of ambiguity, however, and it raises issues that call for clarification, analysis and research. The problem has been exacerbated by the turbulent course of events since September 2001 that made Islam and the *Sharī'ah* targets of suspicion and abuse. Yet a parallel and a more positive development of this period has been the widespread support of Islamic parties and movements for democracy, shown by their enhanced participation in electoral politics.

I have tried to present the *Sharīʿah* in an accessible language that also addresses, within the limitation of a handbook, some of the issues of contemporary concern. This has, in fact, been a motivating factor in writing this book. I may also say that the need for a better understanding of *Sharīʿah* is not confined to Western or non-Muslim readers of this discipline, as the same problem obtains, in varying degrees, among the Muslim masses themselves, who are exposed more to hostile media on Islam than they are to sound and balanced information about it.

At this juncture, I take the opportunity to recount something of my previous experience of relevance to the present publication. I published my *Freedom of Expression in Islam* initially in Kuala Lumpur and later in Cambridge, UK in 1994 and 1997 respectively. And I remember clearly a question I was asked at a pre-publication presentation I gave at the International Islamic University Malaysia by someone who was not a beginner to *Sharīʿah*, but he asked me nevertheless the question 'Is there such a thing in Islam?' To talk about freedom of expression in Islam invited incredulity and surprise. That book provided a detailed presentation of its theme as I knew the nature of the challenge I had to face. Now with the benefit of hindsight I can say with confidence that the work has made an impact; it has been widely reviewed, became an international award winner and by now fairly well-known. Yet the 1990s were not perhaps the most confusing times for Islam and the *Sharīʿah* as the scale of misunderstanding grew wider and wider ever since, especially in the Western world that has become both the victim and the cause of escalating violence. To appeal for a better understanding of Islam and *Sharīʿah* is a more challenging prospect now than it has ever been in recent memory.

My attempt to explore the resources of *Sharīʿah* on themes of relevance to democracy, the rule of law and fundamental rights in this book is meant mainly to address the issues at an introductory level. The subject is exceedingly wide and I have also moved from one stage to another in my research preoccupations since the publication of my *Freedom of Expression in Islam*. For about two decades now I have been engaged in the completion of a multi-volume work on fundamental rights and liberties in Islam. The first four of a seven-volume work I undertook have already been published and, I am pleased to say, well-received. I have already mentioned one of these. The other three are: *The Dignity of Man: An Islamic Perspective* (2002), *Freedom, Equality and Justice in Islam* (2002), and *Equity and Fairness in Islam* (2002), all published by the Islamic Texts Society of Cambridge, UK, and subsequently also for student editions in Kuala Lumpur.

The question I then faced was whether I should extend this endeavour to the various areas and themes of rights and liberties. It is with a sense of relief that I say that I have just finalized the three companion volumes that will complete the seven books in the series. The three yet-to-be published titles are 'Rights to Life, Security, Privacy and Ownership in Islam'; 'Rights to Education, Work and Welfare in Islam'; and 'Freedom of Movements, Citizenship and Accountability: An Islamic Perspective'. The present volume has only touched on some of these themes and I hope will generate initial reader interest for the more detailed coverage of the subject to be presented in the near future. All the three manuscripts are now with the publishers awaiting publication with the Islamic Texts Society of Cambridge during the latter part of 2008.

As earlier mentioned, there is a fresh momentum and interest in democracy among Islamic parties and movements almost everywhere in the Muslim world, most of whom have turned to the ballot box in large numbers not known before. Except for Turkey where the Justice and Development Party has formed a government since its election victory in 2002, the rest are all opposition movements that have voiced criticism and protest against failed governments, dictatorship and corruption in their countries. What we have seen since the turn of the century follows decades of protest and disillusionment of the Muslim populace in the Arab world and beyond over the failure of constitutionalism, democracy and accountable governance. The Islamic revivalism of the past few decades has in the meantime been expressive of a renewed interest in the *Sharī'ah*. Public demand has also grown over the years for the reform of government that needs to be undertaken after the long series of *coup d'etats* by despotic military elites that ruled Muslims for much of the post-colonial period.

To meet public expectations for an enhanced Islamic input in law and government, a great deal of meticulous work needs to be undertaken to clarify the relevance of Islamic principles to the issues involved. This is not an easy task by any means but it has been made more difficult by a combination of negative factors that affected *Sharīʿah's* capacity to relate meaningfully to modern social issues and accountable governance.

The imitative tradition of *taqlīd* that for centuries dominated Islamic scholarship was reinforced by colonialism, which gave rise, in turn, also to a neo-*taqlīd* of a more inimical variety. This was the indiscriminate imitation of the constitutions and laws of Europe that the colonial regimes so avidly encouraged, nay imposed, on their former colonies. The distortion wrought by this manner of importation obviously sowed the seeds of what was to follow. The consistent story of failed constitutionalism and democracy in the Muslim world is necessarily linked with those distortions which robbed Muslims of confidence and initiative and eventually made them feel incapable of taking charge of their own affairs and planning their own future.

Muslims were successful when they were internally coherent and independent, as history provides ample evidence. There are new challenges now and Muslims need to dig deep into their own resources and exercise imagination and initiative to find workable and coherent solutions to their problems. I personally have the impression that a start has already been made and given the necessary political will and popular support for accountable and participatory governance, the desired solutions will emerge, and the twenty-first century may well unfold positive developments that will make it an era of optimism and reassurance for all concerned.

The last three chapters of this volume are devoted to an exposition of *siyāsah shariʿyyah* (*Sharīʿah*-oriented policy); 'adaptation and reform' and 'reflections on some challenging issues' of contemporary concern to Muslim societies. The first of these draws attention to *siyāsah shariʿyyah*, once again a much-neglected yet a vitally important chapter of Islamic public law. For in *siyāsah shariʿyyah* one sees a tendency away from the textualist preoccupations of *Sharīʿah* and the legal theory of *uṣūl al-fiqh* towards greater flexibility, exercise of discretion in government affairs and the administration of justice. Whereas the *Sharīʿah* is often given a rigid and punitive image by its antagonists and rigorously promoted as such in the hostile media – that image is hardly moderated by drawing attention to some of the more flexible components of *Sharīʿah*. *Siyāsah shariʿyyah* encourages flexibility, improvisation, intuitive judgement, and decision-making that may even depart from the text and rule of *Sharīʿah* itself in order to meet unexpected development and vindicate public interest and justice. It also serves to provide a decision-making formula by lawful authorities that may need to respond to emergency situations and make policy decisions where the *Sharīʿah* may be totally silent. Another instance of recourse to *siyāsah* may be when the established *Sharīʿah* provides a response which may, however, be less than satisfactory due to unusual circumstances that may dictate a recourse to *siyāsah shariʿyyah* for a decision that reflects the immediate needs of a just and effective solution.

Chapter 12 of this volume surveys twentieth-century adaptation and reform of Islamic law in basically three areas: law reform, teaching and research, and codification. Codification of Islamic law has a longer history but the account we provided has focused on the emergence of comprehensive civil codes, commercial codes and penal codes which sought to consolidate the *Sharīʿah* for easy access to judges and practitioners. We also discussed the main features of Islamic family law reform of the latter part of the twentieth century with reference to court organization, the emergence of *fatwā* councils and Islamic law academies in the closing decades of the century.

Islamic law teaching at university level has undergone changes and this has also involved adjustment and modernization of scholarship and research in Islamic law. New styles of writing and research in *Sharīʿah* also saw the emergence of Islamic law encyclopedias that present accessible digests of Islamic law that is relatively free of the scholastic bias of the earlier periods. Convenient access to the resources of *Sharīʿah* naturally helps to make the task of researchers easier. This is due, in no small measure, to better classification and more consolidated presentation of topics that records the views and contributions of all the major schools of *fiqh*. Considerable progress has thus been made to facilitate a new era of innovative development and *ijtihād*. This would hopefully move the *Sharīʿah* abreast of the experiences of contemporary Muslims, enhance the Islamic input into statutory legislation, and ultimately bring greater originality and coherence to law and government in Muslim societies.

The last chapter of this book looks into a number of challenging issues and is presented in five sections, each addressing an issue of public concern to contemporary Muslims, individuals and societies and my own brief responses to them. The chapter thus begins with a presentation of the secularist debate concerning Islam, followed by a discussion of issues of gender equality and justice, and then a section on the decline of traditional madrasah education. The disturbing phenomenon of suicide bombing is discussed in section four. And lastly, I present what I regard to be one of the most important, yet much neglected, Qur'ānic principles, that of moderation and balance (*wasatiyyah, i'tidal*), which is the subject of the last section in chapter 13.

In conclusion, I may add that most of the issues I have raised and what I was able to say concerning them, especially with regard to some of the less well-known themes of *Sharī'ah*, should hopefully open up prospects and possibilities for further research. The steps that have already taken place would considerably facilitate the task of exploring the resources of *Sharī'ah* in greater diversity and depth. The Muslim world may well be poised for a fruitful engagement in utilizing the resources of *Sharī'ah* and *ijtihād* that would address the problematics of its recent past and look to a more promising pattern of developments in the future.

BIBLIOGRAPHY

Abd al-Rauf, Imām Feisal. *What's right in Islam is What's Right with America*. Harpersan Francesco, 2005

'Abd al-Salām, 'Izz al-Dīn. *Qawā'id al-Aḥkām fi Maṣāliḥ al-Anām,* ed. Ṭāha 'Abd al-Ra'ūf Sa'd. Cairo: Maktabah Kulliyyat al-Azhariyyah, 1388/1968

Abū Dāwūd al-Sijistānī. *Sunan Abū Dāwūd.* Eng. trans. Aḥmad Hassan, 3 vols. Lahore: Ashraf Press, 1984

Abū Ḥabīb, Sa'di. *Dirāsah fi Minhaj al-Islām al-Siyāsi.* Beirut: Mu'assasah al-Risālah, 1406/1985

Abū Shaqqa, 'Abd al-Ḥalīm. *Taḥrīr al-Mar'ah fi 'Aṣr al-Risālah: Dirāsāt Jāmi'a li-Nuṣūṣ al-Qur'ān al-Karīm wa Ṣaḥīḥ al-Bukhāri wa Muslim,* Kuwait, 1410/1990

Abū Sulaymān, 'Abd al-Wahhāb. *Al-Fikr al-Uṣūli.* Jiddah: Dār al-Shurūq, 1404/1984

—— *Kitābat al-Baḥth al-'Ilm wa Maṣādir al-Dirāsat al-Fiqhiyyah.* Jeddah: Dār al-Shurūq, 1403/1983

—— *Tartīb al-Mawḍū'āt al-Fiqhiyyah wa Munāsabatuh fi al-Madhāhib al-Arba'ah.* Makkah al-Mukarramah: Jāmi'ah Umm al-Qurā, 1408/1988

Abū Yūsuf, Ya'qūb b. Ibrāhīm, *Kitāb al-Kharāj* Iḥsān 'Abbās (ed.). Beirut: Dār al-Shurūq, 1985

Abū Zahrah, Muḥammad. *Abū Hanīfah, ḥayātuh wa 'Aṣruh, ārā'uh wa Fiqhuh.* Cairo: Dār al-Fikr al-'Arabi, 1366/1947

—— *Ibn Ḥanbal, ḥayātuh wa 'Aṣruh, ārā'uh wa Fiqhuh.* Cairo: Dār al-Fikr al-'Arabi, 1367/1947

—— *Al-Jarīmah wa'l 'Uqūbah fi'l Fiqh al-Islāmi.* Cairo: Dār al-Fikr, n.d.

—— *Mālik, ḥayātuh wa 'Aṣruh, ārā'uh wa Fiqhuh*, 2nd edn. Cairo: Dār al-Fikr al-'Arabi, 1952

—— *Al-Shāfi'ī, ḥayātuh wa 'Aṣruh, ārā'uh wa Fiqhuh*, 2nd edn. Cairo: Dār al-Fikr al-'Arabi, 1367/1948

—— *Tanẓīm al-Usrah li al-Mujtama'*. Qāhirah: Dār al-Fikr al-'Arabi, 1965

—— *Tārīkh al-Madhāhib al-Islāmiyyah*. Cairo: Dār al-Fikr al-'Arabi, 1977

—— *Uṣūl al-Fiqh*. Cairo: Dār al-Fikr al-'Arabi, 1377/1958

El-Affandi, Abdelwahab. 'Rationality of Politics and Politics of Rationality.' In John L. Esposito and Azzam Tamimi (eds), *Islam and Secularism in the Middle East*. London: Hurst and Company, 2000

Aghnides, N. P. *Muhammadan Theories of Finance*. Lahore: Premier Book House, n.d.

Aḥmad, Fu'ād 'Abd al-Mun'im. *Uṣūl Nizām al-ṭukm fi'l-Islām*. Alexandria: Mu'assasah Shihāb al-Jāmi'ah, 1411/1991

Ahmed, Leila. *Women and Gender in Islam: Historical roots of a Modern Debate*, New Haven & London: Yale University Press, 1992

'Ālam al-Huda, Abū'l-Qāsim 'Ali Murtaza. *al-Intiṣār*. Qum: Mu'assasa al-Nashr al-Islāmi, 1990

Ali, 'Abdullah Yusuf. *The Holy Qur'ān, Translation and Commentary*

'Ali, Muḥammad Ibrāhīm. *Al-Madhhab 'Ind al-Ḥanafiyyah*. Makkah al-Mukarramah: Jāmi'ah Umm al-Qurā, n.d.

—— 'Al-Madhhab 'ind al-Shāfi'iyyah'. *Majallah Jāmi'ah Malik 'Abd al-'Aziz*, no. 2, Jamadi al Thani 1398/May 1978

'Alwāni, Ṭāhā Jābir. *Adab al-Ikhtilāf fi-l-Islām*. Riyad: Ma'had al-'ḥlam li al-Fikr al-Islāmi, 1992

—— 'The Crisis of *Fiqh* and the Methodology of Ijtihad.' *The American Journal of Islamic Sciences* 8 (1991), 332 f.

—— *Ijtihād*. Occasional Paper 4, Herndon, Virginia: The International Institute of Islamic Thought, 1993

Āmidī, Sayf al-Dīn. *Al-Iḥkām fi Uṣūl al-Aḥkām*. Beirut: al-Maktab al-Islāmi, 1402/1982

Amīnī, Mohd Taqī. *Time Changes and Islamic Law*, trans. from Urdu by Ghulam Ahmed Khan. Delhi: Idarah Adabiyyat Delhi, 1988.

Ansari, Zafar Ishaq. 'The Significance of Shāfi'ī's Criticism of the Madinese School of Law', *Islamic Studies*, 30 (1991), 485–500

Arkoun, Mohammad. *Min al-Ijtihād ila Naqd al-'Aql al-Islāmi,* trans. Hāshim Ṣāliḥ. London: Dar al-Saqi, 1991

Asad, Muhammad. *The Principles of State and Government in Islam*. Los Angeles: University of California Press, 1961

Aṭṭār, 'Abd al-Nāṣir Tawfīq. *Taṭbīq al-Sharī'ah al-Islāmiyyah fi al-'ḥlam al-Islāmi*. Cairo: Dār al-Fadilah, n.d.

Al-Attas, Syed Muhammad Naquib. *Islam and Secularism*. Kuala Lumpur: Muslim Youth Movement of Malaysia, 1978

'Aṭiyyah, Jamāl al-Dīn. *Al-Wāqi' wa'l Mithāl fi'l Fikr al-Islāmi al-Mu'āṣir*. Lebanon: Dār al-Hādi, 2001

—— *Naḥw Taf'īl Maqāṣid al-Sharī'ah*. Damascus: Dār al-Fikr, 2001

—— *Al-Naẓariyyah al-'Āmmah li al-Sharī'ah al-Islāmiyyah.* Cairo: Aṭba'ah al-Madinah, 1407/1988

—— *Tajdīd al-Fiqh al-Islāmi: Silsilah ṭiwārāt al-Qarn al-'Ishrīn.* Damascus: Dār al-Fikr, 2000

—— *Al-Tanẓīr al-Fiqhi.* Doha: n.p. 1407

Awad, M. Awad 'The Rights of the Accused under Islamic Criminal Procedure.' In Cherif Bassiouni (ed.), *Islamic Criminal Justice System.* London: Oceana Publications, 1988

'Awdah, 'Abd al-Qādir. *Al-Tashrī' al-Jinā'i al-Islāmī.* Beirut: Dār al-Fikr, 1403/1983

El-Awwa, Muḥammad Saleem. *Al-Fiqh al-Islāmi fi Ḍarīq al-Tajdīd*, 2nd edn. Beirut: al-Maktab al-Islami, 1419/1998

—— *Punishment in Islamic Law.* Indianapolis: American Trust Publications, 1982

Badrān Abū al-'Aynayn. *Bayān al-Nuṣūṣ al-Tashrī'iyyah, Ṭuruquh wa Anwā'uh.* Alexandria: Mu'assasah al-Shabāb al-Jāmi'ah, 1404/1984

Bahī, Muḥammad. *al-Dīn wa al-Dawlah: Min Tawjihāt al-Qur'ān al-Karīm.* Beirut: Dār al-Fikr, 1391/1971

Bahnasāwi, Salīm 'Ali. *Al-Sunnah al-Muftarā 'Alayhā,* 2nd edn. Kuwait: Dār al-Buḥūth al-'Ilmiyyah, 1401/1981

Bannā, Jamāl. *Naḥw al-Fiqh al-Jadīd.* Cairo: Dār al-Fikr al-Islāmi, 1996

Barikati, Muḥammad Amin al-Iḥsan. *Qawā'id al-Fiqh.* Dacca, Bangladesh: Zeeco Press, 1381/1961

Barsalou, Judy. 'Islamists and the Ballot Box: Findings From Egypt, Jordan, Kuwait, and Turkey.' *United States Institute of Peace, Special Report,* Washington DC, July 2005

Bayhaqī, Abū Bakr Aḥmad ibn al-Ḥusayn. *al-Sunan al-Kubrā.* Beirut: Dār al-Fikr, n.d.

Al-Bishri, Ṭarīq. 'Mua'ssasāt al-Dawlah fi'l-Nuẓum al-Islāmiyyah wa'l-'Arabiyyah.' *Minbar al-ḥiwār*, no. 19 (Summer 1989), 41–2

Brown, Nathan J. 'Constitutionalising Islam in the Arab World.' Paper presented at the International Conference on Religion and State: the Jeffersonian Approach, Prague. March 2007

Al-Bukhari, Muhammad b. Isma'īl. *Ṣaḥīḥ al-Bukhāri.* Eng. tr. Muhammad Muhsin Khan, 6th edn. 9 vols. Lahore: Kazi Publications, 1986

Clayton, John. 'Religions and Rights: Local Values and Universal Declarations.' In Abdullah A. An-Naem, G. D. Gort and Hendrik M. Vroom (eds), *Human Rights and Religious Values: Uneasy Relationship.* Michigan: Wm. B. Eerdmans Publishing, 1955

Coulson, Noel J. *A History of Islamic Law.* Edinburgh: Edinburgh University Press, 1964

Dihlawi, Shah Wali Allah. *Al-Inṣāf fi Bayān Asbāb al-Ikhtilāf.* Cairo: al-Maṭba'ah al-Salafiyyah, 1385 AH

Enayat, Hamid. *Modern Islamic Political Thought*. London: The Macmillan Press, 1982

Esposito, John L. 'Beyond the Headlines: Changing Perceptions of Islamic Movements.' Harvard International Review 2004. (*http://hir.harvard.edu/articles/1116/31*)

Faruqi, Shad Saleem 'Concept of an Islamic State: Problems of Definition, Interpretation and Application in Southeast Asia.' Paper presented at the International Conference on Islam in South-East Asia, Singapore. September 2001

Fatāwa Imām Muḥammad Rashīd Riḍā. Comp. Ṣalāḥ al-Dīn Manaḥḥid and Yūsuf Khuri. Beirut: Dār al-Kitāb al-Jadīd, 1390/1970

Fyzee, A. A. A. *Outline of Muhammadan Law*. New Delhi: Oxford University Press, 1974

Gellner, Ernest. *Conditions of Liberty: Civil Society and Its Rivals*. London: Harmondsworth, Penguin Books, 1996

Al-Ghanouchi, Rashīd. *Ḥuqūq al-Muwāṭanah: Ḥuqūq Ghayr al-Muslimīn fi'l Mujtama' al-Islāmi*, 2nd edn. Herndon, Virginia: The International Institute of Islamic Thought, 1413/1993

Al-Ghazālī, Abū Ḥāmid Muḥammad. *Al-Mustaṣfā min 'Ilm al-Uṣūl*. Cairo: Al-Maktabah al-Tijāriyyah, 1356/1937

Al-Ghazālī, Muhammad. *Mushkilāt fi Ṭariq al-Ḥayāt al-Islamiyyah*. Cairo: Dar Nahdah Misr, 1996

Ghazawi, Muhammad Salim. *Al-Ḥurriyāt al-'Āmmah fi'l-Islam*. Alexandria, Egypt: Mu'assasah al-Shabab al-Jami'ah, n.d.

Gibb, Hamilton A. R. 'Constitutional Organisation.' In M. Khadduri (ed.), *Law in the Middle East*. Washington DC: The Middle East Institute, 1955

Gort, Gerald D. 'The Christian Ecumenical Reception of Human Rights.' In Abdullah A. An-Naem, G. D. Gort and Hendrik M. Vroom (eds), *Human Rights and Religious Values: Uneasy Relationship*. Michigan: Wm. B. Eerdmans Publishing, 1955

Howard, I. K. A. 'Muslim Legal Approaches to Modern Problems.' *Islam 21*, issue 8 (April 2001), 2–3.

Al-Huda, Abu'l-Qasim Murtaza 'Alam. *Al-Intiṣar*, Qum: Mu'assasa al-Nashr al-Islami, 1990

Hughes, Thomas. *The Dictionary of Islam*, Lahor: The Book House (rprt of 1885)

Ibn 'Ābidīn, Muḥammad Amīn. *Majmū'ah Rasā'il Ibn 'Ābidīn*. Lahore: Suhayl Academy, 1396

—— *Ḥāshiyah Radd al-Mukhtār 'ala Durr al-Mukhtār*, 2nd edn. Cairo: Muṣṭfa al-Bābi al-Ḥalabi, 1386/1966

Ibn al-'Arabi, Abū Bakr 'Abd Allah. *Aḥkām al-Qur'ān*. Cairo: Dār al-Sa'ādah, 1330H

Ibn 'Āshūr, Muḥammad al-Ṭāhir. *Uṣūl Niẓām al-Ijtima'i fi'l-Islam*. Ed. Mohamed Tahir al-Messawi. Amman: Dar al-Nafā'is, 1421/2001

—— *Maqāṣid al-Sharī'ah al-Islāmiyyah*. Tunis: al-Sharīkah al-Tunisiyyah li al-Tawzī', 1985

Ibn Farḥūn, Burhān al-Dīn Ibrāhīm b. 'Ali. *Tabṣirat al-Ḥukkām fi Uṣūl al-Aqḍiya wa Manāhij al-Aḥkām*. Cairo: al-Qāhirah al-ḥadīthah li'l Ḍibā'ah, 1406/1986

Ibn Ḥajar al-'Asqalāni. *Fatḥ al-Bāri Sharḥ Ṣaḥīḥ al-Bukhāri*. Cairo: Muṣṭafā al-ṭalabi, 1378/1959

Ibn Ḥazm al-Andalusi, Abū Muḥammad 'Ali. *Al-Iḥkām fi Uṣūl al-Aḥkām*, ed. Aḥmad M. Shakir. Beirut: Dār al-Afaq, 1400/1980

—— *Al-Muḥallā*, ed. Aḥmad Muḥammad Shākir. Cairo: Dār al-Fikr, n.d.

Ibn Kathīr. *Tafsīr al-Qur'ān al-'Aẓīm*. Beirut: Dār al-Andalus, 1966

Ibn Khaldūn, 'Abd al-Raḥman. *Muqaddimah*. Beirut: Dār al-Kitāb al-Lubnāni

Ibn Mājah. *Sunan Ibn Majah*. Istanbul: Cagri Yayinlari, 1401/1981

Ibn Nujaym, Zayn al-'Ābidīn. *Al-Ashbāh wa'l Naẓā'ir*, ed. 'Abd al-'Azīz Muḥammad al-Wakīl. Cairo: Mu'assasah al-ṭalabi li al-Nashr wa'l Tawzī', 1387/1968

Ibn Qayyim al-Jawziyyah. *Al-Ṭuruq al-Ḥukmiyyah fi'l Siyāsah al-Shar'iyyah,* ed. Muḥammad Ḥāmid al-Fāqi. Cairo: Maṭba'āt al-Sunnah al-Muḥammadiyyah, 1372/1993 (I have also used the Cairo edition by Mu'assasah al-'Arabiyyah li 'l-Ṭibā'ah, 1380/1961) and Jiddah edition by Maṭba'ah al-Madani, n.d., edited by Muḥammad Jamīl Ghāzi (I have also used the Mu'assasah al-Madaniyyah publication of this work, edited by Muhammad Jam l Ghazi, as specified in the relevant footnote.)

—— *Ighāthah al-Lahfān min Makāyid al-Shayṭān*, ed. Muḥammad Anwār al-Baltāji. Cairo: Dār al-Turūth al-'Arabi, 1403/1983

—— *I'lām al-Muwaqqi'īn*, ed. Muḥammad Munīr al-Dimashqi. Cairo: Idārah al-Ḍibā'ah al-Munīriyyah, n.d.

Ibn Rushd al-Qurṭubi, Abū al-Walīd. *Bidāyat al-Mujtahid*. Lahore: Faran Academy, n.d.

Ibn Taymiyyah, Taqī al-Dīn. *Iqtiḍā' al-'irāṭ al-Mustaqīm li Mukhālafat Asḥāb al-Jaḥīm*, ed. Nāṣir A. al-'Aql. n.p. 1404/1983

—— *Majmū'ah fatāwā Shaykh al-Islām Ibn Taymiyyah*, compl. 'Abd al-Raḥman b. al-Qāsimi. Beirūt: Mu'assasah al-Risālah, 1398

—— *Minhāj al-Sunnah al-Nabawiyyah*. Bulaq, Egypt: al-Maṭba'ah al-Amiriyyah, 1321

—— *Raf' al-Mulām 'an A'immah al-A'lām*, 5th edn. Beirut: al-Maktab al-Islāmī, 1398

—— *Al-Siyāsah al-Shar'iyyah fi Iṣlāḥ al-Rā'i wa'l-Ra'iyyah*, 2nd edn. Cairo: Dār al-Kitāb al-'Arabi, 1951

Iqbal, Muhammad. *The Reconstruction of Religious Thought in Islam*. Lahore: Sh. Muhammad Asharaf, reprint 1982

Al-Jābiri, Muḥammad 'Ābid. *al-Dīn wa 'l-Dawlah wa Taṭbīq al-Sharī'ah*. Beirut: Markaz al-Dirāsat al-Waḥdah al-'Arabiyyah, 1996

Kabir, Humayun. *Science, Democracy and Islam*. London: George Allen & Unwin Ltd., 1955

Kamali, Mohammad Hashim. 'Law as the Way of God'. In Vincent Cornell (ed.), *Voices of Islam*, 5 vols. Vol. 1: *Voices of Tradition*. Westport, CT: Praeger Publishers, 2007, 149–75

—— 'Islam and Its *Sharī'ah* in the Afghan Constitution 2004 with Special Reference to Personal Law.' In Nadjma Yassar (ed.), *The Shari'a in the Constitutions of Afghanistan, Iran and Egypt–Implication for Private Law*. Tubingen: Mohr Siebeck, 2005, 23–43

—— *Equity and Fairness in Islam*. Cambridge: Islamic Texts Society, 2005

—— 'Personal Law', *The Encyclopedia of Religion*. New York: Macmillan Publishing, 1987, and new edn 2005

—— 'The Ruler and Ruled in Islam: A Brief Analysis of the Sources.' In Abdul Munir Yaacob and Suzailie Mohammad (eds.), *Konsep dan Peranan Ulil Amri di Malaysia*. Kuala Lumpur: Institut Kepahaman Islam Malaysia, 2004

—— 'Civilian and Democratic Dimensions of Governance in Islam.' *Al-Shajarah*, 9 (2004), no. 2, 125–45

—— 'Islam and women's rights in the the constitution of Afghanistan 2004.' *Oxford Journal of Islamic Studies* (forthcoming)

—— *Principles of Islamic Jurisprudence*. Cambridge: The Islamic Texts Society, 2003

—— *Freedom, Equality, and Justice In Islam*. Cambridge: The Islamic Texts Society, 2002

—— *The Dignity of Man: An Islamic Perspective*. Cambridge: The Islamic Text Society, 2002

—— 'Issues in the Understanding of *Jihād* and *Ijtihād*.' *Islamic Studies* 41 (2002), 617–35

—— 'The Johor Fatwa on Mandatory HIV Testing.' *IIUM Law Journal 1* (2001), 99–116

—— 'Issues in the Legal Theory of Uṣūl and Prospects for Reform.' *Islamic Studies* 40 (2001), 1–21

—— *Islamic Law in Malaysia: Issues and Developments*. Kuala Lumpur: Ilmiah Publishers, 2000

—— *Punishment in Islamic Law: An Enquiry into the Hudud Bill of Kelantan*. Kuala Lumpur: Ilmiah Publishers, 2000

—— '*Maqāṣid al-Sharī'ah*: The Objectives of Islamic Law.' *Islamic Studies* 38 (1999), 193–209

—— '*Siyāsah Shar'iyyah* or the Policies of Islamic Government.' *The American Journal of Islamic Social Sciences* 6 (1989), 59–81

—— 'Methodological Issues in Islamic Jurisprudence.' *Arab Law Quarterly* 2 (1996), 1–34
—— *Freedom of Expression in Islam*. Cambridge: The Islamic Texts Society, 1997
—— 'Fundamental Rights and Liberties in Islam: An Analysis of *ḥaqq* (Right).' *The American Journal of Islamic Social Sciences* 10 (1993), 340–367
—— 'Have we Neglected the *Sharī'ah* Law Doctrine of *Maṣlaḥah*?' *Islamic Studies* 27 (1988), 287–304
—— *Law in Afghanistan: A Study of the Constitutions, Matrimonial Law and the Judiciary*. Leiden: E. J. Brill, 1985
—— 'Islamic Personal Law.' *The Encyclopedia of Religion*. Macmillan Publishing Co. New York, vol. 7, 446–53, 1987 and 2005
—— '*Sharī'ah* as Understood by the Classical Jurists.' *IIUM Law Journal*, nos. 1& 2 (1998), 39–88
Karcic, Fikret. 'Applying the *Sharī'ah* in Modern Societies: Main Developments and Issues.' *Islamic Studies* 40 (2001), 207 f.
Karkhī, Abū al-Ḥasan. *Uṣūl al-Karkhī*. Cairo: al-Maṭba'ah al-Adabiyyah
Kāshif al-Ghiṭā', Muḥammad al-Ḥusayn. *Taḥrīr al-Mujallah*. Najaf, 1359
Kawtharāni, Wajīh. *Al-Sulṭah wa'l-Mujtama' wa'l-'Amal al-Siyāsi*. Beirut: Centre for the Studies of Arab Unity, 1988
Keddouri, Ellie. *Democracy and Arab Political Culture*. London: Frank Cass, 1994
Al-Khādimi, Nūr al-Dīn. *'Ilm al-Maqāṣid al-Sharī'ah al-Islāmiyyah*. Riyaḍ: Maktabat al-Abikan, 2001
Khallāf, 'Abd al-Wahhāb. *'Ilm Uṣūl al-Fiqh*, 12th edn. Kuwait: Dār al-Qalam, 1398/1978
—— *Al-Siyāsah al-Shar'iyyah*. Cairo: al-Maktabah al-Salafiyyah, 1350/1931
Lakdawala, M. H. 'It's Time for Justice and Reforms.' http://www.islamicvoice.com/december2002/gwatch.html
Lewis, Bernard. 'Siyasa.' In A. H. Green (ed.), *In Quest of an Islamic Humanism: Arabic and Islamic Studies in memory of Mohamed al-Nowaihi*. Cairo: The American University in Cairo Press, 1984
Madkūr, Muḥammad Salām. *Al-Madkhal al-Fiqh al-Islāmī*. Cairo: Dār al-Qawmiyyah li al-Ḍabā'ah wa al-Nashr, 1384/1964
Mahathir, Mohamad. 'Ulama have distorted Islam.' *New Straits Times*, 4 February 2001
Maḥmaṣṣānī, Ṣubḥi. *Arkān Ḥuqūq al-Insān fi 'l Islām*. Beirut: Dār al-'Ilm li'l Malayīn, Falsafat al Tashri': 1979
—— *The Philosophy of Jurisprudence in Islam*. Eng. trans. F. Zaideh. Leiden: E. J. Brill, 1961

Mallat, Chibli (ed). *Islam and Public Law: Classical and contemporary Studies*. London: Graham and Trottman, 1993

Manzoor, S. Parvez. 'Environment and Values in The Islamic Perspective.' In Ziauddin Sardar (ed.), *The Touch of Midas, Science, Values and Environment in Islam and the West*. Kuala Lumpur: Pelanduk Publications, 1988

Mas'ud, Muhammad Khalid. *Islamic Legal Philosophy, A Study of Abū Isḥāq al-Shatibi's Life and Thoughts*. Islamabad: Islamic Research Institute, 1977

Al-Māwardi, Abu'l Ḥassan. *Kitab al-Aḥkām al-Sulṭaniyyah*. Cairo: Maṭba'ah al Sa'ādah, 1327/1909

Mawdudi, S. A. A. *Human Rights in Islam*. Leicester: The Islamic Foundation, 1976

—— *The Islamic Law and Constitution*, 5th edn. Lahore: Islamic Publication Ltd, 1975

—— *Mawsū'ah al-Fiqh al-Islāmī*. Cairo: Dār al-Kitāb al-Misri, n.d.

Mehden, Von der. 'Islamic Resurgence in Malaysia.' In John L. Esposito (ed.), *Islam and Development*. New York: Syracuse University Press, 1980

The Mejelle. An English translation of *Majallah el-Ahkam el-Adliya*. Trans. C. Y. Tyser, reprint, Lahore: Law Publishing Co., 1967

Motahhari, Ayatollah Mortaza. *Spiritual Discourses*. Eng. truns. Alauddin Pazargadi. Albany, California: Muslim Students Association of Europe, US and Canada, 1986

Moussali, Ahmad S. 'Modern Islamic Fundamentalist Discourse on Civil Society, Pluralism, and Democracy.' In Augustus Richard Norton (ed.), *Civil Society in the Middle East*. Leiden: E. J. Brill, 1995

Moussavi, Ahmad Kazemi *Religious Authority in Shi'ite Islam: from the Office of Mufti to the Institution of Marja'*. Kuala Lumpur: International Institute of Islamic Thought and Civilisation (ISTAC), 1996

Muḥammad Amīn (Amir Bādshāh). *Al-Taysīr Sharḥ al-Taḥrīr*. Beirut: Dār al-Kutub al-'Ilmiyyah, 1983

Mūsā, Muḥammad Yūsūf. *Al-Madkhal li Dirāsah al-Fiqh al-Islāmī*, 2nd edn. Cairo: Dār al-Fikr al-'Arabi, 1380/1961

Muslim al-Nishapuri. *Mukhtaṣar Ṣaḥīḥ Muslim*, ed. Nāsir al-Dīn al-Albāni, 4th edn. Beirut: Al-Maktab al-Islāmī, 1402/1982

Mutawallī, 'Abd al-Ḥamīd. *Mabādī' Niẓām al-Ḥukm fī al-Islām*. Al-Iskandariah: Munsha'at al-Ma'ārif, 1974

Muzaffar, Chandra. 'Tolerance in the Malaysian Political Scene.' In Syed Othman Alhabsy and Nik Mustafa Nik Hassan (eds), *Islam and Tolerance*, Kuala Lumpur: Institute of Islamic Understanding, Malaysia, 1994

Nabhān, Muḥammad Fūrūq. *Al-Madkhal li-Tashrī' al-Islāmi*, 2nd edn. Kuwait: Dār al-Qalam, 1981

—— *Niẓām al-Ḥukm fi'l Islam*. Kuwait: Matbu'at Jami'at al-Kuwait, 1974

Nasr, Seyyed Hossein *Science and Civilization in Islam*. Cambridge: University of Harvard Press, 1968

al-Nawawi, Muḥy al-Dīn. *Riyāḍ al-Ṣāliḥīn*, ed. Muḥammad Nāṣir al-Albāni, 2nd edn. Beirut: Dār al-Maktab al-Islāmi, 1404/1984

Packer, Herbert. *The Limits of the Criminal Sanction*. Stanford: Stanford University Press, 1969

Paton, D. M. (ed.). *Breaking Barriers: Official Report of the Fifth Assembly of the WCC, Nairobi,* 1975. London and Grand Rapids: SPCK/ Eerdmans, 1976

'The Prosperous Justice Party PKS in Indonesia.' http://www.qantara.de/webcom/showarticle.php/c-476/nr-382/i.html

Qaraḍāwi, Yūsūf. *Madkhal li Dirāsat al-Sharī'ah al-Islāmiyyah*. Cairo: Maktabah Wahbah, 1411/1990

——*Al-Fatwā Bayn al-Inḍibāṭ wa'l Tasayyib*. Cairo: Dār al-Ṣaḥwah, 1988

—— *Min Fiqh al-Dawlah fi'l-Islām*. Cairo: Dār al-Shurūq, 1417/1997

—— 'Min al-Ghuluw wa'l-Inhilal ila'l-Wasatiyyah wa'l-I'tidal', in Mu'assa al-Bayt, *Mustaqbal al-Islām fi'l-Qarn al-Hijri al-Khāmis al-'Ashar*. Ammān, 1425/2004

Qarāfī, Shihāb al-Dīn. *Kitāb al-Furūq*. Cairo: Dār al-Kutub al-'Arabiyyah, 1346/1967 (Occasional reference is also made to Cairo edition: Maṭba'ah Dār al-ḥāyā' al-Kutub al-'Arabiyyah, 1386 AH)

Qaṭṭān, Mannā'. *al-Tashrī wa al-Fiqh fi al-Islām*. Al-Qāhirah: Maktabah Wahbah, 1984

al-Qurṭubī, Abū 'Abd Allah. *Al-Jāmi' li Aḥkām al-Qur'ān*. Cairo: Maṭba'ah Dār al-Kutub, 1387/1967

Quṭb, Sayyid. *Fi Ẓilāl al-Qur'ān*, 5th edn. Beirut: Dār al-Shurūq, 1397/1977

Rahman, Tazilur. *Islamization of Pakistan Law*. Karachi: Hamdard Academy, 1978

Rauf, Feisal Abdul. *What's Right with Islam Is Right with America*. New York: Harper San Francisco, 2005

Raysūnī, Aḥmad. *Naẓariyyat al-Maqāṣid 'Ind al-Imām al-Shāṭibi*. Rabat, Morocc: Maṭba'at al-Najāḥ al-Jadīdah, 1411/1991

Rāzī, Fakhr al-Dīn. *Al-Tafsīr al-Kabīr*. Cairo: al-Maṭba'ah al-Bahiyyah, n.d.

Riḍā, Muḥammad Rashīd. *Tafsīr al-Qur'ān al-ṭakīm* (also known as *Tafsīr al-Manār*), 4th edn. Cairo: Maṭba'ah al-Manar, 1737

Al-Ṣābūnī, 'Abd al-Raḥman et al. *Al-Madkhal al-Fiqhi wa Tārīkh al-Tashrī' al-Islāmī*. Cairo: Maktabah Wahbah, 1402/1982

Al-Ṣābūnī, Muḥammad 'Ali. *'Afwat al-Tafāsīr*. Jakarta: Dār al-Kutub al-Islāmiyyah, n.d.

Ṣāleḥ, 'Abd al-Malik. 'The Right of the Individual to Personal Security.' In M. Cherif Bassiouni (ed.), *Islamic Criminal Justice System*. London: Oceana Publications, 1988

Al-Sanhūrī, 'Abd al-Razzāq. *Maṣādir al-Ḥaqq fi al-Fiqh al-Islāmī*. Cairo: Ma'had al-Buhūth wa al-Dirāsāt al-'Arabiyyah, 1967

Sarakhsī, Shams al-Dīn. *Kitāb al-Mabsūṭ*. Cairo: Maṭba'ah al-Sa'ādah, 1324 AH (I have also utilized the Beirut edition by Dār al-Ma'rifah, 1406/1986)

Al-Sayyid, Riḍwan, 'al-'Alamaniyya fi'l-'Ālam al-Islāmi.' In Mu'assasah Alil-Bayt li'l-Fikr al-Islami, *Mustaqbal al-Islām fil-Qarn al-Hijri al-Khāmis 'Ashar*. Ammān, 1423/2003

Schacht, Joseph. *An Introduction to Islamic Law*. Oxford: The Clarendon Press, 1964

—— 'Law and Justice.' In P. M. Holt (ed.), *The Cambridge History of Islam*. Cambridge: Cambridge University Press, 1970

al-Shāfi'ī, Muḥammad b. Idrīs. *Kitāb al-Umm*, ed. Muhammad Sayid Kilani, 3rd edn. Cairo: Mustafa al-Babi al-Halabi, 1403/1983

—— *Jimā al-'Ilm*, ed. Muḥammad Aḥmad 'Abd al-Azīz. Beirut: Dār al-Kutub al-'Ilmiyyah, 1405/1984

—— *al-Risālah*, ed. Muḥammad Sayyid Kilāni. 2nd edn. Cairo: Muṣṭafa al-Ḥalabi, 1403/1983

Shahāwi, Ibrāhīm Dusuqi. *Kitāb al-Shahāwi fi Tārīkh al-Tashrī' al-Islāmī*. Cairo: Sharikah al-Ṭibā'ah al-Fanniyyah al-Muttaḥidah, 1972

Shakalany, Amr. 'Between Identity and Redistribution: Sanhuri's Genealogy and the Will to Islamise.' *Islamic Law and Society* 8 (2001), 219 f

Shalabi, Muḥammad Muṣṭafa. *Al-Fiqh al-Islāmī*. Beirut: al-Dār al-Jami'iyyah, 1982

Shalṭūt, Maḥmūd. *Al-Islām, 'Aqīdah wa Sharī'ah*. Kuwait: Maṭābi' Dār al-Qalam, 1966

Sha'rānī, 'Abd al-Wahhāb. *Kitāb al-Mizān*. Cairo: al-Maṭba'ah al-Ḥusayniyyah, 1329

Sharbinī, Muḥammad al-Khaṭīb. *Mughni al-Muḥtāj ila Ma'rifat Ma'āni al-Minhāj*. Cairo: Dār al-Fikr, n.d.

'Sharī'ah.' The Encyclopedia of Islam. New edn. Leiden: E. J. Brill, 1965

Shāṭibī, Abū Ishaq Ibrāhīm. *Al-I'tiṣām*. Cairo: Maṭba'ah al-Manar, 1332/1914

—— *Al-Muwāfaqāt fi Uṣūl al-Sharī'ah*, ed. Shaykh 'Abd Allah Dirāz. Cairo: Al-Maktabah al-Tijariyyah al-Kubrā, n.d. (I also referred to *Al-Muwāfaqāt fi Uṣūl al-Aḥkām*, ed. Ḥusanayn Makhlaf. Cairo: al-Maṭba'ah al-Salafiyyah, 1341)

Shawkānī, Yaḥyā b. 'Ali. *Irshād al-Fuḥūl fi Taḥqīq al-Ḥaqq ila 'Ilm al-Uṣūl*. Cairo: Muṣṭafa al-Ḥalabi, 1937

—— *Nayl al-Awṭār fi Muntaqā al-Akhbār*. Cairo: Muṣṭafa al-Bābi al-Ḥalabi, n.d.

—— *Al-Qawl al-Mufid fi Adillah al-Ijtihad wa al-Taqlid*. Cairo: Muṣṭafa al-Babi al-Ḥalabi, 1347/1927

Sibā'i, Muṣṭafa. *Al-Sunnah wa Makānatuhā fi al-Tashrī' al-Islāmī*, 3rd edn. Beirut: al-Maktab al-Islām, 1402/1982

Siddiqi, Mazheruddin. *Modern Reformist Thought in the Muslim World.* Islamabad, Pakistan: Islamic Research Institute, 1982

Siegman, Henry. 'The State and Individual in Sunni Islam.' *The Muslim World* 54 (1964)

Sinwan, 'Izz al-Din (ed.). *Jawahir Sahih al-Bukhari.* Beirut: Dar Ihya' al-'Ulum, 1407/1987

Sisk, Timothy. *Islam and Democracy: Religion, Politics and Power in the Middle East.* Washington DC: United Institute of Peace, 1992

Suwaylim, Bandar ibn Faḥd. *Al-Muttaham: Mu'āmalatuhu wa Ḥuqūquhu fi'l Fiqh al-Islāmī.* Riyāḍ: al-Maṭābi' al-Amniyyah, 1408/1988

Al-Ṣuyūṭī, Jalāl al-Dīn. *Al-Jāmi' al-Ṣaghīr*, 4th edn. Cairo: Muṣṭafā al-Bābi al-Ḥalabi, 1954

Ṭabarī, Ya'qūb ibn Jarīr. *Tafsīr al-Ṭabari.* Beirut: Dār al-Ma'rifah, 1400/1980

Tabrīzī, Muḥammad 'Abd Allah al-Khaṭīb. *Mishkāt al-Maṣābīḥ*, ed. M. N. Albāni, 2nd edn. Beirut: al-Maktab al-Islāmī, 1399/1979

Al-Tahānawī, Muḥammad 'Ali. *Kashshāf Iṣṭilāḥāt al-Funūn.* Istanbul: Al-Astana, 1317/1938

Tāj, 'Abd al-Raḥmān. *Al-Siyāsah al-Shar'iyyah wa al-Fiqh al-Islāmī.* Cairo: Maṭba'ah Dār al-Ta'lif, 1373/1953

Tamawi, Sulaymān Muḥammad. *Al-Sulṭāt al-Thalāth fi al-Dasātir al-'Arabiyyah wa al-Fikr al-Siyāsi al-Islāmī*, 2nd edn. Cairo: Dār al-Fikr al-'Arabi, 1973

Tamimi, Azzam and Esposito, John L. *Islam and Secularism in the Middle East.* London: Hurst & Company, 2000

Tanūkhī, Sahnūn ibn Sa'īd. *Al-Mudawwanah al-Kubrā.* Beirut: Dār al-Kutub al-'Ilmiyyah, 1994

Tawḥīdi, Abū Ḥayyān. *Kitāb al-Imtā' wa'l-Muā'nasah.* Cairo: n.p., 1939

Turābi, Ḥasan. *Qaḍāyā al-Tajdīd: Naḥw Manhaj Uṣūl.* Lebanon: Dār al-ḥadīth, 2001

—— *Tajdīd Uṣū al-Fikr al-Islāmi.* Jeddah: Dār al-Su'udiyyah li al-Nashr wa al-Tawzī', 2nd edn, 1987

Voll, John Robert. *Islam: Continuity and Change in the Muslim World.* Boulder, Colorado: Westerview Press, 1982

Zarqā, Muṣṭafa Aḥmad. *Al-Fiqh al-Islāmī wa Madārisuh.* Damascus: Dār al-Qalam, 1416/1995

Zarqā, Shaykh Muḥammad. *Sharḥ Qawā'id al-Fiqhiyyah*, 3rd edn. Damascus: Dār al-Qalam, 1414/1993

Zaydān, 'Abd al-Karīm. *Al-Madkhal li Dirāsat al-Sharī'ah al-Islāmiyyah.* Beirut: Mu'assah al-Risālah, 1998

al-Zuḥaili, Wahbah. *Al-Fiqh al-Islāmī wa Adillatuh*, 3rd print. Damascus: Dār al-Fikr, 1409/1989

—— *Qaḍāyā al-Fiqh wa'l-Fikr al-Mu'āṣir.* Damascus: Dar al-Fikr, 2006

GLOSSARY

ādāb: morality, manners
'ādah: custom, recurrent practice
'adl: justice, uprightness
āḥād: solitary *ḥadīth*, report by a single person or by few individuals
aḥādith (pl. *ḥadīth*): narratives and reports of the deeds and sayings of the Prophet
ahl al-bid'ah: proponents of pernicious innovation
ahl al-ḥadīth: proponents or partisans of Tradition (*Ḥadīth*)
ahl al-ra'y: partisans or proponents of opinion
al-aḥkām al-'amaliyyah: practical legal rules
ahwā' al-nufūs: personal predilection
akhlāq: ethics
'alāmaniyyah: secularism
'amal: act, practice, precedent
amānah (pl. *amānāt*): trust
amārāt: clues or circumstantial evidence
'āmm: general, unspecified
'aql: reason, intellect
Arbāb al-ma'āni: proponents of the meaning and rationale of the law
Arbāb al-ẓāhir: proponents of literalism
'āriyah: temporary loan
al-arkān al-khamsah: five pillars of Islam
asbāb al-nuzūl: causes or occasions of revelation
al-ashbāh wa al-naẓā'ir: resemblances and similitudes
ayāt al-aḥkām: legal verses

bāṭin: concealed, internal, esoteric
bay'ah: pledge of allegiance
bayān: explanation
ḍābiṭah (pl. *ḍawābiṭ*): controller, a rule that controls a certain area of the law
daf' al-ḍarar: prevention of harm
dalālah: meaning, implication
ḍarar fāḥish: exorbitant harm
al-ḍarūriyāt al-khamsah: five essentials protected and advanced in Islam, namely, life, religion, property, intellect and family
ḍarūriyyāh (pl. *ḍarūriyyāt*): essentials, necessities
dhikr: remembrance
diyah: blood-money
faqīh (pl. *fuqahā'*): jurist, one who is learned in *fiqh*
far' (pl. *furū'*): lit. a branch or a sub-division, and (in the context of *qiyās*) a new case
farḍ kifā'i: collective obligation
fatwā (pl. *fatāwa*): legal verdict, legal opinion
fiqh al-Qur'ān: jurisprudence of al-Qur'ān
al-firāsah: intuitive judgement, acumen
fitnah: sedition
ghaṣb: usurpation
ḥaḍānah: custody of a child
ḥadd (pl. *ḥudūd*): prescribed punishment
ḥājiyyāt: complementary, a degree below *ḍarūriyyāt*
ḥajj: pilgrimage
ḥajr: interdiction
ḥalāl: lawful
ḥaqq al-'Abd: Right of man
ḥaqq Allah: Right of God
ḥarām: forbidden, unlawful
ḥawā: whimsical desire
ḥayā': humility, modesty
ḥayḍ: menstruation
ḥibah: gift
ḥikmah: wisdom
ḥirābah: highway robbery
ḥisbah: lit. computation or checking, but commonly used in reference to

what is known as *amr al-ma'rūf wa-nahy 'an al-munkar*, that is, promotion of good and prevention of evil

ḥiyal fiqhiyyah: legal stratagems

ḥudā: guidance

ḥusn al-khulq: pleasant manners

'ibādah (pl. *'ibādāt*): devotional act, worship

ibāḥah: permissibility

'iddah: probation period

iḥsān: beneficence, doing good

iḥtikār: profiteering

ijārah: leasing

ijmā': general consensus

ijtihād: lit. 'exertion', and technically the effort a jurist makes in order to deduce the law, which is not self-evident, from its sources; legal reasoning

ijtihād jamā'i: collective *ijtihād*

ikhlāṣ: sincerity

ikhtilāf: juristic disagreement

'illah: effective cause, or *ratio legis*, of a particular ruling

iltizām: unilateral obligation

intiḥār: suicide

irshād: guidance

isnād: lit. support, chain of transmission

istiḥsān: juristic preference, to deem something good

istinbāṭ: inference, deducing a somewhat hidden meaning from a given text

istiqrā': induction

istiṣḥāb: presumption of continuity, or presuming continuation of the *status quo ante*

istiṣlāḥ: consideration of public interest

I'tidal: moderation and balance, synonymous with *wasaṭiyyah*

jānib ta'abbudi: devotional aspect

jihād: holy struggle

kafā'ah: equality, sufficiency

kaffārah (pl. *kaffārāt*): lit. concealer, penance, expiation

karāhiyyah: reprehension

khāṣ: particular

khilāfah: vicegerency of God in the earth

khiyār al-'ayb: option of defect

khiyār al-sharṭ: option of stipulation
al-khulafā' al-rāshidūn: the Rightly Guided caliphs; the first four caliphs of Islam
kidhb: lying
madhhab (pl. *madhāhib*): juristic/legal school
madhmūm: blameworthy
mafqūd: a missing person of unknown whereabouts
mafsadah: corruption, harm
maḥmūd: praiseworthy
mahr al-mithl: fair dowry
makrūh: abdominable, reprehensible
ma'nā (pl. *ma'āni*): meaning
manāfi' (sing. *manfa'ah*): benefits
mandūb: recommended
mansūkh: abrogated
maqāṣid al-Sharī'ah: objectives of *Sharī'ah*
ma'rūf: decent, fair, customary
maṣāliḥ al-dunyā: worldly benefits
maṣlaḥah: consideration of public interest
mastūr: hidden, occult
ma'ṣūm: infallible
mu'āmalah (pl. *mu'āmalāt*): civil transaction
mubāḥ: permissible
mufassar: clarified text
mufti: jurisconsult
muḥtasib: market controller
mujmal: ambiguous, ambivalent, referring to a category of unclear words
mukallaf: *compos mentis*, a competent person in full possession of their faculties
al-mukhāṣamāt: civil litigation
mulk: monarchy
munākaḥat: matrimonial law
murū'ah: manliness
mut'ah: temporary marriage
mutashābih: intricate, unintelligible, referring to a word or a text whose meaning is totally unclear
mutawātir: continuous testimony
muṭlaq: absolute, unqualified

nadb: recommended
nafaqah: maintenance
nahy: prohibition
al-nāsikh: abrogator
naskh: abrogation
nasl or nasab: family lineage
naṣṣ: clear text
nikāḥ: marriage
niyyah: intent
qabḍ al-fāsid: unlawful possession
al-qaḍā': adjudication
qadhf: slanderous accusation
qāḍi: judge
qaṭ'i: clear and unequivocal, decisive, free of speculative content
al-qawā'id al-kulliyyah al-fiqhiyyah: legal maxims
qiṣāṣ: just retaliation
qiyās: analogy
radhā'il: perfidy, turpitude and degrading conduct
raf' al-ḥaraj: removal of hardship
raḥmah: mercy
ribā: usury
al-riḍā': milk relationship, fosterage
riddah: apostasy
riwāyah: narration, transmission
riyā': hypocricy
ṣadaqah: charity
ṣadaqat al-fiṭr: charity given at the end of the fasting month of Ramadan
sadd al-dharā'i': blocking the means
saf h: idiot
ṣalāh: ritual prayers
shahādah: testimony
shajā'ah: courage
ṣhuf': right of pre-emption
shūrā: consultation
ṣidq: honesty
siyāsah: policy
siyāsah shar'iyyah: *Sharī'ah*-oriented policy
sulṭat al-taḥakkum: power to legislate at will

al-sunnah al-mu'assisah: founding Sunnah
Al-ta'aṣṣub al-madhhabi: scholastic fanaticism
ta'āwun; co-operation
tadarruj or *tanj m*: gradual process
ṭahārah: cleanliness
taḥqīq al-manāṭ al-khāṣṣ: verification of a particular *'illah*
taḥsiniyyāt: embellishments
takabbur: arrogance
ta'līl: ratiocination, search for the effective cause of a ruling
ta'līq: suspension in a contract
taqlīd: unquestioning imitation, following the views and opinions of others
taqwā: God's consciousness
tarjīḥ: giving preference to one legal ruling over another
tawāḍu': humility
tawḥīd: monotheism
ta'zīr (*ta'zīrāt*): deterrent punishment, discretionary penalty determined by the *qāḍi*
'ūlu al-amr: persons in authority and in charge of community affairs
ummah: the faith-community of Islam
'uqūbah (pl. *al-'uqūbāt*): penalty, punishment, penal law
'uqūd al-tamlīk: contracts that involve transfer of ownership
vilāyat-e faqih: rule by jurisconcult
al-wa'd: promise
waḥy: divine revelation
walī: legal guardian
wājib: obligatory
waqf: charitable endowment
wasaṭiyyah: moderation and balance, synonymous with *I'tidal*
wilāyah: guardianship
wuḍū': ablution
ẓāhir: manifest
zakah: legal alms
ẓann : speculative, doubtful
zawaj al-muhallil: catalyst marriage, an intervening marriage intended merely to render a finally divorced woman able to remarry her former husband
zinā: fornication, adultery
ẓulm: oppression

GENERAL INDEX

INDEX OF ARABIC QUOTATIONS

1

2

23 حُرِّمَتْ عَلَيْكُمْ أُمَّهَاتُكُمْ وَبَنَاتُكُمْ.

24 مَّنْ يُطِعِ الرَّسُولَ فَقَدْ أَطَاعَ اللّهَ.

24 وَمَا آتَاكُمُ الرَّسُولُ فَخُذُوهُ وَمَا نَهَاكُمْ عَنْهُ فَانتَهُوا.

27 يَا أَيُّهَا النَّاسُ قَدْ جَاءتْكُم مَّوْعِظَةٌ مِّن رَّبِّكُمْ وَشِفَاء
لِّمَا فِي الصُّدُورِ وَهُدًى وَرَحْمَةٌ لِّلْمُؤْمِنِينَ.

28 إِنَّ الصَّلَاةَ تَنْهَى عَنِ الْفَحْشَاء وَالْمُنكَرِ وَلَذِكْرُ اللَّهِ أَكْبَرُ.

28 إِيَّاكَ نَعْبُدُ وإِيَّاكَ نَسْتَعِينُ.

29 فَأَيْنَمَا تُوَلُّواْ فَثَمَّ وَجْهُ اللّهِ.

30 لَقَدْ أَرْسَلْنَا رُسُلَنَا بِالْبَيِّنَاتِ وَأَنزَلْنَا مَعَهُمُ الْكِتَابَ وَالْمِيزَانَ لِيَقُومَ النَّاسُ بِالْقِسْطِ.

31 يَا أَيُّهَا الَّذِينَ آمَنُواْ كُونُواْ قَوَّامِينَ بِالْقِسْطِ شُهَدَاء لِلّهِ وَلَوْ عَلَى أَنفُسِكُمْ أَوِ
الْوَالِدَيْنِ وَالأَقْرَبِينَ إِن يَكُنْ غَنِيًّا أَوْ فَقَيرًا فَاللّهُ أَوْلَى بِهِمَا.

31 وَلاَ يَجْرِمَنَّكُمْ شَنَآنُ قَوْمٍ عَلَى أَلاَّ تَعْدِلُواْ اعْدِلُواْ هُوَ أَقْرَبُ لِلتَّقْوَى.

31 وَإِذَا قُلْتُمْ فَاعْدِلُوا.

31 إِنَّ اللّهَ يَأْمُرُ بِالْعَدْلِ وَالإِحْسَانِ.

32 لَا يَنْهَاكُمُ اللَّهُ عَنِ الَّذِينَ لَمْ يُقَاتِلُوكُمْ فِي الدِّينِ وَلَمْ يُخْرِجُوكُم مِّن دِيَارِكُمْ أَن
تَبَرُّوهُمْ وَتُقْسِطُوا إِلَيْهِمْ إِنَّ اللَّهَ يُحِبُّ الْمُقْسِطِينَ.

34 لاَ إِكْرَاهَ فِي الدِّينِ.

35 وَمَا جَعَلَ عَلَيْكُمْ فِي الدِّينِ مِنْ حَرَجٍ.

35 إنه ما خيّر من الأمرين إلا أيسرهما ما لم يكن إثما.

36 لاضرر وضرار فى الاسلام.

3

48 بعثت لأتمم مكارم الأخلاق.

51 وَجَزَاء سَيِّئَةٍ سَيِّئَةٌ مِّثْلُهَا.

51 وَإِنْ عَاقَبْتُمْ فَعَاقِبُواْ بِمِثْلِ مَا عُوقِبْتُم بِهِ.

56 وَمَا أَرْسَلْنَاكَ إِلَّا رَحْمَةً لِّلْعَالَمِينَ.

56 وَلَكُمْ فِي الْقِصَاصِ حَيَاةٌ يَا أُولِيْ الأَلْبَابِ.

61 لاطاعة فى معصية، إنما الطاعة فى المعروف.

9

181 لا طاعة فى معصية، إنما الطاعة فى المعروف.

181 لا طاعة لمخلوق فى معصية الخالق.

182 إذا جلس الخصمان فلا تقض بينهما حتى تسمع من الآخر كما سمعت من الأوّل، فإنك إذا فعلت ذلك تبيّن لك القضاء.

182 البيّنة على المدّعى واليمين على من أنكر.

182 لو يعطى الناس بدعواهم لادّعى ناس دماء رجال وأموالهم ولكنّ اليمين على المدّعى عليه.

184 إنما انا بشر أنكم تختصمون إليّ، فلعلّ بعضكم أن يكون ألحن بحجّيّته من بعض فأقضى نحو ماأسمع، فمن قضيت له بحق أخيه شيئا فلا يأخذه إنما أقطع له قطعة من النار.

184 يَا أَيُّهَا الَّذِينَ آمَنُواْ كُونُواْ قَوَّامِينَ بِالْقِسْطِ شُهَدَاء لِلّهِ وَلَوْ عَلَى أَنفُسِكُمْ أَوِ الْوَالِدَيْنِ وَالأَقْرَبِينَ إِن يَكُنْ غَنِيًّا أَوْ فَقَيرًا فَاللّهُ أَوْلَى بِهِمَا فَلاَ تَتَّبِعُواْ الْهَوَى أَن تَعْدِلُواْ.

185 فَمَنِ اعْتَدَى عَلَيْكُمْ فَاعْتَدُواْ عَلَيْهِ بِمِثْلِ مَا اعْتَدَى عَلَيْكُمْ.

185 وَلاَ تَكْسِبُ كُلُّ نَفْسٍ إِلاَّ عَلَيْهَا وَلاَ تَزِرُ وَازِرَةٌ وِزْرَ أُخْرَى.

185 إِنَّا أَنزَلْنَا إِلَيْكَ الْكِتَابَ بِالْحَقِّ لِتَحْكُمَ بَيْنَ النَّاسِ بِمَا أَرَاكَ اللّهُ وَلاَ تَكُن لِّلْخَآئِنِينَ خَصِيمًا.

185 وَمَن يَكْسِبْ إِثْمًا فَإِنَّمَا يَكْسِبُهُ عَلَى نَفْسِهِ...وَمَن يَكْسِبْ خَطِيئَةً أَوْ إِثْمًا ثُمَّ يَرْمِ بِهِ بَرِيئًا فَقَدِ احْتَمَلَ بُهْتَانًا وَإِثْمًا مُّبِينًا.

187 وَمَا كُنَّا مُعَذِّبِينَ حَتَّى نَبْعَثَ رَسُولاً.

187 وَمَا كَانَ رَبُّكَ مُهْلِكَ الْقُرَى حَتَّى يَبْعَثَ فِي أُمِّهَا رَسُولًا يَتْلُو عَلَيْهِمْ آيَاتِنَا.

187 رُّسُلاً مُّبَشِّرِينَ وَمُنذِرِينَ لِئَلاَّ يَكُونَ لِلنَّاسِ عَلَى اللّهِ حُجَّةٌ بَعْدَ الرُّسُلِ وَكَانَ اللّهُ عَزِيزًا حَكِيمًا.

188 قُل لِلَّذِينَ كَفَرُواْ إِن يَنتَهُواْ يُغَفَرْ لَهُم مَّا قَدْ سَلَفَ.

188 وَلاَ تَنكِحُواْ مَا نَكَحَ آبَاؤُكُم مِّنَ النِّسَاء إِلاَّ مَا قَدْ سَلَفَ.

192 وَالسَّارِقُ وَالسَّارِقَةُ فَاقْطَعُواْ أَيْدِيَهُمَا جَزَاء بِمَا كَسَبَا نَكَالاً مِّنَ اللّهِ وَاللّهُ عَزِيزٌ حَكِيمٌ. فَمَن تَابَ مِن بَعْدِ ظُلْمِهِ وَأَصْلَحَ فَإِنَّ اللّهَ يَتُوبُ عَلَيْهِ إِنَّ اللّهَ غَفُورٌ رَّحِيمٌ.

192 الزَّانِيَةُ وَالزَّانِي فَاجْلِدُوا كُلَّ وَاحِدٍ مِّنْهُمَا مِئَةَ جَلْدَةٍ وَلَا تَأْخُذْكُم بِهِمَا رَأْفَةٌ فِي دِينِ اللَّهِ... إِلَّا الَّذِينَ تَابُوا مِن بَعْدِ ذَلِكَ وَأَصْلَحُوا فَإِنَّ اللَّهَ غَفُورٌ رَّحِيمٌ.

289 إِنَّ هَذَا الْقُرْآنَ يِهْدِي لِلَّتِي هِيَ أَقْوَمُ.

290 يُرِيدُ اللّهُ بِكُمُ الْيُسْرَ وَلاَ يُرِيدُ بِكُمُ الْعُسْرَ.

290 فَمَنِ اعْتَدَى عَلَيْكُمْ فَاعْتَدُواْ عَلَيْهِ بِمِثْلِ مَا اعْتَدَى عَلَيْكُمْ.

290 وَلاَ يَجْرِمَنَّكُمْ شَنَآنُ قَوْمٍ عَلَى أَلاَّ تَعْدِلُواْ اعْدِلُواْ هُوَ أَقْرَبُ لِلتَّقْوَى وَاتَّقُواْ اللّهَ.

290 وَقُولُواْ لِلنَّاسِ حُسْناً.

291 وَلَقَدْ كَرَّمْنَا بَنِي آدَمَ.

291 لايؤمن أحدكم حتى يحب لأخيه ما يحب لنفسه.

291 يَا أَيُّهَا الَّذِينَ آمَنُوا اجْتَنِبُوا كَثِيرًا مِّنَ الظَّنِّ إِنَّ بَعْضَ الظَّنِّ إِثْمٌ
وَلَا تَجَسَّسُوا.

291 حسن الظن من العبادة.

292 إِن تَجْتَنِبُواْ كَبَآئِرَ مَا تُنْهَوْنَ عَنْهُ نُكَفِّرْ عَنكُمْ سَيِّئَاتِكُمْ وَنُدْخِلْكُم مُّدْخَلاً كَرِيمًا.

293 يسروا ولاتعسروا و بشروا ولاتعسروا.

293 لايدخل الرفق فيشيئ ولاينزع من شيئ إلا شانه.

293 خُذِ الْعَفْوَ وَأْمُرْ بِالْعُرْفِ وَأَعْرِضْ عَنِ الْجَاهِلِينَ.

294 رحم الله عبدا سمحا اذا باع، سمحا اذا اشترى، سمحا اذا اقتضى.

295 وَالسَّمَاء رَفَعَهَا وَوَضَعَ الْمِيزَانَ أَلَّا تَطْغَوْا فِي الْمِيزَانِ وَأَقِيمُوا الْوَزْنَ بِالْقِسْطِ
وَلَا تُخْسِرُوا الْمِيزَانَ.